Penguin Modern Psychology UPS 6

Abnormal Psychology

Penguin Modern Psychology Readings

General Editor

B. M. Foss

Advisory Board

P. C. Dodwell
Marie Jahoda
S. G. Lee
W. M. O'Neil
R. L. Reid
Roger Russell
P. E. Vernon
George Westby

ABNORMAL PSYCHOLOGY

Selected Readings

Edited by Max Hamilton

Penguin Books

Penguin Books Inc., 3300 Clipper Mill Road,
Baltimore Md 21211, U.S.A.
Penguin Books Ltd, Harmondsworth,
Middlesex, England
Penguin Books Australia Ltd, Ringwood,
Victoria, Australia

First published by Penguin Books 1967

Printed in the United States of America

Contents

Introduction

The day of the text-book is over, say many critics, because by the time it appears in print it is already out-of-date (disregarding those that are out-of-date before they are written). Fortunately, this does not apply to the text-book of 'Readings', which by its nature makes no pretence to be up-to-date, except in the sense of being relevant to present-day problems. On the contrary, it may be said that its value to the senior student is becoming greater. As research increases and the journals, abstracts and reviews multiply, it becomes all the more valuable to stop for a while, to look at the foundations of one's subject, and to see what the original workers wrote and thought, before their ideas became worn smooth by the labours of generations of writers of text-books.

To cope with the difficult task of selecting material for Readings, it is necessary to have rules not only for inclusion but also for exclusion; though it is much easier to adhere to the former than to the latter. If a text is to be confined to one volume, then valuable, interesting, exciting and even favourite works will have to be thrown out ruthlessly. So I started off with a basic requirement that material to be included should be relevant to current problems in abnormal psychology, either directly or because it laid the foundations of fields of present-day study. I gave preference to factual material rather than to theoretical and speculative writing. There is still far too much of the latter based on insufficient of the former. This has made the task of selection even more difficult, for much of the earlier work appeared in the form of text-books rather than as short research papers.

This book is divided into four sections, consisting of clinical descriptions, applications of psychological methods to abnormal psychology, experimental work on animals, and finally, psychodynamic theories. By far the biggest contribution to this volume, and almost the whole of the first section, comes from one writer, Emil Kraepelin. This is deliberate and I make no apologies for it. Kraepelin's work became overshadowed and neglected through the influence of the writings of Adolph Meyer and Sigmund Freud, but the advent of effective methods of treatment has led to a renewed interest in the problems of classification in mental disorder, and even more important, a renewed interest in the clinical phenomena. I am convinced that in the coming decade, the return

7

to the basic principles on which Kraepelin founded his work (rather than to the details of his findings) will be the most significant aspect of abnormal psychology as studied in the clinic. As his writings are out of print, and there is so much misunderstanding and ignorance of his work, I thought it desirable to give fairly extensive extracts.

The section on clinical experimental approaches to abnormal psychology will, I hope, have two unexpected papers both of which are of greater interest at the present than they were when they first appeared. Jung's paper can be regarded as the ancestor of current work on 'perceptual defense' and Moore's paper is the ancestor of a rapidly multiplying progeny. Conversely, the section on experimental work in animals includes papers the importance of which will be accepted by everybody.

The section on psychodynamic theories has attempted to give some impression of pioneering work. This part has given me much difficulty, because small extracts dealing with psychodynamics can very easily produce an impression of absurdity; this is particularly true for the writings of Adler. I hope that those in a position to judge will consider that I have not been unfair.

The basis for exclusion of material is relatively simple. I have made every effort to avoid overlap between this volume and others in the series published by Penguin, not to mention two recent publications (*The study of abnormal behavior* and *Classics in psychology*). This accounts for the absence of work by Bleuler. The paucity of material on clinical psychology is due to the need to keep this volume to reasonable size.

Acknowledgements

I would like to thank Dr Alexander Walk who gave me some very useful general advice, and Mr R. J. McGuire who drew my attention to the paper by Cameron. I would particularly like to express my thanks and gratitude to Miss M. Knott, who has been able to maintain order throughout the chaotic work of preparation, which consisted chiefly of what must have seemed an interminable process of inclusion and rejection, followed by re-inclusion and re-rejection.

References

Shipley, Thorne (ed.), *Classics in psychology*, Philosophical library, 1961.
Zax, Melvin, and Stricker, George (eds.), *The study of abnormal behavior*, The Macmillan Co., Collier-Macmillan Ltd, 1964.

Part One CLASSICAL DESCRIPTIONS OF SYNDROMES

The clinical descriptions by Kraepelin are fundamental to modern psychiatry. If the full range of work were to be included it could be done only in the form of small extracts. It was finally decided to have an adequate account of Kraepelin's description of what is now called simple and hebephrenic schizophrenia, omitting his descriptions of the catatonic and paranoid forms completely. The extracts given have been cut chiefly by excluding most of his clinical examples.

It is likely that some of the case material that Kraepelin included in manic-depressive psychosis was schizophrenic. The extracts given deal with non-controversial material.

It is very uncommon to find a definitive paper in the field of mental disorder and the little paper by Gull is therefore unusual in that it is not only a first description but complete and authoritative.

Far too much work in psychology, and particularly in abnormal psychology, tends to give the impression that the nature of the contents of the skull is irrelevant. The extract from a paper by Kennedy gives more information in less space than almost any other I know of.

1 E. Kraepelin

Dementia Praecox

Excerpts from E. Kraepelin, *Dementia praecox*, E. & S. Livingstone, 1919.

Dementia praecox consists of a series of states, the common characteristic of which is a peculiar destruction of the internal connexions of the psychic personality. The effects of this injury predominate in the emotional and volitional spheres of mental life. To begin with, the assertion that this is a distinct disease has met with repeated and decided opposition, which has found its strongest expression in the writings of Marandon de Montyel and of Serbsky. But even though in many details there are profound differences of opinion, still the conviction seems to be more and more gaining ground that dementia praecox on the whole represents a well characterized form of disease, and that we are justified in regarding the majority at least of the clinical pictures which are brought together here as the expression of a single morbid process, though outwardly they often diverge very far from one another.

The objections have been directed even more against the name than against the clinical conception. I got the starting point of the line of thought which in 1896 led to dementia praecox being regarded as a distinct disease, on the one hand from the overpowering impression of the states of dementia quite similar to each other which developed from the most varied initial clinical symptoms, on the other hand from the experience connected with the observations of Hecker that these peculiar dementias seemed to stand in near relation to the period of youth. As there was no clinical recognition of it, the first thing to be done for the preliminary marking off of the newly circumscribed territory was to choose a name which would express both these points of view. The name 'dementia praecox' which had already been used by Morel (1860)* and later by Pick (1891), seemed to me to answer this purpose sufficiently, till a profounder understanding would provide an appropriate name.

It has since been found that the assumptions upon which the name chosen rested are at least doubtful. As will have to be explained in more detail later, the possibility cannot in the present

---

* Morel, Traité des maladies mentales, 566, 1860.

state of our knowledge be disputed, that a certain number of cases of dementia praecox attain to complete and permanent recovery, and also the relations to the period of youth do not appear to be without exception. I certainly consider that the facts are not by any means sufficiently cleared up yet in either direction. If therefore the name which is in dispute, even though it has been already fairly generally adopted, is to be replaced by another, it is to be hoped that it will not soon share the fate of so many names of the kind, and of dementia praecox itself in giving a view of the nature of the disease which will turn out to be doubtful or wrong.

From this point of view, as Wolff showed, a name that as far as possible said nothing would be preferable, as dysphrenia. The name proposed by Evensen 'amblynoia', 'amblythymia', further the 'demenza primitiva' of the Italians, or the one preferred by Rieger, which meanwhile has certainly been already used in a narrower sense, 'dementia simplex', might also be taken into consideration. Bernstein speaks of a 'paratonia progressive', a name that would suit only a part of the observed cases. Other investigators accentuate the peculiar disturbance of the inner psychic association in our patients and call the disease 'dementia dissociativa', 'dissecans', 'sejunctiva' or with Bleuler 'schizophrenia'. It remains to be seen how far one or other of these names will be adopted.

Psychic Symptoms

The complexity of the conditions which we observe in the domain of dementia praecox is very great, so that their inner connexion is at first recognizable only by their occurring one after the other in the course of the same disease. In any case certain fundamental disturbances, even though they cannot for the most part be regarded as characteristic, yet return frequently in the same form, but in the most diverse combinations. We shall therefore try to give a survey of the general behaviour of the psychic and physical activities before we describe the individual clinical manifestations of the disease.

Perception of external impressions in dementia praecox is not usually lessened to any great extent as far as a superficial examination goes. The patients perceive in general what goes on around them often much better than one would expect from their behaviour. One is sometimes surprised that patients to all appearance wholly dull, have perceived correctly all possible details in their surroundings, know the names of their fellow patients, and notice changes in the dress of the physician. By more accurate observations, however, such as were carried out by Busch and by Gregor, it becomes evident that the extent and especially the trustworthiness of perception are decidedly decreased. This is chiefly so in the acute phases of the malady, and then again in the last periods of its course. It was specially striking in the experiments of Busch to find that the patients usually made, along with a few correct statements, a great many wholly false ones. For instance, in the perception of letters they uttered repeatedly the same arbitrary series or sometimes parts of the alphabet. It was evident that they could not make the effort to retain and to reproduce what they really saw; instead of this they named at random whatever happened to occur to them.

Attention – This behaviour is without doubt nearly related to the disorder of attention which we very frequently find conspicuously developed in our patients. It is quite common for them to lose both inclination and ability on their own initiative to keep their attention fixed for any length of time. It is often difficult enough to make them attend at all. The patients do not look up when spoken to, and betray neither by look nor by demeanour in any way that they are sensitive to external impressions. Although this is so, they have perhaps perceived all the details, but have not experienced any real internal appreciation of their significance. Sometimes in cases of profound stupor or in many other insane states it is no longer possible even by the strongest stimulus to force the patients to show any interest.

But the patients do not take any notice of what they may perceive quite well, nor do they try to understand it; they do not follow what happens in their surroundings even though it may happen to be of great importance for them. They do not pay attention to what is said to them, they do not trouble themselves about the meaning of what they read. On this depends what was observed by Ossipow in some of the patients, 'photographic' reading, the thoughtless repetition of what is printed with all the signs of punctuation. Further there is seen the tendency of groups of patients, when they transcribe to copy carefully all mistakes, corrections, interpolations and marginal notes. In psychological experiments the patients cannot stick to the appointed exercise; they feel no need to collect their thoughts in the appointed manner, or to reach a satisfactory solution. Perhaps the experience related by Dodge and Diefendorff, that patients do not usually follow a moving pendulum continuously, as normal persons do, but intermittently and hesitatingly, may be explained by a similar disorder of attention.

With this loss of capacity to follow a lead is connected *a certain unsteadiness of attention*; the patients digress, do not stick to the point, let their thoughts wander without voluntary control in the most varied directions. On the other hand *the attention is often rigidly fixed* for a long time, so that the patients stare at the same point, or the same object, continue the same line of thought, or do not let themselves be interrupted in some definite piece of work. Further it happens that *they deliberately turn away their attention* from those things to which it is desired to attract it, turn their backs when spoken to, and turn away their eyes if anything is shown to them. But in the end there is occasionally noticed a kind *of irresistible attraction of the attention* to casual external impressions. The patients involuntarily introduce into their speech words that they have heard, react to each movement of their neighbours, or imitate them. Leupoldt describes patients who instinctively had to touch or count objects as they came within their field of vision. On the disappearance of stuporous conditions a distinct inquisitiveness sometimes appears in the patients: they surreptitiously watch what happens in the room, follow the physician at a distance, look in at all open doors, but turn away if any one calls them. We shall later see that all these disorders of that inner activity of volition, which we call attention, represent only partial manifestations of general morbid changes in the processes of volition.

Hallucinations – Sensation is very often profoundly disordered in our patients as is evident by the occurrence of hallucinations. They are almost never wanting in the acute and subacute forms of the disease. Often enough they accompany the whole course of the disease; but more frequently they gradually disappear, to reappear more distinctly from time to time in the last stages. By far the most frequent are *hallucinations of hearing*. At the beginning these are usually simple noises, rustling, buzzing, ringing in the ears, tolling of bells ('death-knell'), knocking, moving of tables, cracking of whips, trumpets, yodel, singing, weeping of children, whistling, blowing, chirping, 'shooting and death-rattle'; the bed echoes with shots; the 'Wild Hunt' makes an uproar; Satan roars under the bed.

And then there develops gradually or suddenly the symptom peculiarly characteristic of dementia praecox, namely, the *hearing of voices*. Sometimes it is only whispering, 'as if it concerned me', as a patient says, a secret language, 'taunting the captive'; sometimes the voices are loud or suppressed, as from a ventriloquist, or the call of a telephone, 'children's voices'; a patient heard 'gnats speak'. Sometimes they shout as in a chorus or all confusedly; a patient spoke of 'drumming in the ear'; another heard '729,000 girls'. Sometimes the voices appear to have a metallic sound, they are 'resonant voices', 'organ voices', or as of a tuning-fork. At other times they do not appear to the patients as sense perceptions at all; they are 'voices of conscience', 'voices which do not speak with words', voices of dead people, 'false voices', 'abortive voices' [...]

The illusions not infrequently are connected with real noises. The clock speaks as if it were enchanted; the rushing of water is changed into words; each step under the patient speaks; a patient 'heard the thoughts of others out of the soles of his boots'. Here and there the voices have a rhythmical cadence, probably in connexion with the carotid pulse.

The voices are often referred to the ear or the head; they are 'voices in the ear'; there are evil spirits in the ear, a telephone, a receiver, a phonograph in the head; 'the brain talks'. One ear may be exclusively concerned in it, or at least more so; sometimes the voices of the two ears have a different character. A patient asserted that the voices went in at one ear and out at the other. Many patients hear the voices in the whole body; the spirits scream in the belly, in the feet, and possibly also wander about; a patient heard them speaking in his purse. Another wrote down:

Voice in the right ear: 'Never,' for example as answer to a wish. Voice in the left ear: 'Stupid – Jesus – God.' Voice in the stomach: 'Blackguard. Point. Good.' Voice in the nose: 'Munich; Oho-boy.' Voice at the heart: 'Boy.' Voice in the right side of the abdomen: 'Yokel.'

But for the most part the origin of the voices is sought for in the external world. The patient feels himself influenced by the telephone, is a 'living telephone'; 'it all came by telephone to the bed'; said a patient. [...]

It is, however, usually difficult to get trustworthy accounts of these occurrences from the suspicious and reserved patients; they usually deny that they still hear voices, and only allow on pressure that yesterday or the day before perhaps something happened. Sometimes the patients are only able to give general information about the voices: 'They were voices as if the battle was lost', 'as if I had set about something'; 'the conversation was about the king and royalty', 'of life and the soul and divine love', of 'marriage and death'; 'the clergyman whispered something into my ear, that could not be understood'. But much more frequently they catch the exact wording as in real perceptions; some patients make notes of what they hear.

15

What the voices say is, as a rule, *unpleasant* and *disturbing*. 'The voices rushed in on me at all times as burning lions,' said a patient. The patient is everywhere made a fool of and teased, mocked, grossly abused, and threatened. People speak about him; everyone is occupied with him; the whole workshop screams; there is 'a petty espionage', 'like legal proceedings'; he hears voices, 'as one reads of them in stories of murder and Indians'. Someone calls out: 'Rascal, vagrant, miserable scoundrel', 'incendiary, parricide', 'good-for-nothing', 'blackguard', 'anarchist, rogue, thieving murderer', 'filthy fellow, filthy blockhead, filthy beast', 'vagabond', 'scamp', 'swine', 'filthy swine', 'sloven fury', 'town whore', 'convict', 'criminal, criminal', 'offended, offended'. The patient is said to have assaulted a child, seduced a girl with 80,000 marks, had sexual intercourse with his children, eaten human flesh. He is threatened with having his ears cut off, his feet chopped off, with being sawn asunder, with being beheaded; there is a command from the Government to stab him. [...]

On the other hand there are also frequently *'good voices'*, 'good wishes', 'praise', 'That's the real Simon Pure'. God makes known to the patient that he will proclaim him, send him into the world as his son. 'Here he is', cries a voice from heaven. [...]

Many of the voices make remarks about the thoughts and the doings of the patient: 'He has good hearing', 'Damn it, what ears the fellow has!' 'He has done for himself; the filthy fellow must get away from this', 'Do you hear the reflector upstairs? Now they have the sound-hole open again' [...] 'The voices knew what I did,' said a patient. Another when she exposed herself to the sun heard, 'She is melting'; to one patient the voices named the people he met, 'analysed his inside'. They narrated events in his life, asked him about family affairs. [...]

Often, however, in the beginning of the disease or in the more advanced stages what the voices say is indifferent or quite nonsensical and incomprehensible. The patient hears a call from England that he is to pay a visit, 'always another way about, always new names'; he hears 'Banker, rich farmer, crash, salt roll'; 'Stallion', 'They help me or they don't help me', 'The military come tomorrow early', 'Education', 'Lavender and crossroads are the strongest explosive', and similar expressions. [...]

Another patient, also quite reasonable, wrote down the following words as being what the voices said:

He – veni – I came – Cham – Saul – Absalom – lyric – dropping – roast – lust – Turks – rukidiku – trilling – singing – tins – tinker - sky – ram – fail – dog – fruit – Ko – vault – complaint – flax – holy water –

pasture – inspired – drone – dull – pressing – funnel – Druid – tremens – squeezing – dropping – quail – clever – formerly – sausage – lynx – vult – question – crime – splendour.

In some places 'veni – kam – Cham', 'Saul – Absalom', 'trilling – singing' – 'tins – tinker', there is a certain connexion, if only external, of the ideas which follow each other. But, except for these, the words are connected without any obvious link of ideas or sound; at most the slight similarity of sound in 'roast – lust' and in the series 'drone' to 'dropping' [in German, Drohne – trübe – drängen – Trichter – Druide – tremens – drücken – tröpfeln] could be regarded as the connecting link. This series reminds one of similar inventions of alcoholics in delirium when they read from a blank sheet of paper; and in reading during dreams such expressions, wholly without connexion, occur.

Many patients hear perpetually, in endless repetition or with slight changes, the same meaningless sentences, so that there is a kind of hallucinatory *verbigeration*. The following notes give an example of it. They were written down by an otherwise thoroughly clear and intelligent patient:

For we ourselves can always hope that we should let ourselves pray other thoughts. For we ourselves wish to wish to know who would let the swine's head be tormented to death with us foolishly. No, we ourselves are no longer so stupid, and do not always trouble ourselves, if we shall let ourselves be spared drinking like beasts. Because we just behave as fools and would let ourselves be cheated like silly swine.

In a series of cases the voices *give commands* which in certain circumstances are very precisely obeyed. They forbid the patient to eat and to speak, to work, to go to church; he must run barefoot. 'Go on, strike him, beat him', it is said, 'go on, go on!' 'Hands up!' 'Slope arms!' 'Put the chair here, stand up!' 'Jump in!' A patient said that he heard: 'You must do that', then 'You must not do that'; 'it is a chaos, one can't get out'.

But it is quite specially peculiar to dementia praecox that the patients' own *thoughts appear to them to be spoken aloud*. In the most varied expressions we hear the complaint of the patients constantly repeated that their thoughts can be perceived. They are said loud out, sometimes beforehand, sometimes afterwards; it is 'double speech', the 'voice trial', 'track-oratory', the 'apparatus for reading thoughts', the 'memorandum'. A patient heard her thoughts sounding out of noises. In consequence of this everything is made public. What the patients think is known in their own homes and is proclaimed to everyone, so that their thoughts are common property. 'I have the feeling, as if someone beside me said out loud what I think,' said a patient. 'As soon as the thought is in my head, they know it too,' explained another. [...]

Influence on Thought – Still more characteristic of the disease which is here discussed seems to be the feeling of one's thoughts being influenced, which often occurs. People speak to the patient in his thoughts, guide them, contradict him, 'offer' him thoughts, suggest them to him, transfer to him words, thoughts, pictures, smells and feelings. A patient said, 'My senses don't belong to me any more, they are being unlawfully taken from me'. Strangers send him thoughts silently and speak in his head, it is 'a remembrance, a memory, a memorial', a 'receiving of thoughts'. In this way his own thoughts are disturbed, 'drilled', 'drawn off'; he cannot think when the voice speaks. A patient explained, 'They take my thoughts from me and nothing comes back but a ragamuffin'. What he thinks himself is distorted; his thoughts are 'plundered, organized and published'. [...] 'It flows into the brain as a thought and expresses itself as words in the mouth,' said a patient. Another heard 'dead' and had to answer 'bread'.

On the other hand the patient sometimes *knows the thoughts of other people*, is 'connected by telephone with M'Kinley', can 'speak with the Kaiser', 'tones constantly with God', is in 'constant communication with the Holy Ghost'. He can also think for others, he passes on the thoughts, carries on conversations, dialogues, with his companions, with people in other houses; it is an 'electrical glee'. [...]

These most extraordinary disorders, quite foreign to healthy experience, are at first usually kept secret by the patient, so that one only hears something about them when they have already existed for a long time. The patients frequently connect them with malevolent people by whom they are 'watched through the telephone', or connected up by wireless telegraphy or by Tesla currents. Their thoughts are conveyed by a machine, there is a 'mechanical arrangement', 'a sort of little conveyance', telepathy. A patient said, 'I don't know the man who suggests that to me'. Another supposed that it might perhaps be done for scientific purposes by a professor. [...]

Many patients feel themselves very much troubled by telephony, they stop their ears, 'do not like such treatment by voices'. One patient begged that 'the blessed nonsense should be taken away'. Others regard themselves as specially privileged. 'I hear from a distance; not everyone can do that,' said a patient. Some patients try, by ingenious devices, to protect themselves against their thoughts being influenced; a patient translated foreign words in order to ward off the receiving of thoughts. Others exert themselves to conceal their real line of thought to a certain degree, by a second carried on alongside of it, which shall then receive the outside influences.

Hallucinations of sight begin with variegated rings in front of their eyes, plays of colour, fiery rays and balls, seeing sparks, everything looks awry and wrong. The patients are troubled by reflections, by blinding light, their eyes are irradiated and blinded by reflectors. On the wall appear white figures, reflections, the mother who is dead, paintings, imaginative pictures, death's heads, a heart with a dagger, ghosts, shadow figures half beast, half human, southern landscapes, saints from all eternity; it is photography at a distance and double sight. [...] Acquaintances look strange, everything is as though accentuated, pieces of furniture are changed into the form of wife and children; the figures in paintings and sculpture make obeisance. A patient saw the 'voices' in the form of small, grey, four-footed beings hopping round about and whirling in the air; they were accompanied by small flames, which could be separated from them. [...]

Smell and *taste* frequently share in the morbid condition. Evil-smelling substances are scattered about; there is a smell of sulphur; of corpses and chloride of lime, of blood, of fire, of the fumes of hell, of 'stinking poison', of dynamite. A patient smelled human souls; another felt the devil standing behind her, 'it stank'. Cold vapours are blown in at the one nostril, warm vapours at the other. Many patients smell the fragrance of roses, or notice that they are being chloroformed or stupefied by perfumed handkerchiefs. The soup has a curious taste of creosote; in the food there is petroleum or arsenic, in the beer morphia or iodoform, the drinking water is brackish, or contains chloroform.

Morbid tactile sensations and *common sensations* meanwhile gain considerable importance in the clinical picture. They are usually very varied. The patient feels himself laid hold of, touched over his whole body, he feels tickling in his thigh and right up to his neck, pricking in his back and in his calves, a curious feeling in his neck, heat in his face; hot sand is strewn over his face, filth is put in his hair; something is squirted on his feet; a hundred mice run over his neck. At night he is pricked with needles, he gets blows in the ribs, invisible powder is sprinkled over him; warm air plays on his body. [...]

Not infrequently these imaginations, connected apparently with organic sensations, receive a very strange *interpretation*. The patient is terribly tormented in his body, notices that something is taken away from him, blood is taken, that 'every part of his body is misused'; he feels 'internal stirrings', emptiness inwardly, currents and strains in his body. Water flows away out of his body, food goes immediately out at his head. His body is twisted; his mouth is torn asunder; his gums are broken open; his eyes are clawed out; his hair is tugged out; his shoulders are pulled apart, his testicles are burst; her ovaries and stomach are torn out; his cheeks are pared off. His brain is crushed, his throat is blown out; his whole intestine is drawn up; fire bursts out at his mouth. The patient has injections made behind; God pierces his foot with a wire; he is disfigured. [...]

Very commonly these sensations are associated with *electricity* and similar action at a distance. The patient feels himself fastened to the receiving and also to the discharging station, electrified from a distance, raised from the ground by electric shocks, blown up by electricity, he feels the current in his pleurae, a prick in his heart from the apparatus, he becomes warm by the rays; electric currents flow through his bed; an electric current comes from the sun. A patient thought that she was illuminated with Röntgen rays under her petticoats and was thus exposed to the general gaze.

As the result of these hallucinations the conviction is often developed in the patients that they have become the sport of all sorts of *influences*. [...]

Sexual sensations play a considerable role in our patients' experiences. The patient has a feeling of contraction in the testicles and penis, experiences 'a sultry feeling' on meeting people, notices signs in his fingers which the girls make. Love-charms are employed, the penis is erected by the electric current, a gold needle is stuck into it. At night lustful deeds are committed, his nature is electrically withdrawn from him; lustful men approach him. A patient felt that she was kissed at night by a Capuchin. Another patient described her experiences at night in the following way:

It seemed to me in the night as though I were divinely and spiritually married, or rather that my innocence was taken from me. The pains were considerable, but I did not scream though for some minutes I had to breathe violently. It then seemed to me as though I were several times married, when I had to lie down on the bed with better clothes on. But there never was a human being with me.

Orientation is not usually disordered. The patients know as a rule where they are, recognize people, are clear about the reckoning of time. It is only in stupor and in states of intense anguish that the correct perception of the environment may occasionally be more profoundly disordered. It is indeed often just the characteristic of the patients that they remain surprisingly clear in spite of the most violent excitement. On the other hand, however, orientation is not infrequently encroached upon by hallucinations. The patients name their place of residence and persons incorrectly, give a wrong date, are in a wrong hospital, in an imitation madhouse, in a prince's house; the physician is God, the attendant Satan; his relatives have been exchanged, his fellow patients are females or disguised policemen. But here it is clearly not a case of falsification of perception but of insane interpretation of impressions in themselves correctly perceived.

The *consciousness* of the patients, if we leave out of account the terminal condition of dementia, is in many cases clear throughout. Only in conditions of excitement and stupor is it occasionally dulled, though the dullness is not usually so great as it appears at the first glance. The patients complain frequently of passing dullness of consciousness which should probably be regarded as a condition of very slight stupor. They say that they were 'stunned', 'disembodied, magnetically repressed'; they became suddenly incapable of thinking or of working. These are 'mental conditions artificially induced through hypnosis', 'spiritual visitations', 'magnetic conditions of sleep', caused by the physician. [...]

Memory is comparatively little disordered. The patients are able, when they like, to give a correct detailed account of their past life, and often know accurately to a day how long they have been in the institution. The knowledge which they acquired at school remains sometimes with surprising tenacity until they are sunk in the most profound dementia. I remember a peasant lad, mentally quite dull, who could point to any town on the map without hesitation. Another startled you by his knowledge of history. Others again solve difficult problems in arithmetic with ease. [...]

Retention is also often quite well preserved. Gregor however, found in his experiments very dissimilar values for successive repetitions in consequence of great wavering of attention. Mistakes and senseless combinations were not corrected, but rather showed an inclination to become established; continuance of the repetition was of comparatively little use. Vieregge also reports great wavering of attention. In spite of that it is usually easy to impress numbers or names even on quite indifferent patients, which they correctly reproduce after days and weeks. Certainly inappropriate answers are often given first, but after more searching interrogation it is clear that the patients have quite understood

21

the exercise. After deep stupor it sometimes happens that the patients have no recollection, or only a very dim recollection, of what has occurred during a long space of time, it may be that because of the dullness of consciousness, they were unable to perceive, or that the impressions were not permanent.

Pseudo-memories – Here and there we meet also with *confabulations* which point to *pseudo-memories*. It must, it is true, seem very doubtful if one ought to speak of such when the patients relate that they have been in hell, in heaven, in America, have travelled over the moon and all parts of the world, that at six years of age the marrow was burned out of their legs, and their feet were chopped off. A patient declared that he had already been beheaded, but his head had not fallen off. In other cases, however, it is easier to assume pseudo-memories. The patient remembers having been in a beautiful castle as a little child and having sat on the knee of a grand gentleman, and to have been kidnapped on a cloudy night. [...] A patient declared he had himself planted the trees in the hospital garden. Usually the tendency to such insane pseudo-memories passes off quickly.

Train of thought – This sooner or later suffers considerably. There is invariably at first a *loss of mental activity* and therewith a certain poverty of thought. The patient 'has little life in him'; his nerves are under such tension that he can no longer think or speak. Thinking is difficult to him; 'he trifles about the whole day', occupies himself 'with tearing off the last leaf of the calendar and tidying up'. His thoughts have been taken out of his head; he has lost the joy of life; it is as if a fur cap were on his brain, he is 'as stupid as a pig'; his head is empty and hollow. A patient complained that 'he had no more earnestness'.

Association experiments – Bouman frequently observed repetition of the word used as stimulus, irrational associations, omissions; disinclination to make the attempt seemed to play a considerable role. Bleuler brings forward, among others, as further peculiarities of 'schizophrenic' associations, great irregularity of association-time, connecting up with former stimuli or answers, frequent repetition of the same associations, tendency to indirect associations, change of answer on repetition of the experiment. Marcus found in his patients specially lively visual ideas. Further, Pfersdorff has proved that in the combination of ideas *linguistic constituents* gain a certain preponderance; the patients show a tendency to rhyme, to introduce assonances, to play with words, to twist them, behaviour to which we shall later have to return.

But above all, as Bleuler especially has shown in detail, the patients lose in a most striking way the faculty of *logical ordering* of their trains of thought. On the one hand, the most self-evident and familiar associations with the given ideas are absent. It seems as if these were only partially illumined, and therefore were not in a position to call into consciousness thoughts that lie quite near. On the other hand again, the most unnatural combinations of heterogeneous ideas are formed, because their incongruity is not perceived on account of some purely external relation, as similarity in sound, or coincidence in time. The most evident truths are not recognized, the greatest contradictions are thoughtlessly accepted. 'Doctor, is your name Julia?' asked a patient, and another called the physician 'Mrs Colonel'. By these disorders, which in many respects remind one of thinking in a dream, the patients' mental associations often have that peculiarly bewildering incomprehensibility, which distinguishes them from other forms of confusion. It constitutes the essential foundation of *incoherence of thought*.

In less severe cases this is shown only in increased facility of distraction and increased desultoriness, in passing without any connexion from one subject to another, in the interweaving of superfluous phrases and incidental thoughts. Similarly, Pfersdorff found in continuous reading a tendency to make meaningless mistakes, to perseveration of certain words, to changes and omissions, even when single words or short sentences were correctly rendered; he concludes rightly that there is a failure of attention. [...]

In certain circumstances the incoherence may go on to complete loss of connexion and to confusion. An example of this is given in the following answer of a patient to the question: Are you ill?

You see as soon as the skull is smashed and one still has flowers (laughs) with difficulty, so it will not leak out constantly. I have a sort of silver bullet which held me by my leg, that one cannot jump in, where one wants, and that ends beautifully like the stars. Former service, then she puts it on her head and will soon be respectable, I say, O God, but one must have eyes. Seats himself and eats it. Quite excited, I was quite beside myself and say that therefore there should be meanness and there is a merry growth over. It was the stars. I, and that is also so curious, the nun consequently did not know me any more, I should come from M. because something always happens, a broken leg or something, they've had a quarrel with each another, the clergyman and she; a leg has just been broken. I believe it is caused by this that such a misfortune happens, such a reparation for damages. I have also said I shall then come in the end last, with the sun and the moon, and too much excitement, and all that makes still a great deal of trouble. Kings do not collect the money, in this way the letters have been taken away from me, as I at last specially think from the that, and all are burned. You can imagine that comes always from one to the other.

In a few places here, a certain connexion between the ideas can perhaps be recognized: 'ill – skull smashed', 'held by my leg – not jump in', 'something happens – broken leg', 'misfortune – reparation for damages', 'excitement – trouble', 'letters taken away – burned', 'excited – quite beside myself'. Also 'silver bullet' and 'stars', and further on 'sun and moon' and 'nun' and 'clergyman', who 'have had a quarrel with each other', point to associations of thought. On the whole, however, we have before us a completely unintelligible and aimless series of words and fragments of thoughts. It must certainly be taken into consideration that the actual train of thought is possibly much less disordered than the expression of it in speech, because the patients, as indeed happened in this case, can in certain circumstances not only perceive correctly, but also further elaborate what they perceive and behave fairly rationally.

Stereotypy – We almost always meet in the train of thought of the patients indications of stereotypy, of the persistence of single ideas. If the patient continues talking, the same ideas and expressions usually turn up again from time to time. Occasionally the persistence gets the mastery of the train of thought to such an extent that the patients for weeks and months always move in the same monotonous sphere of ideas, and cannot be brought out of it by any means.

Evasion – Further peculiar disorders of the train of thought which here and there are observed, are evasion and a feature which Bleuler more accurately characterized as '*intellectual negativism*'. Evasion or *paralogia* consists in this, that the idea which is next in the chain of thought is suppressed and replaced by another which is related to it. It appears most distinctly in the patients' answers to questions; but it might be possible that the complaints of the patients that their thoughts are 'drawn off' from them, 'distorted', refer to similar occurrences. An example is given in the following answers of a patient to the physician's questions:

What is the name of this gentleman? (Dr A.), 'Little man.' What is his name? 'Florschütz' (The name of a fellow patient). How many fingers am I holding up? (3) 'Four.' How many now? (4) 'Five.' And now? (2) 'One.' How much money is that? (three pennies) 'Sixpence.' No, you know quite well. 'Twopence.' No, how much? 'Fourpence.' Now name the number that was left out, how much then? 'Twenty-five thousand.' What do you mean by twenty-five thousand? 'That I'm all right.'

It is here easily seen that the patient deliberately avoids the right answer which he certainly has at his command, a proceeding which at first makes the impression of intentional dissimulation. A patient replied to the question how old she was; 'One day.' Clearly this phenomenon is nearly related to the negativistic disorders of thought. They appear in the difficulty to carry on a series of ideas as one wishes, the patient's thoughts are 'taken' from him. So it sometimes comes to pass that he is obliged to think the opposite of what he really wishes. [. . .]

Constraint of thought – From these and similar experiences the feeling which has already been discussed often develops in the patients, that their thinking is constrained, has been withdrawn from the dominion of their will by irresistible influences. On the one hand thoughts arise in them which they feel as strange, as not belonging to themselves; there is a 'thronging of thoughts', a 'pushing of thoughts', sometimes in tempestuous form. A patient had to 'drive through his brain in four hours nineteen years'; another thought he would have to write a book if he were to note down everything that came into his head. But on the other hand the patients cannot think as they wish; their thoughts are withdrawn from them, slip away from them, although they exert themselves to hold them fast and to think them out. Owing to this there can be a sudden 'blocking' of their thought, producing a painful interruption in a series of ideas.

They never tire of describing this constraint of theirs in ever varying ways. The patient's *thoughts are influenced*, inspired, pressed on him; he must receive them like a telephone; they are forced on him by hypnotism and suggestion, act on him 'by suggestion'. Everything that he thinks or says is thought or said under compulsion. A patient had always to fight against the idea that he was Christ. Reading is interrupted by thoughts and explanations; thoughts are arrested, blurred, the patient has to exert himself to squeeze them out; he must think what people say. He feels as if his brain stood still, as if he had two brains. He is no longer himself, he has a kind of double consciousness; the voices pull a thread, so that he has to think such stupid things. The thoughts can be taken out of people's brains; the patient is confused in his head, he cannot grasp any clear ideas, he cannot bring order into the jumble of his thoughts, there is an 'entanglement in his mind'. [. . .]

Mental efficiency is always diminished to a considerable extent. The patients are distracted, inattentive, tired, dull, do not take pleasure in work, their mind wanders, they lose the connexion, they 'cannot keep the thought in mind', they have no perseverance. It is true they are often able to carry out quickly and correctly tasks depending solely on memory or practice, sums, repetition of what they have previously learned, but fail completely as soon as it is a question of independent mental activity and the overcoming of difficulties. [. . .] In work the patients soon become negligent, they get bad certificates, pass no examinations, are turned off everywhere as useless, and easily fall into the condition of beggars and vagabonds. They sit about idle and the most they do is to turn over the pages of an old calendar or to stare at the advertisements in a newspaper. Others develop great diligence, 'study all night long', but accomplish nothing at all, take up trifling or aimless occupations, begin to compose bombastic, incomprehensible rhymes, to copy a foreign dictionary, or they lock themselves up in order to learn poems off by heart. [. . .]

Judgement – Further the faculty of judgement in the patient suffers without exception severe injury. What always surprises the observer anew is the quiet complacency with which the most nonsensical ideas can be uttered by them and the most incomprehensible actions carried out. One has the impression that the patients are not in a position to accomplish that mental grouping of ideas which is requisite for their survey and comparison, their subordination among one another and for the discovery of contradictions. In this respect they resemble dreamers in whom likewise the ability to sift the ideas which come into the mind, to arrange them and to correct them according to the standards gained by former experiences and general ideas is abolished. These disorders, on whose great fundamental significance Bleuler also lays most emphatic stress, suggest an encroachment on the inner action of will.

The patients often have a distinct feeling of the profound change which has taken place in them. They complain that they are 'dark in the head', not free, often in confusion, no longer clear, and that they have 'cloud thoughts'. They cannot grasp a thought, cannot understand anything; their mind is scattered; their thoughts have flowed away; their brain is no longer competent, is enfeebled. A patient declared she was quite well, but stupid, and would like to be cured, while another begged that she might be freed from spirits, she did not wish to be mad, to be the plaything of other people, but wishes to be like other human beings, she couldn't stand it any longer, she was quite incurable. In contrast to these indications which sometimes characterize the situation with surprising clearness, understanding of the disease disappears fairly rapidly as the malady progresses in an overwhelming majority of cases even where in the beginning it was more or less clearly present.

Delusions, either transitory or permanent, are developed with extraordinary frequency on the foundation of the morbid change which is created by dementia praecox. In the first period of the disease they are usually by preference of a sad character, hypochondriacal, or ideas of sin or of persecution. The feeling of disease takes on insane forms; the brain is burned, shrunken, as if completely gone to jelly, full of water, the mind is 'drawn like rags from the brain'; the patient 'has only a little knuckle of brain left'; the nerves are teased out.

Ideas of sin – These delusions are frequently accompanied by ideas of sin. The patient has by a sinful life destroyed his health of body and mind, he is a wicked fellow, the greatest sinner, has confessed unworthily, has committed lese-majesty, has denied God, scorned the Holy Ghost, neglected his gifts. [. . .]

Ideas of persecution – In connexion with these ideas of sin ideas of persecution are invariably developed, in the shaping of which hallucinations of hearing generally play an important part. The patient notices that he is looked at in a peculiar way, laughed at, scoffed at, that people are jeering at him, are spitting in front of him, the clergyman makes allusions to him in the sermon. He is grossly abused and threatened, his thoughts are influenced, he is surrounded by a 'spiteful revolution'. People spy on him; Jews, anarchists, spiritualists, persecute him, poison the atmosphere with poisonous powder, the beer with prussic acid, generate magic vapours and foul air, do not let him take a single good breath, try to wash him away with musk water. [. . .]

Ideas of influence – From the examples which have already been given it can be seen that very often the delusions of influence through external agents is developed; 'In a natural body such things do not happen.' Many patients are entangled in an inextricable net of the most painful ideas by the feeling of forced and powerless dependence on strange influences.

Exalted ideas – In a large number of cases ideas of exaltation are added to the ideas of persecution, sometimes from the beginning, more frequently first in the further course when they often come quite into the foreground of the clinical picture. Here and there perhaps only ideas of exaltation are observed. [. . .]

Sexual ideas – A conspicuously large place in the clinical picture of dementia praecox seems to me to be occupied by sexual delusions which are often connected with the sexual sensations described above. The ideas of sin are not infrequently connected with this domain. The patient has committed sin with his step-daughter, with his sister, has had intercourse with cows so that hybrids have been produced; he has committed a crime against decency, has ruined himself by sexual excess, is homo-sexual, is a sadist. He has become impotent through onanism, the 'neurosis' proceeds from onanism, onanism can be recognized in his face. [...]

But above all things patients feel themselves sexually influenced in the most varied ways. A neighbour's wife occupied herself at night with the genitals of the patient, nuns constantly withdraw seminal emissions from him and behave immodestly before him. [...] Women feel that they have lost their virtue, that their honour has been tarnished; their father, their clergyman has abused them; their master, the Kaiser comes at night to them. Gentlemen are sent to them for sexual intercourse, someone lies on them every night. [...]

In connexion with these insane ideas an irritable aversion to the other sex is not infrequently developed. A patient spat at the girls he met. Women fall into lively excitement as soon as the physician comes near, speak abusively in obscene language about debauchery and whoredom, will not have anything to do with men. A patient cut off her hair in order to displease her followers.

Ideas of reference – The events of the outside world are brought into manifold connexion with the delusions by means of 'conjecturing thoughts'. Indifferent remarks and chance looks, the whispering of other people, appear suspicious to the patient. 'I feel myself referred to there,' said a patient. A passer-by shows off his big nose, his red face on purpose to mock at the patient. News in the papers contain allusions, he finds in them thoughts which he has had. 'My instinct tells me that,' asserted a patient. His fellow-patients are appointed to watch him; a patient who heard others speaking about him said, 'I think to myself that the doctor gives people the commission to make me mad, the thunderstorm must help too'. [...] Frequently the delusions are connected with dreams which are regarded simply as actual experiences or as significant portents.

The delusions of our patients often show, as the given examples do, an extraordinary, sometimes wholly *nonsensical* stamp. As a rule also they are either not at all, or only in a very superficial way, worked up mentally and are scarcely brought into inner connexion with one another. The patients do not try to give any account of the reliability of their observations and conclusions, do not search for explanations of their remarkable experiences, their persecutions, their good fortune; they make no difficulties and pay no regard if any are pointed out to them, but rather hold the more to their insane ideas without further proof. 'I have innumerable proofs and not one,' said a patient.

But always here and there we meet with a certain systematization of the morbid ideas mostly indeed only temporary; they are connected with one another by all sorts of unwarranted assumptions or subtle arguments. [. . .]

In accordance with their generally very *loose inner connexion* the delusions are for the most part by no means constant, but they change their content more or less quickly by the disappearance of former and the addition of new constituents. At times the patients produce nearly every day new delusional details in spite of certain persistently returning characteristic features, and perhaps let themselves be stimulated to further delusions by suggestion. In the overwhelming majority of cases, however, the delusions which are at first often very luxuriant, gradually cease. At most a few insane ideas are for some time adhered to without being further developed, or they appear once again from time to time, or finally they fall into oblivion permanently and completely. Only in that group of observations with which we shall later become acquainted as paranoid dementia are the delusional ideas generally more connected for a longer time, perhaps for some years, and appear unchanged in the main point, but here also they become gradually more confused and more contradictory.

Emotion – Very striking and profound damage occurs as a rule in the emotional life of our patients. The most important of these changes is their *emotional dullness*. The disorders of attention which have already been mentioned might be essentially connected with the loss of interest, the loss of inner sympathy, with the giving way of those emotional main-springs which move us to exert our mental powers, to accomplish our tasks, to follow trains of thought. The singular indifference of the patients towards their former emotional relations, the extinction of affection for relatives and friends, of satisfaction in their work and vocation, in recreation and pleasures, is not seldom the first and most striking symptom of the onset of disease. The patients have no real joy in life, 'no human feelings'; to them 'nothing matters, everything is the same'; they feel 'no grief and no joy', 'their heart is not in what they say'. [. . .]

Hopes and wishes, cares and anxieties are silent; the patient accepts without emotion dismissal from his post, being brought to the institution, sinking to the life of a vagrant, the management of his own affairs being taken from him; he remains without more ado where he is put 'till he is dismissed', begs that he may be taken care of in an institution, feels no humiliation, no satisfaction; he lives one day at a time in a state of apathy. The background of his disposition is either a meaningless hilarity or a morose and shy irritability. One of the most characteristic features of the disease is a frequent, causeless, sudden outburst of *laughter*, that often is strikingly in evidence already at the very commencement. 'His thoughts always made him laugh,' said the relatives of a patient.

Moral sentiments also and their regulating influence on action suffer severe loss. Not only in the former history of the patient do we find manifold contraventions of the penal code and public order, but also during the disease itself deeds are frequently committed which are dangerous to the common weal. Pighini found that among 114 mental patients who were sentenced, 49·1 per cent were cases of dementia praecox.

Loss of sympathy is shown in indifference and want of understanding for the misfortunes of others, in the roughness with which the patients occasionally ill-use their companions in misfortune on the most trifling occasion; a woman tried to strangle the patient in the next bed in order to free her from her troubles. Even the fate of his nearest relatives affect the patient little or not at all. He receives their visits without a greeting or other sign of emotion, does not inquire how they are, takes no share in their joys or sorrows. A patient remained quite indifferent to the death of his mother, and then excused himself, as he could not help it; 'Life is nothing to me and death is nothing,' he said. A patient who had cut the throats of her three children because they were bewitched and would not be rightly brought up, did not show afterwards the slightest emotion; her children were now angels and well taken care of, she explained.

Another phenomenon of emotional dementia is the *disappearance of delicacy of feeling*. The patients have no longer any regard for their surroundings; they do not suit their behaviour to the situation in which they are, they conduct themselves in a free and easy way, laugh on serious occasions, are rude and impertinent towards their superiors, challenge them to duels, lose their deportment and personal dignity; they go about in untidy and dirty clothes, unwashed, unkempt, go with a lighted cigar into church, speak familiarly to strangers, decorate themselves with gay ribbons. The feeling of disgust and of shame is also lost. The patients do not preserve control of the sphincters. They pass their excreta under them, they ease themselves under the bed, in the spittoon, in their hat, in the dishes, they make little balls of faeces, collect their evacuations in handkerchiefs or cigar-boxes, smear themselves with urine, wash their handkerchief in the full chamber; they take their food with their fingers, they spit in their bed or in their hand, or on their bread, they devour beetles and worms, sip dirty bath-water, or empty at one draught the full spittoon. The want of a feeling of shame expresses itself in regardless uncovering of their persons, in making sexual experiences public, in obscene talk, in improper advances, and in shameless masturbation.

It appears also that the patients often become *less sensitive to bodily discomfort*; they endure uncomfortable positions, pricks of a needle, injuries, without thinking much about it; burn themselves with their cigar, hurt themselves, tear out the hair from their genitals, let the glaring noonday sun shine in their face for hours, do not chase away the flies which settle on their eyelids. Often, however, food retains for a long time a special power of attraction. When their relatives visit them the patients are seen hurriedly rummaging through their bags and baskets for things to eat, which they immediately devour to the last crumb, chewing with their mouths full. In the terminal conditions of the illness, perfect indifference towards all that goes on in the neighbourhood is often enough one of the principal features of the clinical picture.

On the foundation of the more or less strongly marked emotional dullness, however, *sudden oscillations of emotional equilibrium* of extraordinary violence may be developed. In particular, sudden outbursts of rage with or without external occasion are not infrequent and can lead to most serious deeds of violence. The patients destroy objects, smash windows, force open doors, deal out boxes on the ear. A patient stabbed a girl's arm, another killed his master, a third killed a companion by whom he felt himself influenced. On the other hand the patients may suddenly fall into the most unrestrained merriment with uncontrollable laughter, seldomer into states of intense anguish. All these emotions are distinguished by the suddenness of their onset and disappearance and the often quite sudden change of mood. At the same time they have often no recognizable connexion with the experiences or the ideas of the patients. Bleuler, however, brings forward the view that in such states it is usually a case of contact with the 'complexes', the sensitive traumata of life. I have not been able to convince myself of that, but believe much rather that we have essentially to do with the loss of that permanent colouring of the background of mood which in normal people influences all chance oscillations of the emotions, equalizing and checking them and which only then lets them appear in greater strength when an important occasion finds a powerful echo in our being.

Stransky has, therefore, not without justification, said that it is a case in our patients less of an emotional devastation, than of an 'ataxia of the feelings', a loss of connexion with other mental occurrences. I am inclined to assume that this confusion in the emotional life is caused essentially by the weakening of the higher permanent feelings whose task it is on the one hand to check sudden oscillations of feeling, on the other hand to give to our inward states permanently equable tension and temperature, and so to become security for the agreement of our emotional relations with the outer world. Exactly in the terminal conditions with pronounced dementia one frequently observes emotional irritability with sudden, violent outbursts, and also excitement which appears without cause with more or less regular periodicity.

The comparatively great independence on outer influences of the temper has as a consequence that it often remains for a very long time extremely *uniform*. Many patients constantly exhibit a silly cheerfulness, others always a lachrymose dull depression or an ill-humoured strained behaviour. They are not brought out of their careless contentment either by unpleasant occurrences or by the blows of fate, nor can they be comforted, nor can their affection be won. But the course of the illness itself can bring about unexpectedly some day a sudden change in their mood.

Here and there it may be observed that the disposition of the patients is exactly *contrary to the actual state of affairs*. The patients laugh while they narrate an attempt at suicide, or the death of a near relative, and weep bitterly on any occasion for mirth. Sometimes it is only a case of want of relationship between mood and expression – of paramimia. The most frequent occurrence of the kind is senseless laughing without mirthfulness. The patient cannot help laughing; he does it even when he does not wish to; he has 'laughing fever', said a patient. Also the mingling of crying and laughing, crying in tune, dancing about with fixed and furrowed features belong to the paramimic phenomena.

But further there sometimes takes place in the patients a *complete reversal of their emotional relationships*, which may be the first sign of the approaching illness: Former feelings of affection are changed into downright aversion. In especial the nearest relatives suffer frequently. Towards his parents of whom he has hitherto been fond, the patient behaves rudely, haughtily, threateningly;

he abuses them in obscene language; his mother is an old spitfire, his father is a rogue, a perjured dog. [. . .]

Volition – Hand in hand with the profound disorders of the emotional life go the extensive and varied morbid manifestations in the domain of *work and conduct*, which specially give the clinical picture its peculiar stamp. They are composed of a series of diverse fundamental disorders. In the first place we have commonly to do with a general *weakening of volitional impulses*. The patients have lost every independent inclination for work and action; they sit about idle, trouble themselves about nothing, do not go to their work, neglect their most pressing obligations, although they are perhaps still capable of employing themselves in a reasonable way if stimulated from outside. They experience no tediousness, have no need to pass the time, 'no more joy in work', but can lie in bed unoccupied for days and weeks, stand about in corners, 'stare into a hole', watch the toes of their boots or wander aimlessly about. For work they have 'no inclination'; 'their nerves can't stand it'. A patient did no work for two years, 'in order not to deprive people of gain'; another had in view, after having used his last sovereign, to go into the Lake of Constance; a third asked 'for an easy job, perhaps as a clergyman'.

Automatic obedience – This loss of instinct for occupation, even though its clinical manifestations may be inconspicuous, represents without doubt an *unusually severe disorder*, as the activity of the will forms the most important foundation of psychic personality. To it there stands in close relationship that *susceptibility of the will to influence*, which finds its most distinct expression in the phenomena of automatic obedience. As the inner activity of volition fails, the resistance which outside influences meet within us is also easily lost. The patients therefore are usually docile, let themselves be driven as a herd, so that they form the necessary nucleus of those crowds which conform willingly to the monotonous daily round in large institutions. A not inconsiderable number join without resistance the crowd of vagabonds which chance leads today hither, tomorrow thither.

But also fully developed automatic obedience is extremely frequent. It is found in all stages of the disease, at the beginning as well as at the end, not infrequently also as the one noticeable remaining feature of the disease in otherwise apparently complete recovery. It is seen in waxy flexibility, in the preservation of whatever positions the patient may be put in, even although they may be very uncomfortable. Again, automatic obedience, as its name expresses, appears in involuntary obedience when called upon to do things, even those which are visibly disagreeable to the patient. He continues to put out his tongue when commanded to do so although one threatens to stab it, and causes him pain with a needle, as can be seen by the grimaces he makes. It might also be considered as automatic obedience that the patient submits to unpleasant touching of his face, tickling of the mucous membrane of his nose, piercing a fold of his eyelid without defending himself, in as far as these proceedings contain the unspoken command not to prevent them. Again echolalia and echopraxis belong to this group of phenomena, the involuntary repetition of words said to them, the imitation of movements made in front of them, or the continuance of movements passively initiated. 'I do it because you wish it so.' 'I place myself according to what is commanded.'

'I was unconscious, I had to do everything,' say the patients. But in the end a curious constraint of the movements is invariably connected with automatic obedience, which apparently stands in relation to the inner want of freedom of the patient, with the uncertainty of the patient's own will and its susceptibility to influence from all possible accidental occurrences. Often indeed is it so distinctly marked that it makes the conclusion very probable that there will be other disorders of automatic obedience.

Impulsive actions – The weakening of the dominion of will in the psychic life provides further, as it appears, the conditions favourable for the appearance of the impulsive actions which attain such great significance in dementia praecox. The relaxing of those restraints, which keep the activity of normal people in well defined paths, provides chance impulses with the freedom to turn themselves unhesitatingly into action without regard to the end in view or to suitability. So it happens that the patients commit a great many of the most nonsensical and incomprehensible acts of which they themselves are usually unable to explain the cause. 'I have a sort of feeling as if I must do that,' explained a patient who was screaming and biting everything. 'I had no free course left me, I had often to do things without knowing why,' said another. [. . .]

The patients suddenly break a mirror in pieces, knock over tables and chairs, take down pictures, throw objects out at the window, climb on to a cupboard, set fire to their hair, run naked into the street, ring bells, put their heads in the basin of the water-closet, set the chamber on their head, creep under the table, smash a lamp. Usually such senseless actions are carried out with great violence, suddenly, and with lightning rapidity, so that it is impossible to prevent them; the patients also oppose themselves in the most insolent way to every attempt to keep them from doing these things. [. . .]

In certain circumstances the impulsive actions of the patients may become extraordinarily dangerous. The patients suddenly give a box on the ear to anyone they meet, make a furious attack on a neighbour, set fire to beds, tear off a gas-bracket. [. . .]

Often sexual impulses are also very lively. The patients masturbate without regard for their surroundings, or in the examination by the physician, snatch at the genitals of their fellow-patients, take hold of their sister under her skirts. A patient raped his brother's cook and tried to do the same to his sister-in-law. A female patient for years made regardless sexual attacks on the physicians, in order through intercourse 'to be freed from the oppression on her breast'.

Catatonic excitement – The peculiar condition of catatonic excitement consists of a collection of senseless actions and movements with which we shall have later to occupy ourselves in more detail. Besides impulsive actions we meet at the same time in large number and variety with discharges of will-power, in which every relation to the realization of fixed aims is wanting, but which appear in the form of completely aimless movements. They have no connexion either among each other or with ideas or emotions, but have the tendency to repeat themselves very often either in the same form or with all manner of changes. Here and there they still bear the character of mutilated movements of purpose or expression, from which partly at least they may arise. The patients hop, jump, turn somersaults, scream, grunt, see-saw, drum, screech, go through the movements of ringing, of playing the violin, usually with the expenditure of all their energy, but without any recognizable aim.

Stereotypy – With the disorders of volition which have already been considered, there is very frequently connected in dementia praecox, as has already been indicated, another, the tendency to the instinctive persistence of the same volitional movements, stereotypy. It shows itself in continuance in the *same positions* as well as in the repetition of the *same movements* or *actions*. The will is here to a certain extent influenced for a considerable time by previous activities, in the same way as in automatic obedience. Stransky therefore speaks, probably with right, of an 'auto-echolalia' and 'auto-echopraxis'. The patients stand or kneel for hours, days, or still longer, on the same spot, lie in the most uncomfortable positions in bed, fold their hands spasmodically, even till pressure-sores appear, take up the position of fencing. Usually it is possible only with the most extreme force to bring them out of such a position, which they usually take up again as soon as the hindrance has ceased.

Much more varied are the stereotypies of movement which we often meet in the most marked form, especially in states of catatonic excitement. In the milder degrees it is more a matter of a certain uniformity of volitional expression, the persistence of definite activities. The patients always make the same gestures, go the same ways, pull their hair out. [...] In the same category there belong also twitching movements in different groups of muscles, raising a shoulder, 'contortionist movements', waving with the hands, touching definite parts of their bodies with their fingers, conspicuous clearing of their throats, smacking of their lips, snorting. A patient who always twitched with his alae nasi, explained, 'That is just my way'.

Sometimes the whole volitional expression of the patient is dominated by stereotypies for a long time, so that his doings resolve themselves into an almost uninterrupted series of senseless movements which are either monotonous, or repeat themselves with slight changes. A certain *rhythm* invariably results. The patients rock themselves from one leg on to the other, keep time, 'pull letters away from their fingertips', spread out their fingers with a quavering movement, clap their hands, shake their heads, bellow keeping time, give themselves boxes on their ears, run up and down in double quick time. About the motives for these proceedings, no satisfactory account is got from them. [...]

We may well suppose that also the development of such stereotypies which later give such a peculiar appearance to the terminal states of the disease and likewise to many forms of idiocy, is specially favoured by the failure of healthy volitional impulses, perhaps first made possible. Many experiences at least indicate that the mechanism of our will possesses arrangements acquired long ago, which favour a rhythmical repetition of the same discharges; their influence will be able to make itself felt as soon as the impulses disappear which serve for a realization of intentions.

Mannerisms – The uncertainty and weakness of the volitional movements which are accompanied with consciousness of purpose, and further the ease with which all possible impulses can influence volitional expression perhaps explain how it is that the actions of our patients often end in *morbidly changed forms*. Even simple movements can show such changes. Sometimes they are carried out with too great an expenditure of force, or unnecessary groups of muscles take part in them, or too much of the limb is employed, so that they become ungraceful and clumsy; or they are not rounded off, they begin and end jerkily and appear therefore stiff, wooden, and angular. Other patients again arrive at the aim of the movement not by the nearest way, but by round-about ways with all sorts of changes and interpolations; they add flourishes by which the movements become unnatural, affected and manneristic. Through such peculiarities, which are called mannerisms, the processes of breathing, speaking and writing, standing and walking, dressing and undressing, shaking hands and eating, smoking, gestures, and the mode of setting to work, can be influenced and transformed in the most manifold way. [. . .]

The process of taking food especially may be changed by the most manifold side impulses. Frequently the patients simply thrust their hands into their plate, fall upon the common dish, hurriedly stuff their mouths as full as possible and swallow their food down almost without chewing, or the spoon is grasped quite lightly with their finger-tips, often at the extreme end and the handle is used for eating; their food is invariably stirred about with their forks two or three times before each mouthful, the vegetables are divided into a row of equal little heaps, their hands are first wrapped up in their coats, their nose is stuck into the soup, or there must be a mouthful drunk between each two mouthfuls of food till twelve are counted and so on. [. . .]

Not infrequently the aim of the action is wholly or at least partially frustrated by the changes and made unrecognizable, so that the impression arises of oddness and senselessness. [. . .] All these mannerisms have a pronounced tendency to persist, and they may form part of the behaviour of a patient without change for decades. Through them especially arise the half-repulsive, half-ludicrous impressions which strike the laity on visiting an institution for the insane, and it is those therefore above all from which the popular picture of 'lunatic' is usually composed.

It is made still more complete by the oddities in the outer adornment of the patients, the extraordinary modes of dressing the hair, the earrings made of pieces of wire, the gay ribbons in the hair and in the button-hole, the peculiar ornaments of the clothes. [. . .]

Parabulia – Gradual transitions from the simple changes of every-day purposeful actions lead to those disorders of volition which we may gather together under the name of parabulia. The side impulses which at first bring about only flourishes in action may gradually become cross impulses which lead to complete derailment of volition. Some examples belonging to this class we have already brought forward in which to a certain extent a distorted picture of natural actions arises by the employment of unsuitable means. But further, an action at first perhaps correctly begun is turned away in quite another direction by cross impulses or perhaps simply stopped before completion. . . . The hand that will stretch out and take hold of the spoon, goes to the nose to scratch there; the patient who will put on his coat, puts his legs into the sleeves. [. . .]

Whether we have here to do with the turning away of actions in a different direction or with the stopping before completion of actions already begun, the cross or contrary impulse can further suppress the volitional movement itself even as it is already coming into being, so that the action which is about to be done is not even begun, but from the outset is replaced by another or simply suppressed. The patient who is to show his tongue, opens his eyes wide instead, he flings the cup away instead of putting it to his mouth. We shall consider these 'parergasias' more in detail in the discussion of the movements of expression.

Negativism – By far the most important form of parabulia is the suppression of volitional movements by contrary impulses, negativism. It is natural that of the innumerable side impulses which in themselves are possible, those should take up a special position which are exactly *contrary* to the attainment of the end in view; on the appearance of a volitional intention they are at the same time most strongly stimulated in consciousness by the action of contrast. Negativistic obstruction of volition plays therefore an extraordinarily large role in the clinical picture of dementia praecox. [. . .]

It is, however, certain that the disorders commonly collected under the term negativism have not all the same origin, as Bleuler in particular has shown in detail. At first insane ideas or ill-temper, especially anxiety or irritability, cause the patients to shut themselves up from their environment. They do not touch their food because they think it is poisoned, do not lie down in bed because they imagine that they are threatened with the danger of syphilitic infection there, do not shake hands because they distrust the physician, or fear his influencing them, and they will not have anything to do with him. In a similar way probably one should regard the resistant attitude of the bewildered and confused patients to whom everything appears changed, incomprehensible, and mysterious; here also anxious distrust may be assumed as the mainspring of their opposition. In none of these cases is it a question of negativism in the sense of a disorder specially peculiar to dementia praecox. It appears to me also that the behaviour of such patients towards the stimuli which they encounter does not differ from that of other anxious or irritable persons; in especial on stronger provocation they fall into excitement, make lively movements of defence, or even pass over to attack. [. . .]

Autism – The clinical phenomena, in which negativism shows itself, are extremely varied. It is a common experience that the patients with dementia praecox are more or less inaccessible, that they shut themselves off from the outer world. Bleuler has described this important symptom as *autism*. The refusal of all psychic contact is often shown in the whole behaviour of the patients as soon as one begins to occupy oneself with them. They do not look up when spoken to, perhaps turn away their head, or turn their back directly to the questioner. The hand offered in greeting is refused, 'It is not proper', 'In bed the hand is not given', 'Only women greet each other that way', say the patients; they have given the hand too often formerly. Many patients close their eyes, cover their faces with their hands, cover themselves up, draw the bed-cover over their head, and convulsively hold it fast; 'This position is pleasant for the eyes and more restful for the inner life', explained a patient. [. . .]

Stupor – But even when they do express themselves, one notices very distinctly by their niggardly, resisting, forced statements which tell nothing, the resistance which they oppose to any searching into their inner life. Frequently the patients have already shut themselves off from their family and their surroundings long before the appearance of the more striking symptoms, say only the most necessary things, do not appear any more at the common meals, avoid all friendly intercourse, bolt themselves in, take lonely walks. They bluntly refuse visits from the physician and friendly relations with their fellow-patients. As the disorder becomes further elaborated there is developed the picture of negativistic stupor, the rigid, impenetrable shutting up of themselves from all outer influences, which is connected with a suppression driven to the limit of the possible of all natural emotions.

Causation of negativism – As has already been indicated in the general part, the understanding of negativism in the sense here depicted requires to be connected with the fact that our thinking and acting constantly have to make decisions between different, often contrary ideas and volitional resolves. In especial our whole relationship to the environment is governed throughout by volitional movements of inclination and disinclination, and the suitable choice of these possesses fundamental importance for our existence. Bleuler speaks of an 'ambivalence' and an 'ambitendency' of psychical processes, in the sense that they are accompanied at the same time by contrary emotional stresses and can lead to contrary emotional movements. He assumes on the basis of his experiences that this discord in feelings and impulses comes under observation specially frequently and strongly in dementia praecox, and forms an important foundation for the development of negativism.

But of course even if that discord be granted, still further explanations are needed, not indeed why the choice between resistance and yielding oscillates in an unaccountable way which certainly often enough happens, but why so frequently during a long period the negativistic movements govern the sum total of the actions in so decided a way. So far as morbid moods or delusions play a part, I believe, as has been mentioned above, that it is not a case of genuine negativism. At most it might be admitted that with their help the tendency to the appearance of negativistic phenomena, which is present in any case, may be strengthened, as conversely negativism perhaps also exercises some influence on the content of hallucinations and delusions, as on the tone of the mood.

In the last place, however, there must be other causes which determine the governing position of the contrary impulses, because of their instinctive origin and their independence of the remaining contents of consciousness. Besides erotic emotions which are usually even in healthy life already accompanied by discordant processes of emotion and volition, Bleuler regards as such, principally the 'autistic' tendency of the patients to withdraw themselves into themselves, the existence of specially sensitive 'life traumata', and the 'forcing of thoughts', the deficient command over the train of thought. He reckons, however, for the explanation of 'inner negativism' also with influences unknown as yet.

The significance of erotic emotions is in my opinion to be judged of in a similar way to those other feelings and therefore to be left out of account in the fundamental explanation of genuine negativism. That in the behaviour of the patients 'life traumata' play a part to any great extent, so that they shut themselves up from their surroundings as a protection from contact has, as I believe, till now neither been proved nor even made probable; also the fact that negativism frequently appears and disappears so suddenly seems to me to argue very much against such an interpretation. In contrast the 'autism' of the patients stands certainly without doubt in near relation to their negativism, only I should think that it represents not so much a cause but much rather a manifestation of negativism. The tendency to shut themselves off from their surroundings is frequently found in our patients already many years before the real onset of the disease and it is a very common phenomenon in the terminal states. But I very much doubt if it, as Bleuler thinks, is caused by the withdrawal of the patient to his own phantasies, and if he on this account feels every diverting of attention as an intolerable disturbance. Stubborn inaccessibility is often enough shown by patients on the one hand, in whom there can be no thought of special imaginings in which they could lose themselves, and it is lacking on the other hand in innumerable other delusional forms of disease, as specially in paralysis in which the patients certainly do dream themselves into a world of imaginings which are greatly disturbed by the influences of the surroundings.

It seems far more probable to me that negativism and 'autism' which is only its forerunner, are not at all connected with ideas or 'complexes', but with the general constraint of volition which is so specially peculiar to dementia praecox. Already on the most varied occasions we have had to point to the fact that the patients *lose the mastery over volition* and often feel this profound disorder more or less distinctly. They are heard describing their inner constraint always in new and emphatic expressions. Their will has been taken from them; it is weak, they have no will of their own any more, are not masters over it; there is no independence in them. 'I am not melancholy, and not senseless,' said a patient, 'I only lack a will of my own, an impulse of my own.' The patients feel themselves not free, influenced, dominated by external will, by invisible might, by magic powers possessed by superhuman beings 'like an automaton'; they suffer from 'auto-suggestion and high grade suggestibility', stand 'as under compulsion', are in 'slavery to suggestion'; 'I am a man under compulsion,' explained a patient. An external force has power over them under whose ban they must wholly exist and act; they must do what others wish, other people have power over them. [. . .]

We have already mentioned that even the isolated peculiar acts are caused as a rule without further motive by irresistible impulses. [. . .] Here and there the impulses take on the form of auditory hallucinations without the nature of the process being thereby essentially altered; voices summon the patient to do this or that, and he 'must do all that they ask'.

Personality – From these and similar utterances of the patients it clearly follows that their thinking, feeling, and acting have lost the unity and especially that permanent inner dependence on the essence of the psychic personality, which provides the healthy human being with the feeling of inner freedom; 'I can't get hold of my will,' said a patient. We may assume that this profound change in the psychic life, which indicates a complete destruction of the personality, must in itself influence the attitude towards the outer world in the most decisive way. The most natural protective measure of the weak consists in shutting himself up and hiding. The more or less distinct feeling of inner constraint and powerlessness which accompanies our patients along with childish susceptibility to influence could therefore on the other hand play an essential part in the development of their obstinate seclusion. If the disorder of volition can influence the conduct of the patients in both directions and if it at the same time makes it more difficult for them to hold fast to a uniform attitude towards their surroundings, we should also have come nearer to the understanding of the frequent oscillations between heightened sensitiveness to influence and stubborn negativism. It is self-evident here that we must not, as has already been pointed out, think of conscious deliberation. Much rather is it the general change of the personality and its behaviour towards the ordinary events of life that come into consideration as it is conditioned by the perception of its own inner want of independence. If one wishes, one may with more right in my judgement regard the feeling of the destruction of the will, which may precede the real onset of the disease under certain circumstances certainly by many years, as a 'life trauma' which cannot endure any contact and therefore causes the patient to shut himself up, rather than the influence of other chance events of life. That disorder would also to a certain extent explain the tendency of many of the patients to spin themselves round with imaginings; he who is not able to control his own will, and with it his life, gladly takes refuge in the realm of dreams.

Practical efficiency – As the mental, so also the practical efficiency of the patients is invariably greatly encroached on by the disorders of volition. They come to a standstill at every difficulty, must always be driven on again, work extremely unequally, do a great deal of their work wrongly, are completely unreliable, spoil material and tools. At the same time, however, a certain technical skill can be preserved. In their handiwork the loss of taste often makes itself felt in their choice of extraordinary combinations of colour and peculiar forms. [. . .]

Self-expression – The general disorders of volition often take many peculiar forms in the movements of expression of the patients. The cessation of the need to express oneself corresponds to the disappearance of volitional activity. The patients become monosyllabic, sparing of their words, speak hesitatingly, suddenly become mute, never relate anything on their own initiative, let all answers be laboriously pressed out of them. They enter into no relations with other people, never begin a conversation with anyone, ask no questions, make no complaints, give their relatives no news. They write no letters or only those with almost nothing in them, stop after writing a few lines. Their facial expression also is vacant and dull, their gestures are limp, few, and monotonous. On this foundation echolalia easily appears, which makes itself known in the involuntary repetition of questions asked or other things said to them, as well as in the introduction of fragments of speech caught up into their own utterances.

In the states of excitement in place of taciturnity a prodigious flow of talk may appear which does not correspond to a need for expression, but usually unburdens itself without any reference to the surroundings. Often it consists of outbursts of filthy abuse, piercing shrieks or singing; a patient whistled tunes all day on a water-bottle; many patients carry on monologues or answer voices out loud, often cursing and abusing, especially in the night. The following is a record of a fairly lively dialogue of this kind, which a patient carried on with his voices:

What does it matter to me then what you think! That has nothing to do with me, is in the highest degree indifferent to me. What? I must think that? That I must not at all. I can think what I like, and you think what you like! That would be still better? No, that would not be better at all! I can certainly do with my head what I will! I must wholly misunderstand you! That is entirely your affair if you share your thoughts with me! It is not I who am ill. You are the patient! [. . .]

Incoherence of the train of thought, as we have already depicted it, is usually distinctly noticeable in the conversation of the patients. The most different ideas follow one another with most bewildering want of connexion, even when the patients are quite quiet. A patient said 'Life is a dessert-spoon,' another, 'We are already standing in the spiral under a hammer,' a third, 'Death will be awakened by the golden dagger,' a fourth, 'The consecrated discourse cannot be over split in any movement,' a patient, 'I don't know what I am to do here, it must be the aim, that means to steal with the gentlemen.' [. . .]

Stereotypy is shown in the frequent recurrence of the same turns of expression which occasionally are 'done to death'. A patient added on to everything; 'We Germans don't have that,' another always answered, 'Certainly, certainly', a female patient invariably interpolated 'bitt schön'. [. . .]

In this senseless rigmarole single words and phrases are always brought forward again, sometimes exactly the same, sometimes with all sorts of changes, specially 'über sein', 'venerishcrenerisch', 'Arzttalent-Feldherrntalent', 'was ich bin', 'im Geist-am Geist', 'hinausel'.

If stereotypy is still more strongly pronounced, the morbid symptom of *verbigeration* is developed, the endless repetition of the same sentences, usually in measured cadence. A female patient repeated the following sentence from seven o'clock to half-past nine:

> I beg you to put me in another bed, in the bed where it was got ready yesterday; else I shall not get out of hell any more. Jesus, dear Master mine, let me rely faithfully on thee; lead me in the right path, O do lead me heavenward. You are my mother's lady's maid, and my mother is also there. [. . .]

Negativism shows itself in the domain of speech activity, on the one hand in *mutism*, on the other hand in *resistive* or *evasive answers*. Many patients answer every question with another question or with 'How?' and then perhaps without further ado give the required information; others simply repeat the question. Answers are often given that say nothing, are indefinite, or quite without relation to the subject. Negativism appears more distinctly when the patients answer to all remarks, 'I don't know' or 'I don't need to tell you that'. Sometimes the patients obstinately maintain silence, as long as one is occupied with them, and begin to talk when one turns away from them, or they try to speak, utter a few words, but suddenly break off and cannot be moved to any further utterance; a few patients speak with certain people, but are wholly inaccessible to others. Many patients speak low, scarcely move their lips, murmur unintelligibly to themselves. In the end it comes to complete mutism, which lasts for months or years, but which may be suddenly interrupted by outbursts of the most violent abuse or screaming. In certain circumstances the patients in this state still give utterance in writing to their thoughts, sometimes expressing them comprehensively and for the most part very confusedly; a patient declared that he wrote because he could not find words readily. [. . .]

Derailments in linguistic expression form a specially important domain in the speech disorders of dementia praecox. Vocal speech itself can be changed in the most varied way by side and cross impulses. The patients in speaking, bellow, screech, murmur or whisper, scarcely move their lips, keep their teeth closed, or often pass suddenly from low whispering to loud screaming. The flow of speech is frequently hurried and rapid even in low speaking, sometimes varying quite irregularly, or speech is jerkily broken up, or produced keeping time with sharp rhythmical modulation. The cadence often lacks the risings and fallings, the melodies of speech; the timbre of the voice may also be changed. The patients speak in falsetto, through their noses, in an artificial bass voice, pass suddenly from one key to another. [. . .]

Later there are introduced into speech not infrequently clicking and smacking sounds, sniffing, and snorting, bleating words without sense, stock phrases with tiring repetition. Many patients *speak affectedly* with excessively distinct pronunciation, with distortion of single letters and with senseless intonation; [. . .]

In their *writings* there is found an arbitrary, peculiar disorder with whimsical misuse of punctuation marks and orthography invented by themselves.

Neologisms – There are intimations here already of a further form of paraphasic derailment, which may become of very great extent in dementia praecox, neologisms. In several of the examples quoted it was already a case of new unintelligible words, but they were, however, composed of sensible component parts. ('Papstneuner', 'Pgaumenschwach', 'Frevelschnur'.) But there may be produced also quite senseless collections of syllables, here and there still having a sound reminiscent of real words. A patient spoke of the 'Gestübe und Angstbetrieb'; another of the 'Totendumpf'; a third of the 'Lebepuppe'; a fourth of the 'Oxypathie', from which he was suffering; a fifth was 'krikeliert'; a sixth did not want to belong 'zur Tätowie'; a seventh drivelled in an unintelligible way of 'Reichsleben und Gerichtsleben'. [. . .]

The tendency to silly plays on words and neologisms can get the upper hand in our patients to such an extent that they fall into a wholly *incomprehensible gibberish*; they usually then give it out as a foreign language which by slight changes in the syllables may be changed into any other you like. [. . .]

Akataphasia – Not less worthy of note than the disorders in word-finding are those which influence in a morbid way the form of speech. At first we have to do with those derailments in the *expression of thought* in speech which we call akataphasia. In this case the patients either do not find the expression appropriate to their thoughts, but only produce something with a similar sound ('displacement paralogia'), or they let their speech fall into quite another channel ('derailment paralogia'). A patient said he was 'wholly without head on the date' for 'he did not know the date'; another complained he 'lived under protected police' instead of 'under the protection of police'; a third declared to his father he 'was the great judicial murder' instead of 'on him the greatest judicial murder was practised'. [. . .]

Construction of sentences – A further form of impairment of speech springs from *disorder in the construction of sentences*. In the examples of incoherence of the train of thought which were given before, the *syntax* is also confused in different places ('Former service and then she does it,' 'I, and that is also so curious, therefore the nun.' 'I should come from M. because always something happens, leg broken or something, they have quarrelled,' 'as I that at last of those that particularly believe'). [. . .]

Train of thought – The last group of examples brings us to derailments in the train of thought itself, which certainly often accompany the forms hitherto discussed. As already mentioned, we hear from our patients a great many quite incomprehensible and disconnected utterances, in which it can scarcely be only a question of disorders of linguistic expression, even though it is impossible in the individual case to discover the inner mechanism by which the utterances arose. Thus a patient spoke of the 'brain-navel of the merchants' association'; another said, 'One cannot take the direction from the reflection'. But sometimes a derivation of the train of thought from the series of ideas which is immediately present, to another, as frequently happens in dreams, is clearly seen. A patient when asked what year it was, replied, 'It may be Australia,' wandering from the series of years to the series of continents; another to the question what month it was, answered, 'Strassburg'. [. . .]

From these disorders the transition is easy to those phenomena with which we became acquainted before as *speaking past a subject*. Here it is no longer the transference to expression in speech that is morbidly influenced, but the ideas aroused by the circumstances are themselves already in their origin pushed aside or suppressed by ideas related but lying remote or opposed to the original ones.

Clinical Forms

The presentation of clinical details in the large domain of dementia praecox meets with considerable difficulties, because a delimitation of the different clinical pictures can only be accomplished artificially. There is certainly a whole series of phases which frequently return, but between them there are such numerous transitions that in spite of all efforts it appears impossible at present to delimit them sharply and to assign each case without objection to a definite form. We shall be obliged therefore, as in paralysis, to content ourselves at first for the sake of a more lucid presentation with describing the course of certain more frequent forms of the malady without attributing special clinical value to this grouping.

As such forms I have hitherto separated from each other a *hebephrenic*, a *catatonic*, and a *paranoid* group of cases. This classification has been frequently accepted with many modifications, specially concerned with the clinical position of the paranoid diseases, as also by Bleuler in his monograph on schizophrenia; he adds, however, to it the insidious 'dementia simplex' as a special form. Räcke has made other attempts at classification; he separates out 'depressive', 'confused excited', 'stuporous', 'subacute paranoid' forms and a 'catatonia in attacks'. Wieg-Wickenthal differentiates 'dementia simplex', 'hebephrenia' with pseudomanic behaviour, 'depressive paranoid forms' and catatonia.

The undoubted inadequacy of my former classification has led me once more to undertake the attempt to make a more natural grouping, as I have in hand a larger number of possibly more reliable cases. For this purpose there were at my disposal about 500 cases in Heidelberg which had been investigated by myself, in which according to their clinical features, as well as according to the length of the time that had passed, the ultimate issue of the morbid process could be accepted with considerable probability. 'Recovered' cases were not taken into account because of the uncertainty of their significance which still exists, but only such cases as had led to profound dementia or to distinctly marked and permanent phenomena of decreased function. On grounds which will be discussed later, it is, as I believe, not to be assumed that by this choice definite clinical types have quite fallen out of the scope of our consideration; at most a certain displacement in the frequency of the individual forms would be conceivable.

The result of this attempt at a classification agrees in many points with the statements of the above-mentioned investigators. First I also think that I should delimit simple insidious dementia as a special clinical form. Next in the series comes hebephrenia in the narrower sense of silly dementia which was first described by Hecker. A third group is composed of the simple depressive or stuporous forms, a fourth of states of depression with delusions. In a fifth form I have brought together the majority of the clinical cases which go along with conditions of greater excitement; one could speak of an agitated dementia praecox. To it is nearly related the sixth form, which includes essentially the catatonia of Kahlbaum, in which peculiar states of excitement are connected with stupor. A more divergent picture is seen in the seventh and eighth groups, in which the cases are placed which run a paranoid course, according to whether they end in the usual terminal states of dementia praecox or in paranoid, relatively hallucinatory, weak-mindedness. We shall then subject to special consideration the small number of observations which present the remarkable phenomenon of confusion of speech along with perfect sense and fairly reasonable activity.

Dementia Simplex

Simple insidious dementia as it was described by Diem* under the name dementia simplex consists in an *impoverishment and devastation of the whole psychic life which is accomplished quite imperceptibly*. The disease begins usually in the years of sexual development, but often the first slight beginnings can be traced back into childhood. On the other hand Pick has also described a 'primary progressive dementia of adults', but it is certainly very doubtful whether it may be grouped with dementia praecox. In our patients a deterioration of mental activity becomes very gradually noticeable. The former good, perhaps distinguished scholar, fails always more conspicuously in tasks which till then he could carry out quite easily, and he is more and more outstripped by his companions. He appears absentminded, thoughtless, makes incomprehensible mistakes, cannot any longer follow the teaching rightly, does not reach the standard of the class. While pure exercises of memory are perhaps still satisfactory, a certain poverty of thought, weakness of judgement and incoherence in the train of ideas appear always more distinctly. Many patients try by redoubled efforts to compensate for the results of their mental falling off, which is at first attributed by parents and teachers to laziness and want of good will. They sit the whole day over their work, learn by heart with all their might, sit up late at night, without being able to make their work any better. Others become idle and indifferent, stare for hours at their books without reading, give themselves no trouble with their tasks, and are not incited either by kindness or severity.

Hand in hand with this decline of mental activity there is a change of temperament, which often forms the first conspicuous sign of the developing malady. The patients become depressed, timid, lachrymose, or impertinent, irritable, malicious; sometimes

*Diem, Archiv f. Psychiatrie xxxvii. III.

a certain obstinate stubbornness is developed. The circle of their interests becomes narrower; their relations to their companions become cold; they show neither attachment nor sympathy. Not infrequently a growing estrangement towards parents and brothers and sisters becomes noticeable. The patients remain indifferent to whatever happens in the family circle, shut themselves up, limit the contact with their relatives to the least possible. Bleuler brings forward here as a frequent explanation the 'Œdipus complex', the concealed sexual inclination to one of the parents and the jealous emotions which arise from it. I consider that the generalization of that kind of case, which is certainly very rare, as belonging to the system of Freud, is wholly without foundation. It seems much more natural to me to explain the antagonism to relatives by the gloomy feeling of inferiority and the defiant resistance to it, but above all by the common experience that for a long time it has been the habit of the relatives to trace the morbid phenomena back to a moral offence, and to meet them with painful reprimands and measures. Similar antagonism is also seen quite commonly to develop in the relations with degenerate, wayward children.

Ambition and pleasure in the usual games and occasional occupations become extinct; wishes and plans for the future are silent; inclination and ability for useful occupation disappear. The patient has neither endurance nor understanding, works confusedly, begins everything the wrong way about, tries as far as possible to withdraw himself from claims on him. He remains lying in bed for days, sits about anywhere, trifles away his time in occupations of no value, devours perhaps without choice and without understanding chance and unsuitable literature, lives one day at a time without a plan. A few patients have indeed at times a certain feeling of the change, which takes place in them, often in hypochondriacal colouring; but the majority sink into dullness without being in any way sensible of it. Sometimes a certain restlessness is shown which causes the patient to take extended walks, to run away without any plan, to undertake aimless journeys. Alcohol is for him a special danger, he gives way to its temptations without resistance, and then very rapidly comes down in the world, and comes into conflict with public order and criminal law. That happens the more easily as many patients are very sensitive to intoxicating drinks.

In these circumstances the inability of the patient to undergo the preparatory training or to attain to the calling which was planned for him becomes always more clear. He passes no more examinations, is sent away as useless from every apprenticeship, does not fit in anywhere, nor does he feel at home in anything. After all possible unsuccessful attempts to get them settled, many patients in the end remain idle at home, where they either lead a quiet existence without activity and without desire, without any disorder of note, or they live their own lives, and as capricious oddities try the patience of their relatives severely. Other patients succeed in getting a foothold in some subordinate calling, especially in gardening and agriculture, where in narrow surroundings they are in a position to fulfil a limited number of duties. Others again, as no other expedient is known, are provided with some money and sent to America, where they immediately go to the bad; some manage to enter the Foreign Legion and are there again turned away after severe discipline and punishment. A considerable number in the end fall into the crowd of beggars and vagabonds, and oscillate hither and thither in a half-witted state from year's end to year's end between public highway and workhouse, where ever anew the hopeless attempt is made 'to turn them into useful people again'.

The development of this clinical picture invariably takes a series of years. It may stand still for a shorter or longer time, but on the other hand it may occasionally experience a more sudden exacerbation. The terminal result to which the malady leads is of varied character, as it may make a final halt on each step of its development. Thus then we see in a series of cases a very slight loss in the psychic life remain, which only becomes noticeable by comparison with former behaviour, while in others a marked psychic decline comes into existence.

The frequency of the malady is probably fairly large, even if only a small number of the cases are considered as morbid at all or even fall into the hands of the alienist. Who cannot call to mind companions of his youth who at first gave just ground for certain, perhaps brilliant, hopes, but then from some point of their development onwards failed in an incomprehensible way? It is here a question of these young people who, without palpable cause and without any special morbid phenomena, simply trifle away the time, or are only able to gain a position in life far under their original prospects. Neither they nor their relatives have perhaps any idea that a morbid process has taken place; only the knowledge of cases which run a severer course suggests the thought that such slight losses in psychic ability might also be due to dementia praecox. Here and there, perhaps, also individual caprices, peculiarities or temperamental inadequacy in people who are otherwise well developed psychically are to be regarded as residua of slight morbid disorders of the same kind as the disease here discussed, if it can be proved that they were first developed in a definite period of life.

When the disease comes to a standstill, it may mean a final, though incomplete, recovery; but sooner or later the morbid process may again progress. We are not able at present to say whether the latter is always possible, or if in many cases it is excluded. A really profound dementia, without fairly acute exacerbations, with a continuous development of the malady, only slowly progressive, does not seem to occur. On the contrary, a dementia simplex which lasts for many years, even for decades, forms often enough the introduction to one of the forms of dementia praecox which goes on to profound dementia, and which will be discussed later on. If one will, one may also regard dementia simplex in a certain way as the first period of dementia praecox. The cases which belong to it halt on one of the steps which form this period, while in the remaining forms there occurs progress of the malady beyond that point. But a first period in the sense of the term dementia simplex can certainly not always be proved, except in a certain number of observed cases.

Silly Dementia

That form of dementia praecox which we have called above 'silly dementia' is in many respects nearly related to simple insidious dementia. In its clinical picture there appears besides the progressive devastation of the psychic life *incoherence* in thinking, feeling, and action. It corresponds, as already mentioned, in its principal features to the clinical picture of *hebephrenia* which was described by Hecker* in 1871 as a type in connection with the researches of Kahlbaum. Hecker at that time brought together under this term a group of cases in which, after an introductory stage of melancholy, a stage of mania develops and then rapidly makes room for a quite peculiar weak-minded condition. Daraszkiewicz† then enlarged the idea of hebephrenia by including also the 'depressed forms' which lead to profound insanity.

The development of the disease is accomplished in almost four-fifths of the cases quite gradually; often an insidious change of the psychic personality precedes the appearance of more distinct morbid phenomena by many years. In the remaining patients the

* Hecker, Virchows Archiv lii. 394.

† Daraszkiewicz, Über Hebephrenie, insbesondere deren schwere Form. Diss. Dorpat, 1892.

disorder begins in subacute form; in a few cases it breaks out suddenly. In the preliminary stage there are sometimes nervous troubles, complaints of lassitude, headaches, feeling of giddiness, fainting-fits, irritability, disorders of sleep. The patients become absent-minded, forgetful, negligent; they tire easily, they cannot collect their thoughts any more; they appear lacking in ideas and understanding, they are silly and lazy; they fail in daily tasks, change their occupation, because it is too difficult for them, set aside their work, or give it up entirely.

Here and there hallucinations appear. The patients see apparitions, witches, dead people, will-o'-the-wisps, the devil with a white beard, little black mannikins, which sit down on their breasts. A patient saw 'the three most beautiful crowns in the world'; 'black points were flung at' another. [. . .]

Delusions – Not infrequently passing states of depression are developed. The patients are dispirited and dejected, they think they are syphilitic, have got the itch or dyspepsia; they have a feeling of oppression in their brain; they search out all possible physicians and quacks; the disease is in all their limbs. Their morbid sensations sometimes assume the most nonsensical forms. They have no brain any longer; their back is broken in two; their blood has been taken from them; their body has died; their legs are exchanged. A female patient thought that she had the Kaiser in her stomach, every human being in her body, a telephone, small dolls, a bicycle in her head, that she had a wooden head; five people had been made out of her. Other patients become anxious, are to blame for everything, are damned, have committed sins, are said to have killed someone; they wish to make confessions, read the Bible zealously, search out clergymen. People are looking at them, speaking about them, making fun of them, hatching out abominable crimes, are persecuting them, are selling them for immoral purposes, are hypnotizing them, are making fools of them. Little girls make sexual assaults on them; everywhere there are enemies, 'enchanters', conspirators; it is a year of revolution, a hereditary feud; the arch-enemy has a hand in it. [. . .] Thoughts of suicide often rise to the surface; a patient thought he would have liked to kill his child in order that it might not be so unhappy as himself.

Exalted ideas – On the other hand we meet also, but in smaller range with *exalted ideas*. The patient feels that he has a special call, is something more than everyone else, has a proud spirit, an enormous will-power, is 'the ornament of his feelings', is sent from God, will be Christ, receives revelations; the feast of the atonement is there. [. . .] Many patients do not acknowledge their father any longer, they speak of their 'so-called parents'.

At the time the patients are giving utterance to these nonsensical delusions they are for the most part fairly quiet and quite sensible, clear about time and place, about their surroundings and their affairs, but incoherent and desultory in their train of ideas; they are not in a position to occupy themselves seriously and with perseverance in mental work; they are childishly incapable of making a decision and susceptible to influence. Their delusions even appear mostly only as sudden thoughts, which are not further worked up or retained. Memory, especially what was learned at school, and the recollection of recent events may be quite undisturbed.

Emotions – These are for the most part in harmony with the ideas to which the patients give utterance, but are not very deep and they show quite sudden fluctuations. The patients laugh and weep without recognizable cause, sometimes convulsively, fall abruptly into violent excitement, but quieten down again just as suddenly. Sometimes there predominates an imperturbably exalted, self-satisfied mood; in other patients, a childish hilarity which passes easily into a lachrymose state or a pitiable faintheartedness; or the patients are mistrustful, peevish, impertinent, rough and rude, break out into obscene abuse on the most insignificant occasions, threaten and become violent. A patient without more ado shot a railway employee with whom he had fallen into an altercation. A few patients incline to exaggerated religiosity; a patient wished to change his religion; others plan to go into a cloister. Many are sexually excited, plan to be married; show a 'pathetic desire for love', masturbate, expose themselves, make sexual assaults on little girls; a patient wished to go to bed with his mother and sister. [. . .]

Conduct – The disease makes itself noticeable in by far the most striking way in the activities of the patients. Already in the beginning of the malady a change in their behaviour invariably sets in. They become dreamy, shy of their fellow-beings, withdraw themselves, shut themselves up, do not greet their friends any more, stand about in corners, stare intently in front of them, give no answer, talk with themselves. Others become stubborn, self-willed, difficult, insubordinate, or unrestrained, restless, loquacious. Their capacity for work suffers severely. They do not trouble themselves any more about their obligations, do everything the wrong way about; a patient cleaned his boots with mud. They leave everything where it is, suddenly throw the shovel away, go to bed, look out at the window all day long, busy themselves with trifling affairs, make wreaths of flowers; they exert themselves to learn poems off by heart, or to begin Latin; a patient said 'he took as great pains as possible to investigate thoroughly what the real meaning of positive and negative electricity was'. Many patients stop working, because they have enough to live on; others because of their performances being of less value, work 'for board' without wages; they frequently change their situations because they are of no use anywhere. [. . .]

The whole conduct of life of the patients becomes senseless and incoherent. They cannot any longer manage money; they make aimless purchases, give away and squander their property; a female patient threw good fruit to the pigs. A poor patient fooled away an inheritance of 5000 marks within two years; another stopped taking money for the wares which he sold. Many patients fall into drinking habits and in this way come down in the world with remarkable rapidity. In their outer appearance they become disorderly, negligent, dirty, peculiar. They do not wash themselves any more; they wear conspicuous clothing, tie cigar ribbons in their button-hole, stick paper in their ears; a patient put on a truss without any reason. [. . .]

With these are associated a multitude of incomprehensible and childishly aimless actions. The patients throw stones, lie down in cruciform attitude on the floor, cut off their hair, undress, bathe publicly in the middle of the town, begin to play the harmonica at night, run about on the rails of the shunting-station, burn their own hair and beard and those of other people with their cigar, cut up their linen and clothing; they destroy the furniture and throw it about; they lie sprawling on the floor, turn somersaults in bed, climb on to the stove, slide about the room with chairs.

Very frequently we observe in the patients a certain restlessness. They run away suddenly from their work, roam about, wade barefoot in the snow, insist on going out even at night, become deserters, hide themselves away, make senseless journeys, often without money and without a ticket, want to get into the Castle, to go to America; a patient wandered for days in the forest without food. In consequence of this they easily become vagrants, beg, commit small thefts, and land in this way in prison and the workhouse, where then a deterioration of their condition often sets in; nearly a quarter of my male patients met this fate.

The conduct of the patients invariably shows many peculiarities. They are very changeable in their behaviour, sometimes accessible, childlike, docile, at other times repellent, inapproachable, resistive, irritable, flaring up easily, at one moment loquacious and verbose, at another taciturn and mute. Their mode of speech is frequently manneristic, unctuous, didactic, sometimes noisy or purposely obscene. The substance of their conversation is often confused and unintelligible, or there is nothing in it. Frequently they ride to death certain phrases; they indulge in stale jokes and insipid doggerel; they introduce unusual or foreign expressions or dialect.

Writing – These peculiarities often appear more distinctly in the writing of the patients which are usually in 'Karlchen-Miesnik-style', according to Hecker's description. Besides negligent want of connexion in the train of thought, repeated change of construction in long spun-out periods, mixed metaphors, abrupt interspersing of sudden ideas, rhymed effusions, we find a slovenly external form, irregular hand-writing, flourishes on single letters, underlining, deficiency or superfluity in marks of punctuation, and monotonous contents often with verbal repetitions. [. . .]

The *sleep* of the patients is frequently disturbed, sometimes by excitement at night. The *appetite* is irregular; the patients are sometimes voracious; at other times they eat nothing or only certain articles of food, cram them hastily into their mouth, eat in an extremely unmannerly way, seize the food with their hands. A patient declined food, giving as his motive that he lived on the supernatural; another asked for better food and at the same time called out: 'Waiter, a glass of water!'

The *further course* of the disease in the very great majority of cases which I have brought together led to profound dementia in which for the most part the peculiarities of the previous morbid condition, silly conduct and incoherence of the train of thought, were still distinctly recognizable. In a quarter of the cases the patients became wholly dull and devoid of thought, in a further number of cases manneristic or negativistic. Only in about 12 per cent of the observed cases the disorders disappeared so far that a simple weak-mindedness remained without other striking morbid phenomena. Improvement lasting somewhat longer, 8 or 10 years, with later relapse, was ascertained in about 7 per cent of the cases. Not infrequently the condition exhibited fluctuations, sometimes within a fairly regular return, it may be in connexion with the menses. As the *issue* in states of slight weakness was noted in about 19 per cent of the total number of our cases of dementia praecox, and considerable and more lasting improvement occurred in nearly 26 per cent of the cases, we must regard silly dementia as an *unfavourable* form of the disease. It includes about 13 per cent of our observed cases. Seizures, in nearly 21 per cent, appear to be a little more frequent than in the average. The age of the patient corresponds fairly accurately with that of dementia praecox as a whole; 59 per cent of the patients had not yet reached their 25th year; the male sex was represented by 63 per cent, which is considerably more than the average (56 per cent).

2 E. Kraepelin

Manic-Depressive Insanity and Paranoia

Excerpts from E. Kraepelin, *Manic-depressive insanity and paranoia*,
E. & S. Livingstone, 1921.

Definition

Manic-depressive insanity, as it is to be described in this section,
includes on the one hand the whole domain of so-called *periodic
and circular insanity*, on the other hand *simple mania*, the greater
part of the morbid states termed *melancholia* and also a not inconsiderable number of cases of *amentia* (confusional or delirious
insanity). Lastly, we include here certain slight and slightest
colourings of *mood*, some of them periodic, some of them continuously morbid, which on the one hand are to be regarded as
the rudiment of more severe disorders, on the other hand pass
over without sharp boundary into the domain of *personal predisposition*. In the course of the years I have become more and
more convinced that all the above-mentioned states only represent
manifestations of a *single morbid process*. It is certainly possible
that later a series of subordinate forms may be described, or even
individual small groups again entirely separated off. But if this
happens, then according to my view those symptoms will most
certainly not be authoritative, which hitherto have usually been
placed in the foreground.

What has brought me to this position is first the experience that
notwithstanding manifold external differences certain *common
fundamental features* yet recur in all the morbid states mentioned.
Along with changing symptoms, which may appear temporarily
or may be completely absent, we meet in all forms of manic-depressive insanity a quite definite, narrow group of disorders, though
certainly of very varied character and composition. Without any
one of them being absolutely characteristic of the malady, still in
association they impress a uniform stamp on all the multiform
clinical states. If one is conversant with them, one will in the great
majority of cases be able to conclude in regard to any one of them
that it belongs to the large group of forms of manic-depressive
insanity by the peculiarity of the condition, and thus to gain a series
of fixed points for the special clinical and prognostic significance
of the case. Even a small part of the course of the disease usually

enables us to arrive at this decision, just as in paralysis or dementia praecox the general psychic change often enough makes possible the diagnosis of the fundamental malady in its most different phases.

Of perhaps still greater significance than the classification of states by definite fundamental disorders is the experience that all the morbid forms brought together here as a clinical entity, *not only pass over the one into the other without recognizable boundaries, but that they may even replace each other in one and the same case*. On the one side, as will be later discussed in more detail, it is fundamentally and practically quite impossible to keep apart in any consistent way simple, periodic and circular cases; everywhere there are gradual transitions. But on the other side we see in the same patient not only mania and melancholia, but also states of the most profound confusion and perplexity, also well developed delusions, and lastly, the slightest fluctuations of mood alternating with each other. Moreover, permanent, one-sided colourings of mood very commonly form the background on which fully developed circumscribed attacks of manic-depressive insanity develop.

A further common bond which embraces all the morbid types brought together here and makes the keeping of them apart practically almost meaningless, is their *uniform prognosis*. There are indeed slight and severe attacks which may be of long or short duration, but they alternate irregularly in the same case. This difference is therefore of no use for the delimitation of different diseases. A grouping according to the frequency of the attacks might much rather be considered, which naturally would be extremely welcome to the physician. It appears, however, that here also we have not to do with fundamental differences, since in spite of certain general rules it has not been possible to separate out definite types from this point of view. On the contrary the universal experience is striking, that the attacks of manic-depressive insanity within the delimitation attempted here never lead to profound dementia, not even when they continue throughout life almost without interruption. Usually all morbid manifestations completely disappear; but where that is exceptionally not the case, only a rather slight, peculiar psychic weakness develops, which is just as common to the types here taken together as it is different from dementias in diseases of other kinds.

As a last support for the view here represented of the unity of manic-depressive insanity the circumstance may be adduced, that the various forms which it comprehends may also apparently mutually replace one another in *heredity*. In members of the same family we frequently enough find side by side pronounced periodic or circular cases, occasionally isolated states of ill temper or confusion, lastly very slight, regular fluctuations of mood or permanent conspicuous coloration of disposition. From whatever point of view accordingly the manic-depressive morbid forms may be regarded, from that of aetiology or of clinical phenomena, the course or the issue – it is evident everywhere that here points of agreement exist, which make it possible to regard our domain as a unity and to delimit it from all the other morbid types hitherto discussed. Further experience must show whether and in what directions in this extensive domain smaller sub-groups can be separated from one another.

In the first place the difference of the states which usually make up the disease, presents itself as the most favourable ground of classification. As a rule the disease runs its course in isolated attacks more or less sharply defined from each other or from health, which are either like or unlike, or even very frequently are perfect antitheses. Accordingly we distinguish first of all manic states with the essential morbid symptoms of flight of ideas, exalted mood, and pressure of activity, and *melancholia or depressive states* with sad or anxious moodiness and also sluggishness of thought and action. These two opposed phases of the clinical state have given the disease its name. But besides them we observe also clinical '*mixed forms*', in which the phenomena of mania and melancholia are combined with each other, so that states arise, which indeed are composed of the same morbid symptoms as these, but cannot without coercion be classified either with one or with the other.

Manic States

The presentation of the individual clinical states, in which manic-depressive insanity usually appears, will in the first place have to begin with the conspicuous contrasts between *manic* and *depressive* attacks. With these are associated, as third form, the *mixed states* which are composed of states apparently the opposite of each other. Lastly, we shall have to consider the inconspicuous changes in the psychic life which continue even in the intervals between the marked attacks, changes in which the *general psychopathic foundation* of manic-depressive insanity comes to expression. It must, however, be emphasised beforehand that the delimitation of the individual clinical forms of the malady is in many respects wholly artificial and arbitrary. Observation not only reveals the occurrence of gradual transitions between all the various states, but it also shows that within the shortest space of time the same morbid case may pass through most manifold transformations. The doctrine of form given here may accordingly be regarded as an attempt to set in order quite generally with some degree of lucidity the mass of material gathered by experience.

Hypomania

The slightest forms of manic excitement are usually called 'hypomania', mania mitis, mitissima, also, but inappropriately, mania *sine delirio*. The French have spoken of a 'folie raisonnante', an insanity without disorder of intellect. Indeed the sense, the power of perception, the memory of the patients, appear in general not disordered. Psychic activity, mobility of attention, are not infrequently even increased; the patients may appear livelier, more capable than formerly. In especial the ability to perceive distant resemblances often surprises the hearer, because it enables the patient to produce witty remarks and fancies, puns, startling comparisons, although usually not very valid when examined more minutely, and similar products of the imagination. Nevertheless even in the slightest degrees of the disorder the following features are extraordinarily characteristic, *the lack of inner unity in the course of ideas*, the incapacity to carry out consistently a definite series of thoughts, to work out steadily and logically and to set in order given ideas, also the fickleness of interest and the sudden and abrupt jumping from one subject to another. Certainly the patients are not infrequently able with some effort to overcome temporarily these phenomena and to gain the mastery again for some time yet over the course of their ideas which have become unbridled. In writing and especially in rhyming, which is often diligently indulged in, a slight flight of ideas usually makes a distinct appearance. But even in these slight forms fairly severe excitement and confusion may temporarily be present.

Recollection of recent events is not always exact, but is often coloured and supplemented by original additions. The patient is easily led away in his narrations to exaggerations and distortions, which arise partly from mistaken perception, but partly also from subsequent misinterpretation without the arbitrariness of it coming clearly into his consciousness. Although genuine delusions are absent we invariably meet with a very much exaggerated opinion of *self*. [. . .] In eloquent words the patient boasts of his performances and capabilities; he understands everything best; he ridicules the doings of others with aristocratic contempt, and desires special recognition for his own person. He is an 'excellent poet, orator, jester, and man of business', a 'jolly fellow'; he can work like a nigger, can take the place of many a professor or diplomatist. [. . .]

Insight – Of this there is as a rule no question; even by a reminder of former attacks, of which during depression the patient perhaps formed a quite correct opinion, he cannot for a moment be convinced of the real nature of his state. On the contrary he feels himself healthier and more capable than ever, has 'a colossal energy for work', is 'awfully merry', at most is somewhat excited by the unworthy treatment. The restriction of his freedom he regards as a bad joke, or as an unpardonable injustice, which he connects with the perverse ongoings of his relatives or of persons otherwise inimical to him, and he threatens to take legal measures for their removal and punishment. Those, not he, are mentally afflicted, who did not know how to appreciate his intellectual superiority and his gifts, and who tried to excite him by irritating and provoking him. This behaviour reminds one of the experiences so frequently encountered of the self-deceptions of drunkards.

Mood is predominantly exalted and cheerful, influenced by the feeling of heightened capacity for work. The patient is in imperturbable good temper, sure of success, 'courageous', feels happy and merry, not rarely overflowingly so, wakes up every morning 'in excellent humour'. [. . .] For the most part an exuberant, unrestrained mood inclined to practical jokes of all kinds is developed. Occasionally there is developed a markedly humorous trait, the tendency to look at everything and every occurrence from the jocular side, to invent nicknames, to make fun of himself and others. [. . .] On the other hand there often enough exists a great emotional irritability. The patient is dissatisfied, intolerant, faultfinding, especially in intercourse with his immediate surroundings, where he lets himself go; he becomes pretentious, positive, regardless, impertinent and even rough, when he comes up against opposition to his wishes and inclinations; trifling external occasions may bring about extremely violent outbursts of rage. In his fury he thrashes his wife and children, threatens to smash everything to smithereens, to run amuck, to set the house on fire, abuses the 'tribe' of his relatives in the most violent language, especially when under the influence of alcohol. The internal equilibrium of the patient is lost; he is led wholly by momentary impressions and emotions which immediately obtain mastery over his mood and his excited volition. His actions accordingly often bear the stamp of impulsiveness, lack of forethought, and – because of the slight disorder of intellect – of immorality.

Increased busyness is the most striking feature. The patient feels the need to get out of himself, to be on more intimate terms with his surroundings, to play a part. As he is a stranger to fatigue, his activity goes on day and night; work becomes very easy to him; ideas flow to him. He cannot stay long in bed; early in the morning, even at four o'clock he gets up, he clears out lumber rooms, discharges business that was in arrears, undertakes morning walks, excursions. His pressure of activity causes the patient to change about his furniture, to visit distant acquaintances, to take himself up with all possible things and circumstances, which formerly he never thought about.

At the same time the real capacity for work invariably suffers a considerable loss. The patient no longer has any perseverance, leaves what he begins half finished, is slovenly and careless in the execution of anything, only does what he likes, neglects his real duties. A patient spent his whole time in plans for marriage, reading the newspapers, going walks, and playing bowls. Just as it occurs to him, the patient undertakes unnecessary journeys, wanders about, takes drives, pawns his watch, borrows money, makes useless purchases and exchanges, even when he has not a penny in his pocket, because every new object stimulates his desire. Even occasional theft and fraud are sometimes committed in this morbid lust for possession in order to obtain what is desired.

External behaviour – Exalted self-consciousness, the passion to come to the front, is conspicuous, and also restlessness and changeableness. The patient dresses contrary to his usual custom, according to the newest fashion, although perhaps negligently. He often makes himself conspicuous by all sorts of disorderly conduct; he serenades with trumpets, spends the night on benches out of doors, promenades in a dress coat wearing an order made by himself, takes a bath with his clothes on, performs military exercises with a broom, goes about the streets distributing blessings, pays a visit to the archbishop without any occasion. In company the patient behaves without ceremony and morality, tells risky jokes before the ladies, carries on boastful conversations, in wanton merriment behaves with unsuitable familiarity towards strangers or his superiors, is friends with the first person he meets and calls him by his first name. In consequence of his petulance and irritability the patient frequently comes into conflict with his surroundings and with the authorities; he insults officials, demands from the physician satisfaction as a cavalier, runs up debts in public houses, is called to account by his superiors and brought to order. The tendency to debauchery usually becomes especially fatal to the patient. He begins to get drunk frequently, to gamble foolishly, to remain out at night, to frequent brothels and doubtful taverns, to smoke and snuff excessively, to eat strongly-seasoned food. When such states of excitement occur frequently, and are of short duration, a picture very similar to dipsomania may arise.

Sexual excitability experiences a considerable increase. An elderly father of a family, who otherwise lives a very retired life, began to drink champagne with the girl fencers from a circus. A woman declared that she was going to commit adultery in order to get a divorce from her husband.

Rationalization by patients – With extraordinary acuteness the patient can find a reason for all his astonishing and nonsensical doings; he is never at a loss for an excuse or explanation. The exertions of his relatives to quiet him are, therefore, not only ineffectual, but they only irritate him and easily lead to violent outbursts of rage. [. . .]

Movements of expression are as a rule lively and passionate. The patients talk a great deal, hastily, in loud tones, with great verbosity and prolixity, jumping from one subject to another, using sought-out, bombastic expressions, speaking with peculiar intonation, and of themselves often in the third person in order to place themselves in the right light. Silly joking, puns, violent expressions, quotations, scraps of foreign languages play a large part, and occasionally violent abuse and swearing or emotional weeping intervenes. Their writing displays large, pretentious flourishes, many marks of exclamation and interrogation, underlining, besides negligence in the external form. Many patients compose bombastic or humorous documents full of flights of ideas and irritation, in which they narrate without reserve all their family affairs, beg for certificates of sanity, and call for the protection of public opinion.

The variety in detail of this state is, in spite of all the common features, very large. The more slightly the real morbid process affects the individual, the more conspicuous are his personal peculiarities in the form which the manifestations assume. The differences are noticeable especially in the kind and intensity of the emotions. While many patients at this time are amiable, good-natured, docile, sociable, and at most become disturbing to their surroundings by their restlessness, others because of their irritability, their imperiousness, and their regardless pressure of activity, are extraordinarily difficult and unpleasant. It is just the peculiar mixture of sense and maniacal activity, frequently also an extensive experience of institutions, which makes them extremely ingenious in finding out means to satisfy their numerous desires, to deceive their surroundings, to procure for themselves all kinds of advantages, to secure the property of others for themselves. They usually soon domineer completely over their fellow-patients, use them for profit, report about them to the physician in technical terms, act as guardian to them, and hold them in check.

Acute mania

From the slighter forms of mania here described, imperceptible transitions gradually lead to the morbid state of actual acute mania. The beginning of the illness is always fairly sudden; at most headaches, weariness, lack of pleasure in work or a great busyness, irritability, sleeplessness, precede by some days or weeks the outbreak of the more violent manifestations, when a definite state of depression has not, as is very frequent, formed the prelude. The patients rapidly become restless, disconnected in their talk, and perpetrate all sorts of curious actions. They run out of the house in a shirt, go to church in a petticoat, spend the night in a field of corn, give away their property, disturb the service in a church by screaming and singing, kneel and pray in the street, fire a pistol in the waiting-room, put soap and soda in the food, try to force their way into the palace, throw objects out of the window. [. . .]

As a rule, therefore, the patients must be brought to an institution in a few days. Here they show themselves sensible and approximately oriented, but extraordinarily distractible in perception and train of thought. Sometimes it is quite impossible to get into communication with them; as a rule, however, they understand emphatic speech, and even give isolated suitable replies, but they are influenced by every new impression; they digress, they go into endless details, in short, they display more or less developed flights of ideas, as we have already described minutely.

Delusions – Very commonly fugitive delusions are expressed, usually more in a jocular way. The patient asserts that he is descended from a noble family, that he is a gentleman; [. . .] A female patient asserted that she was the Christchild and was three years old. The patients are often disoriented about their own position and their place of residence; they make mistakes about persons, often in a playful way. Now and then isolated *hallucinations* are reported. The patients see horsemen in the clouds, saints, a dead child; they carry on a conversation with their father who is dead, with the Virgin Mary; they feel themselves influenced by something external.

Occasionally the patients narrate all sorts of extraordinary adventures. A female patient asserted that she had been assaulted and abused, but then said that she could not swear that it had not been a dream. [. . .] Many patients have a certain morbid feeling, and at times make fun of the ideas which they bring forward. Great wishes and plans are also developed. [. . .]

Mood is unrestrained, merry, exultant, occasionally visionary or pompous, but always subject to frequent variation, easily changing to irritability and irascibility or even to lamentation and weeping. [. . .]

At the most trifling affront it may come to outbursts of rage of extraordinary violence, to veritable high-tides of clamorous abuse and bellowing, to dangerous threats with shooting and stabbing, to blind destruction and actual attacks. The female sex has a much greater tendency to such outbursts than the male sex. Sexual excitement finds an outlet in obscene talk, forcible approach to youthful patients, shameless masturbation; among the female patients in calling the physicians by their first names, dressing up, taking down their hair, anointing themselves with saliva, frequent spitting, using indecent and abusive language, as well as in sexual calumniation of the nursing staff. [. . .]

Conduct – The behaviour of the patients is, as a rule, free and easy, self-conscious, unmannerly or confiding, importunate. They run after the physician, are always interrupting, let themselves be diverted or influenced by persuasion, imitate other patients, and not rarely display indications of automatic obedience; they do not defend themselves from pricks. But often enough they are repellent, pert, unapproachable; they resist, hide in corners, close their eyes, hold their fingers before their face in order to blink through them. [. . .] The morbid picture is dominated by the rapidly increasing *volitional excitement*, which in its impulsiveness and suggestibility may remind one of alcoholic poisoning. [. . .]

The patient cannot sit or lie still for long, jumps out of bed, runs about, hops, dances, mounts on tables and benches, takes down pictures. He forces his way out, takes off his clothes, teases his fellow-patients, dives, splashes and squirts in the bath, romps, beats on the table, bites, spits, chirps and clicks. These volitional utterances in general usually exhibit the stamp of natural activities and movements of expression, although frequently mutilated and over-hasty. Among these, however, are frequently interpolated movements which can only be regarded as discharges of inner restlessness, shaking of the upper part of the body, waltzing about, waving and flourishing the arms, distorting the limbs, rubbing the head, bouncing up and down, stroking, wiping, twitching, clapping and drumming. Sometimes these movements are conspicuously clumsy and inelegant, or affected and peculiar. [. . .]

Many patients display a great tendency to be destructive. They slit up their suits and bed-clothes in order to use the rags knotted and twisted in a hundred ways for extraordinary decorations. All objects in any way attainable are broken up into their component parts in order to be put together again as new structures of various kinds, according to the inspiration of the moment. [. . .]

Movements of expression are for the most part very vivacious. The patient makes faces, rolls his eyes, assumes theatrical attitudes, stands erect, salutes in military fashion. He usually produces in the shortest interval of time an enormous flood of words with changing intonation, makes jokes, is quick at repartee, swears, scolds, suddenly makes a noise, recites, preaches, mutters to himself, and now and again screams out loud. He bellows, sings music-hall songs, hymns, often for hours the same, prays, imitates the sounds of animals, calls out hallelujah; among these are interpolated roaring, whistling, yodelling, shouting, uncontrollable laughter. But at times, even in spite of lively excitement, the patients may be taciturn; they do not reply to questions or they give short and evasive answers; they perhaps only make a few expressive gestures and then suddenly break out with the greatest vivacity. Jocular speaking past the subject also occurs now and then, right instead of left, six instead of five. A female patient always repeated the question directed to her; another persistently replied, 'How?'; a third, 'I don't know that.' Associations with external impressions and rhyming frequently occur in the conversation of the patients.

Many patients develop a veritable passion for writing, cover innumerable sheets with very large fantastic calligraphy, the words crossing one another in all directions. [. . .] It is remarkable that there are no repetitions as there are in catatonic documents which have a similar appearance. [. . .]

Depressive States

Melancholia Simplex

The slightest depressive states are characterized by the appearance of a *simple psychic inhibition without hallucinations and without marked delusions*. Thinking is difficult to the patient, a disorder which he describes in the most varied phrases. He cannot collect his thoughts or pull himself together; his thoughts are as if paralysed, they are immobile. His head feels heavy, quite stupid, as if a board were pushed in front of it, everything is confused. He is no longer able to perceive, or to follow the train of thought of a book or a conversation, he feels weary, enervated, inattentive, inwardly empty; he has no memory, he has no longer command of knowledge formerly familiar to him, he must consider a long time about simple things, he calculates wrongly, makes contradictory statements, does not find words, cannot construct sentences correctly. At the same time complaints are heard that the patient must meditate so much, that fresh thoughts are always coming to him, that he has too much in his head, that he finds no rest, is confused.

The patients frequently describe that change of their inward state which is usually called 'depersonalization'. Their presentations lack sensuous colouring. The impressions of the external world appear strange, as though from a great distance, awake no response in them; their own body feels as if not belonging to them; their features stare quite changed from the mirror; their voice sounds leaden. Thinking and acting go on without the cooperation of the patient; he appears to himself to be an automatic machine. [. . .]

Mood is sometimes dominated by a profound inward dejection and gloomy hopelessness, sometimes more by indefinite anxiety and restlessness. The patient's heart is heavy, nothing can permanently rouse his interest, nothing gives him pleasure. He has no longer any humour or any religious feeling – he is unsatisfied with himself, has become indifferent to his relatives, and to whatever he formerly liked best. Gloomy thoughts arise, his past and even his future appear to him in a uniformly dim light. He feels that he is worth nothing, neither physically nor mentally, he is no longer of any use, appears to himself 'like a murderer'. His life has been a blunder, he is not suited for his calling, wants to take up a new occupation, should have arranged his life differently, should have pulled himself together more. [. . .]

He feels solitary, indescribably unhappy, as 'a creature disinherited of fate'; he is sceptical about God, and with a certain dull submission, which shuts out every comfort and every gleam of light, he drags himself with difficulty from one day to another. Everything has become disagreeable to him; everything wearies him, company, music, travel, his professional work. Everywhere he sees only the dark side and difficulties; the people round him are not so good and unselfish as he had thought; one disappointment and disillusionment follows another. Life appears to him aimless, he thinks that he is superfluous in the world, he cannot restrain himself any longer, the thought occurs to him to take his life without his knowing why. He has a feeling as if something had cracked in him, he fears that he may become crazy, insane, paralytic, the end is coming near. Others have the impression as though something terrible had happened, something is rising in their breast, everything trembles in them, they have nothing good to expect, something is happening.

Imperative ideas of all kinds occasionally emerge in these states, agoraphobia, the fear of having been pricked by a splinter and having to die of blood-poisoning, the fear of having vicious or 'unclean' thoughts, the idea of throwing people into water, the fear of having stolen bread or money, of having removed landmarks, of having committed all the crimes mentioned in the newspapers. A patient was tormented by the idea of having murdered people with his thoughts. [. . .] The fear of knives, with the idea of being obliged to kill someone, occurs occasionally also. A patient went to bed in order not to do anything of that kind. [. . .]

The *total absence of energy* is very specially conspicuous. The patient lacks spirit and will-power, like a wheel on a car, which simply runs but in itself has no movement or driving power. He cannot rouse himself, cannot come to any decision, cannot work any longer, does everything the wrong way about, he has to force himself to everything, does not know what to do. A patient declared that he did not know what he wanted, went from one thing to another. The smallest bit of work costs him an unheard-of effort; even the most everyday arrangements, household work, getting up in the morning, dressing, washing, are only accomplished with the greatest difficulty and in the end indeed are left undone. Work, visits, important letters, business affairs are like a mountain in front of the patient and are just left, because he does not find the power to overcome the opposing inhibitions [. . .] Finally the patient gives up every activity, sits all day long doing nothing with his hands in his lap, brooding to himself in utter dullness. His sorrowful features show no play of emotion; the scanty linguistic utterances are laboured, low, monotonous and monosyllabic, and even the addition of a simple greeting on a postcard is not attainable or only after much urging. [. . .]

Just because of this severe volitional disorder it relatively seldom comes to more serious attempts at suicide, although the wish to die very frequently occurs. It is only when with the disappearance of inhibition energy returns while the depression still continues, that the attempts at suicide become more frequent and more dangerous. A patient with very slight moodiness hanged himself a few days before his discharge on a free pass when he already appeared quite cheerful.

Insight – Sense and orientation are in spite of the great difficulty in perception and thinking completely retained. Generally a very vivid morbid feeling also exists, not infrequently even a certain morbid insight, in as far as the patients express their regret for former improprieties, and their fear lest they might again let themselves be carried away by excitement. Others, however, think that they are not ill, only destitute of will-power, that they could indeed pull themselves together, only will not; that they are simulating. Frequently the return of moodiness is connected with external accidents, unpleasant experiences, changes in circumstances and such things. To the unprejudiced observer it is clear that the psychic working of those influences has been produced by the morbid clouding of disposition.

Stupor

In the highest grades the psychic inhibition described may go on to the development of marked stupor. The patients are deeply apathetic, are no longer able to perceive the impressions of the surroundings and to assimilate them, do not understand questions, have no conception of their position. A female patient who was made to leave her bed and go into the one beside it, said quite without understanding, 'That is too complicated for me.' Occasionally, it can be recognized that the inhibition of thought is slighter than the volitional disorder. A patient was able to give the result of complicated problems in arithmetic in the same time, certainly considerably prolonged, as that of the simplest addition.

Sometimes the occasional, detached utterances of the patients contain indications of confused, delusional ideas, that they are quite away from the world, have a crack through the brain, are being sold; down below there is an uproar. [. . .]

Volitional utterances are extremely scanty. As a rule, the patients lie mute in bed, give no answer of any sort, at most withdraw themselves timidly from approaches, but often do not defend themselves from pinpricks. [. . .] They sit helpless before their food; perhaps, however, they let themselves be spoon-fed without making any difficulty. They hold fast what is pressed into their hand, turn it slowly about without knowing how to get rid of it. They are, therefore, wholly unable to care for their bodily needs, and not infrequently they become dirty. Now and then periods of excitement may be interpolated. The patients get out of bed, break out in confused abuse, sing a folk-song. [. . .] After the return of consciousness, which usually appears rather abruptly, memory is very much clouded and often quite extinguished.

Melancholia Gravis

The picture of simple depression corresponding perhaps to the former '*melancholia simplex*' experiences very varied elaboration through the development of hallucinations and delusions, which frequently follows; one might here perhaps speak of a '*melancholia gravis*'. The patients see figures, spirits, the corpses of their relatives; something is falsely represented to them, 'all sorts of devil's work'. Green rags fall from the walls; a coloured spot on the wall is a snapping mouth which bites the heads off children; everything looks black. The patients hear abusive language ('lazy pig', 'wicked creature', 'deceiver', 'you are guilty, you are guilty'), voices, which invite them to suicide; they feel sand, sulphur vapour in their mouth, electric currents in the walls. A patient, who reproached himself with having had connexion with a cow, felt a cow's tail flicking his face.

Ideas of sin usually play the largest part. The patient has been from youth up the most wicked being, an abomination, filled with malice, has led a horrible life, as far as possible has let others do his work, has not put his full strength into his calling, has sworn falsely in taking the military oath, has defrauded the sick fund. He has offended everyone, has borne false witness, has overreached some one in making a purchase, has sinned against the seventh commandment. He cannot work any more, has no feeling, no more tears; he is so rough; something is lacking in his disposition. Frequently the self-accusations are connected with harmless occurrences which have often happened long before. The patient, when a child, communicated unworthily, did not obey his mother, told a lie before he was twelve years old. [. . .]

The domain of *religion* is a peculiarly favourable soil for self-accusation. The patient is a great sinner, cannot pray any more, has forgotten the ten commandments, the creed, the benediction, has lost eternal bliss, has committed the sin against the Holy Ghost, has trafficked in divine things, has not offered enough candles. He has apostatized from God, is gripped firmly by Satan, must do penance. The spirit of God has left him; he feels that he dare not enter church any more. He is going to Hell, has only two hours to live; then the devil will fetch him; he must enter eternity with transgression, and redeem poor souls.

His present activities also frequently give the patient the opportunity for continual self-reproach. [. . .] He causes so much trouble, is to blame that the others are so distressed, that they are being taken away. 'I have probably done all this,' said a patient. He has brought in all his fellow-patients, must care for them all, is responsible for them, complains that he is really not able to feed the others, to do the work of the head-waiter, to pay for them all. Everyone must go hungry when he eats. [. . .]

Ideas of persecution frequently exist in the closest connexion with the delusion of sin. Disgrace and scorn await the patient everywhere; he is dishonourable, cannot let himself be seen anywhere any more. People look at him, put their heads together, clear their throats, spit in front of him. They disapprove of his presence, feel it as an insult, cannot tolerate him any longer among them; he is a thorn in the side to all. Speeches in the club have reference to him; there is secret talking of stories about females; he is a bully, should hang himself, because he has no character. Everywhere he notices signs. [. . .] A patient concluded from the remark, 'Still waters run deep', that he should drown himself. The patient therefore asks for an explanation; he did not know that such was his state. 'What is being done with me?' he asks anxiously. Things are so put before him as if every step in his life had been wrong. He defends himself, therefore, in despair against the supposed accusations and declares his innocence. But I have not done anything wrong, have stolen nothing, have not betrayed my country, such patients are heard to lament. They are afraid that on the death of a relative they may be suspected of poisoning ('Has poison been found?'), that they may be called to account for lese-majesty, or for a planned assault.

Everywhere danger threatens the patient. The girls read his letters; strange people are in the house; a suspicious motor-car drives past. People mock him, are going to thrash him, to chase him from his post in a shameful way, incarcerate him, bring him to justice, expose him publicly, deport him, take his orders from him, throw him into the fire, drown him. The people are already standing outside; the bill of indictment is already written; the scaffold is being put up; he must wander about naked and miserable, he is quite forsaken, is shut out of human society, is lost, body and soul. His relatives also are being tortured, must suffer; 'I do hope they are still at home.' His family is imprisoned; his wife has drowned herself; his parents are murdered; his daughter wanders about in the snow without any clothes on. Everything goes the wrong way; the household is going to ruin; there is nothing more there but rags; the clothes have been changed at the laundry.

71

Things have been pawned; the money is not sufficient, is false; everything costs too much; everyone must starve. A woman said that her husband did not like her any longer; he wanted to kill her. Others release their husband, invite him to get a divorce.

His bodily state also appears to the patient to be frequently in a very dangerous condition, which may be connected with the dysaesthesiae formerly described. He is incurably ill, half-dead, no longer a right human being, has lung-disease, a tapeworm, cancer in his throat, cannot swallow, does not retain his food, passes such thin and such frequent stools. Face and figure have changed; there is no longer blood in his brain; he does not see any longer, must become crazy, remain his whole lifetime in the institution, die, has already died. He has become impotent by onanism, has had a chancre from birth, has incurable blood-poisoning, infects everyone, he must not be touched. On this account a woman no longer had the bread baked in the house. The people in his surroundings become ill and yellow through the nasty exhalation of the patient, are already mentally disordered and weary of life. Female patients feel themselves pregnant, have been sexually ill used. [. . .]

Paranoid Melancholia

When ideas of persecution and hallucinations of hearing are frequently present and sense remains preserved, morbid states may occasionally arise, which readily call to mind alcoholic insanity, without alcohol having any causal significance. The patients feel themselves watched, are pursued by spies and threatened by masked murderers; they catch sight of a dagger in their neighbour's hand. On the street, in the restaurant from the neighbouring table, they hear isolated remarks about themselves.

In the course of the forms here described consciousness is mostly clear, and sense and orientation are preserved. The patients perceive correctly the conversations and occurrences in their surroundings and then frequently misinterpret them in a delusional way. Their train of thought is orderly and connected, although mostly very monotonous; on an attempt being made to divert them, they return again immediately to the old track. All mental activity is as a rule made difficult. The patients are absent-minded, forgetful, are easily tired, progress slowly or not at all, and at the same time are sometimes most painfully precise in details.

Mood is gloomy, despondent, despairing. By persuasion or visits from relatives it may usually be somewhat influenced; sometimes on such an occasion lively excitement follows. On the other hand unpleasant news often makes little impression. What happens in the surroundings also usually affects the patients only slightly. [. . .] Many patients in regard to their delusions appear remarkably dull and indifferent, occasionally also perhaps good-humoured and even cheerful.

In the *activities* of the patients, their *volitional inhibition* on the one hand makes itself felt, on the other the influence of their *delusions* and *moods*. They feel tired, in need of rest, are no longer able to take care of themselves, neglect themselves, spend no more money, take no nourishment, wear very shabby clothes, refuse to sign the receipt for their salary, as indeed they have not done any work. They shut themselves up, go to bed, lie there rigidly with a troubled expression in a constrained attitude, sometimes with closed eyes, or sit timidly on the edge of the bed, because they do not venture to lie down. Indications of automatic obedience are not rare. In other patients anxious restlessness is predominant. [. . .] Speech is mostly low, monotonous, hesitating and even stuttering. [. . .]

Suicide – The extraordinarily strong tendency to suicide is of the greatest practical significance. Sometimes it continually accompanies the whole course of the disease, without coming to a serious attempt owing to the incapacity of the patients to arrive at a decision. Nevertheless the danger of suicide is in all circumstances extremely serious, as the volitional inhibition may disappear abruptly or be interrupted by violent emotion. Sometimes the impulse to suicide emerges very suddenly without the patients being able to explain the motives to themselves. Occasionally, after indefinite prodromata, the first distinct morbid symptom is a suicidal attempt. Only too often the patients know how to conceal their suicidal intentions behind an apparently cheerful behaviour, and then carefully prepare for the execution of their intention at a suitable moment. Not at all infrequently the idea occurs to the patients to do away with the family also, because it would be better if none of them were alive. They then try to strangle their wife, to cut their children's throats, they go with them into the water, in order that they may not also be so unhappy, that they may not get step-parents.

Fantastic Melancholia

A further, fairly comprehensive group of cases is distinguished by a still greater development of *delusions*. We may well perhaps call it 'fantastic melancholia'. Abundant *hallucinations* appear. The patients see evil spirits, death, heads of animals, smoke in the house, black men on the roofs, crowds of monsters. God speaks in words of thunder; the devil speaks in church; something is moving in the wall. The patient hears his tortured relatives screaming and lamenting; the birds whistle his name; call out that he should be taken up. 'Do away with him, do away with him,' 'Look, that's the masturbator,' 'Now she's coming, now there'll be blood again.' The patient is electrified by the telephone, is illuminated at night by Röntgen-rays, pulled along by his hair; someone is lying in his bed; his food tastes of soapy water or excrement, or corpses and mildew.

Besides those genuine hallucinations there are also multifarious delusional interpretations of real perceptions. The patient hears murderers come; someone is slinking about the bed; a man is lying under the bed with a loaded gun; an electro-magnet crackles. People with green hats or black spectacles follow him on the street; in the opposite house someone is bowing conspicuously; the motor-cars are making a very peculiar noise; in the next room knives are being sharpened; the conversations on the telephone refer to him. Plays in the theatre, the serial story in the newspaper, are occupied with him; there is gross abuse written on a postcard; a female patient found her hat portrayed in a fashion paper for mockery. There is a great deal of talk, another said, and she imagined that it referred to her. What is said in the surroundings has a hidden meaning. Another one asserted that the physicians spoke a 'universal language', in which they expressed all thoughts in a quite different form not understood by her. The most extraordinary conclusions are drawn from every perception; ravens flying signify that the daughter is being cut to pieces in the cellar; the son when he made his visit was wearing a black tie, so the youngest child must be dead. Everything is 'so fateful', comedy and illusion. [. . .] The food is flesh and blood of their own relatives, the light is a funeral-light, the bed is an enchanted bed, the clattering cart outside is a hearse. It is quite another world, not the right town, quite another century. The clocks strike wrong; the letters are as if from strangers; the mortgages are exchanged; the savings-bank book is not valid. The trees in the forest, the rocks, appear unnatural, as if they were artificial, as if they had been built up specially for the patient, in fact, even the sun, the moon, the weather, are not as they used to be. One of my patients thought that the sun was artificial electric illumination, and he complained about the weakness of his eyes because he could not see the real sun (in the night).

The people who visit the patient are not the right people, are only false show. The physicians are only 'figures'; he thinks that he is surrounded 'by elemental spirits'; the children appear changed. The nurse is a disguised empress; a fellow patient (female) thinks that the patient (also female) is her husband; the attendants have false names. The wife is a witch, the child is a wild cat, a dog. A patient noticed that her husband looked black, and on this account attacked him with a bottle.

The numerous delusions are very extraordinary. The patient has committed mortal sins, has caused a derailment, has killed many people, has brought on himself a primeval sin, has murdered many souls; he has forged documents, been a legacy hunter, caused an epidemic. Because of sins of his youth he is in detention; he has committed bestiality; he is poisoning the whole world by his onanism. He has torn down the firmament, drunk up the fountain of grace, tormented the Trinity; cities and countries are on his account laid waste. The other patients are there by his fault, are beheaded on his account; every time that he eats or turns round in bed, someone is executed; the devil's mill is working over there; they are being killed there. Female patients have committed abortion, have been extravagant, have not been good housewives, must be the devil's whore.

Because he is to blame for all misfortune, the patient is going to hell. The devil slipped down the chimney to take him away, has him by the nape of the neck, sits in his bosom as a black beast with sharp claws, speaks in his heart; he himself is changed into the devil; neither will his dead son come into heaven. His baseness is revealed in his expression; everyone knows of his crime. No one likes him any longer; he is surrounded by spies, is watched by the police, is continually followed by suspicious people; detectives wait for him; the judge is already there. He is dragged off to Siberia, to the convict prison; he is being electrocuted, stabbed, shot, is having petroleum poured over him, is being tied to a corpse, run over by the motor-car, hacked to pieces, cut up into a thousand bits, flayed, devoured by mice; naked in the wild forest he is being torn to pieces by wolves. His fingers are being chopped off, his eyes dug out, his sexual parts, his entrails cut off, his nails torn out; women have their womb drawn out. The last judgement is coming; the vengeance of God is at hand. Today is the death-day, the last meal before execution; the bed is a scaffold; the patient wishes to confess once more. Over his family also misfortune is poured out.

His relatives are crucified by the mob; his daughter is in the convict prison; his son-in-law has hanged himself; parents and brothers and sisters are dead, his children are burned up. The husbands of female patients have been murdered. The sister is cut to pieces, sent away in a box; the son's corpse was sold for dissection.

At home the patient is teased by everyone, regarded as a fool, cheated; people have no respect for him, spit in his face; the servants take everything from him with their finger-tips, because they think that he is syphilitic. All are in alliance together and vent their anger on him; many dogs are the death of the hare. The telephone conversations were listened to; the house was searched; the things sent to the laundry were lost; false keys were found on the ring; at night the children were rendered insensible by gas. The patient is surrounded by an international gang of robbers; his house is going to be blown up into the air. People knew his career and his thoughts. At night he is sent to sleep, taken away and made to carry out practical jokes, for which he is later held responsible. A female patient aged sixty-five complained of improper assaults, thought that she had been brought to a house of ill-fame and was pregnant. Another of the same age fancied that she was exposed to the persecutions of old bachelors, who lay down beside her in bed. A young girl asked if she would get a child. A woman forty-eight years of age declared that she was pregnant and that she had impregnated herself. An elderly man thought that he was dragged about every night in brothels and there infected with syphilis. 'I am here again,' said a female paitent every time she was visited, as she thought that she was always being taken away each hour to a different place.

Hypochondriacal delusions usually reach a considerable development; they often completely resemble those of the paralytic. In the patient everything is dead, rotten, burnt, petrified, hollow; there is a kind of putrefaction in him. He has syphilis of the fourth stage; his breath is poisonous; he has infected his children, the whole town. His head is changing in shape, is as large as Palestine; his hands and feet are no longer as they were; the bones have become thicker, have slipped lower down; all his limbs are out of joint; his body is no longer compact; it stretches out and is shrivelled up. In his skull there is filth; his brain is melting; the devil has displaced it backwards by a discharge of blood. His heart no longer cooks any blood, is a dead piece of flesh; his blood-vessels are dried up, filled with poison; no circulation goes on any longer; the juices are gone. Everything is closed; in his throat a bone is sticking, a stone; stomach and bowel are no longer there. There is a worm in his body, a hairy animal in his stomach; his food falls down between his intestines into his scrotum; neither urine nor faeces are passed; his entrails are corroded. His testicles are crushed, have disappeared; his genitals are becoming smaller. His mucous glands have risen up; his life is lacerated; rolling about is going on at the navel. There is a hole in his nose; there is pus in his jaw, in all his limbs, and it passes away in great quantity with his motions and with hawking; his palate stinks. His skin is too narrow over the shoulders; worms are lying under it and are creeping about. A patient declared that for eleven years he had been a spirit, and had only the internal organs left; when someone died, death passed through him and took away his entrails; he still had the scar. A female patient asserted that there was iron in her and the bedstead attracted her. Another said that she would get a child with a cat's head. Many patients believe that they are bewitched inwardly, changed into a wild animal, that they must bark, howl and rage. Others cannot sit, cannot eat, cannot go a step, or give their hand.

The ideas of *annihilation* already frequently indicated in the foregoing pages, may experience a further, wholly nonsensical elaboration. The patient has no longer a name, a home, is not born, does not belong at all to the world any more, is no longer a human being, is no longer here, is a spirit, an abortion, a picture, a ghost, 'just only a sort of shape'. He cannot live and he cannot die; he must hover about so, remain in the world eternally, is as old as the world, has been already a hundred years here. If he is beaten with an axe on his head, if his breast is cut open, if he is thrown into the fire, he still cannot be killed. 'I cannot be buried any more,' said a patient, 'when I sit down on the weighing-machine, it shows zero!' The world has perished; there are no longer railways, towns, money, beds, doctors; the sea runs out. All human beings are dead, 'poisoned with antitoxic serum', burned, dead of starvation, because there is nothing more to eat, because the patient has stuffed everything down into his enormous stomach, and has drunk the water-pipes empty. No one eats or sleeps any more; the patient is the only being of flesh and blood, is alone in the world. A female patient declared that there was no blood in her internal organs, therefore the electric light caught fire from her, so that the whole human race and the firmament were consumed. Another thought that a thunderstorm would destroy the whole world.

Consciousness is in this form frequently somewhat clouded.

The patients perceive badly, do not understand what goes on, are not able to form clear ideas. They complain that they cannot lay hold of any proper thought, that they are beastly 'stupid', confused in their head, do not find their way, also perhaps that they have so many thoughts in their head, that everything goes pell-mell. Many patients say that they have been made confused by medicines and much eating, that they have been hypnotized, that they continually talk nonsense, must profess sometimes one thing, sometimes another, that they have become crazy. But at the same time, when their delusions come into play, they are incapable of recognizing the grossest contradictions or of correcting them; they assert that they cannot take a bite more while they are chewing with full cheeks. 'This is my last,' said a patient every time the contradiction was pointed out to her. Others beg to be sent out of the world by poison, although they assert that they cannot die at all.

Yet the train of thought is usually in general reasonable. They are frequently also able to give appropriate and connected information about their personal circumstances and more remote things, though certainly they are for the most part little inclined to engage in such conversations, but return immediately to their delusions again.

Mood is sometimes characterized by dull despondency, sometimes by anxious tension or excitement; at times the patients are also repellent, irritated, angry, inclined to violence. But not altogether infrequently we meet in the patients slight self-irony; they try to describe their sins and torments in excessively obtrusive colours, use the language of students, enter into a joke, allow themselves to smile; erotic moods also may be conspicuous. Especially in the last periods of the attack a grumbling, insufferable, perverse mood is developed, which only with complete recovery gradually disappears. A patient declared that she was envious of the other children of God.

The *volitional disorders* are also not quite uniform. The activity of the patients is frequently dominated by volitional inhibition; they are taciturn, even mute, cataleptic; they lie with vacant or strained expression of countenance in bed, often with closed eyes, do not ward off pricks, do not do what they are bidden, are resistive when taking nourishment, hide themselves under the cover, are occasionally unclean. The inward tension is perhaps only revealed by isolated whispered utterances ('Entreat for me,' 'What's the matter?'), convulsive grasping of the rosary, imploring looks, excitement during the visits of relatives. Many patients feel themselves not free, but under the influence of a higher power. A patient declared that people had him in their power, he had lost his will completely, and was a broken man. A female patient was obliged to kiss the floor and altar in church.

Anxious restlessness, however, seems to me to be more frequent, occasionally alternating with slight stuporous states. The patients do not remain in bed; they wander about, bewail and lament, often in rhythmical cadence, 'Sinful creature, wicked creature.' They beg for forbearance as they have not committed any fault; people want to kill them, to bury them alive, to throw them into the outermost darkness, into the river, into the fire, to poison them and then have them dissected, to chase them out naked into the forest, for choice when it is freezing hard. A patient begged to be let down for execution. They refuse nourishment, as they are not worthy of food, do not want to deprive others of nourishment, cannot pay, observe poison or filth in the dishes; they would like to nourish themselves on refuse and to sleep on bare boards. A patient ran about bare-footed in order to be accustomed to the cold when people chased him out into the snow.

At times more violent states of excitement may be interpolated. The patients scream, throw themselves on the floor, force their way senselessly out, beat their heads, hide away under the bed, make desperate attacks on the surroundings. A female patient knelt down in a public warehouse in front of religious pictures and tried to destroy secular ones. Another made herself conspicuous in the tramway car by her loud self-accusations. A third in great anxiety seized the full spittoon and emptied it. A patient, who was wholly disordered, suddenly proposed the health of the Prince Regent. Serious attempts at suicide are in these states extremely frequent. God commanded a female patient to kill her relatives. [. . .]

Irritable temperament

The irritable temperament, a further form of manic-depressive predisposition, is perhaps best conceived as a *mixture of the fundamental states*, which have been described, in as much as in it manic and depressive features are associated. As it was demonstrable in about 12·4 per cent of the patients here taken into account, it appears to be still a little more frequent than the depressive predisposition. The patients display from youth up extraordinarily great fluctuations in emotional equilibrium and are greatly moved by all experiences, frequently in an unpleasant way. While on the one hand they appear sensitive and inclined to sentimentality and exuberance, they display on the other hand great irritability and sensitiveness. They are easily offended and hot-tempered; they flare up, and on the most trivial occasions fall into outbursts of boundless fury. 'She had states in which she was nearly delirious,' was said of one patient; 'Her rage is beyond all bounds,' of another. It then comes to violent scenes with abuse, screaming and a tendency to rough behaviour. In such an attack of fury a female patient threw a whole pile of plates on the ground; she flung a lighted lamp at her husband and she tried to attack him with the scissors. The patients are positive, always in the mood for a fight, endure no contradiction, and, therefore, easily fall into disputes with the people round them, which they carry on with great passion. A female patient who thought that she had been taken advantage of in the purchase of a house, threatened her opponent with a revolver, which, however, was unloaded. In consequence of their quarrelsomeness the patients are mostly very much disliked, have frequently to change their situations and places of residence, never come well out of anything. A patient who was an officer fought a series of duels with swords. In the family also they are insufferable, capricious, threaten their wives, thrash their children, have attacks of jealousy.

Mood – The colouring of mood is subject to frequent change. In general the patients are perhaps cheerful, self-conscious, unrestrained; but periods are interpolated in which they are irritable and ill-humoured, also perhaps sad, spiritless, anxious; they shed tears without cause, give expression to thoughts of suicide, bring forward hypochondriacal complaints, go to bed. At the time of the menses the irritability is usually increased.

Intellectual endowment is often very good; many patients display great mental activity, and they feel keenly the necessity for further culture. But they are mostly very distractible and unsteady in their endeavours. Sometimes they are considered to be liars and slanderers, because their power of imagination is usually very much influenced by moods and feelings. It therefore comes easily to delusional interpretations of the events of life. The patients think that they are tricked by the people round them, irritated on purpose and taken advantage of; occasionally they imagine there is poison in their food. On the other hand they build castles in the air, take themselves up with impracticable plans.

Capacity for work may not show any disorder worth mentioning; many patients are very diligent, indeed over busy, over zealous, but yet accomplish relatively little. In conversation the patients are talkative, quick at repartee, pert. In consequence of their irritability and their changing moods their conduct of life is subject to the most multifarious incidents, they make sudden resolves, and carry them out on the spot, run off abruptly, go travelling, enter a cloister. A female patient 'became engaged before she realized what was happening'. Psychogenic disorders are often conspicuous, convulsive weeping, fainting fits, cramps.

Cyclothymic temperament

The cyclothymic temperament must still be shortly considered. It is characterized by *frequent, more or less regular fluctuations of the psychic state to the manic or to the depressive side.* It was found only in 3 to 4 per cent of our patients, but without doubt in reality is much more frequent as it is the invariable introduction to the slightest forms of manic-depressive insanity which run their course outside of institutions, and frequently leads to them by gradual transitions. These are the people who constantly oscillate hither and thither between the two opposite poles of mood, sometimes 'rejoicing to the skies', sometimes 'sad as death'. Today lively, sparkling, beaming, full of the joy of life, the pleasure of enterprise, and pressure of activity, after some time they meet us depressed, enervated, ill-humoured, in need of rest, and again a few months later they display the old freshness and elasticity.

'I have always throughout life imagined something,' explained a patient, 'one time I thought that everything was soaring, another time it appeared to me as if the sky were falling in.' Another stated that she had times in which 'everything got on so well from herself outwards', and other times, in which 'again everything was so frightfully difficult'. A third said that she was 'like a barometer, one time so, another time different'. A patient described how sometimes at his work 'each grip was difficult', and how then a 'lightening of the brain' came over him.

Wilmanns draws attention to artists, who are only at certain times happy in creating and productive, and in the intervals in spite of all efforts do not get beyond unsatisfying attempts. At first these deviations from the middle line are only occasionally perceptible once in a way and as rapidly passing attacks; but for the most part they have the tendency to return more frequently and to last always longer, indeed finally to fill up the whole life.

3 W. W. Gull

Anorexia Nervosa

Excerpts from W. W. Gull, 'Anorexia nervosa (apepsia hysterica, anorexia hysterica)', *Trans. clin. Soc.*, vol. 7 (1874), pp. 22–8.

In an address on medicine, delivered at Oxford in the autumn of 1868,* I referred to a peculiar form of disease occurring mostly in young women, and characterized by extreme emaciation, and often referred to latent tubercle, and mesenteric disease. I remarked that at present our diagnosis of this affection is negative, so far as determining any positive cause from which it springs; that it is mostly one of inference from our clinical knowledge of the liability of the pulmonary or abdominal organs to particular lesions, and by proving the absence of these lesions in the cases in question. The subjects of this affection are mostly of the female sex, and chiefly between the ages of 16 and 23. I have occasionally seen it in males at the same age.

To illustrate the disease I may give the details of two cases, as fair examples of the whole.

Miss A., aet. 17, under the care of Mr Kelson Wright, of the Clapham Road, was brought to me on Jan. 17, 1866. Her emaciation was very great. (*Vide* figures† Nos. 1 and 2.) It was stated that she had lost 33 lb in weight. She was then 5 st 12 lb. Height, 5 ft 5 in. Amenorrhoea for nearly a year. No cough. Respirations throughout chest everywhere normal. Heart-sounds normal. Resps. 12; pulse, 56. No vomiting nor diarrhoea. Slight constipation. Complete anorexia for animal food, and almost complete anorexia for everything else. Abdomen shrunk and flat, collapsed. No abnormal pulsations of aorta. Tongue clean. Urine normal. Slight deposit of phosphates on boiling. The condition was one of simple starvation. There was but slight variation in her condition, though observed at intervals of three or four months. The pulse was noted on these several occasions as 56 and 60. Resps. 12 to 15. The urine was always normal, but varied in sp. gr., and was sometimes as low as 1005. The case was regarded as one of simple anorexia.

* 'Lancet,' August 1868.

† The figures illustrating this paper are facsimiles of the original photographs exhibited at the time the paper was read.

Miss A. No. 1

Miss A. No. 2

Various remedies were prescribed – the preparations of cinchona, the bichloride of mercury, syrup of the iodide of iron, syrup of the phosphate of iron, citrate of quinine and iron, etc. – but no perceptible effect followed their administration. The diet also was varied, but without any effect upon the appetite. Occasionally for a day or two the appetite was voracious, but this was very rare and exceptional. The patient complained of no pain, but was restless and active. This was in fact a striking expression of the nervous state, for it seemed hardly possible that a body so wasted could undergo the exercise which seemed agreeable. There was some peevishness of temper, and a feeling of jealousy. No account could be given of the exciting cause.

Miss A. remained under my observation from Jan. 1866 to March 1868, when she had much improved, and gained in weight from 82 to 128 lb. The improvement from this time continued, and I saw no more of her medically. The figure, Miss A., No. 2, from photograph taken in 1870, shows her condition at that time. It will be noticeable that as she recovered she had a much younger look, corresponding indeed to her age, 21; whilst the photographs, taken when she was 17, give her the appearance of being near 30. Her health has continued good, and I add a fourth photograph taken in 1872.

It will be observed that all the conditions in these case were negative, and may be explained by the anorexia which led to starvation, and a depression of all the vital functions; viz., amenorrhoea, slow pulse, slow breathing. In the stage of greatest emaciation one might have been pardoned for assuming that there was some organic lesion, but from the point of view indicated such an assumption would have been unnecessary.

This view is supported by the satisfactory course of the case to entire recovery, and by the continuance of good health.

Miss B., aet. 18, was brought to me Oct. 8, 1868, as a case of latent tubercle. Her friends had been advised accordingly to take her for the coming winter to the South of Europe.

The extremely emaciated look (vide figure, Miss B., No. 1), much greater indeed than occurs for the most part in tubercular cases where patients are still going about, impressed me at once with the probability that I should find no visceral disease. Pulse 50, Resp. 16. Physical examination of the chest and abdomen discovered nothing abnormal. All the viscera were apparently healthy. Notwithstanding the great emaciation and apparent weakness, there was a peculiar restlessness, difficult, I was informed, to control. The mother added, 'She is never tired.'

Amenorrhoea since Christmas 1866. The clinical details of this case were in fact almost identical with the preceding one, even to the number of the pulse and respirations.

I find the following memoranda frequently entered in my note-book: 'pulse 56, resp. 12; January 1868, pulse 54, resp. 12; March 1869, pulse 54, resp. 12; March 1870, pulse 50, resp. 12.' But little change occurred in the case until 1872, when the respirations became 18 to 20, pulse 60.

After that date the recovery was progressive, and at length complete. (*Vide* figure, Miss B., No. 2.)

The medical treatment probably need not be considered as contributing much to the recovery. It consisted, as in the former case of various so-called tonics, and a nourishing diet.

Although the two cases I have given have ended in recovery, my experience supplies one instance at least of a fatal termination to this malady. When the emaciation is at the extremest, oedema may supervene in the lower extremities – the patient may become sleepless – the pulse become quick, and death be approached by symptoms of feeble febrile reaction. In one such case the *post-mortem* revealed no more than thrombosis of the femoral veins, which appeared to be coincident with the oedema of the lower limbs. Death apparently followed from the starvation alone. This is the clinical point to be borne in mind, and is, I believe, the proper guide to treatment. I have observed that in the extreme emaciation, when the pulse and respiration are slow, the tempera-ture is slightly below the normal standard. This fact, together with the observations made by Chossat on the effect of starvation on animals, and their inability to digest food in the state of inani-tion, without the aid of external heat, has direct clinical bearings; it being often necessary to supply external heat as well as food to patients. The best means of applying heat is to place an india-rubber tube, having a diameter of 2 inches and a length of 3 or 4 feet, filled with hot water along the spine of the patient, as suggested by Dr Newington, of Ticehurst.

Food should be administered at intervals varying inversely with the exhaustion and emaciation. The inclination of the patient must be in no way consulted. In the earlier and less severe stages, it is not unusual for the medical attendant to say, in reply to the anxious solicitude of the parents, 'Let her do as she likes. Don't force food.' Formerly, I thought such advice admissible and proper, but larger experience has shown plainly the danger of allowing the starvation-process to go on.

As regards prognosis, none of these cases, however exhausted,

Miss B. No. 1

Miss B. No. 2

are really hopeless whilst life exists; and, for the most part, the prognosis may be considered favourable. The restless activity referred to is also to be controlled, but this is often difficult.

It is sometimes quite shocking to see the extreme exhaustion and emaciation of these patients brought for advice; yet, by warmth and steady supplies of food and stimulants, the strength may be gradually resuscitated, and recovery completed.

After these remarks were penned, Dr Francis Webb directed my attention to the Paper of Dr Laségue (Professor of Clinical Medicine in the Faculty of Medicine of Paris, and Physician to La Pitié Hospital), which was published in the 'Archives Générales de Médecine,' April 1873, and translated into the pages of the 'Med. Times,' Sept 6 and 27, 1873.

It is plain that Dr Laségue and I have the same malady in mind, though the forms of our illustrations are different. Dr Laségue does not refer to my address at Oxford, and it is most likely he knew nothing of it. There is, therefore, the more value in his Paper, as our observations have been made independently. We have both selected the same expression to characterize the malady.

In the address at Oxford I used the term *Apepsia hysterica*, but before seeing Dr Laségue's Paper, it had equally occurred to me that *Anorexia* would be more correct.

The want of appetite is, I believe, due to a morbid mental state. I have not observed in these cases any gastric disorder to which the want of appetite could be referred. I believe, therefore, that its origin is central and not peripheral. That mental states may destroy appetite is notorious, and it will be admitted that young women at the ages named are specially obnoxious to mental perversity. We might call the state hysterical without committing ourselves to the etymological value of the word, or maintaining that the subjects of it have the common symptoms of hysteria. I prefer, however, the more general term 'nervosa', since the disease occurs in males as well as females, and is probably rather central than peripheral. The importance of discriminating such cases in practice is obvious; otherwise prognosis will be erroneous, and treatment misdirected.

In one of the cases I have named the patient had been sent abroad for one or two winters, under the idea that there was a tubercular tendency. I have remarked above that these wilful patients are often allowed to drift their own way into a state of extreme exhaustion, when it might have been prevented by placing them under different moral conditions.

The treatment required is obviously that which is fitted for persons of unsound mind. The patients should be fed at regular intervals, and surrounded by persons who would have moral control over them; relations and friends being generally the worst attendants.

Addendum

As a further illustration, I may add the following correspondence on one of these cases with Dr Anderson, of Richmond.

Miss C., aet 15 years 8 months, was sent to me in April 1873. The clinical history was that she had been ailing for a year, and had become extremely emaciated. (Figure, Miss C., No. 1.) The catamenia had never appeared. Pulse 64, resp. 16. Very sleepless for six months past. All the viscera healthy. Urine normal. Lower extremities oedematous. Mind weakened. Temper obstinate. Great restlessness. No family history of disease beyond the fact that the maternal grandmother had had peculiar nervous symptoms. I wrote the following letter to Dr Anderson:

DEAR DR ANDERSON, – I saw Miss C. today. The case appears to be an extreme instance of what I have proposed to call 'Apepsia hysterica', or 'Anorexia nervosa'. (*See* 'Address on Medicine at Oxford', 1868.) I believe it to be essentially a failure of the powers of the gastric branches of the pneumogastric nerve. It differs from tuberculosis, though that state may subsequently arise, by the pulse, which I found to be 64, by the breathing, 16, the cleanness of the tongue, &c. In fact, the disease will be most correctly interpreted if it is remembered that no symptom more positive than emaciation is presented in and throughout its course.

I would advise warm clothing, and some form of nourishing food every two hours, as milk, cream, soup, eggs, fish, chicken. I must only urge the necessity of nourishment in some form, otherwise the venous obstruction, which has already begun to show itself by oedema of the legs, will go on to plugging of the vessels. With the nourishment I would conjoin a dessert-spoonful of brandy every two or three hours. Whilst the present state of weakness continues, fatigue must be limited, and if the exhaustion increases beyond its present degree the patient should for a time be kept in a warm bed. I do not at present prescribe medicines, because the nursing and the food are more important than anything else. Such cases not unfrequently come before me; but as the morbid state is not yet generally recognized, I should be glad if you would second my wish of having a photograph taken of Miss C. in her present state, that we may compare it with some later one, if, as I hope, our plan of treatment is successful, as in my experience it generally is. I would, as I say, enclose a prescription, but I feel it most necessary to insist on food and stimulants, at least for a time.

Yours truly,

April 30, 1873.

Miss C. No. 1

Miss C. No. 2

On May 24 I received the following note from Dr Anderson:

DEAR SIR WILLIAM, – I enclose photograph of Miss C. . . . There is rather an improvement in one respect, viz. there is less aversion to food. Want of sleep and swelling of the feet are the two great troubles. You have given us all new hope, however, and I trust I may one day send you a *plump* photograph, like what she was two years ago. With renewed thanks, I am, dear Sir William, yours very truly,

On October 23, 1873, I received a further report.

DEAR SIR WILLIAM, – Miss C. is now at Shanklin, but returns very soon. I hear she is much better. She had a bad slough on the leg near the ankle, from persisting in wearing a tight boot.

The great difficulty was to keep her quiet, and to make her eat and drink. Every step had to be fought. She was most loquacious and obstinate, anxious to overdo herself bodily and mentally. I will give you particulars when they return, but I am told she is much improved. Rest, and food, and stimulants as prescribed, undoubtedly did her a great deal of good. She used to be a nice, plump, good-natured little girl. Believe me, &c.

The last report I received was on April 15, 1874.

DEAR SIR W., – I am sure you will be delighted to hear that Miss C., in whose case you were so kindly interested, . . . has now made a complete recovery, and is getting plump and rosy as of yore. . . . (*Vide* figure, Miss C., No. 2.)

4   A. Kennedy

The Organic Reaction Types

Excerpts from A. Kennedy, 'The organic reaction types', in *Modern practice in psychological medicine* (ed. J. R. Rees), Butterworth, 1949, chapter 19, pp. 316–25.

Some Principles of Aetiology

Although the relation between the functions of the mind and the activity of the central nervous system is by no means clear in the present state of our knowledge, certain psychological symptom-complexes are known to be frequent in organic disease of the brain, and their appearance must always lead the clinician to suspect that the patient's disorder of thought or behaviour is wholly or in part due to this cause. Whereas at the lower levels of integration in the spinal cord and midbrain, organic changes of the same location and kind may be expected to produce relatively constant effects in different individuals, the principles of diagnosis on a purely anatomical basis break down at the higher levels at which the extent of individual variation is far greater. Although innate differences in mental potential and predisposition are related to variations in central nervous structure and development, the postnatal trend of functional development must be largely dependent upon environmental factors and the conditioning process by which the adult personality and temperament are fashioned from the inborn raw material of mind. The clinical picture of organic disease will therefore always vary in its coloration according to the personality of the patient. In some cases the disease process will do little more than release or accentuate pre-existing tendencies to socially inacceptable behaviour or to neurotic escape, whereas in others the psychological disturbance is highly characteristic of the particular influences at work. In general, however, the basic rules of symptom-formation which apply at lower levels of the nervous system are applicable if due allowance is made for the psychological as well as for the mechanical and humoral reactions of the individual to the disturbing process. In observing any case of organic disease of the nervous system, therefore, the following principles must be constantly borne in mind.

(1) A great part of the central nervous system is organized in developmental levels. The primitive, coarser function of the lower

levels, both sensory and motor, is modified, controlled and inhibited by the higher levels. The clinical effects of any disturbance will vary with its nature (whether degeneration, intoxication, mechanical disturbance, infection or anoxia), its localization and the levels involved.

(2) Symptoms may be of three kinds, *negative* or paralytic, due to loss of function from destruction, intoxication or shock, *positive* due either to irritation of neurones or to the release of patterns of reaction normally held in check by inhibition, or *disordered* due to the abnormal action of units within the nervous system which results from damage to their neighbours.

(3) Any particular clinical state is unlikely to be due to a single cause operating only at one level but will be a composite of different effects at different levels. Knowledge of the detailed localization of purely psychological functions is limited and in some cases purely tentative, and little reliance can be placed upon it in diagnosis, especially when it is considered that the global effect of central nervous activity probably amounts to more than the sum of its functional components. Compensatory mechanisms may completely disguise a loss of function within a very short time of its occurrence. Further in any circumscribed lesion the clinical effects will be due not only to the local disturbances but also to its indirect effect on the whole central nervous system.

(4) Changes in character and temperament due to organic disease are referable not so much to the nature of the lesion but to the previous personality of the individual and his state of mental development at the time of onset. It will depend also upon the opportunities afforded him, after the appearance of the pathological state, of acquiring the behaviour disorders to which that state has predisposed him. In addition to such organic predispositions, personality traits already in existence may be reduced in strength or rendered more prominent by release of inhibition.

(5) Organic disease of the central nervous system is a form of stress which renders normal adaptation to life more difficult, especially when the patient is unaware of the reasons for his growing incompetence. Before diagnosis is made he must labour under his disability without receiving the consideration allowed to a sick man. The symptoms of organic states of gradual onset may, therefore, be obscured by psychogenic mechanisms of a compensatory kind. Further, the presence of organic disease *per se* may lower resistance to psychoneurotic mental mechanisms and these may be responsible for symptoms clinically far more conspicuous

than those due to the underlying condition. Symptoms of functional incapacity (hysteria) of a gross kind appearing in the absence of a fully adequate psychogenesis must always give rise to a suspicion either of an underlying organic state or of the presence of psychogenic factors as yet unrevealed. In organic nervous disease of gradual onset some sort of functional overlay is almost the rule.

Psychological Symptoms of Common Occurrence in Organic Nervous Disease

A number of symptom-complexes are almost pathognomonic of organic disease, whereas others are more frequently associated with it than with the functional psychoses and psychoneuroses. The proportion of these groups of symptoms in any general clini al picture allows of a differential diagnosis by increasing probability. The following, although not entirely specific to organic disease, are frequently found in its various forms.

Disturbances of consciousness

These vary from complete unconsciousness such as is seen in concussion, epilepsy, greatly raised intracranial pressure and the coma of meningitis or uraemia, through the states of altered or clouded consciousness associated with delirium and the twilight states of the epileptic fugue, to minor alterations in which the patient is unable adequately to focus his attention. Feelings of unreality or depersonalization are often present with these minor disturbances as is the *déjà vu* phenomenon, which, although observed in normal individuals, is often associated with dysrhythmic states.

Disturbances of sleep

Hypersomnia is seen in encephalitis, in some tumours of the hypothalamus and in increased intracranial pressure, whereas intractable *insomnia* is found in early arteriosclerotic dementia and in some forms of delirium, notably delirium tremens and the delirium of gas-gangrene intoxication. Such insomnias are not difficult to differentiate clinically from the difficulty in getting off to sleep which is seen in anxiety or in the early morning awakening of depression.

Inversion of the sleep rhythm – This condition is seen in post-encephalitic states and some arteriosclerotic reactions, the patient being sleepy by day and alert and tense at night.

Lethargy – This is a state in which the individual can be roused to answer questions but at once goes to sleep again; it is seen in epidemic encephalitis and in other conditions in which the hypothalamic regions are directly or indirectly involved.

Narcolepsy and cataplexy – These conditions are invariably organic in origin, although cases, especially those secondary to encephalitis lethargica, frequently exhibit a gross functional overlay.

Fatiguability

Rapid fatigue of attention and memory is a prominent feature of the syndrome of *organic vulnerability* to which reference will be made later. It is found during convalescence from severe head injuries and meningitis and is, in fact, seen in any condition – such as latent uraemia, peripheral neuritis or arteriopathic dementia – which is liable, when more marked, to produce evening delirium. Fatigue in such cases is accompanied by mild confusion with difficulty in remembering names and inability to focus the attention.

Perseveration

This condition, in which a movement or thought is repeated whenever the patient attempts to initiate a new one, is most marked when associated with dysphasia, although it is without localizing value and may be seen in a variety of conditions in which the cerebral cortex and subjacent white matter are involved. It is practically pathognomonic of organic disease and is most marked in the presenile dementias.

Impairment of memory

Failure to recall recent impressions is present to some extent in most acute and chronic organic reactions, whereas generalized failure of memory for both recent and remote events occurs in the organic degenerative diseases. *Circumscribed amnesias* are confined to the effects of trauma, including vascular accidents and the primary and symptomatic epilepsies. These consist of *retrograde amnesia* for a period of time before the stress, and *post-traumatic amnesia* and a patchy amnesia for the periods of clouded consciousness which may follow any cerebral disturbance. In the latter form 'islands' of memory occur for isolated events in the period of confusion – a phenomenon which is also observed in the patient's recollection of a period of delirium. Diagnosis from hysterical amnesia is not usually difficult although it must constantly be recalled that superimposed hysterical amnesia is a not uncommon complication of organic conditions in which emotional lability is a feature of the organic syndrome, such as disseminated sclerosis, chronic encephalitis lethargica or slowly increasing hydrocephalus. In organic reactions in which recent memory is lost without gross interference with intellect, and especially in the alcoholic psychoses and post-traumatic deliria, *paramnesias* or false recollections occur in which the forgotten material is replaced by retrospective falsification, or the patient compensates for his lack of content by pseudo-reminiscence. In subacute delirium this confabulation may be carried to a great degree, the patient relating in detail and with conviction events which have had no reality at all. This bears some resemblance to the pseudologia fantastica seen in some psychopathic personalities, but the content is invariably far less probable or consistent in the recent organic state. Since confabulation is often a prominent feature of Korsakow's psychosis associated with alcoholic polyneuritis, the term Korsakow syndrome is often applied to it.

Irritability

Explosive episodes are characteristic of the dysrhythmias, but they are often seen in other organic states such as early dementia paralytica or arteriosclerotic dementia and during the withdrawal of drugs of addiction. The syndrome of cerebral irritation after trauma includes great irritability and negativism. Irritability is often seen in patients with chronic infections, including tuberculosis, and is a prominent feature of organic vulnerability.

Emotional lability

The tendency to a superficial emotional facility (or lability) and over-reaction, in which there are abrupt changes from laughter to tears and fine gradations of feeling are replaced by sudden waves of strong emotion of brief duration, are very common in chronic nervous disorders. In these conditions emotion and sentiment are not fully under the patient's control and the degree of affective response to the patient's thoughts tends to be out of proportion to the stimulus. The prevailing tone in these cases is one of euphoria with a superficial sentimentality which is highly characteristic. Emotional lability is frequently present in the early stages of conditions such as cerebral arteriosclerotic dementia or the presenile psychoses in which feeling later becomes blunted and the patient becomes indifferent. As organic dementia of any kind becomes more advanced there is generally a progressive flattening of affective response and an increasing apathy.

Vulnerability to neurosis

Emotional facility, especially when seen in association with disorders of the basal ganglia and the region bordering the third ventricle, is often accompanied by a vulnerability to hysterical mechanisms, and diagnosis is not infrequently made difficult by the addition of gross conversion phenomena to the clinical picture. This *degenerative hysteria* in which a severe hysterical reaction appears without apparent adequate psychogenic cause is particularly common in disseminated sclerosis, chronic lethargic encephalitis and epilepsy, and even dementia paralytica not uncommonly comes to light through the patient's being brought for examination on account of an amnesia or aphonia. It may be that in these conditions the threshold amount of anxiety necessary to cause the patient to seek escape in functional incapacity is lowered. His response thus becomes comparable to that of an individual with a severe constitutional vulnerability to neurotic escape. In general, the presence of early organic disease without gross dementia acts as a predisposing factor to neurotic reactions of all kinds, although obsessional reactions are rarely seen except in the obsessive-compulsive states which sometimes accompany chronic chorea and disorders of the extrapyramidal motor pathways.

Disinhibition

The release of latent tendencies, although especially associated with damage to the more anterior parts of the cerebral cortex and subjacent white matter, has no reliable localizing value. In the early stages of the presenile cortical atrophies, in arteriosclerotic dementia and in dementia paralytica, for instance, an individual may get into trouble through shameless behaviour which is quite inconsistent with his previous reputation, or he may be thought to be drunk after having taken small quantities of alcohol which he could tolerate previously without visible effect.

Disinhibition is also seen in the release of the tendency to affective psychosis, the mental state being often indistinguishable from an acute melancholia. In the rarer cases when a manic reaction is released by organic disease, as is seen sometimes in senile dementia, hypertension or Wernicke's encephalopathy, the rapid appearance of confusion and exhaustion renders the diagnosis less difficult. Disinhibition reaches its extreme form in the grandiose delusions of dementia paralytica in which failure of self-criticism and euphoria may allow of a fantastic expansiveness.

Character disorder

Quite apart from causing intellectual and emotional decay, organic disease may predispose to a failure of social adaptation which is mainly in the moral sphere. The most marked examples of this are seen in those victims of epidemic encephalitis whose acute attack has occurred between the ages of 8 and 14 years and is far less marked in those who have reached maturity. It is probable that the greater tendency to *moral amentia* in these cases is due to the fact that the disease made its appearance at the time when the child was developing the means of adaptation to life in a civilized community and acquiring the codes of behaviour necessary to such adaptation, for it is just this process which has failed in the post-encephalitic subjects who show delinquent tendencies. These cases show an insightless egocentricity and lack of foresight in their contacts with other individuals and with society in general, and with it a total lack of sympathy with others and a tendency to take what pleasure they can at the moment the opportunity occurs. The resulting hedonism, faithlessness and delinquency are characteristic. A similar syndrome in greater or less degree may be found either associated with congenital anomalies of the nervous system or as a feature of other forms of acquired disease.

In early dementia, especially the arteriosclerotic form, social behaviour is often impaired as egocentricity and lack of consideration for others appear as a compensatory response for lack of mental efficiency.

Delirium

This is an exclusively organic syndrome associated with acute or subacute disturbance in the nervous system as a whole when neurone dysfunction of toxic, anoxic, dysrhythmic or traumatic causation is present. The damaged or degenerating nervous system is vulnerable to delirium and very mild anoxaemia or toxaemia will readily produce delirious episodes in the course of chronic progressive disease. Such episodes are, for instance, common in senile or alcoholic dementia. The clinical features of delirium will be described later.

Some General Clinical Features of Organic Reactions

The clinical picture in any organic nervous disorder which exhibits psychological disturbances may contain some features due to localizable disturbances such as the dysgnosias, dyspraxias and dysphasias and other symptoms such as those mentioned above which, though often associated with organic disease, are of no localizing value. There are relatively few examples of abnormal mental content specific to one disease process and such well-known entities as the expansive grandiosity of the paretic, the dementing religiosity of advanced epileptic deterioration or the confabulations of chronic alcoholism occur in only a proportion of the cases. Certain general syndromes, on the other hand, are remarkably constant and their presence together with other features, localizing and non-localizing, renders diagnosis of the type of process at work relatively easy. Once these have been recognized further investigation will usually establish the cause. The psychological accompaniments of the reaction of the nervous system to physical disturbance may be divided into three main types.

1. *Organic dementia:* the chronic organic reaction form.
2. *Delirium:* the acute or subacute organic reaction form.
3. *Organic mental vulnerability:* a predisposition brought about by the effects of organic disease or of the individual's efforts to adapt to or compensate for its presence.

The three clinical entities described above are likely to enter in varying degree into the mental state of any patient with an organic disturbance. They are far from mutually exclusive, but one form of reaction may be much more in evidence.

The appearance of the three reaction-forms may be compared to the response of any machine to damage, to excessive or too prolonged stress, or to deterioration of its component materials. When the defect is severe and of sudden onset yet insufficient to cause complete stoppage, the fall in output is great and much abnormal noise and heat are generated – an acute reaction. When efficiency falls off slowly, due to the wear and tear of age, the defect can at first be discovered only by carefully measuring the output, and on superficial observation the machine appears to be as good as others of its type. It is only when the end is near that serious disturbances occur. Such an engine is more easily put out of order and even mild overload may be sufficient to produce an acute reaction. When a machine is getting too old for effective service, or when it has suffered acute breakdown which has left it vulnerable, it requires constant care and consideration if it is to pull its weight. Not only is it more easily put out of order but it generates rather more heat and noise than an undamaged machine. Delirium may be compared to the heat and noise of acute engine trouble and in like manner it usually occurs in the final disturbance which leads to cessation of function. If recovery occurs, efficiency is often lowered and a reasonable mental output and adaptation to life can only be secured by means of a series of make-shifts and compensatory mechanisms – the reactions of the mentally vulnerable and inefficient.

Organic dementia

Dementia is the common end-point of a large number of disorders and consists of an irreversible deterioration of mental efficiency due to destruction of neurones. Clinically there is a profound failure of intellect, emotion and social adaptation. In all organic disease there is some degree of irreversible neurone destruction but if the outfall of cells is gradual a considerable portion of the nervous system can be destroyed before there is a clearly demonstrable falling-off in intellectual performance. This is well illustrated by the return to normal life of treated cases of dementia paralytica, in whom very gross damage must have occurred before the disease was arrested. None the less, certain psychological disabilities are constantly found in early dementia. These consist of failure of memory, especially for recent events, and difficulty in recalling names. Any sort of intellectual effort causes fatigue, attention is ill-sustained and there is little initiative. The patient is confused when in strange surroundings and has difficulty in adapting to new places and understanding new points of view. Thus in the early stages of senile dementia spectacles are lost, anecdotes repeated and the individual resents changes in a rigid routine of life. New acquaintances are made with reluctance, and failure of recall is either compensated for by confabulation or avoided altogether by living in the past. New events make little impression emotionally and increasing inadequacy is projected in the form of irritability with others and ill-sustained paranoid ideas. Later, memory is almost lost and there is difficulty even in completing the daily round until an end-state is reached of indifferent, incontinent mindlessness which is common to most progressive organic conditions where life is spared long enough for it to develop. There is no accurate method of measuring the degree of organic deterioration but some guidance can be provided by the use of the Babcock principle, that is to say, the capacity for abstract thinking and mental agility in test situations is more rapidly lost than is memory for the meaning of words. In tests of this kind, of which the Shipley-Hartford is the best known, the score on tests requiring reasoning is compared with the result of vocabulary tests and the result expressed as an index of deterioration known as the *conceptual quotient*.

Delirium: the acute organic reaction

In contrast to dementia which occurs on a background of clear consciousness the acute organic reaction seen in the infections, the encephalopathies and at times in the dysrhythmic and traumatic states, has confusion and disturbance of consciousness as its main features. Although the factors responsible for delirium may also in time cause dementia, its presence in a previously normal person indicates at least a potentially reversible process in which the nervous system is functioning abnormally but has not been destroyed. In the normal individual a considerable anoxia or toxaemia is necessary to produce delirium but the nervous system which is already reduced in efficiency by such dementing agencies as alcoholism, head injury, epilepsy or senile change, may readily react in this way. In bromide intoxication, for instance, the threshold blood-bromide at which different individuals show psychological abnormality differs within wide limits. When the threat to nervous function is severe, however, the acute organic reaction may occur in anyone.

The term delirium may be held to include states of mild degree and long duration as well as those in which the psychological disturbance is acute and profound. Clinically it is characterized by confusion, including disorientation in time and place, difficulty in concentrating the attention or grasping the meaning of what is said, together with impairment of memory, especially for recent events. Disturbances of perception occur and misinterpretations of outside events, based on the patient's mental content at the time, are common. The hallucinations of delirium are usually visual in contrast to those of the functional psychoses, although auditory hallucinations are not infrequent. In some cases the type of hallucination seems to some extent to be specific to the process at work, the animals of delirium tremens, the winged creatures of belladonna poisoning and the haptic (touch) hallucinations of cocainism being examples of this. In acute delirium the confusion is accompanied by a prevailing effect of fear together with restlessness and a feeling that some terrifying experience is imminent. Ideas of reference are often present. In the subacute forms the disturbance of memory is compensated for by a confabulation in which the patient invents material to fill the gaps in his memory. This is particularly well marked in Korsakow's psychosis and after severe head injury. Even in the acute toxic deliria, however, suggestibility and confabulation may also be very striking.

Delirium, when acute, is accompanied by pyrexia and the physical concomitants of toxaemia and shows marked variations in intensity, being usually much more marked in the evenings. When dementia supervenes upon chronic delirium, euphoria may replace the fear and apprehension of the acute state and indifference, character deterioration or systematized delusions may make their appearance.

Organic vulnerability

When organic disease is present which is neither acute enough to cause disturbance of consciousness or delirium nor sufficiently advanced to produce a demonstrable dementia, a condition is often found in which the patient is well enough adapted under conditions of rest without responsibility, worry or toxaemia, but breaks down on exposure to even minimal stress. Such patients appear to be lacking in resistance to neurotic reactions even though they have apparently had little tendency to them before the onset of the illness. In slowly progressive disorders of the nervous system a history of such a state of vulnerability before the advent of severe symptoms can often be elicited. It is found in the early stages of the presenile dementias, in convalescence from severe head injury, in the months preceding the recognition of dementia paralytica, in nutritional deficiencies and, in fact, in any organic state where there exists a mild general degree of mental inefficiency in the absence of gross disorder necessitating either specific treatment or a protected environment.

The commonest complaint in such patients is of headache, often described as pressure on the head or a band round the head, and of inability to concentrate. A feeling of perpetual fatigue or of exhaustion at the end of the day is often mentioned as is inability to remember names in the evenings, together with irritability and depression. Hypochondriacal worries and a feeling of unreality are often present together with quarrelsomeness and infantile behaviour when the patient is with people whom he knows well. A tendency to egocentricity and to the seeking of sympathy often makes its appearance. Marital difficulties may lead one or the other partner to seek separation or advice, and loss of libido is often then found to be present. Moods of depression following trivial setbacks may alternate with an inconsiderate euphoria in which the patient is careless of his future or of the interests of his family. Affective lability may be evident together with a tendency to excessive sentimentality and dependence on others. Patients in this condition are extremely liable to react in neurotic fashion to relatively slight stress, and conversion symptoms may mask the underlying state. When an injury has been received, the grossest forms of traumatic hysteria may make their appearance and, in persons of low intelligence, the clinical picture is often not unlike that of malingering. Such patients have usually little tolerance for alcohol, heat or fatigue and readily become confused. Even a relatively slight infection may produce delirium. Frequently they are reported by those who know them well to have changed in personality during a definite period.

A similar vulnerable state can be induced by continued anxiety, mild depression or undetected physical disease, especially tuberculosis, but a careful neurological and psychological examination may bring the true cause to light. This state of vulnerability is in part due to physical impairment of the function of nervous tissue and in part due to compensatory mechanisms of a psychological kind. A considerable proportion of such cases show abnormality of the electrical rhythms and the fairly frequent occurrence of impulsive behaviour may be related to this.

Localizing Value of Psychological Symptoms

Broadly speaking, psychological symptoms are of localizing value only in the presence of other evidence pointing to the same localization. General mental efficiency and memory are most seriously impaired in conditions where the cortex is attacked or the disorder involves the major association systems (corpus callosum, superior and inferior longitudinal fasciculi and the white matter of the frontal lobe). Emotional disturbance and released neurosis are more common when the disorder is in the neighbourhood of the third ventricle and the thalamus. The gnosias and praxias are, of course, of value in localization, and disturbances of perception related to damage in the neighbourhood of the sensory projection areas of the cortex may help if other evidence is lacking. Motor abnormalities ranging from choreiform movements and spasmodic torticollis to the fantastic methods of progression seen in some post-encephalitic patients may point to involvement of the extrapyramidal motor system. The psychological symptoms associated with localized disturbances will be dealt with below in describing the effects of space-occupying lesions. [. . .]

Classifications

(1) The psychological effects of space-occupying lesions within the skull.

(2) The dysrhythmias.

(3) Post-traumatic states.

(4) The encephalopathies.

(5) The inflammatory conditions of the nervous system, acute and chronic.

(6) The dementias and degenerations.

The Psychological Effects of Space-occupying Lesions within the Skull

The localized effects of tumours will always be obscured to some extent by the effects of raised intracranial pressure. There are no cardinal symptoms in the psychological field comparable to the headache, vomiting, vertigo and failure of vision which usually point the way to a correct diagnosis, but certain non-localizing signs may strongly suggest the presence of a neoplasm. A general lowering of mental alertness and blunting of feeling may lead to inefficiency, indifference and lack of initiative. The patient fails to keep up with topical matters, spends a greatly increased time in sleeping and has difficulty in remembering recent events and recalling names. From time to time he may become muddled in trying to express himself although he is not usually greatly distressed by this. Euphoria may make its appearance at an early stage and this may make him put off seeking advice until his inefficiency is obvious to all but himself. Wandering away from work, or impulsive behaviour, may occur as well as actions into which the patient has no insight, such as talking loudly when silence is indicated or making preparations to retire or undressing far from home. Actions may be needlessly repeated and finally perseveration appears in speech. Cerebral tumours, especially of an infiltrating kind, may occasionally be associated with paranoid states or may predispose to gross hysterical reactions for which advice is initially sought. Although localization on the basis of psychological symptoms is far from reliable, the following are worthy of mention.

The frontal lobe syndrome

The frontal lobe is an anatomical and not a functional unit and the symptoms found when it is involved are related to a number of functional systems. In patients with frontal tumours convulsions are common and in a fair proportion of cases incontinence or enuresis is present. Often there is an increase in appetite and in weight together with euphoria, facetiousness and excessive placidity. Intellectual deterioration is often rapid, and occasionally profound stupor is present. In some cases a marked loss of foresight and of the capacity for ethical valuation may lead to shameless or antisocial conduct.

Temporal tumours

The most characteristic feature of temporal tumours is the uncinate fit. This may commence with an aura in which there are gustatory or olfactory hallucinations and disturbance of consciousness together with unreality feelings or a momentary conviction that everything that is happening has been seen or has happened before – the *déjà vu* phenomenon. [. . .]

Part Two EXPERIMENTS IN RELATION TO ABNORMAL PSYCHOLOGY

The value one gives to the writings of C. G. Jung depends very much on one's taste, but there can be no doubt about the importance of Jung's work on the word-association test when it first appeared. I am sure that this work will be seen, in the future, to be even more important than it was in the past.

So far as I have been able to find out, the paper by Moore is the first attempt to apply the methods of factor analysis to the field of abnormal psychology. The method of 'factor analysis' (really a form of cluster analysis) used is very primitive by modern standards, and even at that time there were better methods available. Nevertheless, this paper (only some of the tables have been cut) must be regarded as a landmark in the history of abnormal psychology.

The little monograph by Cameron is one of the earlier attempts in this field. It is still one of the most interesting and provided much food for thought.

5 C. G. Jung

Studies in Word-Association

Excerpt from C. G. Jung, *Studies in word-association* (translated by Dr M. D. Eder), Heinemann, 1918.

I have endeavoured in the translation to give the ideas of the different contributors as clearly and literally as possible. In a number of illustrative examples of word-associations, when clang-associations, assonances, alliterations, or rhymes occur impossible of literal translation, I have substituted reactions from my own experiments or constructed reactions on the lines of the original model. This nowhere impairs the interpretation or understanding of the text, and it has not been considered necessary to note these substitutions. In a few cases the German has been retained, a translation of the word being also given.

TRANSLATOR

[. . .] Despite the many valuable experiences which Freud has expounded for us, psycho-analysis is a very difficult art, for every beginner rapidly loses courage and orientation in face of the innumerable obstacles. Safe foundations are wanting from whence to start; when you have to begin with a patient at haphazard, so to say, you are often at a loss where to begin the attack.

Association experiments have helped us to get over these first and chief difficulties. I have shown in the chapter on time-measurements (chapter v) that the emotionally charged presentation complexes give rise to characteristic disturbances in the experiment; their presence and probable nature can be recognized from the disturbances themselves. This fact forms the foundation of *The Psychological Diagnosis of Facts* founded by Wertheimer and Klein,[1] Hans Gross,[2] and Alfred Gross.[3] It seems fairly possible by this method to diagnose by the associations the complex of a crime. Everyone has naturally one or more complexes which make

1. Wertheimer, *Experimentelle Untersuchungen zur Tatbestandsdiagnostik* (Dissert: Würzburg, 1905).
   Wertheimer and Klein, 'Psychologische Tatbestandsdiagnostik', *Archiv. für Kriminalanthropologie*, Bd. XV.
2. Hans Gross, 'Zur psychologischen Tatbestandsdiagnostik', *Archiv. für Kriminalanthropologie*, 1905.
3. Alfred Gross, 'Die Associationsmethode im Strafprocess', *Zeitschrift für die gesamte Strafrechtswissenschaft*, Bd. XXVI. Grabowsky, 'Psychologische Tatbestandsdiagnostik', 1905.

themselves manifest in some way in the associations. The background of our consciousness (or the unconscious) consists of complexes of this kind. The whole material of memory is grouped around them. They form higher psychical unities analogous to the ego complex (Bleuler,[1] chapter vi). They constellate the whole of our thinking and doing, hence the associations also. We sometimes join a second experiment to that of the association one, *reproduction*.[2] The experiment consists in making the subject repeat his reactions to the stimulus-words in the first experiment. Where memory fails we have generally to do with a constellation due to a complex. Reproduction, therefore, assists in the closer circumscribing of the complex disturbances.

All psychogenic neuroses contain a complex which is differentiated from normal complexes by being endowed with extremely strong emotional tones, possessing such constellating power that it brings the whole individual under its influence. The complex is hence the *causa morbi* (given, of course, the predisposition). The associations often enable us to recognize the nature of the complex, thus obtaining valuable clues for causal therapy. A by-product, not to be underestimated, is the scientific knowledge which we thus gain of the origin and inner construction of the psychogenic neuroses. Freud has assuredly long since given us the substance of this knowledge, but he has anticipated by a long way the understanding of his time. It will not, therefore, be superfluous if I offer some new approach on the experimental plane to the Freudian store of knowledge. In previous chapters Freud's principles have several times been drawn on in explanation. Here I would present the connexion between psycho-analysis and association experiments by some practical examples. I choose an ordinary case of obsessional neurosis which I treated in June 1905.

Miss E. came to me for hypnotic treatment for sleeplessness of four months' duration. Besides the sleeplessness she complained of inner unrest and excitement, irritability towards her family, impatience and quarrelsomeness. She is thirty-seven, a teacher, cultured and intelligent; has always been nervous; has a younger sister feeble-minded; her father was an alcoholic. Condition: well nourished; physically nothing of moment was found. Her agitated and convulsive movements are remarkable. Whilst talking she seldom looks at the doctor, as a rule not addressing him but speaking out at the window. From time to time she turns away still more, is often obliged to laugh involuntarily, frequently

1. Bleuler, ' Versuch einer naturwissenschaftlichen Betrachtung der psychologischen Grundbegriffe', *Allgemeine Zeitschrift für Psychiatrie.*
2. Jung, 'Experimentelle Beobachtungen über das Erinnerungsvermögen', *Centralb. für Nervenheilk, u. Psych.*, Bd. XXVIII.

shrugs her shoulders as if shaking off something disagreeable, protruding the lower part of her abdomen in a peculiar manner.

The anamnesis which she gives is very incomplete and indefinite. She had formerly been a governess abroad, but had not then been ill. The illness only occurred in recent years and has gradually developed to its present pitch. She says she has been unsuccessfully treated by many doctors. She would now like to try hypnosis, but immediately adds that she is firmly convinced that hypnotism will not succeed. Her disease is incurable and she is sure she will go mad. She has, indeed, often thought that she cannot be normal now and that she is already insane. It here occurred to me that the patient was obviously talking round something, that she would not or could not say. On being urged she finally explained, with many gestures of resistance and constant blushing, that she could not sleep because whenever she disposed herself to sleeping the idea came to her that she would not, of course, be able to sleep, that she would never sleep again until she were dead; she would then wake right up and be unable to sleep again the whole night. Whenever she felt worn out and desired to sleep a terrible fear would rouse her up again – she would never sleep again – until she were dead or mad. She had to wrench this explanation out of herself – in such a way, and with such gestures of aversion, as almost to arouse the impression that she was telling something sexually improper which caused her to be ashamed. Again there were the movements of the abdomen. She frequently laughed as if abashed, which made a peculiar impression of inadequacy. This peculiar state caused me to ask if there were other ideas present which troubled her during the sleeplessness: 'No, I can't remember anything – things just pass through me – oh, it's thousands of things that keep running through my head.' She was unable to recall anything, made gestures of aversion and said suddenly: She has really such stupid thoughts; these force themselves upon her and she cannot possibly shake herself free from them. She is sorry she cannot communicate these ideas to me for she is afraid I would then get these obsessions. She had once told a doctor and a clergyman about her thoughts and now she is always thinking that she had infected those people and they also had obsessional ideas. She was sure she had already infected me. I reassured her; I had already heard many ideas of that kind and they had not injured me in the least. Upon this she admitted with the same gestures that, besides the ideas mentioned with which she had infected the doctor and the clergyman, she was chiefly bothered by the thought that a neighbour, a woman, who had recently died, had on her account died unhappy and had had to suffer all the torments of hell. She had only had that idea since her death; previously, she had had for many years the idea that a boy whom she had formerly educated had subsequently died from the punishments she had occasionally imposed upon him. Her anxiety was so great that she had been obliged to write twice to the family for news about his health. She had done it each time in a way that would not arouse suspicion. The good news which she received each time had momentarily quieted her, but a few days later the anxiety was as great as ever. That idea had now ceased, but she had now to reproach herself with the unhappy death of her neighbour. Reason told her that these ideas were nonsense (she said this in a very uncertain voice) or was it perhaps the truth? (she quickly added). Thus she did not entirely correct herself, but she was obviously completely mastered by the obsessional ideas.

The anamnesis did not succeed in discovering any sexual abnormalities, that is to say, anything which could in any way refer to sexual matters was denied as a matter of course.

Any attempt at hypnotism was useless because she could not fix her attention in any way. Not to spoil this method at the beginning by useless attempts, I decided first to obtain some certainty about the psychical material which was at the root of the illness. I therefore arranged an association experiment with her.

I. The Association Experiment

The whole experiment is reproduced here.

Stimulus-word	Reaction	Reaction-time	Reproduction
1. *Head*[1]	*thoughts*	: 2·2 seconds	hair
2. Green	grass	: 1·8 ,,	†[2]
3. *Water*	*drinker – drink*	: 2·4 ,,	glass
4. Prick	needle	: 3·6 ,,	†
5. Angel‡[3]	heaven	: 2·6 ,,	†
6. Long‡	short	: 4 ,,	†
7. Ship	sea	: 1·4 ,,	†

I note that I am not in a position to give an exhaustive analysis of the associations. The subject met all questions by assuring me that nothing special occurred to her mind at the so-called critical places. In this way it was impossible to discover the determinants of the individual reactions by subjective analysis. But, after all, the objective result of the experiment suffices for a diagnosis, at least in its outlines, apart from the statements of the subject. I should like to give in as much detail as possible how I arrived at my diagnosis.

The probable mean (Kraepelin) of all the reaction-times of the experiment amounts to 2·4 seconds. This mean is far too high for an intelligent and cultured person. The mean figures I obtained in twelve educated persons are 1·5 second. As the effects of emotion are chiefly responsible for the prolongation of the reaction-time,

1. Associations which were absent or incorrect in reproduction are in italics.

2. † denotes correct reproduction.

3. ‡ denotes that the patient quickly repeated the stimulus-word. This phenomenon is frequently encountered both with and after complex reactions.

a marked emotivity of the subject may be concluded from this rather high figure. I beg the reader to keep hold of this figure, 2·4 seconds, during the following consideration of the reactions.

Reaction 1, *head – thoughts*, reproduced incorrectly. The complex of the illness may have been at work here. Reaction 3, *water – drinker – drink*, is verbally disturbed. *Drinker* has been improved to *drink*. Her father was a heavy drinker. The subsequent three reaction-times are all prolonged to over 2·4 seconds; there are besides two repetitions of the stimulus-word. One may therefore accept a perseveration due to emotion after *drinker*.[1] Reaction 5, *angel – heaven*, may have aroused the obsessional idea of the unhappy death of her neighbour.

Stimulus-word	Reaction	Reaction-time	Reproduction
8. Pluck	sow	: 2·2 seconds	†
9. *Wool*	*spin*	: 3·4 ,,	—[2]
10. *Friendly*	*lovable*	: 3·6 ,,	good
11. *Table*	*woman*	: 4·6 ,,	—
12. Ask	answer	: 2·4 ,,	†
13. State	church	: 2·2 ,,	†
14. *Haughty*	*spirited*	: 1·8 ,,	friendly
15. Stalk	flower	: 1·8 ,,	†

What disturbance caused the prolongation at *wool* I cannot say. Experience has shown that with reaction 10, *friendly*, erotic reminiscences readily occur. The striking reaction 11, *table – woman*, which patient cannot explain, seems to refer to an erotic significance of reaction 10. In sensitive persons, as all neurotics are, stimulus-words are always taken personally. One can easily suppose that the patient would like to be the 'lovable, good woman'. That the word *friendly* has a certain tendency to reproduction in the patient is seen in its recurrence in reaction 14. (Naturally emotional presentations have a stronger tendency to reproduction than indifferent ones.)

Stimulus-word	Reaction	Reaction-time	Reproduction
16. Dance	jump	: 1·8 seconds	†
17. Sea‡	water	: 2·4 ,,	†
18. Ill	healthy	: 2 ,,	†
19. Proud	arrogant	: 5 ,,	†
20. Cook	roast	: 2 ,,	†
21. Ink	barrel	: 2 ,,	†

1. I cannot here enter into the justification for this deduction and must refer the reader to Chapter V [not reproduced here].

2. — means not reproduced.

Stimulus-word	Reaction	Reaction-time		Reproduction
22. *Wicked*	*good*	: 3	,,	—
23. Needle	prick	: 2·2	,,	†
24. Swim	water	: 2	,,	†
25. Journey	railway	: 2·2	,,	†
26. Blue	red	: 1·8	,,	†
27. Bread	knife	: 2	,,	†
28. *Threaten*	*naughty*	: 8	,,	—

Reaction 16, *dance*, is prone to arouse erotic reminiscences. This supposition is not unjustified here, for the reaction following is disturbed. Reactions 18 and 19, *ill* and *proud*, may have easily had personal references. With *proud* there are distinct complex signs, likewise *wicked* and *threaten* have obviously aroused feelings. The reaction to *threaten* – *naughty* sounds like the association to the presentation of a child. Perhaps the reminiscence of her pupil has been aroused? *Threaten* is capable of arousing many emotional relationships. People with vivid complexes generally have some anxiety about the future. We often see that they refer *threaten* to the threatened uncertainty of their future. Naturally concrete references frequently underlie this emotion. It should not be forgotten that a word like *threaten* is not quite usual, and by its 'difficulty' alone has a somewhat exciting effect, without there being necessarily a definite complex beneath. All the same, it seems more prudent to put it down to the influence of a complex than to 'difficulty'. (I would remind the reader of Freud's analyses.)

Stimulus-word	Reaction	Reaction-time		Reproduction
29. Lamp	light	: 1·8 seconds		†
30. Rich	poor	: 1·8	,,	†
31. Tree	green	: 1·2	,,	†
32. Sing	dance	: 2	,,	†
33. Pity	poor	: 2	,,	†
34. *Yellow*	*flower*	: 4·2	,,	green
35. Mountain‡	mine	: 2·8	,,	†
36. *Play*	*children*	: 2·2	,,	dance
37. Salt	bread	: 2·8	,,	†
38. New	old	: 1·6	,,	†

In this series *dance*, which was the stimulus-word of reaction 16, recurs twice, betraying a distinct tendency to reproduction, corresponding to the not inconsiderable emotional tone which obviously clings to it. Frequent repetition can betray a person in this way, as the following case indicates: A gentleman, whom I asked to take part in an experiment, was convinced that he would disclose no complexes. On his way to me he thought over what words he would answer to my stimulus-words. It at once occurred to him to say *Paris*, a word that seemed to him void of all personal significance. In the experiment he repeated *Paris* several times, explaining that the word was absolutely accidental. Six months later he admitted to me that, at the time of the experiment, he was entirely absorbed by an affair which greatly upset him which was taking place in Paris. But at the time it seemed to him that *Paris* had no significance at all for him. I have no reason to doubt the truthfulness of this person. Reaction 34, *yellow*, certainly had a personal reference, to judge from the surrounding complex disturbances. Patient has a rather yellowish complexion, giving her an elderly appearance. Women are very sensitive to these things, especially when an erotic complex is present.

That *children* (reaction 36) is not reproduced but is replaced by another of erotic nature is worth mentioning.

Stimulus-word	Reaction	Reaction-time	Reproduction
39. *Habit* ‡	*ugly or bad*	: 12·2 seconds	bad manners
40. Ride‡	drive	: 2·4 ,,	†
41. *Wall*	*room*	: 3 ,,	—
42. Stupid‡	clever	: 2·8 ,,	—
43. Copy-book‡	book	: 3 ,,	†
44. *Despise*‡	*disesteem*	: 15·2 ,,	to disesteem
45. Tooth	abscess	: 1·4 ,,	†

In this series we meet various severe complex disturbances. At reaction 39, *habit*, and reaction 44, *despise*, the patient made gestures of aversion and stamped her foot. An 'ugly or bad habit' can easily be understood in a sexual sense: onanism, for instance, is a bad habit. People are despised who have such bad habits. Reaction 42, *stupid*, can be personal or can be a perseverating emotional tone extending over from *habit*. The movements accompanying the expressions are certainly not against a sexual complex. *Habit* might also be *drinking habit*, and thus have aroused the complex of her drunken father.

Stimulus-word	Reaction	Reaction-time	Reproduction
46. *Right*‡	*I always feel like saying exactly the opposite*	: 7·6 seconds	wrong
47. People‡	father	: 6 ,,	†
48. Smell	pleasant smell	: 4·8 ,,	†
49. *Book*‡	*pen*	: 4·4 ,,	copy-book

Stimulus-word	Reaction	Reaction-time		Reproduction
50. *Unjust*‡	*opinion*	: 3·6	,,	just
51. Frog	green	: 2·4	,,	†
52. Divorce	marriage	: 2·2	,,	†
53. Hunger	thirst	: 1·4	,,	†
54. White	black	: 1·8	,,	†

If, as we presume, the subject takes the stimulus-word person-ally and has a sexual complex in the direction suggested, it will be readily understood that in reaction 46, *right*, she *always feels like saying the opposite*, for that agrees with her actions; it is more suitable also in regard to her father's drunkenness. Double or manifold determinations should not be excluded; according to Freud, they are indeed the rule.

It is noticeable that reaction 47 runs *people – father*. She seems still to be within the region of the emotional tone of *right*. We might conclude that there is some obscure connexion between her self-reproaches and *father*. (This connexion will become clear later.)

What was the nature of the disturbance in *book – pen* is not easy to say. (Book = German *Buch*, and, thus pronounced, means in the Swiss dialect *Bauch* = belly.) An assimilation of this kind could easily occur with a sexual complex. I have often come across it in other persons.

The constant decrease of the reaction-times from *right*, 7·6 seconds, speaks, however, rather in favour of a severe complex disturbance which began at this stimulus-word and gradually decreased in the seven reactions that followed. Reaction 50, *unjust*, seems to be taken personally, which bears out the idea of self-reproach.

Stimulus-word	Reaction	Reaction-time		Reproduction
55. Cattle‡	cow	: 4·2 seconds		†
56. Take care	disobedient	: 4	,,	†
57. *Pencil*	*sharpen*	: 3	,,	pointed
58. Cloudy	weather	: 1·8	,,	†
59. Plum	tree	: 3·8	,,	†
60. Touch	certain	: 1·4	,,	†
61. Law	state	: 2·8	,,	†
62. *Dear*	*good*	: 4	,,	child
63. Glass	wa–water	: 1·6	,,	†
64. *Quarrel*	*dispute*	: 2·2	,,	discord
65. *Goat*	*milk*	: 2	,,	to give milk

I cannot explain the disturbance at reaction 55, *cattle*. Reaction 56, *disobedient*, recalls the previous *naughty*, which one should probably refer to the pupil. The disturbance in the succeeding reactions speaks for perseveration of the emotion. Reaction 59, *plum – tree*, judging from the length of the reaction-time, does not seem to have gone quite smoothly. Plum is not an everyday word, but it is not likely that an educated person would require so much time for the reaction. (In Wehrin's idiots the average times varied from 3 to 3·7 seconds; in an educated person 3·8 seconds thus seems far too long.) *Plum* (like an egg-shaped plum), Swiss *zwetschge*, is a favourite sexual symbol in Swiss colloquial speech.

Reaction 62, *dear*, can be readily claimed as an erotic complex. In reaction 63, *glass*, the complex of the alcoholic father came again to the surface, with the strong emotion bound up with it. (Hence the disturbance of the two subsequent reactions.)

Stimulus-word	Reaction	Reaction-time	Reproduction
66. Big	small	: 2·6 seconds	†
67. Potato‡	mealy	: 0·6 ,,	†
68. Paint	mill	: 2 ,,	†
69. Part‡	small	: 11·6 ,,	†
70. *Old*	*ugly*	: 3 ,,	young, not beautiful
71. *Flower*	*beautiful*	: 2 ,,	scent
72. Hit	cane	: 2·8 ,,	—
73. Chest	table	: 2·8 ,,	—

Reaction 66, *big*, is usually taken personally. The patient is of very small stature. In an erotic complex there will be, as we have already seen, many references to the body. That must be the explanation of the disturbances in the subsequent reactions. Reaction 69, *part*, has a greatly prolonged reaction-time; part(s) taken as sexual part(s) is very common. The strong emotional tone of this is characteristic. That among these constellations reaction 70, *old*, is apprehended in the personal erotic sense is not to be wondered at. How strongly marked the question of personal beauty is in the patient is seen from the perseveration *beautiful* (reaction 71). Reaction 72, *hit – cane*, may have been especially constellated by the obsession that she was responsible for the death of her former pupil.

Stimulus-word	Reaction	Reaction-time	Reproduction
74. Wild	child	: 2·4 seconds	†
75. Family	big	: 2·4 ,,	†
76. Wash‡	clean	: 3 ,,	†
77. Cow	milk	: 1·8 ,,	†
78. Strange‡	home-sick	: 14·8 ,,	†

Stimulus-word	Reaction	Reaction-time	Reproduction
79. Luck‡	ill luck	: 3 ,,	†
80. Relate	stories	: 1·6 ,,	†

The slight disturbance at reaction 76, *wash*, is explicable by the previous *erotic* associations, *child* and *family*. Reaction 78, *strange*, has obviously awakened a personal reference of which we shall get the explanation later.

Stimulus-word	Reaction	Reaction-time	Reproduction
81. Standing	understanding	: 4·6 seconds	†
82. Narrow‡	small	: 3·2 ,,	†
83. Brother	sister	: 1 ,,	†
84. Injure‡	neighbour	: 4 ,,	†
85. Stork‡	church	: 2·4 ,,	†
86. False‡	faithless	: 3 ,,	†
87. Anxiety	feeling	: 2·4 ,,	†
88. Kiss	mouth	: 2·2 ,,	†
89. Burning	fire	: 1·8 ,,	†
90. Dirty	clammy	: 2·2 ,,	†
91. Door	crease	: 1·6 ,,	†

The clang-association *standing – understanding*[1] is very striking; we recall the disturbance evoked by *habit*. We there suspected the *bad habit* of onanism. This complex may have been aroused here also. The popular belief is that onanism destroys the understanding (mind). Remember also the subject's complaint that she feared she would go mad. Reaction 82, *narrow – small*, is under the influence of the previous reaction: *small* probably belongs by analogy with its former occurrence to the bodily complex; *narrow* can be referred, under the constellation of the previous association, to the introitus vaginae and thus be linked with the *small*, which hints at her stature; the suspicious 'part(s)' are *small*. (This supposition will be confirmed.) Reaction 84, *injure*, is probably taken personally. *Neighbour* agrees well with this. She caused immeasurable injury to her neighbour by being the cause of her unhappy death. But *injure* can be also taken personally under the sexual constellation; one causes oneself physical and mental injuries by onanism (as above). The neighbour is thus only a cover person (cp. Freud's similar demonstrations). Her neighbour is an easy means of concealing herself. Subsequent disturbances indicate that an emotional tone set in here.

1 This should be understood as *standing in society*: the German is *Anstand* (station, demeanour, etc.), *Verstand* (understanding). TRANSLATOR.

In reaction 86, *false – faithless*, a definite erotic reminiscence may easily have emerged in an elderly single woman.

Stimulus-word	Reaction	Reaction-time	Reproduction
92. Choose‡	teacher	: 4·4 seconds	†
93. Hay	straw	: 1·8 ,,	†
94. *Still*‡	*stool*	: 13 ,,	child
95. Scorn	derision	: 1·4 ,,	†
96. Sleep‡	wake	: 3·4 ,,	†
97. Month	year	: 1·6 ,,	†
98. Tinted	bright	: 2·4 ,,	†
99. Dog	cat	: 1·2 ,,	†
100. Talk	silence	: 1·4 ,,	†

Reaction 92, *choose*, women are prone to link on to thoughts of marriage. The subject's father was a teacher, she is a teacher. It is a likely supposition that she thinks of marriage with a teacher. Again the father-complex comes up for consideration (see later about this). Reaction 94, *still – stool*, is a striking clang-association. The explanation is given by the eroticism *child*. A child can be *still*, but the dead are also *still* (obsessional idea – she caused the death of her pupil through ill-treatment). But erotic relationships can be also present; for *stillen* means in German to *suckle, nurse, hush* an infant. One can 'still' a child, 'still' the sexual impulses.

Reaction 96, *sleep*, has many sexual references. Patient is unable to sleep. Sleeplessness in younger people is frequently the expression of want of sexual satisfaction (Freud).

Those without experience in the sphere of pathological association-psychology will probably shake their heads at the above suppositions; perhaps they will not only see herein hypothesis, but also fantasies. Very likely the same criticism will be made here as at Freud's *Dream Interpretation*.

We will first recapitulate the result of the association and reproduction experiment. As already mentioned, the patient gave no explanations; I am thus thrown entirely upon the objective data of the experiment, and on my experience.

The probable mean of the reaction-times amounts to 2·4 seconds; 44 per cent of the reaction-times exceed 2·4 seconds. Among these are figures up to 15·2 seconds, from which we may deduce a considerable emotion, or, in other words, a considerable want of command over the psychical material.

We have pointed to the existence of various complexes during the analysis. The erotic complex seems to play a chief part. It will not be superfluous if I again summarize the individual complex reactions so as to obtain a better perspective.

The following refer to an erotic complex[1]:

Stimulus-word	Reaction	Reaction-time		Reproduction
10. *Friendly*	lovable	: 3·6 seconds		good
11. *Table*	woman	: 4·6 ,,		—
12.		: 2·4 ,,		
13.		: 2·2 ,,		
14.		: 1·8 ,,		
16. Dance	jump	: 1·8 ,,		†
17. Sea‡	water	: 2·4 ,,		†
34. *Yellow*	flower	: 4·2 ,,		green
35. Mountain‡	mine	: 2·8 ,,		†
36.		: 2·2 ,,		
39. *Habit*	ugly or bad	: 12·2 ,,		bad manners
40. Ride‡	drive	: 2·4 ,,		†
41. *Wall*	room	: 3 seconds		—
44. *Despise*‡	disesteem	: 15·2 ,,		to disesteem
45.		: 1·4 ,,		
59. Plum	tree	: 3·8 ,,		†
62. Dear	good	: 4 ,,		child
66. Big	small	: 2·6 ,,		†
67. Potato‡	mealy	: 6 ,,		†
68.		: 2 ,,		
69. Part	small	: 11·6 ,,		†
70. *Old*	ugly	: 3 ,,		young, not beautiful
71. *Flower*	beautiful	: 2 ,,		scent
72. *Hit*	cane	: 2·8 ,,		—
73.		: 2·4 ,,		
74. Wild	child	: 2·4 ,,		†
75. Family	big	: 2·4 ,,		†
76. Wash‡	clean	: 3 ,,		†
81. Standing	understanding	: 4·6 ,,		†
82. Narrow‡	small	: 3·2 ,,		†
83.		: 1 ,,		
86. False‡	faithless	: 3 ,,		†
87.		: 2·4 ,,		†
88.		: 2·2 ,,		
89.		: 1·8 ,,		
92. Choose‡	teacher	: 4·4 ,,		†
93.		: 1·8 ,,		
94. *Still*‡	stool	: 13 ,,		child
95.		: 1·4 ,,		
96. Sleep‡	wake	: 3·4 ,,		†
97.		: 1·6 ,,		

[1] To emphasize the complex disturbances I add the phenomena of perseveration, especially the gradually decreasing times of the succeeding reactions.

118

These reactions, all showing characteristic disturbances which are *ex hypothesi* of a sexual nature, can be linked together into the following story:

The subject feels that she is *old, ugly*; she finds her *yellowish* complexion very disagreeable and her physique, upon which she bestows anxious attention, displeases her as being too *small*. She has a great longing for *marriage*, she would be a *loving wife* to her husband and would like to have *children*. Beneath these erotic yet quite innocent symptoms there seems to be a sexual complex which the patient has every reason to suppress more strongly. There are hints from which it may be inferred that she bestows unusual attention upon her genitalia; in a respectable and educated single lady that can only signify *onanism*, of course, in the wider sense of perverse sexual self-satisfaction.

Onanism is one of the most frequent sources of *self-reproach*[1] and self-criticism. We find suggestions of this complex, or rather this side of the sexual complex, in the associations:

Stimulus-word	Reaction	Reaction-time	Reproduction
14. *Arrogant*	*courageous*	: 1·8 seconds	friendly
19. *Proud*	spirited, stupid	: 5 ,,	†
22. Wicked	good	: 3 ,,	—
23.		: 2·2 ,,	
42. Stupid‡	clever	: 2·8 ,,	—
43. Copy-book	book	: 3 ,,	†
46. *Right*‡	*I always feel like saying exactly the opposite*	: 7·6 ,,	wrong
47. *People*‡	*father*	: 6 ,,	†
48. Smell	pleasant smell	: 4·8 ,,	†
49. *Book*‡	*pen*	: 4·4 ,,	copy-book
50. *Unjust*‡	*opinion*	: 3·6 ,,	just
51.		: 2·4 ,,	
52.		: 2·2 ,,	
53.		: 1·4 ,,	

Referable to the complex of the alcholic father are:

3. *Water*	*drinker – drink*	: 2·4 seconds	*glass*
4.		: 3·6 ,,	
63. Glass	wa-water	: 1·6 ,,	†
64. *Dispute*	*quarrel*	: 2·4 ,,	*discord*
65. *Goat*	*milk*	: 2 ,,	*to give milk*

[1] The reproaches need not, of course, be limited entirely to the sexual complex but are rapidly generalized.

It is obvious from this summary that the sexual complex is very prominent. Although, as has been said, no direct confirmation of this interpretation could be obtained from the subject, I regard the complex diagnosis as certain upon the basis of the considerations I have advanced.

I therefore said to her: 'I am certain that your obsessional ideas are merely excuses and screens; in reality you are tormented by sexual ideas.' The subject contested this explanation with affect and sincere conviction. If I had not been persuaded by the association experiment of the existence of a strongly marked sexual complex my conviction would probably have wavered. I made an appeal to her intelligence and her love of truth: she assured me that if she knew of anything of the kind in herself she would say it, for she knew it would be stupid to conceal such thoughts from the doctor. She had thought of marriage 'like every one else, but not more.' I then ended the interview, and made an appointment for two days later.

II. The Psycho-analysis

In psycho-analysis the mental condition of the patient is important, but still more important is the mental condition of the doctor. This must assuredly be the reason why Freud's psycho-analysis is treated by science with silence. The analyst who goes into a case without assured conviction is soon lost in the pits and snares which the hysterical complex constructs at every turn. He must know beforehand that everything in the hysteric resists the bringing forth of the complex. When convenient, not only do interest and sympathy for the doctor disappear, but the subject loses the power of thought, the possibility of recollection, and finally even speech. But it is exactly these peculiar measures of defence that serve to betray the complex.

Just as in the association experiment hesitation, prolongation of time, absence of reproduction occur when the complex is aroused, in analysis likewise difficulties occur where the complex is being approached. To circumvent these difficulties Freud insists upon 'free association'. It is a very simple method which has only to be used a few times to be understood to a certain degree. In this case I undertook the psycho-analysis, following exactly Freud's method. I made the subject sit in a comfortable chair and seated myself behind her so as not to confuse her. I asked her to tell me quietly everything that came into her mind, to be quite indifferent as to what it was. The subject laughed: 'One can't tell every bit of nonsense that occurs to one.' I stood to my demand. A couple of times she tried to say something, but broke off each time with the excuse that it was silly, that I should be obliged to laugh and would think that she was a stupid or ungrateful person. I confined myself again to urging her to speak out, and finally she brought out these sentences: 'I think that I never shall be well – now you'll laugh – but I'm convinced that I shall never be well. You can't hypnotize me, for I'm convinced that nobody can hypnotize me. You'll not be able to cure me any more than any other doctor. It will only be worse for me, for I shall reproach myself for having taken up your time unnecessarily with my rubbish.' This idea was not quite unjustifiable, for the patient only threw the sentences out after long pauses, so that we had required almost half an hour to produce this meagre result. She went on: 'I am now thinking of the people at home, how they are working and require me whilst I am here for nothing but my own silly thoughts – of course, you'll be infected by them – now I am thinking that I cannot sleep, that last night, despite your order, I took a gramme of veronal – of course I shall never be able to sleep again, how will you cure me then? – what am I to say to you? (There was here noticeable a certain restlessness.) I can't tell you all the silly thoughts that come into my head. (Restlessness increases, shrugs her shoulders, stamps up and down, shakes herself as if in great depression.) Now this is rubbish – I don't know anything more – nothing else occurs to me – let me go home now, nothing else comes to me.' (Very restless – turns about on the chair, gestures of disgust, shaking the upper part of her body to and fro and her elbows moving as if thrusting aside; at last she jumps up to leave.) Nothing else comes to her. With gentle force I persuade her to sit down again and point out to her that she has really come to get better, so she must carry out my prescription. After much discussion as to the purpose and meaning of my method she finally agrees to remain and continue. But the same depression and gestures of disgust soon recommence; she twists about on the chair, from time to time sitting upright with a forced movement as if after a great victory she had come to a determination, and finally says despondingly: 'Something silly comes to me – you will certainly laugh – but you must not tell it to anybody else – no, I really can't tell you, never – it is something very simple – it has nothing to do with my illness – I am robbing you of your time – it is nothing important – am I really obliged to tell it you? It is not easy to say it – here goes: Well, once I was in France – it won't come, not if I sit for a month in this chair – (then with sudden determination) well, once I was a governess in France – no, I really can't tell it – there was a servant there – no, there was a gardener there – my God, what will you think of me! – this is martyrdom – I have never thought of anything like this.'

Amid such interjections of distress there came out in the end, with innumerable stoppages and interruptions in which she swore that this would be her last consultation, that tomorrow she would go away, the following story:

There was among the servants a gardener who once said to her he would like to sleep with her. Whilst saying this he tried to kiss her, but she pushed him away. At night on going to bed she listened at the door and imagined what it would be like if he were to come and sleep with her; she got fearfully excited lest he might come. In bed her thoughts again turned to what it would be like if he were to come, and then she drove these ideas away. But she could not get rid of thinking what it would be like, although she again and again shuddered at the idea that she could be thinking of anything of the sort. In this turmoil of thought she could not get to sleep until the morning.

This first sitting had lasted no less than an hour and a half. The result was a sexual history. Especially interesting was the fact of the disclosure being accompanied by the same mimetic manifestations which I had noticed at the first consultation. These tic-like phenomena were thus in very close and easily explicable connexion with the repressed sexual incidents. I made an appointment for the day after next, which she at once agreed to, seeming much relieved, and saying no more about going away.

At the time of her appointment I was engaged with some urgent work, and therefore requested her to come in the evening. But she sent me a message that it was impossible for her to wait, it was absolutely essential for her to talk to me. I supposed that something special had happened and went to her. I found her greatly excited; she had not slept at all, not a minute; she had been obliged to take sleeping medicines. I asked her if she had been again worried about her obsessions: 'No, something much worse; my head is now full of that nonsense about which I spoke to you last time. Now I can only think of these stories and of nothing else; all night I have been tossing and turning about and cannot banish the thoughts for a minute. I must have a talk with you at once; it gives me no peace.' She stated that on the last occasion she had felt much relieved and calmer and had gone home in good spirits, hoping that she would now be able to sleep; but then she recalled an affair which she ought really to have mentioned last time, but which she thought wasn't worth while. She was now firmly resolved 'not to act so stupidly' as last time but to speak out freely whatever came up into her mind. In this way the confessions would soon be ended. I began the analysis again, hoping that it would now go smoothly without the endless preliminaries of the last time. But I was hopelessly mistaken. The patient went through almost exactly the same interjections as in the first sitting. After an hour and a half of real spiritual torment I had brought out the following history:

In the same house where my patient was a governess there was a servant-girl* who had a lover; the girl had also had sexual intercourse with the gardener. The patient had frequent talks with her about sexual matters, especially about the sexual intercourse of the master and mistress. She and the servant had from time to time even examined the bedding of their master and mistress for spots of semen and other signs of coitus. After these conversations the patient used every time to reproach herself bitterly with her immorality, and passed sleepless nights in which she would be tossed by painful reproaches and voluptuous fantasies.

When the story was brought to an end after wearisome struggles, the patient said 'that was the last, there was nothing more in her mind.' If only she could sleep; repeating these events was no help at all.

Two days later she came for the third sitting and stated: After the last interview she felt fairly calmed, but hardly had she got into bed when another event at once occurred to her which had tormented her ever since, together with the self-reproach of not having told me everything the last time. She was not certain that today she would tell me about it quickly, without the constant resistance of the previous occasions. But the third sitting was exactly the same: continuous interjections, excuses, etc. Most remarkable was a tendency to present the affair as a matter of course, as if there were nothing in it. It concerned a second servant-girl in the same house. The master had a page-boy who pursued the girl, but did not succeed in seducing her. Finally, one evening when there was a party going on he managed to seduce the girl in the garden. But the couple were taken unawares by the mistress at the critical moment. The lad is said to have exclaimed, 'What a pity! I was just ready.' The governess had been told this story by the servant-girl first mentioned. At first she pretended that the story had no interest at all for her, as if it were disagreeable, but she was lying, for in reality she had the greatest interest in it; she

* Cp. the mention of this servant at the first sitting.

had tried a couple of times to bring the girl back to the story so as to learn all the details. That night she could scarcely sleep on account of her curiosity and was ceaselessly asking herself 'what the couple were doing in the garden, in what position were they when the mistress discovered them, for what was he ready if his mistress had not arrived?' Although she knew the answers to these questions quite well, she could not rest without putting the questions to herself over and over again. Then she was constantly considering what she would have done in such a position. The excitement lasted several days.

In telling the story her attitude was, as mentioned, that it was a matter of course. For instance, under great resistance she told how the boy had pursued the servant. From the resistances one supposed that something unpleasant was to come; but then she went on in a tone of indifference: 'True, the page-lad was in love with the girl; there's nothing wonderful in that; that frequently happens, doesn't it? Ah! now something else comes – oh well, that's nothing.' During the recital she tried again and again to minimize the importance of the event to herself by throwing in general rhetorical questions of this kind.

From that time on the former obsessional ideas were absent during the whole time of the analysis (three weeks), but the sexual ideas took their place; as soon as one story was finished another took its place, worrying the patient with a real obsession. She found no peace again until it had been told. She expressed herself as much astonished at the change; the stories would come up like clockwork, just as if they had been 'experienced yesterday'. Things came back to her of which she had lost all remembrance, but which she now recognized again (Freud's hyperamnesia). These excuses must naturally be accepted with the same reserve as were the common 'I don't know'. The subject may easily have nourished and jealously cherished all the sexual ideas up to the present moment without on that account being able to recall them when she has to speak of them objectively. Her mimetic expressions during the talks are often in themselves sufficient to let me know what is coming, whilst she assures me a dozen times that she really can remember nothing more. Her ordinary self and her sexual self are really two distinct complexes, two different consciousnesses, which neither desire nor dare to know anything of each other. There is here but a suggestion of the dissociation of personality (as, moreover, in every vivid complex whose peculiarity is a striving after autonomy). But it is only a step to the classical cases of dissociation of personality, which are naturally all conditioned by Freud's mechanisms.*

A certain termination had been reached in these three sittings, so far as concerned the obsession that she was responsible for the death of her former pupil and the self-reproaches connected with her sexual stories. The patient felt this obviously, for she stated herself that many years had passed since these affairs, and the idea that she was responsible for her pupil's death had not troubled her for a long time. Probably to circumvent the unbearable sexual ideas she had transferred the reproaches from this sphere and fastened them on to her educational methods, in the well-known way. If one has constantly to reproach oneself about one set of ideas compensation is sought elsewhere as if a similar defect were present there. This is especially noticeable in onanists (hyper-criticism, obsessions of cleanliness and tidiness). It does not seem to be mere accident that those incidents were first related which lay at the root of a past obsessional idea. As in her actual consciousness no obsessional ideas were present which could directly support these incidents, no special inhibitions were present. These incidents were therefore relatively indifferent material.

I do not want to describe the succeeding sittings in detail; they all followed the type described. No exhortation, no allusion to the ridiculous nature of her stereotyped resistances, could induce the subject to a quicker and less embarrassed narrative. Each fresh sitting was a fresh torture, and in nearly every one the subject assured me that it was the last. Usually the night following new material came up which afforded her no rest.

To the governess's reminiscences there were appended a series of indecent stories which had served as the themes of talks with her neighbour for whose unhappy death the patient reproached herself. The dubious past of her neighbour was whispered on every hand. The subject, who is a highly respectable person and comes of an honourable family, has in her sense a dubious past also; she indeed reproached herself about it. It was therefore not psychologically wonderful that she had been immediately attracted by her interesting neighbour. The *chronique scandaleuse* was discussed there, and the patient was obliged to narrate a whole series of highly obscene stories and jokes which I need not repeat here. To this she had again linked a number of self-reproaches. When the neighbour rapidly succumbed to an illness the subject transferred the reproaches, really due to her own sexual curiosity, on to the

* Cp. Jung, *Collected Papers*, 'The Psychology and Pathology of Occult Phenomena' (Baillière, Tindall and Cox; 1916).

death of her neighbour, who must have died unblessed since the patient's visits had induced her to sinful talk. The nature of the reminiscences and of the chain of thought seems to be in favour of the view that these obsessional ideas were simply a new edition of her earlier ideas about her pupil's death. She had brought the religious obsessional ideas first to the clergyman and then to the doctor. To both she linked the presentation that she had infected them with her obsessions, to a certain extent in the same way as she had infected her neighbour, and originally her pupil. At the root of all this there is the general idea that she is a terrible creature who infects every one with her own corruption.

In the following sittings the patient chiefly disclosed a number of incidents which she had talked over in earlier years with a friend. This friend had a position in the office of a large business. There she heard all kinds of piquant things from gentlemen, which she brought post-haste from time to time to the patient. One day her friend said she would like to have relations with a man to see what it was like. This idea excited the patient powerfully; she was obliged to keep saying to herself she would like to do the same. That was reason enough for renewed reproaches. From this narrative onwards the sexual incidents become more distinctly fastened on to her own person, although at nearly every sitting obscene jokes and the like had to be reproduced. Of the stories referring to her own person there were first of all reminiscences of earlier love affairs and expectations. The reproduction of these events, innocent enough on the whole, went pretty smoothly. Only one story had a more marked emotional tone. She had been in love with a young foreigner and believed he wished to marry her. But afterwards he left without a good-bye and she heard no more of him. She waited a long time, always hoping that he would write again to her. Reaction 78, *foreign – home-sick*, 14·8 seconds, refers to this affair. As already mentioned, the subject could not at the time explain the meaning of this reaction. Whilst the old love affairs were related without too great difficulties, there recurred at the end of this phase considerable resistances. The subject wished absolutely to leave; she had nothing more to tell. I suggested to her that I had heard nothing about her earlier youth. She thought that would soon be got over, for she had not much to say about her youth. Hardly had she spoken this sentence when she was obliged to repeat a couple of times her tic-like gestures of disgust – an infallible sign that some important material was to be expected. Amid inconceivable stoppages and painful twistings she told me, by fits and starts, about a book that at the age of ten she had found at home called *The Way to a Happy Marriage*. She assured me that she had no longer any idea of what was in the book. But as I remained inexorable, memory after a time returned, and it was seen that the patient remembered all the details, frequently indeed the very words. She described the first coitus and its complications; this academic description seemed to me peculiar and unusual. I suspected that at the back of this general description much must lay concealed. There was not long to wait before the patient related how at the age of fourteen she had found in the pocket of her elder brother a small book in which a letter was pressed. The letter was addressed by a young woman to a bosom friend and treated the secrets of the wedding night in a very obscene and lascivious way. As this showed, I was obviously on the right path. The next thing that came to the patient referred to erotic dreams which she had had in earlier days. The dreams were distinct pollution dreams and represented coitus without disguise. She then confessed to having sometimes tried to retain the dream-picture and to masturbate. Bound up with the onanism was a constant thinking about her own genitalia; she was concerned as to whether she was 'properly formed', if her introitus was not somewhat too narrow, and she felt compelled to investigate this problem with her finger. She was frequently obliged to look at her naked body in the looking-glass, and so on. She felt compelled to make a whole series of imaginary pictures about coitus – how she would behave at the first coitus, etc. Finally she acknowledged feeling violent sexual libido (which she had at first vehemently denied), admitting that she would very much like to marry, and had sexual images about most of the men with whom she had associated. She could not resist putting herself in the leading part in all the sexual events which she had piled up. For instance, she told about a young, naïvely frank acquaintance who in an excursion in an overfilled railway carriage had sat her teacher on her lap. The girl said afterwards, laughingly, that the teacher never failed to play his part, he had even taken a ruler with him in his trousers pocket. The patient was always thinking how pleasant it would be for her also if a teacher sat upon her knees, and she would know then what the ruler in the trousers pocket signified. (The earlier reaction, *choose – teacher*, must have been constellated by this incident.)

Amid great resistance she related how at the age of fourteen she had once lain upon a younger sister 'as if she were a man'. In one of the last sittings she succeeded in recalling an event which agrees in every way with the importance attributed by Freud to early psychical trauma. At the age of seven or eight she had on several occasions overheard the coitus of her parents. Once she heard her mother preventing it and refusing to give in to her father at all. After that it was a long time before she could look at her parents. Her mother became pregnant and gave birth to the patient's younger sister. She hated her sister from the first moment and was only able much later to overcome a deep antipathy to the child. It is not at all improbable that the subject had imagined herself as the second person in this affair, and she has indeed taken over the role of mother. The strong emotional tone which occurred in all the associations to 'father' is readily comprehensible from this intimate link.

The psychological trauma of a perception of this kind is naturally preserved in the child's mind as an extremely emotional complex which constellates thinking and doing for years. This was classically the case in this patient. Her sexual function was thus given a very definite direction.* The analysis of her repressed presentations shows this; it is chiefly concerned with the grubbing out and picturing of coitus situations. It is remarkable that despite her extraordinarily vivid fantasy, she had never got deeply entangled with men and had rejected all attempts at seduction. On the other hand, she has been attracted by women of dubious character and equivocal conversation with an almost magical compulsion, an unexpected tendency in a woman of her education and intelligence. The two last sittings were peculiarly instructive in this respect. She reproduced a cunning accumulation of the most disgusting indecencies which she had occasionally heard in the streets. What was common to all these indecencies, the repetition of which we may be spared, was the different abnormalities of coitus (too wide or too narrow an introitus, coitus of a young man with a big, fat woman, etc.). The amount and the deep vulgarity of these jokes seemed to me almost incomprehensible in so cultured and respectable a lady. The phenomenon is, however, explained by the early perverse direction of the sexual function, which was chiefly concerned with the hunting out of sexual filth, that is, the symbolical repetition of the overheard coitus. This complex has therefore affected the whole of her previous life and determined a mass of sexual doings and associations in its particular form. That is, for instance, why the patient carried out a kind of coitus action with her little sister, why her
)

* With this may be compared the fact that many sexual perverts (fetishists) have acquired their abnormality through an accidental sexual event. Cp. v. Krafft-Ebing, *Psychopathia Sexualis.*

listening at the door to find out whether the gardener is coming is still so impressed upon her, why she engaged in the disgusting business of snuffling in the bed of her master and mistress, why she sought the company of sexually despicable people. Her defensive gestures and the peculiar projection of her abdomen show the effect of the complex at work everywhere. It is also very noticeable that at every sitting she appeared in another dress.

Such a use of the sexual function is bound to be unbearable to an otherwise finely planned character; a repugnance to and repression of the tendency, as absurd as it is detestable, must arise. It is impossible that an educated and finely sensitive woman could bring these obscenities into union with the rest of her mental content. These things can therefore only exist in repression. But they do exist, they carry on a separate existence, they form a state within a state, they constitute a personality within a personality; or, otherwise expressed, two consciouses are present which are kept apart by violent emotional inhibitions. One mind can and does know nothing of the other mind. That is the explanation of the remarkable disturbances in reproduction which work against analysis. The ethically higher mind does not deal with the associations of the other mind; that is why it seems to her that she has forgotten these ideas, as if she had never known about such things. I am inclined to agree with her conviction that she really knew nothing more, that it was not a lie when she assured me with the greatest obstinacy that she had nothing more to say.

But although a complex be repressed ever so much from normal consciousness it must still influence and constellate the content of normal consciousness – for the deepest dissociation of the conscious does not extend to the unitary basis of personality. Repression must therefore leave behind a certain residue in the functions of the conscious; normal consciousness must in some way direct the state of feeling which a repressed complex leaves behind. What is simpler than for any one of the ideas compatible with normal consciousness to be projected and accepted as the explanation of the constant self-reproaches and discontented mood? To find a motive for the pangs of conscience attributable to her sins at the time she was a governess, the patient projects her reproaches on to her methods of education. These must have been bad is the view taken by her conscious self, for she would not otherwise have a constant feeling of reproach when she recalls memories of that time. As we have already seen, the origin of this obsession becomes the model of the obsession about her guilt for the unhappy death of her neighbour. The accumulation of obsessional ideas around the doctor and clergyman were well grounded, for, as the subject confessed to me, these persons were not sexually indifferent to her. Inasmuch as they affect her sexually they are quasi-accessories in her depravity; hence they must also be reproaching themselves.

After this analysis we can understand the part her father played in her erotic complex, a part that was not clear in the associations. The analysis confirms, in the fullest way, the suppositions aroused by the associations. The associations served me as a safe signpost in the maze of moving fantasies which sought to put the analysis at each step on a wrong road.

The analysis was undertaken during three weeks every second day and lasted each time from an hour and a half to two hours. Although at the end of the three weeks there were neither proper sleep nor real quiet, I dismissed the patient from further treatment and did not hear from her till the end of November. In the last days of November 1905 she came to see me unexpectedly and announced that she was cured. After breaking off the analysis she said she was in the most violent, agitated mood, and remained thus for some four weeks. At night she was either tormented by her sexual images or by the re-emergence of her obsessional ideas. The obsessions about her neighbour were particularly frequent and gave her no rest until she had again visited the daughter of the deceased, to be told for the xth time about the death scene. When the daughter again assured her that her mother had died quietly, the subject became suddenly convinced that the woman had died at peace. Then at one blow all her obsessions disappeared. Sleep returned and was only on rare occasions troubled by sexual images.

To what is this fortunate end of the treatment to be attributed?

Obviously the daughter's version, which the patient had repeatedly heard without result, was only the occasion of the removal of the obsessions. A real turn for the better took place at the beginning of the treatment, when the sexual images replaced the obsessional ideas. The confession of her sinful thoughts must have enormously lightened the patient. But it seems improbable that it was to this speaking out or to the 'abreaction' alone that the cure was attributable. To keep down such fancies permanently great energy is required. People with obsessions are weak, they are incapable of holding in their images with a tight rein. Treatment therefore always works best with them. The best treatment is to compel them, with a certain ruthlessness, to reproduce and display all the presentations incompatible with their consciousness.

The energy is thus not only put to a severe test, but the conscious gets accustomed to the existence of images formerly repressed. The mental separate existences become crushed, since they are dragged by an effort of will from repression into daylight. In the process they lose considerably in nimbus, and hence in danger; the subjects receive at the same time the feeling of being masters of their images. I therefore lay stress upon the strengthening of the will, and not upon the mere 'abreaction', as Freud did formerly.

It seems from some recent works that Freud's theory of obsessional phenomena is still systematically ignored. It is hence a great satisfaction to me to be able to recall attention to Freud's theories – even at the risk of falling into the sphere of this systematic amnesia.

Summary

(1) The complex appearing in the associations of a psychogenic neurosis exhibits the *causa morbi* (excluding the predisposition).

(2) Associations can be a valuable aid for the discovery of the pathogenic complex as well as serving for the shortening and lightening of Freud's psycho-analysis.

(3) Associations give us experimentally an insight into the psychological structure of the neurotic symptoms: Hysteria and obsession phenomena arise from one complex. The physical and psychical symptoms are but the symbolical pictures of the psychogenic complex.

6 T. V. Moore

The Empirical Determination of Certain Syndromes
Underlying Praecox and Manic-Depressive Psychoses*

Excerpts from T. V. Moore, 'The empirical determination of certain
syndromes underlying praecox and manic-depressive psychoses',
Amer. J. Psychiatry, Vol. 9 (1929–30), pp. 719–38.

If a clear and definite pathology, such as we have for valvular diseases of the heart, were established for the various mental disorders,
such a study as the present would be superfluous. But we have as
yet only the vaguest notions about the pathology of the mind, and
as a result the diagnostic entities of psychiatry are so poorly
defined that the attempts to associate physical symptoms with
definite mental conditions have been most disappointing. Likewise, psychological measurements of memory, association, reaction-time, etc., have been difficult of interpretation, when they
had to be attached to the vague, overlapping, indeterminate
entities of clinical psychiatry.

The present study is an attempt to see whether or not it is
possible to determine in a purely empirical manner any syndromes
at all in the mental disorders. The final results only are here reported. But the preliminary stages were:

(1) The working out of a scheme for measuring quantitatively
various emotional manifestations of the mental disorders. This
will be published shortly in our *Studies in Psychology and Psychiatry* (Williams & Wilkins, Baltimore, Md.).

(2) The development of a method for measuring reasoning,
perception, the span of memory and the rate of forgetting as indicators of cognitive defect. The reasoning test was published recently.[1] The tests for perception and memory were used on a
previous occasion.[2] We are well aware that the tests we have used
are capable of being vastly improved, but they have served their
present purpose and clearly defined certain psychiatric syndromes. They may, therefore, be employed for the detection of
other syndromes in the future; and that too with considerable
reliability.

(3) The recording of a number of symptoms as present or absent.
A quantitative measurement of these was not attempted, partly

* Read at International Congress of Psychology, Yale, September 5, 1929.

because of intrinsic difficulty, partly because the labor of the research was necessarily limited.*

In all, 367 patients were examined though not all had every item recorded. The items most often lacking were the cognitive measurements. This was due mainly to the time taken by such tests, partly to the necessity of full cooperation on the part of the patients. Refusals were surprisingly seldom, for after a little an interview with the psychologist came to be regarded as an opportunity of demonstrating the soundness of one's mentality. About 208 patients were given the cognitive tests and about 350 had the full emotional record.

After the measurements had been completed the attempt was made to intercorrelate 41 symptoms finally selected as a basis for the empirical determination of the syndromes of psychiatry.

When curves of distribution were made it was found that in all the emotional symptoms we had the positive side only of a normal curve with the negative cases heaped up at the zero point. This was due to the assumption made in our quantitative schema that, e.g., the depressions would show a mean frequency at a point indicating a depression of average intensity and taper off on either side to zero depressions and those of maximal intensity. Depressions, however, do not do this; nor do any other emotional symptoms in our schema. The maximum frequency is not far from our zero point. This is in itself a very interesting fact and indicates that normal mental life is at a zero point of emotional equilibrium.[3] When a psychotic condition develops, the plane of emotional equilibrium is tilted to one side or the other. Slight tilts are more frequent than any other just as small excesses of the probable number are more frequent in the tossing of coins. An abnormal emotional condition is, therefore, not a new psychological growth but an excess or defect of a normal mental condition.

It might have been possible after some study to determine the precise opposite of depression, 'shut-in', irritability, euphoria, etc., but unless this were done without any ambiguity the results would have been seriously clouded. Consequently, we made use of the

* I must here make acknowledgement to the authorities of Mt. Hope Retreat, Baltimore, Md., for the appointment of a psychologist, Miss Gertrude Reimann, to carry out the tests and measurements as a part of the routine examination of patients; to Dr William A. White, who allowed me to examine a number of patients at St Elizabeth's Hospital; to the rector of the Catholic University for a grant of $500; and to Sister Rosa McDonough for considerable help in the calculations; and to Miss Evangeline Sheibley. The sorting of the cards for the correlations, which would have been an almost impossible task by hand, was kindly done for me by the Remington Rand Business Service on the Powers Sorting Machine.

data obtained by the quantitative schema we had developed. It enabled us to clearly define the symptoms studied and to say whether or not a patient manifested one of these symptoms in definite excess. This information led to the formation of fourfold tables in which patients were placed with a fair degree of certainty in one of the four compartments that compared the presence and absence of two traits. We were thus enabled to make use of Pearson's method of tetrachoric correlation. The correlations so obtained are theoretically the same as the product moment r when the distribution is normal.

There are 820 possible intercorrelations for a total of 41 symptoms. Naturally we are interested mainly in those of significant magnitude. To select these without having to go through the labor of calculating r the following expedient was used.

Consider for a moment the accompanying fourfold table for 'Auditory Hallucinations' and 'Loss of Finer Sensibilities'.

	Auditory Hallucinations		
	Absent	Present	
Loss of Finer Sensibilities, *Absent*	160	138	298
Loss of Finer Sensibilities, *Present*	13	34	47
	173	172	345

In the group of insane patients that had no 'loss of finer sensibilities' $\frac{138}{298}$ showed auditory hallucinations. Taking this as the probability of the occurrence of auditory hallucinations as a chance phenomenon in the insane we would expect, if the same chance obtained in patients with 'loss of finer sensibilities', an incidence of 22·224 in our group of 47 cases in the above table. (Incidence = probability times number of throws plus one.) As a matter of fact we find 34 cases. Would this excess of 11·776 be likely to occur by chance? The probability of this excess as a chance phenomenon is obtained by calculating its sigma value.

$$\sigma = \sqrt{p(1-p)n}.$$

That is to say σ equals the square root of the probability that the event will occur (p) times the probability that it will not occur ($1-p$) times the number of cases or throws.

In the case $\sigma = \sqrt{(\cdot46)\,(\cdot54)\,(47)} = 3\cdot417.$[4]

Various tables[5] are available for the calculation of the probability of an error or excess which is given in terms of σ. The probability of such an excess as a mere chance event is only about three in ten thousand. It is, therefore, likely that any correlation that may be found between the above two symptoms is not due to chance. As a matter of fact the tetrachoric r amounts to ·352. By means of this method we spared ourselves the labor of calculating the tetrachoric r wherever the excess of the incidence divided by the sigma value $\dfrac{x}{\sigma}$ was not above 2·67 that is above a chance incidence of about one in a hundred.* Some few with smaller values were later calculated in determining the tetrad differences discussed below.

The table of probability values and correlations obtained in this way is very suggestive of many interesting problems but it does not of itself enable us to pick out the clinical entities of psychiatry. We first thought of taking each symptom in turn and paralleling its associates with those of other symptoms, hoping in that way to pick out symptoms that group together or are mutually exclusive. Or one might arbitrarily choose a symptom that figures in classic discussions of the psychoses and take its associates as the determinants of the condition in question, e.g. depression.

It was thought, however, best to apply the tetrad difference criterion of Spearman to the knotty problem of the mental disorders.[6]

According to this criterion, if a, b, p, q, represent four abilities or variable quantities of any kind, and r stands for the correlation value, then there is one common underlying factor in all four specific manifestations if $r_{ap} \cdot r_{bq} - r_{aq} \cdot r_{bp} = 0$.

Furthermore, all possible combinations of these correlations in any table of four or more variables give zero values within the limits of sampling error.

In the application of such a formula to a series of 41 variables it is out of the question to calculate the tetrads for the whole table which would mean the solution of hundreds of thousands of equations. There is, furthermore, little likelihood that there is one and the same general factor underlying all the psychoses. The practical method of procedure is to take each symptom and look for its highest correlation and then its next highest. Having found a

* In any fourfold table there are always two ways of calculating $\dfrac{x}{\sigma}$. We always chose the one which involved the greater number of cases for the fundamental p value.

135

series of four such closely related symptoms, one arranges their table of intercorrelations. If such a table manifests an evident 'hierarchy' it is worth while calculating the tetrads. By hierarchy Spearman means the proportionate gradation of all the columns and rows from higher to lower values.* If the tetrad values fall within the limits of sampling† one then seeks a fifth variable and so on. In our material we were unable to group together more than five variables.

In this way we have been able to pick out eight general factors that are present in the psychotic conditions from which our patient suffered. In all probability they are fundamental psycho-biological conditions that are involved in the 'manic-depressive' and 'praecox' psychoses. Having found these conditions or general factors we wished to go further and discover a way for measuring the degree in which any given patient manifests them.

The first step towards this end was given by Dodd[7] though he merely conceived of it as a means of demonstrating the presence of a general factor.

The second step was taken by Sister Rosa McDonough[8] who recently applied the technique to the measurement of character traits.

Dodd's work was founded on the method given by Spearman for measuring the correlation between a specific ability and the underlying general factor.‡ Having determined these values he used the ordinary formula for partial correlation and obtained the correlation between the specific abilities after the general factor had been partialed out. If a general factor is present and the specific factors do not overlap (that is, are truly independent) then the average of all these partial correlations will approximate zero.

In the paper above referred to, Sister Rosa McDonough proceeded from this point and (1) conceived of the general factor as the criterion in a multiple regression equation; (2) determined the appropriate weights for the individual measurements so that the

* Consult the tables given below and it will be seen that with few exceptions all the values grade down from the upper left-hand corner below and to the right. All columns, from above downward and all rows from left to right grade more or less proportionately downward. This hierarchy of values was Spearman's original criterion for the presence of a common factor. When, however, the hierarchy was imperfect there was no way by the old technique of telling how much could be allowed to chance errors of observation.

† According to Spearman no tetrad difference should be five times its probable error. This is a reasonable criterion when there are a large number of variables, but is rather lax for only four.

‡ Cf. The Abilities of Man, Appendix, p. xvi.

sum of the weighted values would be the measure of the individual's participation in the general factor.

We have done the same thing for the psychotic symptoms that are indicators of underlying general factors in the tables that are herewith presented.

Unfortunately, however, for a number of our symptoms we have as yet no quantitative measure* and our results in these instances only show how accuracy may be obtained by a psychological study of the symptoms of the psychoses. Symptoms marked with an asterisk in the following tables of intercorrelations had no quantitative measure. The limit of the probable error is taken, for convenience, as that of the product moment formula. The tetrachoric probable error is about double that of the product moment.

Table 1 †
The Cognitive Group
A. Intercorrelations (Tetrachoric)

	Reasoning	Perception	Total memory	Memory ratio	Shut-in
Reasoning	—	·593	·515	·358	·398
Perception	·593	—	·380	·338	·344
Total memory	·515	·380	—	·339	·207
Memory ratio	·358	·338	·339	—	·189
Shut-in	·398	·344	·207	·189	—

B. Tetrads for Intercorrelations in Table 1

Average of tetrads	·034
P. E. of tetrads	·021

C. Correlations of Variables with G

r_{ag}	·853	·720	·583	·481	·425

* Furthermore, except in the cognitive symptoms all negative values are recorded as zero. Practically, however, this need not be of serious difficulty for it would be possible to measure quantitatively the symptoms actually presented by any individual.

† Tables 1–6 have been abridged from the original edition.

Table 2
The Catatonic Group
A. Intercorrelations (Tetrachoric)

	Mutism	Negativism	Refusal of food	Stereotypism of attitudes
* Mutism	—	·817	·687	·627
* Negativism	·817	—	·666	·628
* Refusal of food	·687	·666	—	·572
* Stereotypism of attitudes	·627	·628	·572	—

B. Tetrads for Intercorrelations in Table 2

t_{1234}	·035
t_{1243}	·062
t_{1342}	·027
P. E. of tetrads	·016

C. Correlations of Variables with G

r_{ag}	·896	·883	·773	·717

Table 3
The Uninhibited or Kinetic Group
A. Intercorrelations (Tetrachoric)

	Stereotypism of actions	Destructive	Giggling	Talking to voices
* Stereotypism of actions	—	·667	·523	·566
Destructive	·667	—	·402	·395
Giggling	·523	·402	—	·366
Talking to voices	·566	·395	·366	—

B. Tetrads for Intercorrelations in Table 3

t_{1234}	·038
t_{1243}	·017
t_{1342}	·021
P. E. of tetrads	·019

C. Correlations of Variables with G

r_{ag}	·937	·686	·585	·603

Table 4
Manic Group
A. Intercorrelations (Tetrachoric)

	Irritable	Tantrums	Destructive	Euphoria
Irritable	—	·611	·492	·473
Tantrums	·611	—	·438	·364
Destructive	·492	·438	—	·303
Euphoria	·473	·364	·303	—

B. Tetrads for Intercorrelations in Table 4

t_{1234}	·015
t_{1243}	·020
t_{1342}	·035
P. E. of tetrads	·018

C. Correlations of Variables with G

r_{ag}	·865	·716	·586	·524

Table 5
Deluded-Hallucinated Group
A. Intercorrelations (Tetrachoric)

	A. H.	B. D.	O. H.	St. W.	D. S.
Auditory hallucinations	—	·740	·699	·455	·359
Bizarre delusions	·740	—	·692	·436	·360
'Other' hallucinations	·699	·692	—	·344	·236
Stereotypism of words	·455	·436	·344	—	·281
Disorientation in space	·359	·360	·236	·281	—

B. Tetrads for Correlations in Table 5

Average of tetrads	·049
P. E. of tetrads	·020

C. Correlations of Variables with G *

r_{ag}	·893	·878	·695	·528	·418

* Some partials are too high to allow the assumption to hold that there is no bond between the specific other than the general factor.

Table 6
The Constitutional Hereditary Depression Group
A. Intercorrelations (Tetrachoric)

	Anxious	Depressed	Tearful	Previous attacks	Insane relatives
Anxious	—	·725	·564	·221	·194
Depressed	·725	—	·475	·288	·187
Tearful	·564	·475	—	·175	·104
*Previous attacks	·221	·288	·175	—	·127
*Insane relatives	·194	·187	·104	·127	—

B. Tetrads for Intercorrelations in Table 5

Average of tetrads	·029
P. E. of tetrads	·016

C. Correlations of Variables with G

r_{ag}	·832	·841	·543	·362	·257

Table 7
The Retarded-Depressed Group
A. Intercorrelations (Tetrachoric)

	Depressed	Retarded	Neurasthenia	Suicidal
Depressed	—	·743	·372	·328
Retarded	·743 *	—	·328	·141
Neurasthenia	·372	·328	—	·060
Suicidal	·328	·141	·060	—

B. Tetrads for Table 7

t_{1234}	·0079
t_{1243}	·0630
t_{1342}	·0551

Probable error of tetrads	·0222 (Spearman's formula)
Probable error of t_{1234}	·0246 (Kelley's formula)

* The correlation between depressed and retarded is so high that when one attempts to work out the partials as in the other tables one gets incompatible results. It is probable that in this group there is one general factor plus a special group factor between depressed and retarded.

The Probable Nature of the General Factors in the Psychoses

The above tables demonstrate only the existence of certain general factors underlying the specific manifestations of various mental disorders. The bare facts that a hierarchical order comes out in the tables of correlation, that the tetrad differences are zero, within the limits of errors of sampling, that the partial correlations between the specific symptoms approach zero when the general factor is partialed out, while each specific symptom has a significantly high correlation with the general factor, all these facts together may be taken as conclusive evidence that certain general factors exist in the mental disorders.

We are naturally interested in learning something about the nature of these general factors.* We shall deal first and mainly by way of example with the cognitive general factor.

Let us take up in the first place the evident character of the specific symptoms. In the cognitive group with one exception they have to do with cognition. The fact that our statistical technique has assembled these in one group instead of scattering them indiscriminately among all groups is evidence that a natural law of some kind is responsible for the grouping of the symptoms.

At first sight it seems strange that the symptom 'shut-in' should appear with the cognitive group. That it does, must be taken to mean that 'shut-in', as a pathological symptom, is an indication of cognitive defect. In our quantitative schema 'shut-in' was a measure of the poverty of emotional expression, the mask-like facies so common in praecox patients. Now according to the data presented in the above tables 'shut-in', as so defined, is an indicator of cognitive defect. Furthermore, it has positive correlations with all the cognitive measures we employed.† It may, therefore, be conceived of as a measure of cognitive defect. But how is this possible?

There is good reason to suppose that intelligence is the fundamental causal factor in emotional experience.[9] If intelligence is shallow, emotional experience must also be reduced. With a defect

* The names given to the various factors were suggested by looking at the general character of the specific symptoms.

† Besides those found in our tables these measures were: (1) ability to detect logical and (2) autistic fallacies and (3) absence of insight. 'Detection of fallacies' gives high tetrads when thrown into the cognitive group, probably because this ability involves reasoning and, therefore, is not independent of the other measures, a necessary condition. Absence of insight is such a common symptom in all forms of mental disorder that it is not a good diagnostic criterion.

of intelligence and of emotional experience there should go hand in hand an impoverishment of emotional expression.[10] If this is the case, it is not surprising that 'impoverishment of emotional expression' should appear in the multiple regression equation as an indicator of cognitive defect.

This fact will be of value in understanding the nature of dementia praecox. For cognitive defect, as will be seen by Table 8, is related to the praecox rather than the manic-depressive psychoses. This table gives us the intercorrelations of the general factors of the psychoses. Examining this we find that cognitive defect has a negative correlation with the retarded depressions and the constitutional hereditary depressions. It has positive correlations with what are probably two phases of *dementia praecox*: the uninhibited and the catatonic. This, along with the fact that 'shut-in', the classic symptom of the praecox, enters into the syndrome of cognitive defect, is strong evidence of impairment of intelligence in a group of patients that would be ordinarily classified under the heading of *dementia praecox*.

It is not necessary that this impairment of intelligence should be permanent. Thus, for instance, a patient with delusions and

Table 8

Intercorrelations of the General Factors *

	I	II	III	IV	V	VI	VII	VIII
I. Retarded depression	—	·688	—·046	—·119	—·178	—·415	—·441	—·517
II. Constitutional hereditary depression	·688	—	—·369	—·019	—·439	—·346	—·315	—·117
III. Catatonia	—·046	—·369	—	·401	·331	·651	·383	·039
IV. Non-euphoric manic	—·119	—·019	·401	—	—·154	·205	·029	X
V. Cognitive defect	—·178	—·439	·331	—·154	—	·439	·322	·272
VI. Uninhibited	—·415	—·346	·651	·205	·439	—	·305	·024
VII. Deluded-Hallucinated	—·441	—·315	·383	·029	·322	·305	—	·169
VIII. Euphoric manic	—·517	—·117	·039	X	·272	·024	·169	—

* The manic group was split into two; the euphoric and non-euphoric manics. This was suggested because most euphoric patients are irritable but not vice versa; and because the distribution of patients scoring above the mean in euphoria is bi-modal with marked hump at the extreme of the distribution. The retarded depressions are here included but a table giving the multiple regression constants were not calculated because correlation of the syndrome with other symptoms seemed to imply the possibility that the same general factor is involved in the constitutional hereditary depression.

Table 9

Cognitive Improvement in 'Dementia Praecox' with Clearing of the Psychosis

	Total memory	Memory ratio	Perception	Reasoning	Autistic fallacies	Logical fallacies	Absence of insight
October, 1928	·56	·50	·56	·58	·75	·75	+
May, 1929	·38	·075	·28	·14	·50	·38	—

auditory hallucinations, who was 'shut-in', talking to voices and manifested stereotypisms of actions and attitudes was diagnosed in October, 1928 (after an acute onset six weeks previous), as suffering from dementia praecox, catatonic form. In the following May the condition had considerably cleared. Table 9, in which the figures denote percentages of defect, shows a marked cognitive impairment in October, 1928, which had been to a large extent overcome in May, 1929.

If dementia praecox involves an acute or chronic impairment of cognitive function it probably has some kind of organic factor in its etiology, and cannot be regarded as a wholly psychogenic mental disorder.

A discussion of the ultimate nature of the cognitive general factor would lead us too far afield. It is at present being actively investigated by many psychologists.

It might not be out of place, however, to suggest:

(1) The cognitive general factor which is impaired in certain mental disorders is the same general factor that psychologists have found to underlie the most various and widely different psychological performances.

(2) It is likely that this general factor is what has been found to be inherited in various studies of the mental inheritance of genius and feeblemindedness.

(3) Should the work of Travis and Hunter be confirmed[11] or any similar correlation between neurological factors and intelligence, it would be possible to specify more definitely what is the nature of this cognitive general factor.

(4) Whatever the nature of this general factor, it cannot be any one of the specific mental abilities which enter into the formation

of the tetrads nor their sum total, nor can it overlap to any significant degree with any one of them for this would lead to large tetrad differences which is contrary to the findings.

(5) Many experiments have been made and a great variety of mental abilities have been found to involve an underlying general factor. The general factor is not, therefore, any one of these mental abilities. Furthermore, it is not likely that the general factor in intelligence will turn out to be any known human mental ability.

(6) That which is not likely to be a mental ability, a power, a faculty, but which can be inherited and can be attacked by the causal factors of the psychoses is probably of a definite neurological nature.

It may be well to point out here the conditions which the cognitive factor in the psychoses must satisfy if it can ever be measured directly.

Using the battery of tests that have given us our correlations (or a similar battery *mutatis mutandis*) the measure of the general factor must, within the limits of sampling:

(1) Correlate with Reasoning, $\cdot 853$; Perception, $\cdot 720$; Memory Span, $\cdot 583$; Rate of Forgetting, $\cdot 481$; Shut-in, $\cdot 425$. (*Cf.* Table 1.)

(2) Correlate with the group weighted and used as a battery, $\cdot 914$.

(3) When an attempt is made to treat the measure of the general factor as a specific element and tetrad differences are calculated a number of them will then be larger than the limits allowed for errors of sampling and the correlations of the variable with G partialed out will no longer approach to zero.

If the cognitive general factor is neurological in nature it is likely that the other general factors are also neurological rather than mental. The nervous system has more than one general property. It may be that some of these general factors will prove to be positive and negative variations of the same quantity. This may be the case in our catatonic and uninhibited groups and in the depressions and euphoric excitements.* It is a difficult matter from the purely statistical point of view to say that the general factors

* A word of explanation will be helpful in understanding some of the correlations in Table 8. In recording our data some stand had to be taken about conditions that showed reversals of the psychotic picture. It was decided that reversals separated by genuine recovery would be recorded only in one phase or the other. Reversals not separated by complete recovery would be averaged and the symptoms of both phases recorded. Thus there is a positive correlation between the uninhibited and the catatonic, but a negative between euphoric mania and depression.

present in any two groups are the same or different,* because of the fact that though the two groups may have the same general factor, when an attempt is made to combine them, high tetrad differences are found which may be due either (a) to two general factors, or (b) to the overlapping of the specific factors.

For the present we suggest from inspection of the specific traits that: (1) There is a cognitive general factor; (2) there is a catatonic general factor which may be the negative phase of the uninhibited or kinetic factor; (3) there is a manic factor which for reasons alleged in the legend to Table 8 is generic having two forms, the euphoric and non-euphoric; (4) there is a factor underlying the delusioned hallucinatory condition; (5) there is a constitutional hereditary factor manifesting itself as depression. This is not the cognitive factor with which it has a negative correlation, but probably an inheritable defect of the nervous system which does not affect cognition but weakens emotional control, or actually increases native emotivity.

Let us for a moment consider Table 8, in order to gain some information concerning the relationship between the *dementia praecox* group and manic-depressive insanity. The retarded depression and the constitutional hereditary depression have with each other a high significant correlation. This may be because there is one and the same general factor underlying both. The correlations of the depressions, however, with the 'praecox' general factor or factors (Nos. III–VI) are not all zero. But they are all negative and though two are rather low (·046 and ·019) some are significantly high.† This must mean that praecox psychoses are in some way intimately associated with the manic-depressive disorders. For some reason, one condition excludes the other. This is a very important fact in the interpretation of these conditions; but we have not been able to discover why these two conditions should be in contraposition to each other rather than simply lacking in any relationship.

Summary

(1) A technique, based upon Spearman's tetrad difference

---

* A technique is available (an improvement on Kelley's given in *Cross Roads in the Mind of Man*, p. 69 ff.), but we have not yet applied it to our data. *Cf.* McDonough, Sister Rosa: *Studies in Psychology and Psychiatry*, Baltimore, II, 2: 186, 1929.

† Thus, for instance, the probable error for the correlation (—. 415) between retarded depression and uninhibited (364 cases) is ·081 about 5 times the probable error; that for the correlation (— ·439) between constitutional hereditary depression and cognitive defect (185 cases) is ·085.

criterion, has been evolved for the empirical determination of the syndromes of psychiatry.

(2) This technique has given in a purely empirical manner eight syndromes and their constituent symptoms.

(a) The Syndrome of Cognitive Defect which is positively related to praecox conditions but, negatively, to manic-depressive.

(b) The Catatonic Syndrome, probably the inhibitory phase of dementia praecox.

(c) The Uninhibited or Kinetic Syndrome, probably the excited phase of dementia praecox.

(d) The Non-Euphoric Manic Syndrome, which is probably also a phase or form of dementia praecox.

(e) The Euphoric Manic Syndrome, which is probably the underlying condition in the manic form of manic-depressive insanity.

(f) The Delusional Hallucinatory Syndrome, also a factor in dementia praecox.

(g) The Syndrome of Constitutional Hereditary Depression, which indicates an hereditary factor that attacks the controlling mechanism of emotional life or heightens emotivity, but leaves the cognitive general factor untouched.

(h) The Syndrome of Retarded Depression, which is not as yet clearly differentiated.

(3) Reasons are given for regarding these syndromes as neurological defects of a definite nature.

(4) The measures used in the determination of the general factor can now be applied to the diagnosis of the above syndromes. The development of a procedure for doing this in a definite and simple manner is now in progress.

References

1. Studies in Psychology and Psychiatry, 2, No. 2, 1929.
2. Moore, Thomas: Psychol. Mon., Princeton, 27, 301, 1919.
3. This recalls Wundt's tridimensional theory of feeling which maintains that the simple feelings pass over to their opposites through a zero point of indifference. *Cf.* Wundt, Wilhelm, Gründzüge der physiologischen Psychologie, 5th Ed., 1902, p. 337 ff.
4. *Cf.* on this, *e.g.*, Handbook of Mathematical Statistics, ed. by H. L. Rietz, 1924, p. 72 ff.
5. For example, in the appendix to the work of Rietz above cited.
6. *Cf.*, Spearman, Charles: The Abilities of Man, 1927; Kelley, Truman Lee: Cross Roads in the Mind of Man, Stanford, 1928.
7. Dodd, Stuart: Jour. of Ed. Psychol., 19:217, 1928.
8. McDonough, Sister Rosa: Studies in Psychol. and Psych., II, No. 4, 178, 1929.

9. See the work of Morrison, B. M.: Univ. of Calif. Publ. in Psychol., 3:73, 1924, which shows that with morons emotionality is negatively correlated with the degree of mental defect so that the deeper the degree of mental defect the more shallow the intellectual life of the patient. *Cf*, also, Pages, L.: Affectivité et intelligence. Étude psycho-pathologique, Paris, Alcan, 1926. *Cf.*, also, discussion Moore, Thomas: Dynamic Psychology, 101–15, 1924.

10. The Lange-James theory of the emotions can no longer be taken seriously. *Cf.* T. V. Moore: Dynamic Psychology, Part III, Ch. ii. For the opinion of a Neurologist *cf.* Wilson, S. A. Kinnier: J. Neurol. and Psychopath, 4:299, 1924.

11. Travis, L. E., and Hunter, T. A.: J. of Exp. Psychol., 11:342, 1928.

7 N. Cameron

Reasoning, Regression and Communication in Schizophrenics

N. Cameron, 'Reasoning, regresssion and communication
in schizophrenics', *Psychological Monographs*, no. 1,
vol. 50 (1938), pp. 1–34.

Introduction*

In recent years the study of the psychology of reasoning has been
enriched by contributions from the fields of the genetic and the
abnormal. The comparison has frequently been made between the
thinking of children and of psychopathic persons, particularly
those suffering from schizophrenic illnesses in whom striking
disorders in the form and content of thought occur as, for instance,
in the papers of Piaget[14] and of Wildermuth[27]. The purpose
of the investigation reported in this paper was twofold: (1) To
study reasoning, under controlled conditions, as it appears in
adults whose thinking has undergone modifications in a rather
common form of disorganization; and (2) by analysis of the form
and structure of schizophrenic reasoning and the relation of its
content to the stream of personal preoccupations, to attempt to
introduce greater clarity and definition into conceptions of this
notoriously vague type of human thinking. Although our material
is derived for the most part from a study of abnormal persons, the
results by no means stand outside the realm of the normal psychology of reasoning. We shall have special occasion to draw
comparisons with the results obtained by others in their study of
children; but there are definite points of contact also with the
normal adult. The personal preoccupations of normal adults very
commonly intrude themselves to a certain extent into reasoning
even in relation to relatively neutral topics. Moreover one may
observe at times a certain degree of disorganization, not altogether
unlike that which we shall see in this study, occurring in otherwise
normal persons under conditions of distraction, in fatigue (C.
Schneider[20]), under emotional stress and in toxic and infectious
states. Some of the characteristics to be described in this paper are

* We are indebted to the Supreme Council, 33° Scottish Rite Masons of the
Northern Jurisdiction, U.S.A., for the financial help granted for our
research work in schizophrenia.

also found among quite normal persons and under normal conditions, but to a lesser degree. The occurrence of these characteristics in a more exaggerated form in our material may bring them into a bolder relief and perhaps aid in their further study among normal subjects.

One of the most outstanding characteristics of schizophrenic thinking is its disjointed and apparently incoherent structure for which the term 'scattering' has been commonly employed. As Sullivan[24] has remarked, the difficulty in communicating with schizophrenics has been in some respects an important obstacle in the way of the physician's maintaining a general interest in them; but at the same time this very characteristic has stood as a provocative challenge that has been often and variously answered. Our task was to induce simple reasoning in persons known to exhibit this type of incoherence in their stream of talk, and then to subject the product thus obtained to a functional analysis on the basis of the form it assumes, its relevance to the problem, its efficacy as communication, and its relation to the habitual language responses and individual preoccupations of the person. The question of communicability was regarded as of prime importance. It has the advantage of being susceptible of objective evaluation; it is closely tied up with the more general problem of the asocial characteristics of schizophrenics; and it has been the subject of rather extensive study in connexion with normal children, particularly by Luquet, Piaget, Huang, Abel, and Hazlitt.

Piaget[14] has made some interesting comparisons between normal adult thinking, that of the child, and that of the schizophrenic in an early article where he has drawn the general conclusion that the child's thinking lies midway between autistic thinking and the logical thought of the adult. In a later work[16] he sums up his studies on communication in the child. Beginning with the fundamental questions, 'Why does the child talk?', 'What are the functions of language?', and 'Under what circumstances does it occur?', he goes on to consider what purpose language serves for the child and to what extent it fulfils its purpose. On the basis of his results he divides language functionally into asocial and social, that is, into incommunicable and communicable. As asocial forms he recognizes in ascending order of complexity (1) *repetition*, a remnant of early prattle having little or no relation to present activity; (2) *simple monologue*, in which talk is a mere accompaniment or a part of general activity, the child talking to himself about what he is doing very much as many adults do while working at something; and (3) *collective monologue*, bearing in it the germs of rudimentary conversation but having as yet no function of genuine interchange. In this last form the child apparently feels no need of being listened to, nor yet of being understood, and indeed shows no expectation of either; the presence of others seems to serve merely as a stimulus for talking. Each child in a group talks only about himself, sticks to his own point of view, and makes no effort whatsoever to understand the others. Numerous interesting examples are given by way of illustration. These three forms taken together Piaget calls *asocial* because they are not genuinely communicative. Repetition as prattle is obviously asocial; the monologue is addressed to no one but the speaker; the collective monologue, while apparently addressed to others, involves no interchange of information and has for all practical purposes no effect upon others excepting to act as an almost undifferentiated general mutual stimulation. The remaining functional classifications of language he groups as social in that they represent true interchange, wherein information and attitudes are conveyed, and common activities are talked about – all with the obvious intention on the part of each speaker of being heard and of being understood.

From further studies of conversation, and of attempts at demonstration and exposition, Piaget drew interesting conclusions regarding communication which are of importance in connexion with our own study. The young child, Piaget finds, takes it for granted that he will be understood and is astonished when, after giving a hopelessly inadequate rendition of a story, for example, he discovers that his hearer has not grasped the relationships that he himself certainly felt were implied. Moreover there is a curious lack in the children's talk of that order and sequence one is accustomed to find in adult narrative or exposition; and there is an outstanding absence of causal links. In the explanations he gives, the child evidently 'feels' that certain things belong together; but he doesn't make this connexion in any way explicit. He simply juxtaposes related material in whatever order it happens to occur, instead of arranging it in a natural or a logical order and connecting it by explicit causal links. He is apparently unable to place himself in the position of others, to imagine their point of view, and so to realize their needs and his own gaps. The end-result is that in place of well-integrated concepts that can be expressed in a conventional form and thus used as common currency for communication between individuals, there is a loose conglomerate personally quite satisfying to the as yet asocial child, but failing in what should be its essential characteristic – communicability.

In his work on judgment and reasoning in the child Piaget[15] has attacked the problems of causal reasoning, the use of connectives and the ability to handle inclusion and exception on the part of children. It was his study of the causal relationships and the concept of exception that indicated the method for our own study. The interpretations, however, have a different emphasis and focus as will be outlined in connexion with our own results and their discussion.

Huang[8], in an extensive series of experiments on the explanations of strange phenomena, found the same tendency of children to juxtapose statements without their apparently recognizing the need to reconcile or integrate them. The older children were able to supply intermediary links when specifically questioned, but the younger ones were utterly incapable of it even when asked. Among young college women Huang found that when adequate complex principles were not available in their past experiences, these adults often fell back upon whatever simpler concepts they might happen to have; and sometimes they, also, were unable to supply adequate explicit connexions afterwards. These results seem to favor the view that the difference between child and adult in this respect is one of degree rather than that of the appearance of an abrupt qualitative change during development. Definite examples of juxtaposition did appear in Abel's experiments[1] in which adults were obliged to render passages from the *Scientific Monthly* to each other, but they were very rare. Hazlitt[7], in a study of generalization in children, attributes much to the role of prior education and training in the handling of concepts. Other investigators also emphasize the role of accumulated experience in adult thinking, and some even go so far as to ascribe differences in the responses of mature and immature persons mainly to differences in understanding questions and to experience in knowing how to look for the required answers.

In our own study we were dealing with persons of mature years who had already been exposed to the usual experiences associated with ordinary living. At some phase of their development, long after childhood had been passed through, an illness appeared, bringing with it some degree of disorganization. Moreover, in one of our cases the same person has been studied by the same methods at the height of his illness and again during a period of decided remission or improvement, affording an unusually fortunate opportunity for a comparison that possesses more than the average degree of validity.

Vigotsky[25], apparently stimulated by Piaget's work on children, has made a study of the formation and disintegration of concepts in schizophrenia. He feels, with Kretschmer, that 'the development of concepts, like the appearance of other higher psychologic functions, is accomplished by the formation of new layers over the old ones, with the preservation of the older layer of thought in a subordinate function.' Storch[22], after referring to a similar view of layer-formation held by Reiss[18], speaks of 'the decomposition of schizophrenic thought into complexes' which 'corresponds to a regression to the stage of development where the activities are limited to the sphere of affect and instinct.' Von Domarus[4] has built up hypotheses relating schizophrenic disturbances to a hierarchy of 'demonic', 'paralogic' and logical thinking and expressed an 'Anlagequotient' in terms of their relative proportions. Implicit in these and other widely held views concerning schizophrenic regression is the assumption that in developing disorganization of thought the patient goes through what has often been termed colloquially a 'peeling-off' process, in which the outer layers of racial or of individual maturity are lost and the primitive or the child-like nucleus laid bare. Bleuler[2] questions our right 'to assume that primitive peoples were in themselves less able to think sharply than we.' White[26] has also suggested caution in connexion with the same theories by remarking, 'I shall not further discuss this analogy except to say that the end-result in our [normal] thought and speech, whatever it may be, contains phylogenetic and ontogenetic factors inextricably mixed,' to which we would add that the same might be said of the process of schizophrenic regression as it appears in reasoning.

In this paper we are primarily concerned not so much with the formation of concepts as with their use. We shall see in our own results that, at least functionally considered, increasing disorganization does not result in the schizophrenic adult's retracing in the reverse direction those phases which characterized the development of his reasoning in childhood. There is little evidence to be gathered through a study of causal reasoning and antithetical relations in schizophrenia to support the assumption that one is witnessing a 'peeling'; the disorganization seems to be really a process of disintegration rather than one of delamination.

Method

Our chief interest lay in the psychology of reasoning. In order to induce simple reasoning in our subjects we confronted them with a series of previously prepared uncompleted causal sentences, after the manner of Piaget[15]; and these were sometimes supplemented by direct questions or followed up by further interrogation and requests for explanations. This study was extended further to gather material on the notion of exception or discordance and the concept of relationship. The material was obtained under as nearly uniform conditions as possible. Of the twenty-five cases studied, all but one were worked with alone in an office or in a small reception room with the door closed. In this way extraneous noises and distracting occurrences were reduced to a minimum. Since none of the work was delegated to others it was possible to maintain uniformity of technique throughout, a factor of considerable importance in any human psychological procedure. The technique necessary for such discussion and cooperative working with schizophrenic persons in a hospital environment had been acquired by the experimenter through responsible daily contact with psychiatric patients over a number of years.

It did not prove especially difficult with most of the subjects to establish a satisfactory informal working rapport that focused attention upon the task rather than upon the experimenter. With very few exceptions the patients were quite interested in the procedure and their responses and solutions were much more often carefully considered than merely off-hand. Sometimes hostility prevailed, particularly in two of the cases; but hostility is not always as uncompromising and asocial as it seems, since in order to be hostile one must as a rule at least take the other person into account. In one case an openly threatening attitude was partly responsible for bringing out, in a different form, illustrations of the interpenetration of personal- and problem-themes that were just as useful and informative as were those of a very friendly and cooperative patient.

The responses and remarks of the subjects, together with those of the experimenter, were recorded verbatim on the spot in a form of 'speedwriting' shorthand. The material thus obtained was examined for its yield and the results grouped for comparison; analysis of this material and its presentation as a basis for discussion will be taken up later under the separate divisions. The case records and the impressions of other physicians and of nurses were available to the writer as sources of auxiliary information. Only those patients who were quite unmistakably schizophrenic, who showed definite scattering at the time of the investigation, and who were able to cooperate, were included in the results. The study, originally suggested by Dr Adolf Meyer, was carried out at the Henry Phipps Psychiatric Clinic and at the Spring Grove State Hospital; the writer wishes to acknowledge also the helpful cooperation of Dr S. Weltmer, Superintendent, and of Dr Derbert Harms, Clinical Director, of the latter institution.

The results will be presented in the following order:

1. The study of *causal relationship*, which is taken up first, makes possible the comparison in point of maturity between the reasoning of our subjects and that of normal children.

2. The next subject, a study of the *relationship of discordance* or *antithesis*, permits an interesting further comparison with the results in the preceding section on causal relationship and, as will be seen, throws further light upon the question of regression. For Piaget has been able to show that there is a distinct difference in the ages at which the different forms of causal reasoning preponderate and at which antithesis or discordance is satisfactorily appreciated, and from the variation in their genetic development to distinguish levels of maturity in reasoning.

3. Under the term *asyndetic thinking* we have presented a genetically important phenomenon. This is a form of deficiency in integration at the level of language behavior in which elements are merely juxtaposed, placed next to each other without adequate linkage between them. This form is also socially significant because the product is defective from the standpoint of communication.

4. The peculiar but distinctive vagueness that sets up a nebulous barrier around the schizophrenic receives a certain degree of definition in the analysis of the role of *metonymic distortion*. This is seen to be a rather characteristic displacement of a precise term by an approximation through the partial disintegration of concepts. The individual elements making up the clusters that replace concepts acquire an apparent equivalence for the patient which makes it first difficult and then impossible for that elimination to take place which is the very essence of choice.

5. Finally, the occurrence of an *interpenetration of themes* is exemplified and briefly discussed. By our method of setting a specific problem it is possible to demonstrate the manner in which the theme dominated by the problem presented is received into that of the prevailing preoccupations of the patient.

Causal Relationship

In his study of the expression of causal relationships in children,

Piaget found it necessary to recognize a threefold division based upon the different functional uses of the term *because* in their reasoning. He presents results[15] from which he derives the thesis that as the child matures his reasoning undergoes a phasic change, in part expressed by the development in his comprehension and utilization of these genetically different forms. (*a*) The type of logical reasoning which he regarded as most mature is that indicating a relationship of *cause and effect* (e.g. 'A man fell down in the road because he stumbled'). Piaget found this to be of very infrequent occurrence among children younger than seven years. (*b*) A somewhat less mature form he designates as that of *logical justification*, in which the appeal is made by the subject from one principle to another principle (e.g. 'That animal is not dead because it is moving'). (*c*) His third type he calls *psychological motivation* (e.g. 'A boy threw a stone at me because he wanted to hit me'). In his results he finds this to be the predominant form in young children appearing where an adult would be expected to supply one of the other two types.

Piaget attributes the prevalence of the relation of psychological motivation that he found to the egocentricity of the young child, whose dominant standard at this period seems to be that of his own feeling of satisfaction with the result. It is only later on, through the child's coming into conflict with the reactions and opinions of others, that he is forced to recognize the need for convincing others of the validity of his own conclusions, a process which also favors development toward the further objectivation of events as a part of his reasoning.

Singer[21] stresses a fundamental point in his paper on regression in schizophrenics when he says, 'These people use childish tools but do they use them in a childish way?' Our subjects reason in a peculiar way but is this an approximation to the child's usage? That is the core of our problem. It will be approached from several directions, but the first and the simplest comparison is that between the success of the schizophrenic in handling these types of causality and the data on hand concerning the success of the child. It goes without saying that the older less mature forms of reasoning persist along with the development of the newer; but their relative prevalence diminishes with growing maturity and its attendant socialization. The following table gives a rough comparison of the frequency of the occurrence of each of these three forms in the spontaneous reasoning of six-year-old children, and in the induced reasoning of our schizophrenic adults who exhibited scattering.

Table 1

Relative Occurrence of Types of Causal Relationship in Young Children and in Adult Schizophrenics

Type of Causal Relationship	Percentage in Six Year Old Children	Percentage in Adult Schizophrenics
Cause-and-effect	7·5	45
Logical justification	9·0	23
Motivation	83·5	32

The striking predominance in young children's logic of the expressions of *motivation* we do not find matched by anything comparable in our schizophrenic material where motivation accounts for only about one-third of the causal relations that were unambiguously expressed. The *cause-and-effect* relationship, on the other hand, accounts for nearly one-half of the schizophrenic responses but for less than one-thirteenth of the children's. Evidently these two forms are fundamentally quite different.

A still more pertinent question is that of the relationship between degree of disorganization of the language function and the relative proportion of the types of causal reasoning within our own group of subjects. This was met by arranging the cases in order in accordance with the severity of their disorganization, as expressed in the degree of scattering shown by each, and then forming sub-groups to include the mild (7 cases), the moderate (10 cases), and the severe (8 cases) degrees of disorganization. The evaluation of each of the 375 items involved was made separately by two different persons familiar with Piaget's work and trained in psychopathology. The percentages given in Table 2 indicate the proportion of all the unambiguously expressed causal relationships assigned to each of the three types of reasoning.

It is quite evident that there is no decrease in the capacity of our subjects to handle *cause-and-effect* relations effectively as one passes from the mild to the severe degrees of disorganization provided, of course, they will attempt the problem at all, which was our chief basis of selection. *Motivation* likewise does not show a decrease. The capacity for *logical justification*, however, suffers relatively a marked drop in the severely disorganized group. The conclusion one can draw from this is that in our own material the form of causal relationship which is the last of the three types to develop genetically, *cause-and-effect*, shows no apparent relation to the degree of disorganization of thinking.

Finally we shall make a comparison sentence for sentence with data presented by Piaget to show the definite superiority his children up to nine years show in their ability to handle motivation. His data are based upon a study of 180 children. There are two

Table 2

Relative Occurrence of Types of Causal Relationship in Different Degrees of Schizophrenic Disorganization

	Percentages of Total Causal Relationship Expressed		
Types of Causal Relationship	In Cases With Mild Disorganization	In Cases With Moderate Disorganization	In Cases With Severe Disorganization
Cause-and-effect	39	43	58
Logical justification	32	25	10
Motivation	29	32	32

uncompleted sentences used by Piaget, one demanding a cause-and-effect relationship (i.e. 'That man fell off his bicycle because . . .'), and another calling for motivation (i.e. 'I shan't go to school today because . . .'). Among our fifteen uncompleted sentences we have the equivalents of each, in cause-and-effect (i.e. 'A man fell down in the road because . . .'), and in motivation ('A boy threw a stone at me because . . .'). The comparative results are given in Table 3.

Table 3

Relative Success in Cause-and-Effect and in Motivation Shown by Children and by Schizophrenics

Type of Causal Relationship	Children		Schizophrenics
	Age 7 Years	Age 8–9 Years	
Cause-and-effect	70%	77%	52%
Motivation	85%	95%	44%

The essential contrast in these results lies in the relatively poorer showing the schizophrenic patients made in the genetically immature type of *motivation*. In no sentence of this type did the figures rise more than four per cent above those for cause-and-effect. When we again inquire into the performance in the severely disorganized patients, we find in this group only a single satisfactory example of induced reasoning by motivation; yet the same persons succeeded in completing satisfactorily eleven examples showing the cause-and-effect type of relationship. Thus one fails to find in this part of the study any confirmatory evidence for the simple form of regression implied in a delamination that would remove, layer by layer, the more mature forms of reasoning as disorganization proceeds. Even in our severely disorganized group there is nothing to suggest a puerile nucleus laid bare.

Relationship of Discordance

In the preceding section we discussed the relative expression of the three types of causal relationship by our subjects and compared these results with those for young children. It was evident that our schizophrenics did not show a greater tendency for the less mature form, the relation of motivation, to persist as compared with the more mature cause-and-effect relationship. We shall now present some data of a different kind that serves to support these earlier conclusions.

The use of antithetical terms expressing *discordance* seems to belong to a still more mature phase in the development of reasoning than does the use of any of the causal relationships already considered. Whereas children begin the correct use of *because* in one sense or another from a very early age, the use of discordance appears at a much later period. Our specific interest here is to see whether in schizophrenic disorganization this later acquisition suffers more than the earlier appearing causal relationship. To this end we confronted our patients with a number of uncompleted sentences ending in *although* and *even though*. These involve the principle of exception which, for young children, proves a very difficult task and one which they are evidently able to handle increasingly well as they mature. A comparison, in our results, between the ability to handle causal relationships with the ability of the same persons to handle discordance or exception brought out an interesting contrast. If, as in the preceding section, the patients are arranged in order according to the degree of disorganization they show, a consistent difference appears between the mildly scattered, the moderately scattered and the severely scattered. In Table 4 are given the percentages of causal and discordant relationships that were correctly expressed in the three groups.

Table 4
Relative Occurrence of Causal Relationships and of Discordance in
Different Degrees of Schizophrenic Disorganization

| Degree of Disorganization | Percentage Expressed Correctly | |
	'Because'	'Although'
Mild	57	38
Moderate	41	32
Severe	11	35

Here we see *discordance* or exception, which Piaget found developing late in children's reasoning, showing in our schizophrenic patients a negligible reduction as the disorganization increases; while the *causal relationships* are definitely reduced in the moderately disorganized group and drop off abruptly in the severely disorganized. Thus we find the severely disorganized group doing more than three times as well with the more mature logical relation of discordance than with that of causal relationship.

If the assumption is correct that discordance really represents a more mature phase in the development of reasoning, then our results point to an important fact. Our schizophrenics show relatively a definitely superior preservation of their ability to deal with the discordant over that of the causal relationships. Thus we have another indication that in the disorganization of their thought processes they do not retrace the steps of development which children pass through in the growth of reason. More mature forms of reasoning are better preserved than the less mature as one passes from mild toward greater disorganization of thinking.

Up to this point we have been focusing attention upon whatever seemed definite and precise in the reasoning of our schizophrenics. We have now to direct attention to factors involved in the characteristic vagueness, the prevailing lack of precision and of unity which make schizophrenic logic so difficult to follow. This is a study of the geography of schizophrenic reasoning. From the analyses of our material we were able to pick out three factors distinct enough to justify separate discussion. These are: (1) the appearance of loose clusters of terms in place of organically integrated concepts; (2) the use of terms or phrases that approximate the meaning, striking somewhere on the periphery of the target instead of at the bull's eye; and (3) the concomitant appearance of coordinate themes interweaving with each other and through mutual interference producing what at first glance looks like a mere jumble of words.

Asyndetic Thinking

The appearance of loose clusters of terms instead of the more organically integrated concepts represents in fact a special case of the general disorder of fusion so commonly encountered in schizophrenia. The most outstanding characteristic is a striking paucity of genuinely causal links which, if present, would function in binding the whole together into an integrated concept. The elements of such a loose cluster, although quite evidently felt by the subject to be related, are not explicitly bound together. For this type of logical structure the term *asyndetic* has been adopted. Asyndesis is something more than the simple 'juxtaposition' of Luquet[10] because, as we shall see in our examples, the terms thrown together are actually related to one another. It is something less than Renan's 'syncretism' as presented by Piaget[16] in which a special form of assimilation to global schemas in child reasoning is assumed, for which there is no convincing evidence in our material. Asyndetic thinking, nevertheless, is a form that is not at all uncommon among the juxtapositions of children, where it seems to represent a prelogical phase in the development of reasoning. That in our cases it is in some way the outcome of schizophrenic disorganization appears especially clearly in a case from which we shall present data later, showing its presence during the height of the illness and its absence after partial recovery.

The following examples of asyndesis taken from our own material illustrate at once the relevancy of the elements and their lack of effective integration.

Case 9 says the wind blows 'because it's time to blow.' (What makes it blow?) 'The air.' (The air?) 'The sky.' (How does the sky make it blow?) 'Because it's high in the air.'

The reference to 'time' is the result of perseveration from a previous answer regarding sunrise and can be ignored. For the rest, we find an agglomeration of words loosely connected with wind in general – *wind, blow, air, sky, high*. These are not just any words appearing at random, but terms that are related to the general feeling one might have about wind; and the patient evidently feels that somehow these elements belong together. At the same time there is no genuine causal connexion indicated, even in the last clause where the term 'because' is spontaneously used. It is precisely this failure to bind together explicitly into an integrated concept terms felt as belonging together that constitutes the important feature of this form of reasoning. Here is another example in answer to the same problem:

Case 16 says the wind blows 'due to velocity.' (Why does the wind blow?) 'Due to loss of air, evaporation of water.' (What gives it the velocity?) 'The contact of trees, of air in the trees.'

Again the result, however inadequately put together, is not a random product. The phenomena appealed to are those commonly experienced directly or indirectly in connexion with wind – *velocity, loss of air, evaporation, contact of trees, air in the trees*. The form is not unlike that found among children; but the vague reference to other atmospheric changes bears the stamp of the wider experience that obviously belongs to a more mature phase of life. A third example is somewhat different from the preceding ones:

Case 17 asserts that the wind blows 'because it howls.' (But why does it howl?) 'Lack of cooperation with the rain and sun.' (And why does that make it howl?) 'I don't know.'

The loose relation expressed here in the initial 'reason' is followed by a statement involving other natural events – *wind, howl, rain, sun*. Animism may possibly be implicit in the 'lack of cooperation' referred to but it is difficult to say. The final phrase expresses not indifference but a genuine inability to account logically for a relation which is only felt. The whole response remains asyndetic because the patient is ordinarily no longer able to exercise the functions of selection, restriction, and orderly arrangement necessary in the process of logical thinking. The result is a conglomerate instead of an integrate.

Sometimes the patients expressed more openly this apparently quite common feeling that somehow certain things seemed to belong together; and at the same time they showed clearly their inability to select and to eliminate in the interest of deriving such a clean-cut precise result. Case 23 says his hair is fair '*because of something else; because it's on my head; it came from my mother.*' These statements, given in quick succession, represent a hit-or-miss recital of notions vaguely connected with what he knows about his hair. In the phrase 'because of something else' he expresses the feeling of a belonging together without being able, however, to supply satisfactory content. Case 5 has brown hair. (Why?) 'I don't know. It has something to do with lights.' Case 15 says a boy threw a stone at him '*because stones, or jealous, or something*'; he seemed entirely satisfied with his reply. Case 22 says of the wind's blowing, '*Something about the clouds move it*.' (How do they do that?) 'They move all around and that's why.' The self-satisfaction was evident in this person's manner as well as in her phraseology, an attitude towards very imperfect productions which when present is quite important.

It is impossible in these answers to miss the relevance, a certain restriction to the problem and even some degree of clarity in expression, with at the same time an obvious want of direction and of an effective final pulling together of the elements into a well-integrated whole. These characteristics appear over and over again. They are not so clearly expressed in the following examples but these are included to indicate the commonness and variety of asyndesis in the schizophrenic material.

Case 23 says the sun comes up in the morning 'because it's a gas'; Case 22 'because it's windy and the sun goes down at night'; Case 15 responds, 'Lazy or something, – laziness'; and Case 19 says simply 'Sun and light and heat.' The wind blows, according to Case 18, 'because we want air.' (What makes it blow?) 'You wouldn't say the vapor, would you?' Case 10 says 'the summer.' (What makes it blow?) 'The coolness.' Case 15 says a fish can live in the water 'because they breathe under air, water or something'; Case 20 remarks 'his length and the way he breathes and his gills,' illustrating the lack of a sense of causality in her structure and by the use of 'and' as a connective. Case 4 (male) reasons 'I have fair hair because I brush it.'

What can we conclude from these results? First of all, our material shows surprisingly little real irrelevance. It is evident that even when dealing with hypothetical and very abstract matters in problems imposed from without, our schizophrenic patients show for the most part a prevailing tendency to stick to the subject. While their attempts do not satisfactorily dispose of the problem, their content hovers around it. The answers are by no means sheer nonsense as may at first glance have appeared to be the case. The relatedness of the material is, however, often very distant, the restriction to the problem is loose and too inclusive, and the clarity referred to above does not imply precision. In short we find the schizophrenic offering, in place of an integrated functional whole, something that is a collection of fragments. In asyndetic reasoning something has been lost – the capacity for organization.

What is this functional disturbance in reasoning and to what may it be ascribed? We have said that asyndesis seems to be a part of that general disorder of fusion characteristic of schizophrenic activity. In our own material we have found an inability to bind together explicitly the terms that are felt to be related;

and with this inability goes a defect in selection and elimination. Competing terms cannot be completely discarded, there is a spurious equivalence given to several terms in a given cluster, and the product remains a more or less unorganized conglomerate. Fusion in our sense implies antecedent extension. Schizophrenic reasoning permits in many instances the co-existence, without fusion or elimination, of elements that are even opposed, provided that in some way they seem related. Thus with shifting emphases contradictions appear that are akin to ambivalence. Fusion of these elements, with explicit causal linkages, would inevitably call forth a language structure expressing definite and relatively exclusive relationships without contradiction and without ambivalence. There seems to be in our material a fundamental disorder of concept-formation, in which the function may be considered either as arrested at an intermediate stage before it can be completed, or as reduced through disintegration to a simpler level of pre-logical reasoning.

The last assumption raises the important question of reversibility. Is there any evidence that disorganization of thinking leading to the unmistakable appearance of asyndesis can be followed by reorganization and the return of ordinary concept-formation? This is a fundamental point because on it also hinges the decision as to whether or not this asyndetic disorganization can be correlated with schizophrenic developments. We have by way of evidence a comparison between the performance of the same patient during a severe phase of his illness and later after partial recovery.

Case 23

During Height of Illness	After Partial Recovery
My hair is fair because . . .	
Because of something else; it's on my head; it comes from my mother.	*Because I inherited it from my parents.*
A man fell down in the street because . . .	
Of the World War.	*Because he slipped.*
The sun comes up in the morning because . . .	
Because it's a gas.	*Because the earth goes around the sun.*
The wind blows because . . .	
Just cosmic dust.	*Because of atmospheric air-currents changing.*

Quite obviously in the asyndesis of schizophrenia we are dealing with a process that may become reversible and coincide roughly with the general disorganization of the patient. We have witnessed here the spontaneous disappearance of asyndesis, coincidentally with marked general improvement, in a person who had previously exhibited it rather prominently. Evidently in the development of his illness there resulted a specific type of disorganization of reasoning into that peculiar form of vagueness in which a loose clustering replaced the concept-formation of the normal adult; and then, as recovery began, the process apparently became reversed and definitive concepts reappeared. This observation points the way to another possible measure of schizophrenic disorganization and recovery. It also furnishes some evidence in support of Gruhle's assertion in the course of his criticism of Kleist, 'that the total speech function complex remains potentially present in the schizophrenic'.[5]

The appearance of asyndetic reasoning in such profusion has a special significance in schizophrenics. It is a characteristic far more common in normal young children than among adults: for example, in 600 examples of causal and antithetical expressions we have collected from normal adults it appears only 6 times. Piaget has adduced an impressive array of evidence for his dominant thesis that adult logic is born of necessity, the necessity for influencing or convincing others. It is thus to a large extent the result of socialization, the outcome of social impact. Its absence in children he regards as evidence that they are still to that extent asocial, and its development he takes as a measure of their socialization. The least that can be said of the attitude of our patients is that in connexion with their responses they commonly exhibited a strikingly easy satisfaction with inadequate and often unintelligible products. Some of them showed a haughty unconcern or a flat indifference. Others in better rapport obviously took it entirely for granted that they were being understood and, as we shall see in connexion with metonymic distortion, their attempts at further explanation were often much less intelligible than the original response had been.

Metonymic Distortion

Metonymic distortion consists of the substitution of an approximate but related term or phrase for the more precise definitive term that normal adults would presumably use in the same setting. Unlike asyndesis it has no exact counterpart in the reasoning of children; it represents indisputably a species of disorganization rather than a mere reduction to a lower level of organization. It is related to asyndesis in that it also is in part the outcome of an incapacity for selecting, restricting, and eliminating. The consequence of this is that here also the schizophrenic attributes a false equivalence to several terms or phrases which in the normal person might belong to the fringe of his conceptual structures. Instead of the precise term at the bull's eye, the patient strikes the target elsewhere toward the periphery. It is this peripheral use of approximation metonyms that lends to schizophrenic expression a great deal of its peculiar flavor of elusiveness. The products of metonymic distortion can within limits be translated into conventional logical English. This is essentially a translation of idiom – an idiom so highly individualistic that it cannot serve effectively for social communication. To the translator it brings the same feeling of effort that attends the translation of foreign idiom into one's own tongue. Here are some examples:

Case 16 says he is alive 'because you really live physically because you have menu three times a day; that's the physical.' (What else is there besides the physical?) 'Then you are alive mostly to serve a work from the standpoint of methodical business.'

The first sentence obviously means that on the physical side you live because you eat (*have menu*) three times a day. '*You really live physically because*' conveys the sense of 'on the physical side you live because', but the actual phraseology is distinctly metonymic and until translated into a more conventional logical structure, leaves one with an uncomfortable sense of uncertainty as to the exact intention of the speaker. In the second sentence, '*to serve a work*' represents an inadequate fusion of *to serve* and *to work*, in which the normal elimination of one phrase or the other is wanting. The remainder, '*from the standpoint of methodical business*', is this patient's idiom for daily routine.

Case 7 thinks his body makes a shadow 'because it hides the part of the light that is used for full room capacity or area capacity which you intervene.'

The metonymic term *intervene* is almost correct, but it should be 'intercept'. *Full room capacity* and *area capacity* both give one the feeling of completeness and expanse; they imply the total surface from which part of the light is cut off by the intervention of your body but they don't actually say it. Here, as in many of the asyndetic forms, it is impossible to regard any of the explanation as irrelevant. One feels the reasoning is basically correct but the structure in which it appears can satisfy only the speaker;

as an instrument of social communication it is almost worthless.

Case 7 says that the sun comes up in the morning 'because it is the actual rotation of its axis between the arctic and the antarctic zone, the differences between the stages of its axis during different eclipses of the moon.'

This is a structure built up chiefly of metonymic approximations. '*The actual rotation of its axis*' undoubtedly refers to the rotation of the earth on its axis, although earth is never mentioned by the patient. '*Between the arctic and antarctic zones*' is a very nice example of the substitution of wide geographical areas for the narrower and more precise north and south poles. The general sense of phases in the earth's rotation is conveyed hazily in '*the stages of its axis*'; and the '*eclipses of the moon*' are included because the patient feels vaguely that they belong to the picture. He fails to eliminate this because he is incapable of sharpening his focus and rejecting the fringe.

The same patient says a fish can live in the water '*because it's the natural resource of life*' instead of the far simpler 'because that's its nature' which another one gives. '*Natural resource of life*' is an unprecise metonymic phrase in which 'its nature' and 'its resources' are inadequately blended. Case 13 thinks it can live in the water '*because having no eyes to see on land if it crawls*', expressing in his own individual phraseology its lack of equipment for a life on land where it would have to crawl. The focus is on the wrong aspects of the situation, and the whole image is blurred to an even greater extent than in most of the preceding; but the feeling his explanation conveys in its personal idiom shows relevancy and at least some grasp of the problem.

Case 3 says his body makes a shadow '*because of my flesh, my skin*', metonymic terms for 'body' which convey the sense of solidity but are still only peripheral approximations. When Case 19 says hers makes a shadow '*because it's like the sun*', she evidently means that it is *in relation* to the sun, just as another patient does when he says his body is *in contact with* the sun. Case 6 uses an habitual personal idiom for 'body' when she says 'I am good because I think it's best for any *physical flesh*.'

Case 16 responds to 'I am a man because . . .' with this: 'Trying to find me or way of trying to get a proper vision.' (What does that mean?) 'Working for an assignment where I can be placed somewhere to be of service.' (What 'assignment' would you like?) 'The way I feel I'm not very capable.'

The first sentence expresses an attitude of trying to find himself and of trying to gain adequate perspective. In the second sentence he follows the same sense through to the wish to be of some use; and he ends with a statement of quite justifiable futility. In this example the strikes are preponderantly on the periphery of the target. Without translation into a more logical structure the whole response has very little value to this patient's hearers; yet he is quite satisfied with his product and indicates no uneasiness concerning his own intelligibility. This is the core of the problem. Since communication is the essential social function of language behavior, the ability to define and sharpen one's concepts further when one's hearer shows the need for it gives a rough indication of sociability. It depends primarily upon the capacity for putting one's self in the place of another.

It is therefore worth mentioning that disorganization seems to be favored by extension or amplification of responses. In some cases further questioning that was intended to lead the subjects to greater precision and definitiveness served only to introduce a more pronounced vagueness. The loose organization of their thinking makes the addition of fringe elements irresistible and the delimitation to simple unextended statements very difficult. After a fairly satisfactory response the person goes on needlessly to add related but less relevant terms; the result may be first a good phrase and then something that sounds like a jumble. This apparent jumble is made up of elements belonging to the periphery of the concept and undoubtedly shared in common with other loosely organized clusters or concepts. A few illustrations bring out this common phenomenon of *scatter by amplification*:

I am alive 'because I was born a human *and animal life and normal life*.'

A man fell down in the street 'because he stumbled *or else fell*.' (Did he stumble and then fall?) 'I don't think he stumbled.'

I took a bath 'because it's purifying to *shine of body flesh*.'

A boy threw a stone at me 'because he had mischief and *arm exercise to exercise the body*.'

I am good 'because brought up right *and strictly confidential*.'

I get warm when I run 'because I like careless exercise.' (Why do you get warm?) '*Well, I think it's more the same ailment, takes terrible bites. It happens to many people*.'

The general attitude of these persons toward their productions is a very significant point. In the last example above, for instance, this rather amicable patient spoke in her usual quiet confidential manner, perfectly satisfied with what she was saying and in her entire manner indicating plainly that of course she was being understood. Like Piaget's young children, these patients take it quite for granted that they are understood. They seem unable to assume their listener's point of view, and often fail to see any necessity for even trying to do so. There remain now still other and more involved instances to be discussed briefly, in which the theme of the problem keeps reappearing, while fragments relating to the dominant preoccupations interpenetrate and form at times a rather intricate pattern.

Interpenetration

Preoccupation with personal themes may be definitely asocial but it is not in itself abnormal. Who has not at one time or another found his thinking about relatively neutral matters colored by an unrelated topic of high personal value? When, however, during waking life the intrusion of personal material functions as a disorganizing factor in reasoning, and particularly in communicated reasoning, then it becomes definitely abnormal. This is a characteristic of schizophrenic thinking that is found well-developed only in severe disorganization. In its well-developed form it consists of the interpenetration of the elements or fragments of different themes, sometimes of a theme and a counter-theme – in our material the one concerned primarily with the immediate problem that we have introduced from the outside – and the other deriving from persistent preoccupations of a personal nature. It is another form of the schizophrenic disorder of fusion which does not permit the normal subordination of one theme to another, or the elimination or deferring of one in favor of the other. The undigested elements of both proceed along together as coordinates, and the result is a conglomerate without synthesis.

Here is a clear example. The habitual preoccupations of this woman cannot be eliminated or deferred. They become interpenetrated by terms relating to the intruding concept of the problem we have presented: How is it that a fish can live in the water? One gets, in place of a conclusion in directive form, what turns out to be a sprinkling of vaguely related words in a disorganized setting. The example strikes one at first glance as mere jabber:

(A fish can live in the water because ...) 'Because it's learned to *swim*.' (What if it couldn't swim?) 'Not naturally, he couldn't. Why do certain gods have effects on *seas* like that? What does the *earth* have such an effect to break their backs? The *fishes* near home *come to the surface* and break.' (Why?) 'I think it is due to bodies that people lose. A body *becomes adapted to the air*. Think thoughts and break the *fishes*.'

The personal preoccupations of this person are very bizarre. They center largely about her body and imaginary injuries to it, of which being bitten and having her back broken are prominent. The appearance in this stream of references to *certain gods*, *bodies*, *back*, *effect*, *lose*, *break*, result from the material of her usual personal themes with which her medical attendants are quite familiar. The terms and phrases italicized in the example above belong to the intruding problem and these are sprinkled throughout the stream to the very end. Both lines of thought are evident in these traces. If one thinks very loosely of fish in water and what happens to them on land it will be appreciated that much of this material is vaguely relevant. '*Why does the earth have such an effect to break their backs?*' represents an inadequate fusion of what happens to fish thrown out of water, with the patient's own concern over her supposed broken back. A similar fusion appears in, '*The fishes near home come to the surface and break*', where the previous vein manages to distort 'breathe', which was probably intended. Later on, in the last phrase of all, '*break the fishes*', the two themes are juxtaposed. In '*a body becomes adapted to the air*' the problem has become displaced instead to a corollary of the aquatic adaptation of fishes, very likely as a result of her recurrently shifting focus to vague concern over her own body.

Another example, taken this time from our most hostile patient, will be briefly analyzed. His emotional reaction is, in fact, not at all inconsistent with the general content, but the disorganization is marked. This is interesting in view of Stransky's emphasis upon the role played by inadequate feeling-tone upon the production of disorganization, for which he uses the analogical term 'intrapsychic ataxia'.[23] This patient's dominant theme is that he is God, never stated very definitely or explicitly, but given quite unmistakably by implication. He is always at war with the devil, he always remarks on the key to the outside, and he reacts with definite resentment to any change in personnel or routine on the ward. Here is his statement, given slowly, forcibly, and with strong emphases.

(I get warm when I run because . . .) 'Because you possessing a position of a doctor have the key. The devil *seeing you run* becomes ired. God doesn't get ired because it doesn't have any effect. He doesn't want a *railroad* or an *express company* in this place.'

The influence of the problem is evident in the italicized words. The running is ascribed to me. It is the devil who 'becomes ired' at my running and not God (i.e. the patient) who is superior to such things and therefore unaffected by them. His own genuine annoyance at my being in the place and questioning him slips out at the end in an interestingly distorted form in which he very pointedly and emphatically states that God doesn't want this running-person (*railroad*, *express company*) around the place. By way of further example of his attitude, this patient at a later date ordered a small group of my students out of a corridor, where they were quietly going over their notes, on the grounds that God didn't want 'a reading class' in the place.

Finally a third example will be given this time from the solutions offered by a young man with unrealized ambitions to be an engineer. He met each of the problems in this study with modesty and close attention, couching his explanations in pseudo-scientific terms from which it was obvious that he was deriving a quiet satisfaction. There is a strong metonymic component throughout. This is a sample:

(My hair is brown because . . .) 'Because it is a sort of hydraulic evering.' (What does that mean?) 'It means that it gives you some sort of a *color-blindness* because it works through the *roots of the hair* and hydrasee – that is a study of the *growth of plants*, a sort of *human* barometer, hydraulic hydroscenic method.'

The persistent personal theme in this young man takes the form of what he regards as engineering. His lack of a sufficient supply of technical terms in the face of his scientific pose is responsible for the neologisms *evering*, *hydrasee*, *hydroscenic*; these and the term hydraulic form the thread of the distorting personal theme. The terms italicized in the example relate to the intruding problem. The color of the hair is related correctly to the roots and to growth. But color extends to *color-blindness* and the growth cannot be restricted to the narrower concept in question but must go on to *growth of plants* and the *human barometer*, the latter representing inadequate fusion of the problem-theme and the pseudo-scientific theme.

These are examples of a type of distortion of reasoning through interpenetration, in which personal preoccupations form a theme that competes seriously with the problem-theme for the stage. It gives one the impression of even greater irresistibility than in the vague but not entirely abnormal asyndesis and in the unclear groping of metonymic thought. The world of fantasy here forms more nearly a coordinate system and maintains an influence that is more continuous over the stream of talk initiated by this presentation of a problem in reasoning. Interpenetration occurs chiefly in severe degrees of disorganization where, however, there is still

170

preserved some remnant of the capacity for limiting one's self to a topic imposed arbitrarily from without. When this capacity becomes negligible or disappears little or nothing remains of reasoning in its social forms. Of this phase we have specimens also, but they fall outside the scope of this study.

Summary and Discussion

The prime significance of symbolization has been especially stressed by Adolf Meyer as 'the fundamental and specific feature of psychobiological integration' which brings on the same level 'reference to reality and fancy, past, present and future, personal and social, as if it were all present' here and now in a single individual. It is 'the characteristic psychobiological . . . activity that we call mentation'.[12] In our study we have focused attention upon disturbances in the functional use of symbolization, as they appear in schizophrenic disorganization, and have compared our results with the data of genetic psychology.

The reasoning of the child has been shown to follow a certain general order as he progresses toward maturity. Quite early he develops an ability to handle causal relationships. This can be demonstrated by the way he makes use of the organizing function of *because* in binding together dynamically related terms. At first he shows a very marked preference for ascribing motivation as his leading causal principle; only later on does he give an adequate place to the relationship of cause-and-effect. From such facts as these it has been concluded that the latter represents a definitely more mature phase of reasoning, and that the genetic development of reasoning may in part be followed by observing the waning emphasis upon motivation and the growth of the use of cause-and-effect. Still later in development is the notion of discordance, and so this serves as another milestone in the reasoning of the child.

It is self-evident that such data suggests a clue to the study of schizophrenic disorganization, which has been looked upon by some as a process of regression retracing in a reverse direction the path of development that runs from infancy to maturity. If this be a true picture of regression, one may expect the process of disorganization to result in the successive reappearance of genetically earlier forms of reasoning, roughly in the reverse order of development, as successive 'layers' were peeled off. This does not apparently take place. Instead, the disorganization that we find proceeds as a whole, and results in something quite unlike the reasoning of children. Evidently regression does not simply retrace the path of development but follows instead a pattern of its own.

In the first place, it is motivation as a causal principle that suffers most in the schizophrenic disintegration of reasoning, in spite of its being genetically least mature; while cause-and-effect is relatively well preserved. Moreover, within the schizophrenic group, as one passes from those with mild to those with severe disorganization one still finds no decrease in the relative utilization of the cause-and-effect relationship. Finally, in comparing the whole group of causal relationships with the still more mature discordance we find still further corroboration; with increased severity of disorganization there is a progressive loss in effectiveness, not of discordance, but again of the less mature causal relationships. In short we are witnessing something that is not simply a return to the infantile, but is the functional disintegration of a remarkable, mature organization which is the result, as Meyer says, of 'that tremendous development which has as its essence the use of symbols'.[11] The functional disintegration of such an organization yields products which, far from duplicating those of puerile reasoning, remain in many respects quite unique and together account for the more or less specific character of schizophrenic thinking disorders.

The asyndetic clusters that, among schizophrenics, tend to replace synthetic concepts are not altogether foreign to children's reasoning. Their outstanding characteristic is that of a paucity of functional connecting links which if present would bind together some of the elements that are evidently 'felt' to belong together. Indeed, they usually are related to the problem and to each other; they are not simply random terms, but represent unorganized relatedness – a collection of fragments that cannot be welded into a whole. Indeed, when the attempt was made by subjects to give a further explanation, less instead of greater definition usually resulted with the amplification; and it is possible also in Hadlich's study of the schizophrenic interpretation of proverbs[6] to detect in the verbatim material he quotes a similar phenomenon. A synthetic whole of this sort can become organized only through selection and elimination. Just as soon as functional connecting links are introduced it follows that one element will be retained and others will have to be excluded; but this selection and elimination is just what the schizophrenic is often unable to do.

Schizophrenic thinking tends to stick to everything it touches. Its loose structure permits the presence at the same time of potentially contradictory elements. This is possible simply because the actual contradiction which would arise in the process of the functional organization of concept-formation does not come to pass.

A false equilibrium results which then no longer requires the elimination of one term simply because it is not brought explicitly into relation with its opponent. The result is incongruity and ambivalence. That asyndetic thinking is part of the schizophrenic process is evident from its appearance in one of our cases at the height of the illness and its spontaneous disappearance with partial recovery. This points the way to another measure of disorganization and recovery; and it deserves further emphasis because in the asyndetic form of reasoning one may recognize evidences of that mild language disorganization which often heralds an early schizophrenic development.

Kraepelin, in his discussion of dementia praecox,[9] has described the misuse of terms from a somewhat different point of view, using the concept of *derailment* (Entgleisung). Under this conception he includes such disturbances as changes in pitch, rate, rhythm, loudness and timbre of spoken words, the introduction of sniffing, smacking the lips, etc., and the use of affectations and tiresome repetitions. He includes as well what he regards as forms of paraphasia and of paralogia. The paraphasic forms include simply mutilations, alterations, or partial fusions of commonly used words, and the formation of unintelligible words from constituent syllables which, however, have sense; and neologisms he regards as a further form of the same thing in which even the syllables are senseless. He describes displacement paralogia in which the patient, unable to find the expression appropriate to his thought, produces something having a similar sound, and derailment paralogia in which the patient lets his thoughts fall into quite another channel. According to Kraepelin the patient 'deliberately avoids the right answer which he certainly has at his command'. Finally, under derailment of the train of thought, there is described the derivation of one series of ideas from another near by, as when the patient answers the question, 'What is the year?' by saying, 'It might be Australia', substituting for a series of years the series of continents. Kraepelin feels that where 'a negativistic evasion of the right answer is not clear' one can assume that the form is derived from a 'talking past the subject', in which the ideas have been pushed aside or suppressed by remote or opposing ones.

This explanation of Kraepelin's is based upon the older psychological conception of thought as a concatenation of more or less separate associative units, and the examples are largely derived from isolated samples of the stream of talk. Bleuler[2] developed the hypothesis that associations formed through experience were held in their tracks by 'a dynamic something' – *die Assoziations-spannung* – which was diminished in sleep and distraction, and that probably its weakness was basic for the specific schizophrenic phenomena, 'because from these anomalies almost all the known schizophrenic symptoms can be derived'. In the fifth edition of his textbook,[3] however, the discussion of schizophrenic disorders of association has omitted reference to this hypothesis.

'Reasoning,' Pillsbury says, 'like any other mental operation, can be understood only in its setting.'[17] We feel that by our method of restricting the setting in giving the subjects a pre-determined problem, by taking account at the same time of their attitude and their intent, a more fruitful conception may evolve that brings out in these phenomena rather a functional significance, and relates them to the development of communication as a social product.

Naturally, the lack of definitive organization in children, as in schizophrenics, means impairment in communication. It has been abundantly shown that the development of adult logical form is the product of necessity and develops with the increase in the child's socialization. The young child characteristically takes it for granted that he understands and is understood. He is at first quite unable to put himself in another's position and see things from another's perspective. He does not mould his individualistic thought into conventional logical form before presenting it to his hearers; he 'sees' or 'feels' the relationship and that is evidently all that he needs to satisfy himself of its effectiveness. It is only after repeated conflicts and failures to get cooperation with others that he discovers the necessity for adhering to certain social conventions of expression for the communication of attitudes and information. The child's efforts at communication are deficient because he has not yet achieved effective social contact with others. The schizophrenic has given it up. Minkowski[13] makes the acute observation that 'The blind, the mutilated, the paralysed are able to live in just as close contact with their surroundings as individuals whose sight is intact and who have lost their four limbs; the schizophrenics, on the other hand, lose this contact without any alteration in their sensorimotor apparatus, their memory or even their intelligence.'

In metonymic distortion the divergence from the normal is already very marked. In place of a correct term, the schizophrenic patient offers a poor approximation, usually without becoming in the least disturbed if his listener is unable to grasp his meaning. Like the child he may be quite unable to place himself in the place of his hearer; and usually he recognizes no need to do so. He shares with the child an easy satisfaction with totally inadequate verbal productions, which he may then proceed to amend with a statement which often conveys to the hearer less than the original exposition. But these metonymic forms, in our material, with rare exceptions, satisfied the patients completely; it was the experimenter who was confused and not the subject. Some of them were considerate enough to elaborate here and there, adding incidentally to the unclearness; others did not conceal their contempt or anger at the experimenter's inadequate grasp. Reasoning expressed in this way and with this attitude can fairly be termed asocial in proportion as it becomes relatively uncommunicable. Unlike most aphasics, with whom C. Schneider[19] has contrasted them, these patients make no spontaneous compensatory efforts to bridge the gap between you and them left by their inadequate use of language. The common occurrence of metonymic distortion throws further light upon the problem of regression. It, too, represents a product of a true disintegration rather than a delamination, and it is not comparable to puerile forms.

There seems to be even less concern over the other person's understanding in metonymic distortion than in asyndesis. The equivalence of related terms may so be taken for granted that the patient's statements fairly bristle with approximations and yet cause him no apparent uneasiness. Finally, in what we have called interpenetration, reasoning has reached a stage where new material may enter only if it submit to being broken up and given a place here and there in the more compelling stream of asocial preoccupation. Asocial fantasy has at last become sufficiently dominant to resist subordination to an intruding problem and succeeds in fragmenting it, while partially assimilating it to the prevailing system of preoccupation. The real can no longer displace the fanciful; everything introduced must be related to whatever is present. Objectivation becomes lost and each thing must be explained by such a process of assimilating it to the all-absorbing dream-life in force at the time. In this way external problems, subjected to the criteria of imagination, come out like a dream. From the standpoint of social communication and its disorganization in the schizophrenic, it can be said that in *asyndesis* the patient finds it inconvenient to put himself in another's place; in *metonymic thinking* he does not feel that it is necessary; and in *interpenetration* he is no longer able to effect it.

References
1. Abel, T. Unsynthetic modes of thinking among adults: A discussion of Piaget's concepts. *Amer. J. Psychol.*, 1932, **44**, 123–32.

2. Bleuler, E. Störungen der Assoziationsspannung ein Elementarsymptom der Schizophrenien: Eine Hypothese. *Allg. Zsch. f. Psychiat.*, 1918, **74**, 1–21.

3. —— *Lehrbuch der Psychiatrie*. 5th ed. Berlin, 1930, 50–53.

4. Domarus, E. von. Das Denken und seine krankhaften Störungen. *Würzb. Abh. aus d. gesamtgeb. d. Medizin*, 1929, New Series, **5**, 369–456.

5. Gruhle, H. In O. Bumke's *Handbuch der Geisteskrankheiten*. Spezieller Teil V: Die Schizophrenie. Berlin, 1932, 135–210.

6. Hadlich, H. Schizophrene Denkstörung. *Psychol. Forsch.*, 1931, **15**, 359–73.

7. Hazlitt, V. Children's thinking. *Brit. J. Psychol.:* General Section, 1930, **20**, 354–61.

8. Huang, I. Children's explanations of strange phenomena. *Psychol. Forsch.*, 1931, **14**, 63–182.

9. Kraepelin, E. *Dementia Praecox and Paraphrenia*. [Tr. by R. M. Barclay from the 8th German ed. of *Lehrbuch der Psychiatrie*.] Edinburgh, 1919.

10. Luquet, G.-H. *Les Dessins d'un Enfant*. Paris, 1913.

11. Meyer, A. Interrelations of the domain of neuropsychiatry. *Arch. Neurol. & Psychiat.*, 1922, **8**, 111–21.

12. —— The Fourteenth Maudsley Lecture: British influences in psychiatry and mental hygiene. *J. Ment. Sci.*, 1933, **79**, 435–63.

13. Minkowski, E. *La schizophrénie: Psychopathologie des Schizoïdes et des Schizophrènes*, Paris, 1927, 82–3.

14. Piaget, J. La pensée symbolique et la pensée de l'enfant. *Arch. de Psychol.*, 1923, **18**, 273–304.

15. —— *Judgment and Reasoning in the Child*. New York, 1928.

16. —— *The Language and Thought of the Child*. New York, 1932.

17. Pillsbury, W. *The Psychology of Reasoning*. New York, 1910.

18. Reiss, E. Zur Theorie der schizophrenen Denkstörung (Abstract). *Zentbl. f. d. ges. Neurol. u. Psychiat.*, 1921, **25**, 432–4.

19. Schneider, C. Über die Unterscheide zwischen schizophrener Sprache und Aphasie. *Zsch. f. d. ges. Neurol. u. Psychiat.*, 1925, **96**, 251–74.

20. —— Beiträge zur Lehre von der Schizophrenie: Über die allgemeine Theorie der Schizophrenen Symptome. *Zsch. f. d. ges. Neur. u. Psychiat.*, 1925, **96**, 572–602.

21. Singer, H. D. Is dementia praecox properly described as an infantile mode of reaction? *J. Abn. Psychol.*, 1917, **11**, 305–8.

22. Storch, A. The primitive archaic forms of inner experiences and thought in schizophrenia. *Nerv. & Ment. Dis. Monog.*, 1924, No. 36.

23. Stransky, E. Zur Kenntnis gewisser erworbener Blödsinnsformen: Zugleich ein Beitrag zur Lehre von der Dementia praecox. *Jahrb. f. Psychiat. u. Neurol.*, 1903, **24**, 1–149.

24. Sullivan, H. Peculiarity of thought in schizophrenia. *Amer. J. Psychiat.*, 1925–6, **5**, 21–86.

25. Vigotsky, L. S. Thought in schizophrenia (trans. by J. Kasanin). *Arch. Neurol. u. Psychiat.*, 1934, **31**, 1063–77.

26. White, W. The language of schizophrenia. In *Schizophrenia (Dementia praecox): An investigation of the most recent advances, as reported by the Association for Research in Nervous and Mental Disease*. New York, 1928, 23–43.

27. Wildermuth, H. Schizophrene Zeichen beim gesunden Kind. *Zsch. f. d. ges. Neurol. u. Psychiat.*, 1923, **86**, 166–73.

Part Three CONDITIONING AND BEHAVIOURISM IN RELATION TO ANIMAL DISTURBANCES

The two extracts from the work of Pavlov give an account of the first experimental work in animals which bear relevance to abnormal psychology. Everybody has heard of them but few have read them.

The paper by Maier needs no introduction. It forms the basis for some of the most important animal experimental work in abnormal psychology.

The work of Masserman is unique in the way it combines experimental work on animals, both theoretical and clinically relevant, with direct clinical work on patients suffering from mental illness. It is hoped that this extract does justice to his work.

8 I. P. Pavlov

Relation between Excitation and Inhibition and their
Delimitations; Experimental Neuroses in Dogs

Excerpts from I. P. Pavlov, *Lectures on conditioned reflexes* (translated
by W. Horsley Gantt), International Publishers, 1963, Lawrence & Wishart,
1929, chapters 36 and 39.

(*Dedicated to the memory of my revered friend, Robert Tigerstedt, to
whom physiology owes so much, not only for his investigations, but for his
promotion of physiological knowledge and research.*)

Introduction – First Law of Relationship between Excitation and
Inhibition – Second Law (Delimitation) – The Conflict, and the
Destruction of Normal Nervous Activity – Two Experimental Examples
(Difficult Differentiations) – The Resulting Nervous Disorders caused
by the Collision of Excitatory and Inhibitory Processes – An Experiment
showing four stages in the Abnormal Relations between the Effect of
Strong and Weak Stimuli Resulting from a Collision of Excitation and
Inhibition – Nervous Disorders were produced in the Experimental
Animals by the Leningrad Flood – Lesions of the Cortex following
Extirpation – Senility – Thyroid Insufficiency – Classification of the
Cortical states – Examples of Partial Sleep or Isolated Inhibition (Sleep
Walkers, The Miller and The Mill, etc., Catalepsy, Suggestibility) –
Physico-chemistry of the Nerve Fibre is Necessary.

All the following facts have to do with the functions of the cerebral
hemispheres and have been obtained by the method of conditioned
reflexes, i.e. reflexes formed during the individual life of the
animal. [...]
  By the great difference in facts we were compelled to assume in
the work on the cerebral hemispheres two different kinds of
inhibition, and we called them *external* and *internal*. The former
appears in our conditioned reflex at once; the second develops in
time and is gradually elaborated. The first is an exact repetition
of inhibition, well known for many years in the physiology of the
lower parts of the central nervous system when stimuli, acting on
various nervous centres and provoking various nervous activities,
meet; the second may relate only to the cerebral hemispheres.
Probably, however, the difference between these two inhibitions
has to do only with the conditions of their origin, but not necessarily with the process itself. We are still investigating this question.

Here I shall speak only of internal inhibition, referring to it however, without its adjective, simply as inhibition.

There are two conditions, or better one condition, the presence or absence of which determines whether the impulse brought from the outside into the cells of the cerebral hemispheres will excite in them a process of stimulation or a process of inhibition; in other words, whether this impulse will become positive or negative. This fundamental condition consists in the following: if a stimulus entering into a cerebral cell coincides with some other extensive stimulation of the hemispheres or some lower parts of the brain, then this stimulus is a positive one; under the opposite conditions (i.e. when it acts alone), it becomes sooner or later a negative, an inhibitory stimulus. Relating to this indisputable fact there arose the question, 'Why is this so?' But until now there has been no answer. Therefore we must begin with this fact without having analysed it. Such is the *first basic relation between excitation and inhibition.*

Physiologists have for many years been familiar with the spreading of excitation processes. The study of the higher nervous activity led us to a conclusion concerning the spreading also of the inhibitory process from the point where it first originates. The facts from which this conclusion is drawn are simple and obvious. Now, if from one point an excitatory process spread, and from another an inhibitory, then they limit each other, each confining the other to a definite space and within definite borders. In this way it is possible to obtain a very delicate functional delimitation of the separate points in the cerebral cortex. If we have to do with such separate points in the cortex which under corresponding conditions are subjected to stimulation, then this result can be easily explained by the plan of the cellular construction. This interpretation meets with difficulties when we have to deal with an excitatory or an inhibitory process corresponding to various intensities or other similar variations (for example the different frequencies of the strokes of a metronome) of one and the same external stimulating agent. In order to explain this according to the simple cellular scheme, it is necessary to presuppose as a point of application of this agent not a single cell, but a group of cells. In every case, as a matter of fact, it is possible to associate with a certain intensity of a known elementary agent the excitatory process, and with another intensity of the same agent the inhibitory one. Therefore, the second general relation between stimulation and inhibition in the cortex is their mutual limitation in space, their *delimitation.* The most evident demonstration of this is obtained in the experiments with mechanical stimulation of various points on the surface of the skin.

From this we are forced to presuppose some struggle between two opposing processes, ending normally in a certain equilibrium between them, in a certain balance. This conflict and this balancing are not too easy for the nervous system. We have seen this from the very beginning of our work and we see it constantly even until now. The animal often expresses this difficulty by motor disquietude, by whining and dyspnoea. But in the majority of cases the equilibrium is at last established, each process is allotted its proper place and time, and the animal, after becoming perfectly quiet, reacts to the corresponding stimuli by the process of excitation or of inhibition.

Only under special conditions does this conflict of the two processes lead to destruction of the normal nervous activity and then there originates a pathological state which may last for days, weeks, months, and perhaps even years. This may of itself gradually return to the normal when the experiments are interrupted and the animal is given a considerable rest, but if the conflict is too violent, it can only be removed by definite means, and the animal must be given regular treatment.

These special cases at first arose accidentally and unexpectedly but afterwards we reproduced them intentionally in order to study them. Their description follows in chronological order.

The first of these cases we came upon many years ago (in the experiments of M. N. Yerofeyeva). The conditioned food reflex was elaborated not from an indifferent agent but from a destructive one, evoking an inborn defensive reflex. The skin was irritated by an electric current and at the same time the dog was fed, although at first the feeding had to be forced. A weak current was applied which was later increased to the maximum. The experiment ended thus: with the strongest current, as well as with burning and mechanical destruction of the skin, there could be provoked only the food reaction (the corresponding motor reaction and the salivary secretion) and there was no trace of any interference by the defensive reaction, there were no changes in breathing or heart beat, characteristic of this last reaction. It is clear that this result was attained by the transference of the external excitation to the food centre and that simultaneously with this an inhibition of the centre for defensive reactions must occur. This special conditioned reflex persisted for some months and probably might have remained stable under the given conditions had we not changed them so that the electric irritation was systematically transferred at every excitation to another new point on the skin. And when the number of these points became considerable, then in one of our dogs the condition suddenly changed. Everywhere, beginning with the first location of the skin stimulus and even with the weakest current there was manifested only the strongest defensive reaction, and not a single trace of the food reaction.

By no means were we now able to reproduce the former results. The dog which in the former experiments had been quiet became very excited. In another dog this result came about only when – in addition to the considerable number of places on the skin from which we evoked only the food reaction in spite of the very strong current – during one and the same experiment the irritation was often and quickly moved from one place to another. Both dogs had to be rested for some months, and only in one of them were we able, by proceeding slowly and cautiously, to restore the conditioned food reflex to the irritating agent.

The second case of the same sort was observed a little later (experiments of N. R. Shenger-Krestovnikova). A conditioned food reflex as elaborated in a dog to a circle of light projected on a screen in front of it. Differentiation of the circle from an ellipse of the same size and intensity was afterwards tried, i.e., the circle was always accompanied by feeding; the ellipse, never. Differentiation was thus elaborated. The circle called forth the food reaction, but the ellipse remained without effect, which is, as we know, a result of the development of inhibition. The first ellipse applied was markedly different in shape from the circle (the proportion of its axes was as 2:1). Afterwards as the form of the ellipse was brought closer and closer to that of the circle, we obtained more or less quickly an increasingly delicate differentiation. But when we used an ellipse whose two axes were as 9: 8, i.e., an ellipse which was nearly circular, all this was changed. We obtained a new delicate differentiation, which always remained imperfect, lasted two or three weeks, and afterwards not only disappeared spontaneously, but caused the loss of all earlier differentiations, including even the less delicate ones. The dog which formerly stood quietly on his bench, now was constantly struggling and howling. It was necessary to elaborate anew all the differentiations and the most unrefined now demanded much more time than at first. On attempting to obtain the final differentiation the old story was repeated, i.e., all the differentiations disappeared and the dog fell again into a state of excitation.

After these observations and experiments we recently undertook the investigation of the described phenomena more systematically and in more detail (experiments of M. K. Petrova). As it is possible to assume from the above facts that the destruction of the normal relations occurred as a result of the collision between the excitatory and the inhibitory processes in certain difficult circumstances, we performed in two dogs of different types – the one very lively, the other inactive and quiet – special experiments with various inhibitory agents and their combinations. Together with the conditioned reflexes which had been retarded for three minutes, i.e., when the unconditioned stimulus was followed by the conditioned only three minutes after the beginning of the latter, as a consequence of which the positive effect appeared only after a preliminary period of inhibition of one to two minutes, there were applied other kinds of inhibition (differentiations, etc.). But this problem was solved by these different nervous systems, although with varying facility, yet without damaging the normal relations. Then we began to elaborate the conditioned food reflex with a destructive agent. Now it was sufficient, having formed this reflex, to repeat it several times on the same spot on the skin, in order that the pathological state might appear. This deviation from the normal proceeded in the two dogs in opposite directions. In the lively dog the elaborated inhibitions suffered to a considerable degree or even disappeared entirely and changed into positively acting stimuli; in the quiet dog, on the contrary, the positive conditioned salivary reflexes markedly decreased in strength and disappeared. And in both cases these changes were very stable, they lasted for months and did not alter or vanish without special treatment. In the lively dog with the weakened inhibitory process, there was in the course of a few days a permanent return to the normal, brought about by means of rectal injections of potassium bromide. It is interesting to observe that together with the appearance of normal inhibition, the strength of the positive conditioned action not only was not decreased, but was even somewhat augmented. On the basis of these experiments we are, therefore, compelled to think not of a decrease of one nervous excitability under the influence of bromide, but of a true regulation of the nervous activity. In another dog we failed to restore a permanent and measurable salivary reflex, in spite of various means which we employed for this purpose.

The following experiments done on a third dog for another purpose, however, gave similar results but more instructive details (experiments of I. P. Razenkov). Many positive conditional reflexes were elaborated on the animal, from various receptors or from the same receptor with varying intensities of one and the same agent. Among others a reflex was obtained to a definite frequency of a mechanical stimulus of a certain place on the skin. After this we began to elaborate differentiations from the same place on the skin, but with a mechanical stimulation of another frequency. This differentiation was attained also without great difficulty, and without noticeable changes in the general nervous activity of the animal. But when immediately after the application of completely inhibited rhythm of the mechanical skin stimulus, there was tried without delay stimulation by a positively acting rhythm, the dog manifested a peculiar disturbance, lasting five weeks, and only gradually disappearing. Restoration to normal was perhaps aided by our special measures. For the first days after the experiments in which there was a collision of the nervous processes, all positive conditioned reflexes disappeared. This state lasted for ten days. Afterwards these reflexes began to reappear, but in a peculiar order; contrary to normal, strong stimuli were without effect, or acted minimally, and considerable effect was obtained only from the weak stimuli. This state continued for fourteen days. Again ensued a special phase. All stimuli now acted equally, and with about the same force as strong stimuli in the normal animal. This extended over a period of seven days. Finally came the last period before the normal, characterized in that the stimuli of moderate strength were greater than in the normal state, strong stimuli were less than in the normal, and weak ones had lost their action entirely. This too lasted for seven days, and then there was a return to normal. With the repetition of the foregoing procedure which evoked the disturbance described above, i.e., the repetition of an immediate transition from the inhibitory-acting mechanical stimulation of the skin to the positive-acting stimulation, there occurred the same disturbance with the same phases, but running a shorter course. With further repetitions the derangements became more and more fleeting, until finally the same application provoked no disturbance. The decrease of the pathological state was expressed not only in the shortening of the duration of the abnormal condition but also in the reduction of the number of phases, and the disappearance of the more abnormal phases.

Thus with the collision of the excitatory and the inhibitory processes, there appears either a predominance of the stimulating process, disturbing the inhibition (it is possible to say, a lingering increase of the tonus of the excitation); or in other cases a predominance of the inhibitory process, with its preliminary phases, disturbing the excitatory process, i.e., an increase in the tonus of the inhibition.

But we have seen the same phenomena under other conditions than the above. Under the action of exceedingly unusual directly inhibiting stimulations affecting the animal, there occurs a chronic predominance of the inhibitory process. We observed this in a high degree in some dogs after the great inundation in Leningrad of 23 September 1924, when our experimental animals were rescued with great difficulty and subjected to quite exceptional conditions. The conditioned reflexes disappeared for some time and only slowly reappeared. For a considerable period after this reappearance each more or less strong stimulus, which was formerly followed by a considerable conditioned effect, as well as the application of an earlier elaborated and even well-concentrated inhibition, provoked again this chronic state of inhibition; either as a complete inhibition or as its preliminary phases mentioned above (experiments of A. D. Speransky and V. V. Rikman). In less degree and for a shorter time the same is often observed under more usual conditions, as the removal of a dog to a new environment, or his transference to a new experimenter, etc.

On the other hand, a slight change in the application of a well-elaborated positive conditioned reflex, viz., an unconditioned stimulation following immediately the beginning of the conditioned, so increases the tonus of the stimulation that if the elaborated inhibitions are now tested, they are seen either to have entirely disappeared or to have suffered a great loss in constancy and regularity. Also a frequent interchange now of positive and negative reflexes leads, especially in lively dogs, to a high degree of general excitement (experiments of M. K. Petrova and E. M. Kreps).

The facts given above do not exhaust our material concerning the relation between excitation and inhibition. In the course of our work we have met with many quite peculiar cases of just this very same kind.

It was noticed in many instances that in certain phases of drowsiness in normal dogs there occurred a distortion of the effects of conditioned stimuli. The positive stimuli lost their effect, but the negative became positive (experiments of A. A. Shishlo). In the light of this knowledge, we can understand the frequent fact that in the drowsy state of the animal an apparently spontaneous salivary secretion sets in, which is absent in the waking state. The explanation consists in this – that at the beginning of the elaboration of the conditioned reflexes of a given animal many accessory stimuli, indeed the whole *entourage* of the laboratory, become conditionally connected with the food centre, but later all these accessory stimuli are inhibited, owing to the adaptation to which we subject the conditioned stimuli. In drowsiness these inhibited agents recover, as we are inclined to think, temporarily, their original activity.

The temporary transformation of the elaborated inhibitory stimuli into positive ones is observed also in pathological attractions of the cerebral cortex produced by post-operative cicatrization, especially during the intervals between convulsions. It is interesting that along with these elaborated inhibitory stimulations during this time only the weakest positive stimuli act, viz., light, whereas all other positive conditioned stimuli of moderate or of considerable strength remain without effect (experiments of I. P. Razenkov). Here belongs the former fact, frequently reproduced by us, that new stimuli provoking one or another reflex of moderate strength during their action convert the conditioned inhibitory reflex into a positive reflex (our so-called inhibition of inhibition—dis-inhibition).

In lesions of the cortex, on the other hand, which follow extirpations, the positive conditioned stimuli belonging to the injured cortex become inhibitory. This I have already mentioned in my foregoing article on sleep. The phenomenon is especially marked in the skin region of the hemisphere, where it has been best studied (earlier experiments of N. I. Krasnogorsky and newer ones of I. P. Razenkov). If the lesion is inconsiderable, the previous positive conditioned mechanical skin stimulus produces an effect less than the normal, and if repeated during the course of one experiment soon becomes inhibitory, i.e., being joined with other effective stimuli it weakens their action, and applied alone produces in the animal a state of sleepiness. If the destruction is more serious, it has, under usual circumstances no positive action, being purely inhibitory, and causes after its application a complete disappearance of all positive conditioned reflexes in other parts of the brain.

But this inhibiting agent, being now inhibitory, can nevertheless, under certain conditions manifest a positive effect. If the animal becomes sleepy, then this stimulus, as well as the elaborated inhibitory agent, as mentioned above, manifests a small positive effect. But this effect can be brought about in the animal by still another procedure. If this stimulus is repeated several times, with only this slight change, that it acts alone for 5 seconds instead of the usual 30 seconds (i.e., if the unconditioned stimulus is added 5 seconds instead of 30 seconds after the beginning of the conditioned), then after displacing it to 30 seconds, we may have a positive effect, which, however, is very unstable. When it appears quickly enough after the beginning of the stimulation, it begins to fall rapidly during the continuation of the stimulation and finally entirely disappears (a markedly weakened excitability). Such a transitory effect may be obtained also by a preliminary injection of caffein, or by many other similar measures (experiments of I. P. Razenkov).

Somewhat different but still related to this theme are the following facts. With a very weak general excitability of the cortex, as is observed in senility of animals (experiments of L. A. Andreyev), and also in animals from which the thyroid has been removed (experiments of A. V. Valkov), or in certain states brought about by convulsions in post-operative scarring of the cortex (experiments of Razenkov), the inhibitory process is either much weakened or becomes impossible. In these cases only by an increase of the irritability of the cortex by the application of stronger unconditioned stimuli can we sometimes provoke an inhibitory process.

Here belongs the phenomenon of reciprocal induction, which I have mentioned in the previous chapters (experiments of D. S. Fursikov, V. V. Stroganov, E. M. Kreps, M. P. Kalmikov, et al.). And finally the last fact consists in the following: if by a corresponding procedure, separate points of the cortex are reinforced for a long time, some always as points of excitation, some others always as points of inhibition, then they gradually become highly constant in their effects, and stubbornly resist the influence of the opposite processes. Extraordinary means are sometimes required in order to bring about a change of their function (experiments of B. N. Bierman, U. P. Frolov).

All these facts permit us, I think, to classify the various conditions to which the cortex is subjected in a certain consecutive order. At one pole of this system stands the state of excitation, an extraordinary increase of irritability, when an inhibitory process becomes very difficult or impossible. After this is the normal waking state, the state of normal equilibrium between the processes of excitation and of inhibition. Then follows a long but also consecutive series of states transitory to the inhibition, of which the following are the most characteristic: a state of equalization, when in contradistinction to the waking state all stimuli, independent of their intensities, act exactly equally; the *paradoxical phase* when only weak stimuli act and when strong stimuli either have no action at all or have a barely noticeable effect; and finally the *ultraparadoxical phase*, during which only the previously elaborated inhibitory agents have a positive effect. After this follows a state of complete inhibition. The explanation is not yet clear of that other state in which the excitability itself is so low that inhibition in general becomes very difficult or impossible, just as in the case of the state of extreme excitation.

At present we are occupied among other things with the experimental decision of the question: In all cases of normal transition from the active state to that of inhibition as in the state following sleep or in the process of elaboration of negative conditioned reflexes, etc., are there to be found transitory states which are so sharply expressed in pathological cases? Already we have some clues to the answer to this question. If this should prove to be so, then only as a prolongation of the transition from one state to another, a certain isolation and fixation of those transitory states which normally change quickly or almost imperceptibly, can be considered as pathological.

The above facts open the way to the comprehension of many phenomena of both the normal and pathological activity of the higher nervous system. I shall give some examples. In foregoing articles I have shown how normal conduct is based on the elaborated delimitation of the points of excitation and of inhibition, on that magnificent mosaic in the cortex, and how sleep is to be considered as irradiated inhibition. Now we may add some details showing how it is easy to understand certain variations of normal sleep as well as separate symptoms of hypnosis when they are considered as different degrees of extensiveness and intensity of the inhibitory process.

Cases of sleep while walking or riding horseback are well known. In other words inhibition is limited to the confines of the cerebral hemispheres, and does not spread below over the subcortical centres established by Magnus. Further we know of sleep with partial waking in relation to special stimuli, although they may be feeble: the sleep of the miller who wakes when the noise of the mill ceases; the sleep of the mother who awakes on the faintest sound coming from her ill child, but whose rest is not disturbed by much stronger sounds from other sources, i.e., sleep in which easily excitable points stand on guard.

Catalepsy in hypnosis is evidently an isolated inhibition of only the motor regions of the cortex, not spreading to the centres of equilibrium, and leaving free the remaining parts of the cortex. Suggestion in hypnosis can also be considered as such a phase of inhibition, in which weak conditioned stimulation (words) acts more effectively than stronger direct external stimuli. The symptom established by Pierre Janet of the loss of the sense of reality during many years of sleep can be explained as a chronic inhibition of the cortex interrupted only for short intervals, and especially in the presence of feeble stimuli (usually at night), this inhibition concerning particularly the skin and motor regions, which are the most important for the influence of reality on the organism and for the action of the organism on the outer world. Senile talkativeness and dementia too find a simple explanation in an extraordinary weakening of inhibition resulting from the feeble excitability of the cortex. Finally our experiments on dogs give us the right to consider those changes which we produce – the chronic deviations of the higher nervous activity from the normal – as pure neuroses, and some light can be thrown on the mechanism of their origin. In this way the action of an exceedingly strong and unusual stimulation (for example the flood of 1924) on dogs with a weak nervous system, having a predominant inhibitory process, in other words, on a central nervous system with an increased tonus of inhibition, reproduces the etiology of a special traumatic neurosis.

It is obvious that the time has not yet come for a theory to explain all the enumerated phenomena and to assign them a common basis, although many hypotheses have been proposed, each one of which has a certain justification. In the present situation, one may use various conceptions in the work if only they permit a systematization of the material and suggest new and detailed problems.

Thus in our experiments we think of different phases which develop under special conditions in the cortical cells, from extreme excitation to the deepest inhibition, and which depend upon the intensity and duration of the corresponding stimulation and upon the conditions under which this stimulation occurs. The manifest analogy between the changes which we have observed in the function of the cerebral cortex and in the changes of the nerve fibre inclines us to this view. The latter changes occur under the influence of various strong influences; they are aptly described by N. E. Vvedensky, in his well-known work, *Excitation, Inhibition, and Narcosis*. We do not agree with his theory, but we have grounds on which to refer all the observed transitions from excitation to inhibition to one and the same elements, the nerve cells, as Vvedensky has rightly done in the case of the nerve fibre.

One can hardly deny that only a study of the physico-chemical processes taking place in nerve tissue will give us a real theory of all nervous phenomena, and that the phases of this process will provide us with a full explanation of all the external manifestations of nervous activity, their consecutiveness and their inter-relations.

The Inhibitory Type of Nervous Systems in the Dog

(*Read before the Psychological Society, Paris, December, 1925, on the occasion of the election of Prof. Pavlov to honorary membership.*)

Description of an Inhibitory Type of Dog – Experimental Analysis of the Effect of the Leningrad Flood on this Dog – Passive Defensive Reflex (Fear) Appears – Interpretation of the Experiment – Stimulatory Substances and Fatigue – Resemblance between the Passive Defensive Reflex and Inhibition – Phobias – Analogy of Temperaments (Sanguine, Equilibrated, Melancholic) to Pavlov's Types of Dogs – Discovery of the Social Reflex.

I wish to express my sincere thanks for the great honour you have shown in giving me this opportunity to address you. In the study of the nervous system physiology and psychology must, I am confident, be sooner or later united in an intimate and friendly work. Now, however, let every one of us try in his own way, to marshal his special resources. The larger the number of approaches, the greater the chances that we shall finally unite and proceed together, each helping the other.

In the study of the activity of the brain in the higher animals (in particular, the dog), I and my collaborators, as you know, have adopted a purely physiological point of view, and the terms and explanations we use are exclusively physiological.

The more we investigate, by our method, the higher nervous activity of dogs, the oftener we come upon considerable and striking differences in the individual qualities of the nervous systems of these animals. These differences, on the one hand, added difficulties to our investigation and often disturbed the complete reproduction of the results in other dogs: on the other hand, they were extremely advantageous, as they strongly emphasized a certain aspect of the nervous activity.

Finally, we have been able to distinguish several definite types of nervous systems. To one of these types, then, I take the liberty to direct your attention. This type of dog is one which judging by his behaviour (especially under new circumstances) everyone would call a timid and cowardly animal. He moves cautiously, with tail tucked in, and legs half bent. When we make a sudden movement or slightly raise the voice, the animal draws back his whole body and crouches on the floor. We now have in the laboratory an extreme example of such a type. The dog – a female – was born in the laboratory and has lived there five or six years. Never have we subjected her to anything unpleasant. The only thing required of her was this: we put her periodically on the stand and offered food in the presence of certain signals – our conditioned reflexes. But even up to this time, at the sight of any of us, although constant members of the laboratory staff, she starts, and slinks off as if from dangerous enemies. Such an animal is very useful for work on conditioned reflexes, but not at once. At the beginning it is exceedingly difficult to form conditioned reflexes; the animal resents being placed on the stand, the attaching of the various pieces of apparatus and especially the feeding, etc. But when all this difficulty is at last overcome, the dog acts like a perfect machine. Especially notable is the stability of the inhibitory conditioned reflexes – when conditioned agents call forth not the process of excitation but of inhibition. In dogs of other types, on the contrary, it is the process of inhibition which is the more labile and the more easily destroyed. When on a dog of this type there falls, under the usual experimental conditions, some inconsiderable new stimulus, for example the presence of a stranger outside the door of the experimental chamber, only the negative conditioned reflexes are fully maintained; the positive ones immediately weaken or vanish.

I shall now discuss a dog of this type. My collaborator, Dr Speransky, performed the experiments. Six positive conditioned reflexes were formed: to a bell, a metronome, a whistle, an increase of the general illumination, to a circle of white paper, and to the appearance of a toy rabbit. Differentiations were formed, i.e., inhibitory stimuli were elaborated to a metronome of another frequency, to the decrease of the illumination, to the shape of a paper square, and to a toy horse. The size of the positive reflexes varied as follows: All the auditory reflexes were one and a half times or twice as great as the optical. The bell occupied first place among the sounds, next came the metronome, and the weakest of all was the whistle. The optical were all of nearly the same size. As has been already stated in general (and this dog worked perfectly), all the described relations could always be reproduced uniformly.

In September of last year (1924) there was in Leningrad a great flood. The dogs were saved only with difficulty and under extreme circumstances. Five to ten days later, when they were returned to their usual kennels, the dog under discussion was, to all appearances, perfectly healthy, but in the experimental room it perplexed us not a little. All the positive conditioned reflexes were completely annihilated; not one drop of saliva flowed, and the dog refused to take food offered in the customary manner. For a long time we could not guess what was the matter. All our first suppositions about the cause of this phenomenon could not be substantiated. Finally we came upon the idea that the strong effect of the scene of the flood still persisted.

Then we adopted the following course. Our experiments with conditioned reflexes are now usually conducted so that the dog remains alone in the experimental chamber, while the experimenter is seated outside the door in another room. From here the various agents are made to act on the dog: by a certain mechanical device the vessel of food is swung under his nose, and here on the outside of the door are registered the results of the experiment. For this dog we altered the circumstances. Dr Speransky sat quietly inside the room with the dog, but did nothing else, while I, instead of him in the outer room, performed the experiment. The conditioned reflexes, to our great satisfaction, reappeared, and the dog began to take the food. We repeated this experiment (at first rarely and then more often) over a period, and then gradually weakened or modified it by sometimes allowing the dog to remain in the room alone: in this way we restored the animal to his normal condition. Next we tried the effect of a certain component, so to speak, of the inundation, by reproducing it in miniature. Under the door of the experimental chamber we allowed a stream of water to trickle. Perhaps the sound of the running water or its reflection threw the dog into the former pathological state. The conditioned reflexes vanished as before and their restoration had to be brought about by the means employed previously.

Moreover, when the dog had recovered, it was impossible to elicit an effect from the former strongest of all the conditioned stimuli, viz., the bell. It inhibited itself, and afterwards there was inhibition of all the remaining conditioned reflexes. A year elapsed after the flood, and during this time we carefully protected the dog from every kind of extraordinary stimulus. Finally in the autumn (of 1925) we were able to get the old reflex, even to the bell. But after the very first time the reflex began gradually to decrease although it was employed only once a day; and at last it disappeared entirely. At the same time all the remaining reflexes suffered, now temporarily vanishing, now passing into various hypnotic phases ranging between the waking state and sleep, although in this dog the latter state was never fully attained. During this condition of the animal we again tried two methods in order to restore the normal reflexes. The inhibitory reflexes in this dog were, as has been said, stable to an unusual degree. But concerning the well-inhibited stimuli, we know that they are able by induction to strengthen the process of excitation. Therefore we applied those differentiated stimuli (negative, inhibitory) mentioned above. And we actually saw many times that after this the reflexes reappeared and the dog took the food, although before the reflexes had been absent and the food refused, or in the presence of transitory hypnotic stages, under influence of induction, the phase was transposed toward the normal state.

The other method is only a variation of the one described previously. Into the dog's chamber we introduced not the experimenter *in toto* but only a part of his clothing. This was sufficient to increase markedly the reflexes. As the piece of clothing was not visible to the dog it was evidently the scent of it which acted.

To the experimental facts, which I have purposely kept clear of suppositions, it is necessary to add the following. If we turned our attention to the movements of the dog when the conditioned reflexes had disappeared and he refused to eat, then we saw not the food reaction but the *passive defensive*, according to our terminology, or as it would be called ordinarily, the reaction of *fear*. This is particularly striking when the dog falls into one of the hypnotic stages, or as we call them, *paradoxical*, i.e., when only weak conditioned stimuli act, but not the strong ones. With optical stimuli (these are in general weak) there is an evident motor-food reaction, while immediately after with auditory (strong) stimuli there is a striking passive-defensive reflex: the animal moves the head uneasily from side to side, crouches with head hung down, and does not make the slightest movement towards the food box. Nevertheless, the animal when outside the experimental room is very lively and greedy.

The animal described, however, is by no means an exception. We have had several dogs of this type, as I mentioned earlier, upon which the flood and its variations had a similar influence.

I shall now pass on to our interpretation of all the above facts.

For us it is perfectly clear that this type must be the opposite of all other types, in which it is frequently impossible to elaborate full inhibitory reflexes, or in which, although they may be well elaborated, they are very unstable and are quickly impaired. This means that in the described type the inhibitory process is predominant, while in all the remaining types the process of excitation either prevails or is in more or less equilibrium with that of inhibition.

How can we approach to the understanding of this type, and of its deeper mechanism? We recognize as the most constant and general law in the physiology of the conditioned reflexes the fact that an isolated conditioned excitation conducted into the cerebral cells inevitably leads, sooner or later, and sometimes astoundingly quickly, to an inhibitory state of the cells and perhaps even to its uttermost degree – to the sleeping state. This fact can best be understood thus: these cells being extremely sensitive and quick to react, rapidly expend their *excitatory substances* under the influence of stimuli, and then there sets in another process, in a certain degree conserving and economic, the process of inhibition. This process cuts short a further functional destruction of the cell, and thereby accelerates the restoration of the expended substances. In favour of this speaks our fatigue after the day's work. It is removed by sleep, which, as I have shown before, is an overspread inhibition. Evidently the same is proved by the striking fact, demonstrated in our laboratory, that after damage of certain parts of the hemispheres, for a long time it is impossible to obtain positive conditioned reflexes from the receptors (sense organs) connected with these parts, their stimulation producing only an inhibitory effect. And when later a positive effect of these stimuli appears, it lasts for only a short time and quickly passes over into inhibition. This is an effect typical of so-called nervous exhaustion. Here should be mentioned an observation which we made during the recent difficult years of my native country when the state of exhaustion which the dogs shared with us caused them to fall quickly into different stages of inhibition, and finally into sleep, under the influence of the conditioned stimuli, so that there was no possibility of carrying on researches with the positive conditioned reflexes.

We may conclude, therefore, that the cortical cells, in the type of dog we have described, possess only a small reserve of the excitatory substances, or that these substances are extraordinarily destructible.

A state of inhibition in the cortical cells may be produced by either very weak or by very strong stimuli; only with stimuli of average strength may the cells continue for a long time in a state of excitation without passing over into different degrees of inhibition. With weak stimuli the process of excitation passes over into inhibition only slowly, but with strong stimuli the change is rapid. These degrees of strength of stimulus are, of course, relative, i.e., a strong stimulus for one type of nervous system may be only of average strength for another type. The great inundation produced inhibition only in the type under discussion, while on the other dogs it had no perceptible influence. A bell did not act as a strong stimulus on the subject under consideration until the neurosis appeared (which can be put in a class with human traumatic neuroses), but after the flood, which caused the neurosis, the bell acted definitely as a strong stimulus – as an inhibitory one. The same may be stated in regard to one of the normal hypnotic phases, the paradoxical, when only the weak stimuli acted positively, and the strong led to inhibition.

Then it is impossible not to be struck with the resemblance between the passive defensive reflex in dogs and the inhibitory process. And our dog, we observed, possessed a nervous system in which the process of inhibition predominated. The constant presence of this passive defensive reflex is a common and constant characteristic of the general behaviour of such dogs. At the height of development of the neurosis with all conditioned stimuli, and afterwards in the paradoxical phase during the action of only the strong stimuli, the passive defensive reaction constantly occurs. A remarkable thing! Even in dogs which do not as a rule manifest the passive defensive reflex this reaction characteristically appears, nevertheless, during the time of the paradoxical phase in the presence of strong conditioned stimuli.

On these grounds, we may, I think, assume that at the basis of normal *fear* (timidity or cowardice) and in particular of the pathological fears (*phobias*), there lies a predominance of the physiological process of inhibition, an expression of the weakness of the cortical cells. In this connexion I ask you to recall the aforementioned case of induction, when a purely physiological application temporarily removed the inhibition and with it the passive-defensive reflex.

As I gradually analysed the types of nervous systems of various dogs, it seemed to me that they all fitted in well with the classical description of *temperaments*, in particular with their extreme groups, the *sanguine* and the *melancholic*. The first is the type for which there is continually necessary varying stimuli, and furthermore this type indefatigably seeks such stimuli and is itself under these conditions capable of expressing great energy. With monotonous stimuli, however, it quickly and easily falls into a state of drowsiness and sleep. The melancholic type is the one with which we experimented. You recall the extreme representative of this group described in the beginning of my lecture. Is it not natural to consider this as melancholy and to term it so, when at every step, at every moment, the surrounding medium calls forth in the animal always the same passive-defensive reflex?

Between these extremes stand the variations of the balanced or *equilibrated* type, where both the process of excitation and the process of inhibition are of equal and adequate strength, and they interchange promptly and exactly.

Finally, we have come across in our dogs a definite *social* reflex, operative under the influence of an agent of the social surroundings. Dogs and their wild ancestors, wolves, are herd animals, and man, owing to their ancient, historical association together, represents for them a '*Socius*'. Dr Speransky, who always brought this dog into the experimental room, who played with him, fed him and petted him, represented for him a positive conditioned stimulus, heightening the excitatory tonus of the cortex, and dispersing and overcoming the inhibitory tonus. That Dr Speransky acted on the dog only as an external synthetic stimulus, consisting chiefly of optical, auditory and olfactory components, was proved by our recent experiment in which the scent alone of Dr Speransky had the same effect (though, of course, weaker) on the nervous system of the dog as he did himself.

This experiment taken together with other similar experiments, brings us, finally, into the field of social reflexes, which we shall include in the future programme of our experiments. It is hardly possible now to doubt that by the help of the method of conditioned reflexes, for the purely physiological investigation of the activity of the cerebral hemispheres, there is opened a limitless region.

9   N. R. F. Maier, N. M. Glaser and J. B. Klee

Studies of Abnormal Behavior in the Rat. III The Development of Behavior Fixations through Frustration*

N. R. F. Maier, N. M. Glaser and J. B. Klee, 'Studies of abnormal behavior in the rat. III The development of behavior fixations through frustration', *J. exper. Psychol.*, No. 6, vol. 26, (1948), pp. 521–46.

Introduction

Many investigators have observed that the pre-solution period of a discrimination problem is often accompanied by persistent position habits (e.g., see Spence,[15]). Recently Maier and Glaser[10] and Maier[12] have pointed out that a discrimination problem if made insoluble results in position habits which are so strong that they can be abolished only with great difficulty. Since a problem which cannot be solved results in continued frustration, it is of importance to examine these position habits to determine whether they are the product of ordinary mechanisms involved in learning or whether they are an expression of mechanisms related to abnormalities in behavior. We speak of fixation in learning, meaning that habits have been well established, and we speak of fixations in abnormal psychology and mean that non-adaptive forms of behavior have become persistent parts of behavior. In the one sense fixation is a term used in normal psychology; in the other it refers to something abnormal.

It is the purpose of the present study to compare the strength of the same response when produced under the ordinary conditions of learning and when produced under conditions of frustration and see whether the resulting fixations are of the same order.

Methods

The Lashley jumping apparatus was used for establishing the position habits. The essential feature of the technique is to require the animal to leap from a jumping stand at cards placed in the two windows cut in an upright screen. These cards may be latched or unlatched. If the unlatched card is struck it falls over and the animal gains access to food placed on a platform behind the window, but if the latched card is struck the animal

* This study was supported by grants to the senior author from The Horace H. Rackham School of Graduate Studies of the University of Michigan and from the John and Mary R. Markle Foundation of New York City. The authors wish to express to the donors their sincere appreciation for this assistance.

receives a bump on the nose and falls into a net below. The distance between the jumping stand and the card was 9 inches in these experiments.

Preliminary training

To induce animals to jump at the cards in this apparatus requires some preliminary training. The procedure used in these experiments was adapted to suit the purposes of the experiments.

After having been fed on the food platform of the apparatus for the three preceding days, the first stage of training was to place the jumping stand close to the open windows of the apparatus so that the animal could walk across. Gradually the stand was moved back until the animal was required to leap across the gap. The number of trials required to cause the rat to make the leap varied from animal to animal, but in general from 2 to 3 days of 10 trials per day were adequate to accomplish this. Guidance with the hand was used to cause the animals to jump through both windows.

The second stage consisted of placing cards (15 cm. sq.) in the windows. One card contained a black circle (8 cm. in diameter) on a white background, the other a white circle (of the same size) on a black background. These were changed from side to side in an irregular order. During the first trials the cards were so placed as to cover only part of the window and gradually more and more of the card was exposed. Since both cards were unlatched the cards readily fell over whenever struck by the rat. Soon the window could be covered completely by the card and the rat responded by leaping at the card. To prevent the animal from jumping consistently to one side or to one of the cards manual guidance was introduced whenever the animal began to express a preference for one side or one card. This guidance consisted of pushing the rat away from the preferred window or card as soon as it prepared to jump and was continued until each rat readily reacted by jumping at the cards, which now completely covered the windows. In general 2 or 3 days of training were adequate to accomplish this. In a few cases the first stage was repeated if guidance failed to overcome position habits.

During the third stage the procedure consisted of guiding the animal's choices so that an equal number of responses was made to each card and to each position. The choice was thus determined by the experimenter. This procedure was continued for 4 days and 10 trials were given daily. In this stage all animals received identical treatment.

With the preliminary training completed the rats were divided into 3 groups and each was given special training in the establishment of a position habit. This special training was continued until 98 per cent of the last 160 trials were responses to position. Thus the training extended over a period of 8 days or more and 20 trials were given per day. Preliminary experimentation demonstrated that approximately 160 repetitions of the position habit were adequate for producing group difference.

With the introduction of special training, air led by a tube to the jumping stand was used to induce the animals to jump. The air was applied according to the following schedule: (1) no air for 30 seconds, (2) mild air blast for 30 seconds, (3) medium air blast for 30 seconds, and (4) full air pressure (10 to 14 pounds) for the remainder of the period of resistance. (The intensity of the air was conditioned by marked positions on the valve.) As soon as the animal made a choice the air was turned off and the rat's resistance was rated according to the amount of air required to induce a response.

Special training

Group I. Position habit – preferred side. – The rats in this group, after choosing either the right or left card on their first free choice after the above preliminary training, were forced to continue to respond to the same side. This was done by latching the window on the side opposite to that chosen on the animal's first jump (e.g., if an animal jumped through the right window on its first jump to a card the left window was thereafter latched). Thus a jump to the other side became associated with striking a card fixed in position with the resulting bump on the nose and fall to the net below. The cards were changed from side to side in an irregular sequence so that position rather than the character of the card became associated with success.

Group II. Position habit – reversed preference. – This group of rats was treated in a manner similar to Group I except that both windows were latched on the first jump and the side to which the rat jumped became the latched side thereafter. If the first jump is considered to be an expression of a natural preference the rats in this group were required to form a position habit which was opposed to their natural preferences, whereas the rats in Group I formed position habits which coincided with their natural preferences. In both groups a consistent response to position was rewarded 100 per cent of the time.

Group III. No-solution problem. – In this group the experimenter locked one of the windows at the outset. Thereafter either the right or left window was latched in a random order. As above, the cards were changed from side to side in an irregular sequence. In each series of trials the two sides and the two cards were latched and unlatched an equal number of times. This group was thus rewarded on half its trials and punished on the other half no matter on what basis the choices were made. This situation readily resulted in the appearance of position habits in 11 out of 13 animals. The two others reacted on the basis of the characteristics of the card and were excluded to make possible comparisons with Groups I and II.

Tests on the persistence of the position habit

Since each of the groups developed position habits the following tests were designed to measure the strength of the habit in each of the groups.

Discrimination problem. – Upon completion of the special training all rats were presented with a discrimination problem. The card with the black circle on the white background was made the positive stimulus and a response to it led to reward whether on the right or left side, whereas the card with the white circle on the black background was made negative and a response to it always led to punishment. Under ordinary conditions of learning the average rat in our colony requires 88 trials before making 30 consecutive errorless jumps. To allow ample time for learning the three groups of rats were therefore given 200 trials (20 trials per day) to learn this problem. If the animals persisted in their position habits under these conditions they received punishment on 50 per cent of their trials. For Groups I and II this would result in a change in their pattern of punishment and for Group III the proportion of punishment would remain the same but punishment would now occur in an orderly fashion.

Position response consistently punished. – Animals failing to show evidence of learning the discrimination problem were transferred to a new problem in which the negative card was always on the side to which they reacted consistently and of course this card was always latched (e.g., an animal with a right position habit always received punishment when it chose the negative card on the right). This problem was continued for 10 days and 10 trials were given daily. Clearly this manner of punishment should have discouraged the position habit and encouraged the formation of a response based upon the characteristics of the card.

Subjects Used

Complete records were obtained on a total of 31 rats. Groups I and II each contained 10 animals and Group III contained 11. The age range was from 4–9 months and the average age for Groups I, II, and III was 5·4 months, 6·4 months, and 5·6 months respectively. Of the 31 animals 21 were males and 10 were females. The proportions of males to females for Groups I to III were 7:3, 6:4, and 8:3, respectively. Both white and pigmented animals chosen from the regular laboratory colony were used.

Results

Comparison of groups in the persistence of the position habit – Maier[11] has pointed out that the fixation of a response may be measured by the resistance which a given mode of behavior shows to modification. Since all of our groups of rats developed position habits and since this mode of response was repeated without alteration for about 160 consecutive trials (the criterion was a response to a position in 98 per cent of the 160 trials) these groups may be compared in their degree of fixation. Because the introduction of the discrimination problem makes possible a new form of behavior which is adaptive in nature one might expect the adaptive response to be learned and the unadaptive response to be replaced by it. If such a change in the habit fails to take place one might expect that 100 percent punishment of a fixated response would cause it to be abandoned. If both treatments fail to cause a given mode of behavior to be abandoned one must recognize the existence of a kind of fixation which requires careful analysis since it is not deducible from our knowledge of learning.

Table 1 shows that all but one of the rats in Group I abandoned the position habit during the 200 trials but only 4 of the 11 rats in Group III made this adjustment. The rats in Group II fall between these extremes but are more similar to Group III than to Group I.

The females seem to have a greater tendency than males to persist in their position habits since 6 out of 10 females persisted and only 7 out of 21 males did so. Since Group III had the smallest percentage of females, the difference between Groups II and III is perhaps greater than shown in Table 1. Considering males only, 1 of 7 in Group I, 2 of 6 in Group II and 4 of 8 in Group III persisted.

If the animals in each of the groups differ in the relative amount of persistence, then more drastic treatment should cause additional animals to abandon their position habits. The last column

Table 1
Comparison of Groups in Extent of Fixation

Group	Number of Rats Learning Discrimination	Number of Rats Failing to Learn Discrimination	Number of Rats Persisting after 100 Percent Punishment
I	9	1	1
II	5	5	5
III	4	7	7

of Table 1 shows that this was not the case, however. Animals which failed to learn the discrimination continued to show a position response throughout the 100 punishment trials as well as during the 200 trials on the discrimination problem. This suggests an all or nothing character of the persistence of the positional response.

We may also study the animals which learned the problem and compare the groups with regard to the readiness with which these animals formed the discrimination habit.

From Table 2 we see that the position habit was abandoned after 55 trials in the case of Group I, after 49·8 trials in the case of Group II, and after 98·0 trials in the case of Group III. With respect to the animals which learned, Groups I and II are approximately alike and differ from Group III to the extent that the score ranges show practically no overlapping (only one case in Group I

Table 2
Trials Required to Learn the Discrimination Habit

Group	Percent Solving Discrimination Problem	Average Number of Trials in Which Position Habit Persists	Range	Average Number of Additional Trials to Reach Criterion (Exclusive of Criterion Trials)
I	90·0%	55·0	20–105	27·2
II	50·0%	49·8	21–80	16·2
III	36·4%	98·0	85–117	4·5

falls within the score range of Group III). In all cases, however, in which learning occurs it takes place well before the end of the 200 trials allowed for learning. Thus the animals which learn and those which persist in the position habit seem to differ qualitatively, a point which further substantiates the conclusion that persistence may take on an all or nothing character.

The groups also differ in the manner in which the new discrimination is established once the position habit is abandoned. This is shown in the last column of Table 2. Group I requires an average of 27·2 trials before it consistently reacts to the positive card; Group II requires 16·2 trials; and Group III requires only 4·5 trials. Thus Group III shows sudden learning after abandoning the position habit, despite the fact that it is more reluctant to abandon it.

To throw further light on the group differences as well as on the question of the all or nothing character of the learning within the groups let us turn to the original learning of the position habit. These data are shown in Table 3. It will readily be seen that Group I, whose position habit corresponded to its preference, continued to react on the basis of this preference without ever adopting another mode of response. Group II on the average required 9 trials before it settled down to a positional response opposite to its first reaction. Group III, which was punished on half its trials no matter upon what its reaction was based, reacted in terms of position after 20 trials.

We may therefore say that Group III had the greatest opportunity to eliminate alternative modes of behavior (hypotheses) before consistently reacting to position. The position habit thus

becomes a last resort and resists being displaced by another reaction tendency. The elimination of certain behavior tendencies
at the outset explains why Group III rats are the slowest learners
on the discrimination problem and may also explain why this
group has the smallest number of learners. The fact that the
animals of this group which solved the discrimination problem
formed their position habit after 7·5 trials and those which failed

Table 3
Trials Required to Form Position Habit

| | Average Number of Trials Before Criterion is Reached (98 Percent in 160 Trials) | | |
	All Animals	Animals Solving Discrimination Problem	Animals not Solving Discrimination Problem
Group I	0	0	0
Group II	9	8	10
Group III	20	7·5	27·1

to solve formed their position habit after 27·1 trials supports this
interpretation. The explanation for the sudden learning of the
animals which learned the discrimination in Group III is also
simplified if we grant that certain behavior tendencies have
already been eliminated. Krechevsky[9] has shown that during
the pre-solution period a problem may be changed without reduc-
ing the final rate of learning.

A similar analysis may be applied to Group II. The average
number of trials preceding the formation of the position habit for
the animals in this group lies between that of Groups I and III and
their tendency to persist in the position habit also lies between
these two groups. The learners and non-learners, however, are
not differentiated here.

Evidence for suppressed learning of the discrimination

As already pointed out the introduction of the discrimination
problem changed the pattern of punishment and reward for
Groups I and II but since Group III was previously punished half
the time the proportion of reward and punishment remained the
same for it. Thus it might be said that Group III tended not to
learn the discrimination problem because the opportunity for
learning did not become apparent and hence there was no reason

for abandoning the mode of behavior which was established. If this explanation is sound then Groups I and II should have learned the discrimination problem equally well. Further Group III should have abandoned the position habit when 100 per cent punishment of the position habit was introduced since this condition changed the pattern of punishment. On both of these counts the experimental findings are in disagreement with the demands of this theory.

As a matter of fact it can be demonstrated that the animals which failed to abandon their position habits actually learned the discrimination.

Throughout the experiment the resistance to jumping was overcome by the application of the air blast. By increasing the air intensity at certain intervals, ratings for resistance could be made on the basis of the length of resistance and air intensity used before the jump occurred. The following ratings for resistance were used:

Rating 0.	No air.	Jump occurring between	0– 30 sec.
Rating 1.	Mild air blast.	Jump occurring between	31– 35 sec.
Rating 2.	Mild air blast.	Jump occurring between	36– 60 sec.
Rating 3.	Medium blast.	Jump occurring between	61– 90 sec.
Rating 4.	Full blast.	Jump occurring between	91–120 sec.
Rating 5.	Full blast.	Jump occurring between	120–150 sec.

If a rat always jumped to one side but consistently showed greater resistance to jumping when one of the cards was on the position-response side than when the other card was on that side, then a discrimination between the cards must have been made. We have therefore analyzed the resistance shown to the positive and negative cards during the discrimination test to determine whether the animals which failed to choose the positive card expressed greater resistance for the negative than for the positive card.

For comparison we have also studied the resistance to the two cards during the special training period to see whether a preference for one of the cards was evident before reward and punishment were introduced in connexion with one of the cards. These results are shown in Table 4. For each group of rats the average resistance to each card as well as the difference in resistance is shown. It will be seen that all 3 groups failed to show differential resistance to the two cards during the special training period in which the position habit was being established. The groups differ somewhat in the amount of resistance, however. Group I had a rating of practically zero which means that this group responded before air was applied. However, the data on this group have limited value since

Table 4
Resistance Behavior of Rats Persisting in Position Habits

Number of Trials	Group I (1 rat) Average Resistance Rating			Group II (5 rats) Average Resistance Rating			Group III (7 rats) Average Resistance Rating		
	Positive Card	Negative Card	Difference	Positive Card	Negative Card	Difference	Positive Card	Negative Card	Difference
Special Training Period									
160	0	·01	·01	·57	·55	–·02	·82	·91	·09
Discrimination Problem. Position Habit Punished on Half the Trials									
1–40	2·00	2·05	·05	1·05	1·07	·02	·89	·95	·06
41–80	1·60	3·10	1·50	·76	1·41	·65	·68	1·04	·36
81–120	1·55	3·15	1·60	·97	1·72	·75	·65	1·52	·87
121–160	·55	3·80	3·25	1·17	1·74	·57	·80	1·66	·86
161–200	·40	3·10	2·70	·80	1·88	1·08	·68	1·62	·94
Average	1·22	3·04	1·82	·95	1·56	·61	·74	1·36	·62
Position Habit Punished on All Trials									
1–40	Data not			1·72			1·58		
41–80	available			1·78			1·82		
81–100				1·42			2·36		
Average				1·68			1·83		

they are based on one rat, all the others having learned the problem. Group II with a rating of a little over 0·5 required air about half the time and Group III, which was punished on half its trials, had a resistance rating of nearly 1 which means that on the average these rats jumped as soon as air was applied.

As soon as the discrimination problem was introduced all groups of rats were punished on half the trials until they solved the discrimination problem. As a consequence resistance immediately rose for rats in Groups I and II which experienced a change in the punishment pattern and remained about the same for Group III which had no change in the frequency of punishment.

With the introduction of the discrimination problem the black circle on the white card became the positive stimulus and the white circle on the black card became the negative stimulus. Since all rats consistently jumped to the right or left side they were punished whenever the negative card appeared on the side of the positional response. In order to show the change in the relative resistance to jumping at the positive and negative cards the data on resistance are given for each 40 trials.

From Table 4 it will be seen that during the first 40 trials the resistance to the two cards was about the same. The next four groups of 40 trials, however, show a change in the relative resistance which is maintained throughout the remaining 160 trials. The difference in reaction in all groups is due in part to the increase in resistance for the negative card and in part to a reduction in resistance for the positive card.

When the position habit is punished 100 per cent of the time rather than 50 per cent, as was the case during the discrimination problem period, only a slight increase in resistance to jumping to the negative card occurs despite the fact that the expectancy of punishment for each positional response increases. Brunswik[1] has shown that the probability of reward and punishment is a determining factor in learning and under ordinary circumstances such a change in procedure should have an influence on behavior.

The data on resistance analyzed above show that a discrimination response has been superimposed upon the position habit. Apparently a choice based on the difference between the cards is not able to replace the position habit and thus the differentiation expresses itself in the resistance to jumping to the negative card.

For rats solving the problem the data on resistance must be treated somewhat differently since the number of trials to solve varied from individual to individual. We have, therefore, broken the discrimination period into three parts: (a) the pre-solution phase during which the position habit persisted; (b) the solution phase during which the position habit was abandoned and before the positive card was consistently chosen; and (c) the criterion phase during which the positive card was consistently chosen. Since these animals abandoned the position habit and learned the discrimination they were not presented with the period in which the position habit was punished 100 per cent of the time.

The data for these animals are given in Table 5. As in the case of rats not solving the discrimination problem the resistance behavior towards the two cards is about the same during the special training and is higher for rats in Group III which received punishment for their position responses.

With the introduction of the discrimination problem only a slight difference in resistance for the positive and negative cards appears during the period in which the position habit continues to function. Table 5 shows these differences to be 0·17, 0·36, and 0·45, for Groups I, II and III respectively, whereas Table 4 showed differences of 1·82, 0·61 and 0·62 for the non-solving animals in these same groups.

Table 5
Resistance Behavior of Rats Which Abandoned the Position Habit for the Discrimination Habit

Number of Trials	Group I (9 rats) Average Resistance Rating			Group II (5 rats) Average Resistance Rating			Group III (4 rats) Average Resistance Rating		
	Positive Card	Negative Card	Difference	Positive Card	Negative Card	Difference	Positive Card	Negative Card	Difference
Special Training Period									
160	·30	·31	·01	·30	·45	·15	·18	·92	·04
Discrimination Problem. Position Habit Punished on Half the Trials									
Pre-solution phase	·88	1·05	·17	·63	·99	·36	·89	1·34	·45
Solution phase	1·00	·60	−·40	·93	1·25	·32	·88	0	−·88
Criterion phase	·67			·65			1·13		

During the solution period the resistance to the negative card rises for Group II but falls in the cases of Groups I and III. However, these differences in resistance to the two cards have little significance since very few responses were made to the negative card after the positional responses were discontinued. As shown in Table 2, Group I, after abandoning the position habit, learned in an average of 27·2 trials; Group II in 16·2 trials; and Group III in 4·5 trials. As a consequence of this rapid learning the average number of responses to the negative card during the solution period was 3·6 for Group I, 1·6 for Group II, and 0·25 for Group III.

Thus we see that although the discrimination learning was slightly expressed during the pre-solution phase the position habit was discontinued before the differential resistance became as pronounced as in the case of animals failing to solve. This fact clearly shows that the animals which failed to solve the discrimination problem failed because they were unable to abandon their position habits and not because they did not sufficiently differentiate between the positive and negative cards.

After the animals solved the problem and consistently chose the positive card (the criterion phase) the resistance to jumping showed no change of sufficient magnitude to require elucidation.

Evidence for discrimination on the part of animals failing to abandon the position habit may also be derived from their manner of jumping to the negative and positive cards. Abortive jumps, consisting of (a) jumps to the ledge, (b) striking the card with the side of the body, (c) leaps to the right or left of the cards, and (d) jumps which are very light and not adequate for knocking over an unlatched card, often replace the normal response which consists of a fairly vigorous leap at the center of the card. We have therefore analyzed the data to determine the percentage of abortive responses to each of the cards. These data are presented in Table 6.

This table shows that during the special training abortive behavior was practically absent with the exception of Group III, which received punishment on half the trials and in which nearly 10 per cent of the responses were abortive. With the introduction of the discrimination problem abortive behavior became more common and became applied to the negative card. Groups I and II showed a differential response to the two cards after 80 trials and Group III after 40 trials. Thus all groups expressed a discrimination between the two cards by developing an abortive response for the negative card although this expression of the discrimination occurred somewhat later than the differential resistance (see Table 4).

With the introduction of the period of 100 per cent punishment Groups II and III showed an increase in abortive behavior and for Group II it rose as high as 83·6 per cent. These data are not available for Group I, and since only one rat in this group failed to solve the problem the figures for Group I should be taken as an individual rather than as a group trend.

It appears that abortive behavior is a form of adjustment to the situation. The fact that Group II showed a high percentage of such behavior in the 100 per cent punishment series with very little rise in resistance, whereas Group III showed a lesser per cent of abortive behavior and a significant rise in resistance during this period, supports this contention.

Table 6
Abortive Behavior of Rats Persisting in Position Habits

Number of Trials	Group I (1 rat) Per cent Abortive Jumps			Group II (5 rats) Per cent Abortive Jumps			Group III (7 rats) Per cent Abortive Jumps		
	Positive Card	Negative Card	Difference	Positive Card	Negative Card	Difference	Positive Card	Negative Card	Difference
Special Training Period									
160	0	0	0	4·8	4·1	–·7	9·7	9·6	–·1
Discrimination Problem. Position Habit Punished on Half the Trials									
1–40	0	0	0	19	13	–6	13	14	1
41–80	0	0	0	5	4	–1	0	11	11
81–120	0	20	20	7	27	20	0	19	19
121–160	0	95	95	1	58	57	0	23	23
161–200	0	95	95	1	54	53	1	37	36
Average	0	42	42	6·6	31·2	24·6	2·8	20·8	18·0
Position Habit Punished on All Trials									
1–40	Data not			71			32		
41–80	available			90			41		
81–100				96			42		
Average				83·6			37·6		

The abortive behavior of animals solving the discrimination problem is shown in Table 7. As in the case of animals failing to solve this problem these animals show practically no abortive behavior during the special training but unlike them, these animals do not develop it as a differential reaction when the discrimination problem is introduced. Groups I and II apparently learn the discrimination before abortive behavior appears and Group III (which required about twice as many trials as Groups I and II for learning the discrimination [see Table 2]) shows abortive behavior for both cards but this behavior drops out as evidence for learning appears. Apparently the abortive behavior appears only after a certain amount of frustration and ceases as soon as an adjustment occurs. The animals which fail to solve persist in abortive behavior not because they cannot react differentially to the two cards but because they cannot achieve an adjustment as long as the position habit dominates their behavior.

Table 7
Abortive Behavior of Rats Which Abandoned the Position Habit for the Discrimination Habit

Number of Trials	Group I (9 rats) Per cent Abortive Jumps			Group II (5 rats) Per cent Abortive Jumps			Group III (4 rats) Per cent Abortive Jumps		
	Positive Card	Negative Card	Difference	Positive Card	Negative Card	Difference	Positive Card	Negative Card	Difference
Special Training Period									
160	·3	0	−·3	1·5	1·5	0	2·2	2·9	·7
Discrimination Problem. Position Habit Punished on Half the Trials									
Pre-solution phase	4	5	1	1	0	−1	23	28	5
Solution phase	1	0	−1	0	0	0	0	0	0
Criterion phase	3			0			0		

The evidence on resistance and abortive jumping shows that the animals failing to solve the discrimination problem actually formed the discrimination and expressed the discrimination by reacting differently to the positive and negative cards. Of the 13 animals in the three groups which failed to abandon the position habit, 9 expressed their differentiation both in their resistance and in their abortive behavior, 3 in their resistance behavior only, and 1 in its abortive behavior only. In no case did an individual fail to express a differentiation between the cards.

Although a variety of forms of abortive behavior appeared in these experiments each animal developed its own individual abortive pattern to which it strictly adhered.

Additional experiments on frustration

Thus far our experiment has been carried to the point of demonstrating the unusual persistence of a habit produced by frustration. To throw further light on behavior arising from frustration, 4 additional animals were studied over a longer period of time. During this period the effects of breaking the position habits was also studied.

In 2 animals (rats 1 and 2) the no-solution problem was introduced after the animal was trained to jump and was continued for 450 trials (20 trials per day). One of the cards contained a large black circle and the other a small black circle and both were on grey backgrounds. The position of the cards was changed irregularly and either one or the other was latched on each trial. One rat immediately took a left position habit going left 9 times in the first 10 trials and to the left on the remaining 440 trials. The other likewise chose the left 9 times on the first 10 trials, then chose both sides, but after 30 trials it always chose the card to the right.

After this period of frustration the card with the large circle was made positive. For the next 460 trials both rats continued to choose on the basis of position, never once deviating from this mode of behavior.

The window opposite the position preference was then left without a card and the rats were induced by means of guidance to jump through the open window. After 20 such trials the positive card (large circle) was placed in the open window. Both rats chose the positive card and continued to choose it during the next 120 trials regardless of the side on which it was placed.

The no-solution problem was then introduced again and for 200 trials both of the rats consistently chose the positive card of the discrimination.

In this experiment persistence behavior was shown to appear in the no-solution problem on both occasions, but on the first occasion the position habit persisted and on the second the discrimination persisted. Thus persistence may be shown for an obviously acquired preference as well as for what may appear to be a natural preference, and hence the persistence behavior must be regarded as a product of frustration rather than the expression of any natural strength the position habit may possess. In the previous experiment it was shown that there was greater persistence for a position habit which opposed the animal's natural preference than for one which corresponded to it.

To further isolate the causes that determine which habit will persist the remaining 2 rats (numbers 3 and 4) were tested in the following manner.

A discrimination between the small black circle and the large black circle on grey backgrounds was established, the former being the positive stimulus. After the discrimination was established to the criterion of 30 errorless trials the no-solution problem was introduced. Rat 3 lost the discrimination habit after 140 trials and rat 4 after 40 trials and both reacted thereafter by showing left positional reactions. Rat 3 was given 250 trials and rat 4, 80 trials, and both consistently reacted on the basis of position during this period.

The original discrimination problem was then reintroduced. Rat 3 continued its position habit for the 330 trials it was tested and Rat 4, for the 150 trials it was given.

Since neither of the animals deviated from the position habit, the response was broken by means of the open window procedure described above. As soon as the positional response was abandoned reactions on the basis of the discrimination appeared without any pre-solution trials. Rat 3 was given 80 repetitions and Rat 4, 150, and both consistently chose the card with the small circle.

The no-solution problem was again introduced. Both rats failed to abandon the now irrelevant discrimination habit although Rat 3 was given 450 trials and Rat 4, 630 trials.

The experiments on Rats 3 and 4 show that frustration produces a position habit even when preceded by a discrimination. It is only when the fixation of the position habit has been broken that the rats fail to return to it. In such cases frustration results in the persistence of some other mode of behavior. In both forms of behavior the persistence is abnormally strong and can be broken only by special means. Ordinary conditions for learning do not furnish the necessary instigation for abandoning the habit which becomes fixated. It is only when an alternative is specifically presented by the experimenter (guidance) that a shift in response is made. The animals' own resources apparently are not adequate for taking an alternative even when the inadequacy of a response is experienced repeatedly. This conclusion is supported by observations on additional rats not included in this study.

Discussion

The nature of abnormal fixations
We have found that some animals show a marked reluctance to abandon their position habits. This persistence in a mode of

behavior has an abnormal appearance for the following reasons:

1. Animals persisting and those not persisting form a distinctly bimodal distribution in the sense that all of the latter abandon the position habit in 117 trials or less and all of the former fail to abandon it in 200 trials. Even the addition of 100 trials of 100 per cent punishment fails to destroy the persistence of the position habit.

2. Inability to distinguish between the positive and negative cards does not account for the failure to learn the discrimination habit. The analysis of resistance and of abortive behavior revealed that each animal which failed to form the discrimination habit actually learned the discrimination. Failure to express this discrimination seemed to be due to the dominance of the position habit. Thus the discrimination, even when present, was unable to break through the position habit.

3. Ordinarily the strength of a habit varies with the frequency with which a response has been rewarded. Brunswik[1] has demonstrated varying rates of learning by varying the proportion of reward for the positive card and punishment for the negative. In the present experiment the condition of 50 per cent reward and 50 per cent punishment for the position habit produced a position habit of greater tenacity than did an equal number of trials with 100 per cent reward. Such a condition should produce no learning if we are to accept the principles of learning supported by many studies. Hence the fixation here produced cannot be of the same kind as the fixation produced under ordinary conditions of learning.

To reconcile these results with those of other experiments it is necessary to postulate a different mechanism which has been brought to expression. Our Group III and to some extent our Group II animals were in a frustrating situation. If we suppose that frustration may lead to fixation, this fixation may be of a qualitatively different nature than that produced by learning. In the sense that such fixations are not the ordinary ones produced by learning they may be called abnormal fixations. Frustrations also lead to other forms of behavior which have been called abnormal (and in a sense extreme resistance and abortive jumping are abnormal) and it therefore seems justified to so classify these fixations. Case histories of neurotic people contain much evidence of persistence of unsuccessful modes of behavior and when these arise through frustration they are readily classified as belonging to the abnormal.

4. Although positional responses usually occur in frustrating

situations, fixations are not limited to this mode of behavior. The experiment on the last four rats shows that a discrimination habit may also become fixated but this occurs only after the position fixation has been abandoned. Once a fixation is abandoned there seems to be no tendency to return to it. Rather the fixation shifts to another mode of behavior which is in the animal's repertoire. In each case the basic cause of the abnormal fixation seems to be the no-solution problem which is frustrating.

5. The abandonment of a fixation occurs suddenly if at all and then it constitutes a shift to a different mode of behaving. This fact is illustrated by the behavior of the four animals which were extensively studied and by the sudden learning of the Group III animals which abandoned their position habits. The corresponding animals in Groups I and II which were frustrated to a lesser degree abandoned their position habits after experiencing failure and before a new habit was found. They therefore required trials in which to learn a new response. Thus the animal which forms an abnormal fixation retains its mode of behavior until another is substituted. In this sense the fixation is an adjustment which the animal retains and as a consequence it is incapable of further learning by trial and error under the usual conditions for learning.

6. Because all pre-solution periods in learning are in essence no-solution problems for a time one might expect fixations to occur in all learning situations. This, however, is not the case. Apparently frustration leads to fixation only when it reaches a certain point (let us say a point of saturation for that individual). To put it differently, continued failure causes the animal to 'give up' and when this point is reached the mastery of a new problem no longer takes place. Instead the animal has formed an adjustment which is a fixed mode of behaving.

That individual differences occur is apparent from our results. All animals in Group III did not develop fixations and one animal in Group I did form a fixation. Everall[3] pointed out that some animals perseverate no matter what the conditions are and Hamilton and Krechevsky[6] selected their animals to avoid such individuals. Because some animals are so prone to fixation we feel justified in confining our discussion to the role played by the situation in producing fixations.

Since we believe that frustration must reach a saturation point in order to become effective, we are inclined to disagree with the stimulating volume by Dollard, Doob, Miller, Mowrer, and Sears[2] in so far as these authors insist that all unrewarded experiences are frustrating. We prefer to limit the term frustration to designate the state where continued failure causes learning functions to cease operating and other mechanisms of adjustment to begin operating. In this sense abnormal behavior becomes qualitatively different from normal.

Fixation and regression

Although our experiments have been confined to the study of fixations, they show a similarity to some recent experiments on regression in which punishments caused rats to abandon one mode of behavior and fixate a previously learned habit. The strength of the fixation was not determined in these studies, but rather they were pointed to bring out the regressive feature of behavior. Since our experiments demonstrate the continuance of a given mode of behavior during frustration, it is desirable to compare methods and results to see if the apparent difference in the findings can be clarified.

Hamilton and Krechevsky[6] developed in rats a preference for a right turning response in a simple maze and then altered the situation and developed a left turning response. When shocked at the choice-point 11 out of 18 rats consistently chose the right turn as in the first habit and discontinued the second habit. When animals with no previous training were shocked a good proportion of them showed consistent position preferences. These authors speak of the fixation of the earlier habit as regression. Everall[3] raised the question whether the reversion was to an earlier response or to some natural preference and concluded the former to be the case.

Sanders[14] used a similar procedure and in addition to verifying the earlier work found that the relative strengths of the two position habits had no effect on the tendency to revert to an earlier habit. Furthermore shocking the rats during the second habit caused reversion to the first but when the first habit was again established the introduction of electric shock failed to cause a reversion to the second habit. She therefore believes that regression rather than disinhibition is demonstrated by these experiments.

The fixation of behavior described in the above experiments has been produced by electric shock and the authors believe the emotional effect produced by the shock to be responsible. Hamilton,[5] some years ago, emphasized the perseverative effect of emotional excitement on behavior. Recently Patrick[13] verified Hamilton's work by demonstrating that college students become less rational and more random and stereotyped during emotional excitement. Our experiments have likewise demon-strated fixation but the causal factor seems to be frustration. It is possible that emotion is involved in both cases but in our experiment the accumulative effect rather than the direct arousal of intense emotional excitement has been the dominant feature. Furthermore our fixations have shown greater resistance to change. Even when animals developed a discrimination and had an adaptive mode of behavior available the fixated response dominated the choices of the animals.

It is not our opinion that we have demonstrated regression in behavior. Rather we have found that frustration causes a position habit to become fixated. Once a position fixation is broken, however, another mode of behavior can become equally fixated and in this respect our findings differ from those of Sanders. Any situation which disrupts one mode of behavior must give rise to another and this other available mode of behavior may be a previous one. The appearance of a previous mode of behavior, however, is not necessarily evidence for regression if by regression one wishes the term to imply a reversion to a more primitive behavior tendency. To demonstrate that the reversion is a return to primitive behavior supplementary evidence should be pre-sented which indicates that the behavior is not only an earlier form but a more primitive form.

Because the work on regression has dealt with position habits and because we have found that these become formed and fixated in a frustrating situation, the appearance of a position habit may not be a return to an earlier response but rather the formation of a new one which happens to correspond with the position habit previously formed.

In all of the above experiments animals learned a right position habit and then a left position habit. When shocked they responded with the right position habit. If another group had formed the left position habit only and if it was then shocked, would this group also respond by going to the right in the same proportion? If so the shock would seem to cause the abandoning of one position habit and the appearance of a new one. The appearance of the right position habit in the first case would then not seem to be a return to an earlier habit but rather the formation of a new habit which happened to correspond with the first.

Sanders' inability to cause a return to the second habit may be due to the fact that the same animals had previously abandoned this habit in the punishment situation. This could be tested by developing a left position habit, then, a right, and then retraining on the left habit. After this retraining, would shock cause a right going habit to appear? According to Sanders' interpretation, the left habit should continue since the left habit was the earliest. We suspect that in this case the right habit would appear.

Of course one may say that all animals have natural position preferences which are the earliest and most primitive modes of behaving. Hence the formation of a position habit is a regression to these early tendencies. We have shown, however, that the size discrimination habit may become fixated and this form of reaction is far from primitive since such a habit is learned by rats with considerable difficulty. We therefore believe that fixation but not necessarily regression has occurred in our experiments, and it is possible that the same interpretation holds for the punishment experiments since the regressive feature may be an artifact due to the use of position habits. In any case the relationship between fixation and regression must be studied further and for the present we wish only to make a case for fixation.

Humphreys[7] has recently shown that a conditioned eyelid response in the human is more difficult to extinguish if it is formed on the basis of 50 per cent reinforcement than if formed on the basis of 100 per cent reinforcement. This is true even when the number of reinforcement trials are equated in the two conditions. Humphreys[8] explains this on the basis of expectancy of reinforcement. A response which is reinforced part of the time continues to be effective when reinforcement is completely withdrawn because reinforcement is not always expected and hence failure is not demonstrated. But when reinforcement is withdrawn from individuals which have experienced reinforcement on all occasions a change in experimental conditions is more readily apparent to the subject. The mechanism of expectancy could explain why our Group III animals which did not fixate learned the discrimination less readily than the corresponding animals in Groups I and II but it would not account for our fixations.

Humphreys' findings are consistent with the implication that persistence is due to the tendency not to vary behavior. Maier[11] has pointed out that behavior may continue unaltered either because variability in behavior is not called out in the situation or because a particular response tends to dominate over other modes of behavior. The latter form of behavior should be called stereotypy since it dominates because of its own properties rather than because other behavior alternatives were not called out. Humphreys' form of persistence is evidence for a response which continues because nothing in the situation calls out a different form of behavior. In our experiments we have shown that another form of behavior (discrimination) had actually been aroused but failed to come to complete expression because the position habit could not be replaced. As a consequence the new form of behavior became superimposed upon the position habit. We are therefore inclined to believe that Humphreys was not dealing with an abnormal form of fixation. This is also shown by the fact that all his subjects finally did extinguish the conditioned response, and only additional trials were required by the 50 per cent reinforcement group.

Gottsdanker[4] studied the fixation of college students in a multiple choice problem in which each of a certain group of keys was correct 75 per cent of the time. He found that blindfolded students were more disposed than non-blindfolded ones to confine their choices to a particular key rather than to the group of keys which had the same probability of being correct. He concluded that the fixation was 'explainable on the basis of lack of differentiation among choice possibilities on the part of the subjects.' Since our animals which fixated did show a differentiation between the choice possibilities this explanation does not hold for our data.

Because fixation is both a concept in learning and in abnormal behavior and because the mechanisms upon which these fixations depend are very probably quite different, it is important to differentiate between them. The belief that fixations appearing in certain experimental conditions invalidate the laws of learning is reasonable only when such a distinction is not made. The postulation of two kinds of fixations seems more sound than the throwing aside of a large body of concepts developed through ordinary learning experiments.

Summary

In this experiment rats were forced, by means of an air blast, to choose between 2 cards in the Lashley jumping apparatus. When the problem was insolvable position habits were formed, the strengths of which were greater than those of position habits formed under the usual conditions of learning.

A study of the persistence of position habits formed under 3 experimental conditions revealed that animals in each group could be classified into (a) those which solved a new discrimination problem readily and (b) those which failed to solve the new problem in more than ample learning time. Even the addition of 100 trials of 100 per cent punishment failed to cause a displacement of the persistent type of position habit. Since no intermediate cases were found it became evident that we were dealing with a discontinuous distribution of individual characteristics. This led us to postulate that the fixations in many individuals take on an abnormal character.

The data were then analyzed to determine the cause of the persistence of the position habits. It was shown that the animals which fixated actually solved the discrimination problem but nevertheless continued their positional behavior. In such cases the discrimination was evidenced by (a) the differential resistance to jumping to the positive and negative stimulus cards (when they appeared on the position side) and (b) the different manner (normal or abortive) in which the animals jumped at these two cards. Thus the discrimination habit became superimposed on a fixated position habit. This demonstrated that the persistence of the position habits was not due to the absence of alternative modes of behavior but rather to the strength of the position habit.

Since all learning situations involve some frustration and since a no-solution situation involves greater frustration than solvable problems, the fixation behavior became explainable only when we postulated that fixation is the result of frustration. The individual differences were explained by considering frustration as accumulative. Only when failure is repeated to the point of the individual's level of tolerance does it constitute frustration; but once the level of frustration is achieved, fixation appears.

Under ordinary conditions the fixation expressed itself as a persistent position habit. It is only when the position fixation was broken that another mode of behavior became fixated. When this occurred the other fixation also was of abnormal strength.

The data were also considered in relation to regression produced in situations of emotional stress and although certain doubts concerning regression were entertained no definite conclusion was expressed.

The consequences of frustration must be distinguished from those of conflict since frustration as such does not appear to result in experimental neurosis.

References
  1. Brunswik, E., Probability as a determiner of rat behavior, *J. exper. Psychol.*, 1939, **25**, 175–97.
  2. Dollard, J., Doob, L. W., Miller, N. E., Mowrer, O. H., and Sears, R. R., *Frustration and aggression*, New Haven; 1939, Yale Univ. Press, 209.
  3. Everall, E. E., Perseveration in the rat, *J. comp. Psychol.*, 1935, **19**, 343–69.

4. Gottsdanker, R. M., An experimental study of fixation of response by college students in a multiple-choice situation, *J. exper. Psychol.*, 1939, **25**, 431–44.

5. Hamilton, G. V., A study of perseverance reactions in primates and rodents, *Behav. Monogr.*, 1916, **3**, 65.

6. Hamilton, J. A., and Krechevsky, I., Studies in the effect of shock upon behavior plasticity in the rat, *J. comp. Psychol.*, 1933, **16**, 237–53.

7. Humphreys, L. G., The effect of random alternation of reinforcement on the acquisition and extinction of conditioned eyelid reactions, *J. exper. Psychol.*, 1939, **25**, 141–58.

8. Humphreys, L. G., Acquisition and extinction of verbal expectations in a situation analogous to conditioning, *J. exper. Psychol.*, 1939, **25**, 294–301.

9. Krechevsky, I., A study of the continuity of the problem-solving process, *Psychol. Rev.*, 1938, **45**, 107–133.

10. Maier, N. R. F., and Glaser, N. M., Experimentally produced neurotic behavior in the rat, Film, Bethlehem: 1938, A. Ford, 600 ft 16 mm.

11. Maier, N. R. F., The specific processes constituting the learning function, *Psychol. Rev.*, 1939, **46**, 241–52.

12. Maier, N. R. F., *Studies of abnormal behavior in the rat*. I. The neurotic pattern and an analysis of the situation which produces it, New York: 1939, Harper and Bros., 81.

13. Patrick, J. R., Studies in rational behavior and emotional excitement. II. The effect of emotional excitement on rational behavior in human subjects, *J. comp. Psychol.*, 1934, **18**, 153–95.

14. Sanders, M. J., An experimental demonstration of regression in the rat, *J. exper. Psychol.*, 1937, **21**, 493–510.

15. Spence, K. W., The nature of discrimination learning, *Psychol. Rev.*, 1936, **43**, 427–49.

Experimental Neuroses and Therapy*

Excerpt from J. H. Masserman, *Behavior and neurosis*, Hafner Publishing Co., 1964, chapter 4.

The experimental studies cited in the preceding chapter demonstrated that the stereotyped pseudo-affective reactions obtained by hypothalamic stimulation, despite their emotional-mimetic characterization as 'sham rage', lack motivational connotation or 'meaning' and therefore can neither be 'conditioned' nor made the basis for an experimental neurosis. This is in agreement with the first psychobiological principle of behavior developed in chapter 1 [in *Behavior and neurosis*]. However, according to the other principles, 'conditioned' behavior – i.e., adaptive responses to significant symbols – should occur if the stimulus-situation *is* made meaningful, and, further, the behavioral responses should become 'neurotic' in character if the motivational connotations of the situation are made conflictful to a sufficient degree. In this chapter various series of experiments to determine the validity of these premises will be described and typical results will be presented.

Control Observations
The conditioned feeding response
Cats were taught to associate a feeding signal, which usually consisted of a light-flash and the simultaneous ringing of a bell for about two seconds, with the manual or automatic delivery of food into the food-box of the apparatus. The typical course of adaptive learning in an animal placed in the experimental situation is illustrated in the history of Cat 29.

During several weeks in a cage in the animal room, Cat 29 became accustomed to the daily ration of food: a mixture of solid 'Kiblets', 'Ideal' dog food, and salmon.† After twenty-four hours of starvation she was taken to the experimental room and placed in the conditioning apparatus. The lid on the food-box was raised and a ration of the food

* Thanks are due to Mr Paul Siever for assembling some of the data for this section from our laboratory records.
† Our cats have been kept in good health for as long as four years on this diet with the occasional addition of condensed milk.

mixture was placed in the box; during the subsequent course of the experiment she was fed only in the conditioning apparatus. On the first day the cat showed little interest in the food-box but, instead, spent the time exploring and sniffing all parts of the cage. The following day she ate the entire ration from the open food-box, but again left it after every few mouthfuls to explore the cage further. The next day, simultaneously with the feeding signal, a small portion of food was dropped into the open food-box through the funnel. The cat reacted with a startled jump to the first light-flash and bell-sound but began to come to the box to secure the food after subsequent signals. After twelve such trials the cat regularly suspended any other activity at the feeding signal in order to come to the box and wait for the food offering, which was now delayed for about a second. The lid of the box was then gradually lowered during five or six trials until the cat became accustomed to elevating it with her head from an almost closed position. The following day the lid was started from the half-way mark before it was again lowered, trial by trial, to full closure; in this manner, the cat was induced to raise the lid from a lower position at each feeding signal. After ten such responses the next day, the automatic feeder was put into play. The slight clicking noise of the feeder caused some hesitancy at first, but the lid-raising response was soon re-established. From this time on her response was direct, with no hesitancy or missed trials.

The time required to learn the conditioned feeding response ranged from one to eight days in different animals. Most cats used the nose to raise the lid, although some also employed a prying motion of the paw. After two or three days even active animals would stop their exploration or play to rush to the food-box at the feeding signal. Most cats which tried to open the food-box between signals soon abandoned this activity when they found no food; others were effectively discouraged after a few trials if the lid were held shut by a string device.

Cats which developed normal feeding responses jumped into the experimental cage with apparent eagerness as soon as they were permitted to do so and strongly resisted being removed from it. Such animals apparently awaited the feeding signals with equal avidity and showed in their behavior a definite capacity to anticipate accurately signals given at regular intervals of one or two minutes. After a period of responsiveness to the complex feeding signal—light, bell, and subsequent feeder noise—the animals would also respond to any one of the components of the complex; in this case, however, the auditory stimuli given alone were invariably more effective than the visual. In general, from thirty to fifty feedings per day were necessary to maintain the animal's weight and condition.

222

Control of the feeding signal by the animal

Eighteen animals were trained to actuate their own feeding signals by manipulating a disk control switch placed inside the cage; this activity was rewarded by the deposition of a pellet of food in the food-box. The procedures employed varied as follows: in some cases, such as Cat 15, the animal, which had already been trained to respond to the signals, accidentally rubbed against the switch and thus spontaneously established the association between depression of the switch, the signals, and food. In other instances a larger platform was superimposed upon the switch disk and the animal's paw was placed on it many times in succession by the experimenter; in this way, the connexion between 'paw-placing on disk' and the signal for feeding was made. For more refractory animals salmon juice was placed in a small cup attached eccentrically to the disk so that the cat, in attempting to lap the juice, depressed the switch, gave itself the feeding signal, and thus tentatively established the switch-signal-food sequence. After several repetitions the pattern was retained after the juice and later the cup were removed. This training process in different cats took from eight trials in one day to over a hundred trials over nine days. The well-established pattern consisted of activating the signal switch, an immediate feeding response, rapid return to manipulate the switch, and so on for as many feedings as would be allowed or as necessary for satiation.

The mode of depressing the control switch varied with the learning process. The cats which learned to depress the switch with the paw generally used that motion thereafter; those which learned by accidentally rubbing against the switch continued to rub against it, usually with the head, occasionally with other parts of the body; and those which had to be enticed to the disk with salmon juice invariably used the head to depress the switch.* The number of times per minute the animal depressed the switch and the speed of reaction to the signals increased with hunger but varied with the

* Dr Frank Fremont-Smith, when viewing the motion-picture films of these experiments, pointed out that the cats seemed actually to 'fondle and caress' the switch while manipulating it, as though it were a cherished possession. In a sense it could be said that the instrument, since it mediated the satisfaction of deeply felt needs in our animals, had acquired as great an intrinsic value for them as a Stradivarius violin would have in the eyes of a devoted virtuoso. In the words of William James: 'To the broody hen the notion would probably seem monstrous that there should be a creature in the world to whom a nestful of eggs was not the utterly fascinating and precious and never-to-be-too-much-sat-upon object which it is to her.'

temperament of the animal.† Other phenomena of this manipulative control of the situation on the part of the animal will be considered later.

Extinction of normally adaptive behavior

To determine the effects of the individual procedures later combined to produce neuroses in our animals, various control experiments were performed, of which the following are typical:

Extinction of the effects of sensory signals in the absence of motivational goals – Cat 34 was subjected to the light-and-bell signal used in most experiments but was given no food reward. At first the signals startled the cat, and he sat up suddenly and tensely each time they were given. However, after several trials the animal became accustomed to the stimuli and merely raised his head at their occurrence or else ignored them completely. This rapid extinction of reaction appeared in other cats before the signals had acquired any significance as a preliminary to food.

Extinction of signal and air-blast combination in the absence of motivational conflict – That the type and duration of the reactions to the conditional signal are contingent on its motivational-perceptive-associative context was shown in the same cat when an air-blast was given together with the signal. This produced marked cowering and trembling at the rear of the cage, and these responses were accentuated during subsequent light-and-bell signals given the same day without accompanying air-blasts. However, after several trials this fear reaction to the light and bell diminished and then disappeared even with frequent reinforcement by the blast, so that on succeeding days signals given even while the cat was feeding produced no visible effects. In contrast, if the first air-blast were given while the animal was eating – i.e., if a motivational *conflict* was thereby introduced – no adequate adaptions to the signals occurred, and the animal continued to cower and show marked anxiety in response to all subsequent feeding signals (see below).

In other control experiments six cats were exposed to the air-blast alone at irregular intervals without preceding signals; all these cats readily became accustomed to the stimulus and, after from five to eighteen trials, showed no further disturbance in behavior when it was exhibited. Nevertheless, the carry-over of the cowering reaction to the air-blast if complete adaptation did not occur was seen in Cat 34 one day when the animal room was being sprayed; as the blast from the sprayer was directed towards his cage the cat cowered and trembled in a far corner until the spray passed on to the next cage. A similar generalization of blast-phobia was seen in the crouching, trembling, and escape behavior of neurotic animals when they were accidentally or intentionally

† Cf. Skinner's (1938) concept of 'reflex reserve'.

subjected to air currents from an electric fan or from an open window.

Although several possibilities were explored, our experiments failed to determine why nearly all cats reacted to the first few air-blasts with marked evidences of anxiety and fear. On the supposition that the high-frequency tone of the blast was a factor, six cats were exposed to the sudden sounding of a Galton whistle; after five trials these animals paid no further attention to the supersonic stimulus, whereas from eight to thirty trials were required to extinguish the responses to the air-blast. Month-old kittens born in the laboratory and exposed to the blast for the first time reacted with varying degrees of fear, indicating the genetic, and possible atavistic, as opposed to the experientially determined, nature of the response.

Effects of space-constriction on the normal animal

Three modes of space-constriction in the conditioning apparatus were utilized in various combinations: (a) the transparent barrier was gradually moved to the left against the food-box, permitting vision of the entire cage and passage around the sides of the barrier from one compartment to the other; (b) the guards were placed on one or both sides of the barrier, restricting passage but not interfering with vision; or (c) the opaque screen was placed over the glass of the barrier, barring vision of the other section of the cage. In the normal animal and in the animal responding normally to the feeding signals restriction of space by any of these variants caused no significant disturbances in adaptation. When the side guards were not mounted, the animal passed freely between the compartments and circumvented the opaque barrier with alacrity to get to the food-box when the feeding signals were given. If, under such circumstances, access to the food-box was prevented by the side guards when the feeding signal was given, the animal clawed at the barrier vigorously, vocalizing and pacing from one side to the other trying to get past. When the animal finally found that passage was impossible, this behavior rapidly abated until, in from eight to twenty trials, the feeding signals no longer produced a response. However, in no case did manifestations of anxiety, fear, or conflict develop, i.e., the animal adapted readily to the external frustration.

Other feeding frustrations

In addition to barring passage to the food-box, which, as noted, induced extinction of goal-directed behavior but no residual neurotic changes, the following modes of frustration were employed, in each of which the animals were physically prevented from obtaining their objective after the conditional feeding-signals:

1. *Locking the lid of the food-box* – Twelve well-trained cats were kept from feeding by holding the lid of the food-box down with a cord manipulated from outside the cage. Typical responses were these:

Cat 31 kept scratching and prying at the lid and box and trying to open it; this behavior was elicited for seven feeding signals, but at each succeeding one it diminished in duration and intensity. After this the active response was totally extinguished, although the cat continued to glance up at the feeding signals for several subsequent trials. To test the significance of these control observations, the lid was again opened, and the animal once more began to feed immediately on signal. A two-second air-blast was then administered during a normal feeding response; the animal promptly abandoned the food, retreated to a corner with marked manifestations of anxiety, and thereafter responded to all feeding signals only with crouching, clawing, vocalizations, and attempts to escape, even when the food was directly displayed and easily available.

Frustration of the feeding responses by a similar technic in Cat 60 resulted in the extinction of the lid-opening behavior in seven trials. When the response was re-established by releasing the lid and retraining the animal, five trials with the lid again locked sufficed to eliminate the response a second time; at the third repetition of the procedure, three trials were sufficient. None of these frustrations produced discernible behavior changes other than extinction of feeding, whereas when the same cat was later subjected to air-blasts during feeding, she responded with almost complete passive loss of normal activity and many neurotic aberrations of conduct.

2. *Irregular food rewards* – Eight cats were subjected to random feedings, i.e., food was placed in the cups of the automatic feeder in irregular sequence so that, when the animal responded to the feeding signal by opening the box, the reward was unpredictably withheld. Two examples follow:

Cat 32, a rather restless and active animal, developed some signs of agitation when fed irregularly after a bell-and-light signal; she moved about restlessly, vocalized frequently, and occasionally even attempted to escape from the cage. However, after sixty-four successive feeding signals on one day and seventy-five on the other, none of which was followed by food, she continued to open the lid to search for the reward without showing any evidence of hesitation or extinction of the feeding response or of adverse reactions to the feeding signal.

Similarly, Cat 35 showed some increased restlessness and vocalizing after irregular feedings, but over a twelve-day period continued to respond perfectly to each signal, whether accompanied by food or not. Moreover, at the end of this period of 'fractional frustration' there were no evidences of neurotic behavior, and the animal still resisted being taken out of the experimental cage for removal to the animal room.

These control experiments demonstrated that mechanical interference of goal-directed behavior produces adaptive extinction of the conditional response, whereas irregular rewards, if anything, tend to crystallize and intensify the behavior patterns. It is important to note, however, that neither procedure produced the marked neurotic aberrations that appeared when the goal-seeking behavior, instead of being externally frustrated, was made conflictful by the elicitation of opposing motivations in the animal itself. Experiments designed to elicit these conflictful and incompatible adaptations are described in the succeeding sections.

Production of 'Experimentally Neurotic' Behavior

Technic

To produce motivational conflicts in animals trained to feed on signal, the animal was subjected either to an air-blast or to a grid-shock at the moment of feeding. A combination of both conflict-producing stimuli was also utilized, but the results did not differ markedly from those of the grid-shocks alone. Of the two stimuli, the grid-shocks undoubtedly induced a more intense and persistent motivational conflict; however, since the air-blast produced no noxious somatic effects and seemed to act mainly, if not entirely, as a physically harmless but fear-engendering 'emotional' trauma, experiments with this modality were psychologically more significant.

Air-blasts – Blasts of air were applied across the food-box at the moment the animal opened the lid or immediately afterward as the cat was about to feed. The duration of the blast varied; usually it was applied for only one or two seconds; but in some cases, especially when the initial reaction was insufficient, it was maintained for as long as five seconds. With most animals the blasts were given at two or three successive feeding responses, but in some experiments they were applied at inconsistent intervals so that the animal could accustom itself to no regularity of pattern. Flights from the air-blast usually took the form of a sudden rush to crouch at the far side of the cage. However, the few animals (six out of fifty-eight) which developed greater tolerance of the air-blasts merely cowered momentarily, withdrew from the food-box a short distance, and even re-explored the box in the face of the blast or at the moment the blast subsided.

Grid-shocks – In twenty-four experiments two or three high-voltage, low-amperage condenser pulsations from the fence-shocker were given through the grid-floor of the cage at the feeding signals or at the moment of food-taking; in the five refractory animals which continued to feed despite this, the shocks were prolonged as long as necessary to cause cessation of feeding and retreat from the box. The usual reaction was a startled jump as each impulse was felt, followed by a slow dignified stalking-away from the food after the shocks ended. Quite often, however, the animal would crouch, close its eyes, tense its musculature, and curl its paws to diminish the faradic sensations and would then maintain this position for a variable period after the shocks ended. Only occasionally was the precipitate scramble that so character-istically followed an air-blast seen after a shock, although eight animals did become sufficiently excited after a repetition of the shock to dash about the cage seeking escape. Snarling and intense vocalization often characterized reactions to shocks, in contrast to the usual lack of such vocalizing immediately after a blast of air. Conditioned escape reactions to an insulated platform placed on either side of the barrier were easily established in seven animals.

Air-blasts accompanied by grid-shocks – Twenty-four animals were subjected to both air-blasts and grid-shocks simultaneously, both being administered as the lid was opened or as the food was being delivered. In these instances the duration was restricted to the time required by two or three shocks. The reactions in nearly all cases closely resembled those to the unreinforced shock, although subsequent administrations of the air-blast alone pro-duced the combined effects.

Types of behavior changes induced

Several categories of 'neurotic' behavior changes were elicited in the various animals, but the individual patterns varied extensively from cat to cat, and the presence of one type of disturbance did not preclude the simultaneous or later presence of others in the same animal. Moreover, various 'neurotic symptoms' could develop under different precipitating circumstances, e.g., in the interval between feeding signals, at the time of the signal, at the opening of the food-box, during space constriction, or in response to experi-ences outside of the experimental apparatus. Categorically, the behavior disturbances may be classified as follows:

Changes in spontaneous activity – In general, normally quiet cats subjected to motivational conflicts tended to show restlessness or agitation, whereas habitually active cats developed marked restriction of activity and a tendency to passivity.

For instance, Cat 53 was a moderately quiet animal in which two air-blasts abolished further feeding responses but produced a fidgety, incessant pacing and shifting from side to side, alternating with periods of horripilation, pupillary dilatation, hyperpnea, and characteristic postures and activity mimetic of anxiety. In contrast, Cats 14 and 52 were highly excitable and easily distractible animals, which reacted with frenzied leaping at the air-blasts but which thereafter refused to feed with food easily available and lay passive and immobile between feeding signals in any portion of the cage in which they were placed. Another normally active animal, Cat 26, lay so still after two grid-shocks that he appeared to be asleep; moreover, he could be placed in various cataleptic postures for periods of from ten to twenty minutes. Nevertheless, despite such reactions of apparent external passivity, many of these animals showed chronic disturbances of pulse and respiration and could be reactivated to states of restless anxiety by stimuli associated with the experimental situation.

'Phobic' responses to the feeding signals – In animals which were subjected to air-blast or shock at food-taking the feeding signal which formerly had occasioned an immediate rush to the food-box, now induced crouching, hiding, vigorous attempts to escape from the apparatus, rapid and irregular pulse and respiration, trembling, and other behavior suggestive of marked anxiety or even panic. In some animals these reactions were especially pronounced in the trials just following the noxious stimulus, and then slowly abated during the succeeding weeks; however, even in these animals attempts to resume feeding were immediately discontinued in favor of retreat from the box if the food-signals were again given. In most animals phobic reactions to the feeding signals, once well established, persisted almost unchanged for months without further reinforcement by shock or air-blast. In fact, in animals made severely neurotic a repetition of the original conflict-producing situation even after the lapse of from four to thirty months would reprecipitate a state of severe anxiety or panic.

Illustrative are the protocols of Cats 23 and 15. The former, after a grid-shock at feeding, was unusually quiet between feeding signals, but as each signal was given he crouched tensely, showed piloerection and pupillary dilatation, mewed piercingly, and made frantic efforts to open the door of the cage and escape. Cat 15, after the first shock at feeding, was exposed to another as he approached the food in the open food-box, but this only brought about a momentary withdrawal of his head as he cowered. In contrast, a feeding signal given as he watched the food precipitated an immediate rush to the rear of the cage and behavior similar to that of Cat 23.

Cats which did not show these acute responses to the signals nevertheless refrained from feeding despite prolonged hunger. An outstanding example of this was seen in Cat 26. This animal was subjected to only two grid-shocks at feeding, yet for sixteen days thereafter he refused to feed from the open food-box on signal; instead, he continued to crouch and cower each time the feeding signal was given, despite the fact that he was fed only one-tenth of his normal ration outside of the experimental situation and lost one-third of his original weight during the experimental period.

A more limited range of inhibition of normal feeding was seen in Cat 20, which, after exposure to two air-blasts, refused to approach the food-box, yet ate ravenously from a beaker placed elsewhere in the cage, provided that the food placed in the beaker was powdered and thereby differed (although in form only) from that previously offered in the box. Such animals, however, were exceptional, since most of the cats refused food in any form in the apparatus and were sparing and choosey in their food intake elsewhere during the period of their experimental neurosis. Other animals responded to the light-and-bell signals with ambivalent or abortive behavior, which ended without the attainment of food. This type of reaction followed a single grid-shock in Cat 15; at later feeding signals he made a prompt forward movement but suddenly hesitated and sat down. Later, this response diminished to mere blinking at the signal. Cat 21, following grid-shocks, showed the same type of reaction to the signal and often even came up to the food-box and muzzled it meditatively but did not open it to feed.

Delayed reactions to the noxious stimulus were exhibited by a few animals. For instance, Cat 60 was given an air-blast as she opened the lid of the food-box, but, except for a sudden, startled, momentary tensing of her body, she showed no reaction and continued feeding. When she had consumed the pellet, however, she went to the rear of the cage, sat down to preen, and at following feeding signals cowered slightly but refrained from coming to feed despite several days of starvation.

'Counterphobic' behavior patterns – Significantly, some animals placed in the conflictful situation rapidly developed stereotyped behavioral mannerisms which, though biologically frustraneous and thereby 'neurotic', nevertheless constituted a defensive adaptation in that they seemed to diminish the animal's tension.

A response of this nature was shown by Cat 22, which, after the second air-blast, compulsively crouched in a fixed posture behind the food-box *on the side of the blast*. A similarly 'counterphobic' reaction was exhibited by Cat 60, which, at the feeding signal, would run to the food-box, insert his head beneath the lid, and then, instead of feeding, would remain immobile staring at the experimenter for prolonged periods; this pattern did not change even when the animal was maximally hungry and the box was filled with food. Similarly, a rigid fixation of a response pattern after it had lost its adaptive usefulness was shown by Cat 101, which persisted in a difficult, painful method of escape past the barrier even when an easy avenue of egress through the open cage door was made available.

'*Regressive*' *behavior* – After being subjected to the hunger-fear conflict for several days many animals displayed a fairly well-marked tendency to self-preoccupation and autistic indulgence, apparently in substitutive satisfaction for drives rendered impossible of direct consummation.

Thus, Cat 60, after two air-blasts, discontinued her feeding responses to the light-and-bell signal and at first showed considerable anxiety in the experimental situation. When placed in the cage on the third day, however, she began to clean and lick herself almost continually; when the feeding signals were given she would merely glance at the food-box, vocalize plaintively, and then intensify her preening behavior, which continued when she was removed from the cage. Other animals subjected to the most motivational conflict developed a rather distinctive play-fulness and a tendency to court increased attention and fondling from the experimenter. Cat 14, a normally independent and self-sufficient animal, after three air-blasts became excessively timid, invariably tried to hide his head under the experimenter's arm while being handled, and would rub against the experimenter's legs or climb on his shoulder as an invitation to be fondled and petted. Nevertheless, some animals which previously had been meek and docile became aggressive and vicious under the experimental conditions. Thus, Cat 22, after a single feeding frustration by the air-blast, not only refused to eat for several days but would snarl and attempt to bite and scratch anyone who offered him food. Other animals under similar conditions would attack pre-viously tolerated cage-mates and therefore had to be isolated in single cages in the animal room.

That 'regression' under environmental stress or motivational conflict constitutes the readoption of behavior patterns found more satisfactory in earlier experience – *but that these behavior patterns need not necessarily be more 'primitive' or 'infantile' than those they replace* – is illustrated by some incidental observations in a series of experiments on 'inter-cat relationships'.

Cat 201, an ordinarily friendly and gentle animal, had been taught by the method of alternate feedings over a period of nine weeks to depress a signal-switch twice in succession before attempting to secure the food reward. This special training was then dis-continued, and for five weeks the animal was again fed after every manipulation of the switch, with the result that the single-depression pattern was quickly re-established. The signal-switch was then moved behind the passable barrier to a part of the cage opposite the food-box, and Cat 201 was placed in the cage together with Cat 60, a female, who had also learned the switch-manipulation technic. Cat 201, the more active of the two, promptly walked around the barrier to the switch and depressed it a single time; however, before he could return to the feed-box, the food had been secured and eaten by Cat 60, who had more quickly responded to the feeding signals actuated by her partner. After a series of such frustrations over a period of several days Cat 201 began to alter his behavior in a number of interesting ways, some of which indicated a significant change in 'inter-cat relationships'. For instance, he began to refuse to work the switch for Cat 60's benefit, attacked her on two occasions, and finally hit on the device of forcing her behind the barrier next to the switch and away from the food-box. However, one intercurrent behavioral response was especially significant: often Cat 201, after repeated frustrations by Cat 60, began to depress the switch *twice in succession*, as though the resumption of this earlier, temporarily 'forgotten', and more complex pattern – certainly not one that could be called 'simpler' or more 'primitive' – would re-establish the secure, happy days when individual effort was invariably followed by just reward. Significantly, also, Cat 201 never resorted to the double-depression pattern unless his environment was disturbed by the 'social' frustrations represented by Cat 60.

Other experiments – Observations as to the effects of various drugs on normally adaptive or neurotic behavior and separate experiments to determine the influence of neuroses on dominance-submission patterns and other inter-cat 'social' relationships will be reported in their appropriate connexions in Part II [of *Behavior and neurosis*.]

Factors Tending to Accentuate the Neurotic Behavior

I. Increase of one of the conflict drives

Significantly, any manipulation in or out of the experimental situation that increased the intensity or immediacy of the motivational conflicts in our animals correspondingly augmented their neurotic behavior. Thus, anxiety, phobic reactions, compulsive phenomena, and other behavioral aberrations were most marked on the third or maximal day of hunger, especially when, in the face of strong feeding inhibitions previously developed by the animal, the food-box was filled and left temptingly open. As hunger was maintained at a somewhat lower level with subminimal feedings on subsequent days, the neurotic behavior persisted and became stereotyped, although less acute in expression.

II. Immediacy of environmental press and impossibility of escape

If a neurotic animal were pushed toward the food-box by the movable barrier and thus made to approach the locus and psychological nidus of the conflict, its agitation increased in intensity, especially immediately after repetitions of the feeding signals. The neurotic manifestations were further exacerbated when escape was prevented by the side guards or when the barrier was made psychologically more confining by an opaque screen; under such circumstances animals showed reactions suggestive of extreme 'claustrophobia' and responded to the feeding signals with states of almost uncontrollable panic. The following observations are illustrative.

Cat 29 was a very active animal, which after being subjected to the air and shock combination during a conditional feeding response, developed typical anxiety and phobic reactions. When, after two days of self-starvation, the animal was replaced in the apparatus and pushed halfway toward the closed food-box by the transparent barrier, her restlessness increased markedly and the light-and-bell signals elicited tense crouching and anxious cries. If the motivational conflict was now further accentuated by raising the lid of the box so that the hungry animal could see the food, the feeding signal precipitated frenzied clawing at the barrier and violent attempts to escape.

An episode from an experiment on Cat 56 may also be cited as typical of the excitatory effects of space-constriction. This cat was given an air-blast as she came to feed on signal and promptly responded with a violent retreat. Feeding signals thereafter produced anxious vocalization and agitated rushing about in the cage, although the animal invariably avoided the food-box. Slight extraneous noises likewise caused startled jumping, horripilation, and pupillary dilatation. Space-constriction was then employed, at first with the barrier uncovered and transparent and with the passages at either side open. No change in behavior was seen as the space next to the food-box was reduced by one-half, but with three-fourths restriction there was increased restlessness and vocalizing. When the opaque screen and the side guards were mounted on the barrier, constriction to the halfway mark of the cage occasioned a markedly greater degree of anxiety and restlessness. This was further accentuated by forcing the cat closer to the food-box, but it was immediately relieved if the barrier were again moved to the right, even when the animal did not change its own position. Maximum excitement was induced, when after two days of starvation, the animal was constricted three-fourths of the day toward the box, which was left open to display easily available food. On this occasion the feeding signals which were given once a minute, invariably caused maxima lpupillary dilatation, crouching, trembling, horripilation, and furious attempts to claw the barrier or escape out of the cage.

Less violent reactions were shown by Cat 24 which, after being restricted to half the cage space by the barrier, began scratching at the sides, pulling the sliding door open, or escaping around the barrier as it was pushed closer to the food-box. When the side guards were mounted and the cage door was locked, the animal reacted with more frantic scratching and clawing at both obstructions, especially after each feeding signal, but only while space-constriction was in effect. As the barrier was pulled back to the right the cat followed it to the end-zone and sat there quietly except for a slight shift in position at the light-and-bell signals.

Yet another significant behavior pattern induced by space-constriction appeared in Cat 54, a rather quiet and passive animal, which was exposed to three air-blasts during successive feeding responses. Upon being moved closer to the food-box by the barrier, the animal began to mew plaintively and to develop a progressively more rigid posture and a cataleptic type of resistance to manipulation. These manifestations diminished as the barrier was again moved to the right and reappeared when the geometric and psychological *Lebensraum* of the animal was once more constricted.

Methods of Alleviating Experimentally Neurotic Behavior

I. Effect of rest periods

Thirty of thirty-seven neurotic animals, when returned to the experimental cage for further work after rest periods of from two weeks to five months, manifested the same types of abnormal behavior in almost the same intensity as on the last day of the previous period of experimentation.

An example is Cat 25 which had been made neurotic by the air-blast technic and then given three months' vacation in the animal room, during which time she gradually reacquired apparently normal behavior and spontaneous feeding habits. Nevertheless, on her first re-entry to the experimental cage she immediately went to a far corner and crouched there quietly, refusing to accept food from the open food-box. For two days she was given no food, and on the third day, even when left alone in the room for three hours with plenty of food in the box, she still abstained from touching it. On this day, moreover, she showed a reactivation of her previous anxiety and phobic responses to the feeding signals.

However, although in seven animals a prolonged period of rest from experimentation produced some alleviation of the neurotic behavior, other 'therapeutic' procedures, alone or in combination, were found to be of more immediate and lasting effectiveness in nearly every case. In conformity with the psychobiologic principles of behavior, these procedures, although they apparently differed greatly from one another, had a common characteristic in that they all tended to mitigate or abolish the specific motivational conflicts that had been induced in the neurotic animals and thereby ameliorated the resultant anxiety and its aberrant behavioral expressions. Categorically, the other procedures employed may be classified as follows.

II. Reduction of one of the conflictful drives

An animal in which the hunger drive had been made conflictful by the administration of an air-blast or grid-shock during feeding nearly always showed an alleviation in neurotic behavior if it were manually or even forcibly fed just before being replaced in the cage.

Thus, Cat 106, after two air-blasts administered during conditional feeding, developed marked food inhibitions and showed restlessness, wincing, and crouching at every feeding signal; however, when she was induced to eat in the animal room just before being brought to the experimental cage, she often lay quietly relaxed away from the food-box and showed only minimal phobic or compulsive reactions, such as slight startle or blinking to the light-and-bell signals. Nevertheless, normal feeding responses in the cage were never re-established by this method, and the neurotic behavioral aberrations returned as the hunger of the animal again increased.

III. 'Reassurance' and 'persuasion' through 'transference relationships'

Another method of diminishing anxiety in some neurotic animals was to permit the development of a dependent confidence in the experimenter, who customarily fed and cared for them, and to utilize this relationship to diminish the insecurities and anxieties the animals later developed in the motivationally conflictful situation.

For example, Cat 60, after her feeding responses had been inhibited by the air-blast, could often be brought to the food-box and coaxed to feed again during reassuring handling, stroking, and petting by the experimenter, although at first the feeding responses continued to be disrupted by the animal's phobic reactions to the conditional signals. Nevertheless, even when the animal had been induced to feed between signals and had done so for two weeks in the apparatus, she would stop feeding immediately when the experimenter's hand was taken away or when the next feeding signals were given. Moreover, this type of 'transference therapy' could not be effectively instituted or employed when the animal had spontaneously or neurotically developed a distrust or fear of the experimenter.

IV. 'Forced' solution of the motivational conflict by environmental manipulation

A third general method of dissipating the fear-hunger impasse in the neurotic animals was to increase the intensity of the hunger drive to the point at which it would break through its inhibitions and be discharged in consummatory activity. It was thought at first that an intense enough degree of hunger to accomplish this could be attained simply by starving the animal; however, as previously noted, the craving for food, even when at its maximum at about the third day, was only occasionally sufficient to induce the animal to feed even between signals; on subsequent days the hunger apparently diminished and the neurotic inhibitions again held sway. As a result, many neurotic animals, if permitted to do so, starved themselves into a severe cachexia over periods of from eight to twenty-two days and probably would have died of feline 'anorexia nervosa',* had they not been forcibly fed outside the experimental cage. Fortunately, it was found that the drive to secure food, as measured behavioristically, could apparently be increased not only by mounting hunger but even more effectively by the sight and smell of the food or by sensory stimuli associated with satisfactory feeding rather than with the noxious factors in the hunger-fear conflict. Again, the urge to eat could be greatly increased – seemingly in geometric ratio – by forcing the hungry but neurotically inhibited animal ever closer to the food objective. Combinations of these various methods were therefore employed in the following experiments.

Prolonged hunger – Cat 26 has already been cited with respect to the long period of near-starvation which followed grid-shock application and during which he lost one-third of his original weight. For twenty days this animal ate only one-tenth of his normal ration of food in the animal room. In the apparatus he displayed marked anxiety and crouched, trembled, and cowered at the feeding signal, although the reaction diminished somewhat in time. On the sixteenth experimental day he responded only once to a signal by coming to feed, but this tentative response was promptly abolished by another mild shock. During the next two weeks of near-starvation the animal again refused to feed even from the open food-box and, instead, paced about the cage, mewed plaintively, pawed restlessly at the grid, and froze to inactivity at the feeding signals.

* Fear of what food may symbolically represent is a frequent mechanism in the severe functional disorders grouped under the symptom-complex of 'anorexia nervosa' in the human (Brosin, 1940, 1941; and Masserman, 1941).

Cat 52, following a hunger period of twenty days, finally responded to the light-and-bell signal with a delayed and cautious approach to the box. Nevertheless, after two days of furtive, irregular feeding, the responses to the signal again disappeared during the two succeeding days and were replaced by a constant restless shifting of position and phobic and compulsive reactions. After a vacation of three months, however, feeding was gradually re-established by the transference technic, and the habitual pacing, cringing, mewing, and pawing disappeared.

Percipience of food – Occasionally during the course of an experiment an animal which would not respond to the feeding signals because of an induced inhibition came to the food-box and made abortive attempts to feed as the lid was raised from outside the experimental cage. This almost invariably took place near the middle of the period between signals, in which case the next signal disrupted the hesitant attempts to open the box and sent the cat scurrying to the rear. The quantitative aspects of this method of obtaining feedings were graphically illustrated in several experiments.

Typical was Cat 55, in which the feeding response had been abolished by two air-blasts. After space-constriction had induced occasional feedings, the barrier was removed, and the following reactions were observed over a period of about ninety minutes:

Lid one-quarter open	60 per cent feeding responses to signal, with marked hesitation
Lid one-half open	80 per cent feeding responses to signal, with slight delay
Lid fully opened	100 per cent feeding responses to signal, with no delay

Moreover, if the lid was then again gradually lowered, the normal feeding response was retained for two or three trials.

The case of Cat 20, which refused its regular diet after exposure to air-blasts but which accepted the food in different form, has already been cited. After several days of constriction the new diet was taken from the *open* food-box, the signal responses were restored, and the cat also began to tolerate the air-blasts during feeding (see below).

Forced proximity to the food-box. – Cat 24, a fairly active animal, developed total inhibition of feeding responses after only three air-blasts. Constriction to the halfway point by the transparent, passable barrier caused some muzzling of the food-box; with three-fourths constriction the cat tried to escape around the side of the barrier at the feeding signal but, failing to do so, suddenly turned, opened the box, and fed in furtive, hurried gulps. When the opaque screen and guards were then mounted on the barrier at the position of three-fourths constriction, the animal began vocalizing and crouching; finally he opened the box and peered at the food but withdrew without touching it. During the following nine days that cat showed increasing signs of excitement and attempts to escape during periods of space-constriction, especially at the feeding signals. On the tenth day, with further constriction, feeding responses to the light-and-bell signals occurred; moreover, the animal returned to feed after an air-blast ended and then began to withdraw its head only partially during the blast. Next, he developed complete tolerance of air-blasts when constricted, but would not show such tolerance if he had the full length of the cage in which to retreat. Finally, he fed at every signal, despite air-blasts given regularly or irregularly and in the absence of space-constriction. From this time on he showed no further neurotic symptoms and reverted to his normal spontaneous activity. An incidental but psychologically significant observation during the later period of constriction was that a slight forward movement of the barrier usually induced at least one feeding, even though the additional constriction so produced was negligible. This interesting phenomenon appeared in several other animals; indeed, the feeding response was often precipitated just as the barrier began to move and occurred without a simultaneous feeding signal or even after a feeding response had been inhibited by such a signal. Thus a movement of the barrier *either to the right or left* of less than one-fourth of an inch sufficed to send the cat rushing forward to feed, i.e., apparently the symbolically induced anticipation of further space-manipulation, as well as the actual constriction itself, was effective in precipitating a counterphobic feeding response.

Another type of counterphobic reinforcement was seen in Cat 23. This animal was initially kept from feeding by air-blasts, but space-constriction eventually induced tolerance of the blasts and re-establishment of the response. Nevertheless, during this period of enforced *rapprochement* he manipulated the food-box hesitantly and often delayed taking the food. During such delays an interesting and significant phenomenon appeared: as the cat stood with his head just above the food, a sudden blast of air invariably precipitated a lunge *toward* the food, which the cat then hastily gulped, i.e., the traumatic stimulus itself had now become the needed 'counterphobic' reinforcement for feeding. Three days later this gave way to a normal feeding response without recourse to the air-blasts.

One cat was unique in his response to space-constriction. After air-blasts had abolished his feeding response, barrier movements which brought him close to the food-box at first elicited transitory feedings. However, the constriction suddenly lost its effectiveness, and for three weeks the feeding responses occurred only when the barrier was moved back. In this animal also, restriction of space markedly increased the restlessness, vocalization, and random movements between feeding signals; whereas in the absence of such restriction he sat and preened. In contrast, visual reinforcement – opening the lid of the box – was usually effective in inducing feeding.

Reciprocal relationship between degree of space-constriction and percipience of food. – In Cat 29, after abolition of feeding responses by the air-blast plus grid-shock combination, no further reaction to the feeding signals occurred as long as the animal was permitted to retain a quietly hunched position at the rear of the cage. When she was forced three-fourths of the way against the food-box by the barrier, no feeding occurred, but the signals now induced intense clawing and whining. Conversely, as constriction was diminished, she continued to tremble and cringe close to the retreating barrier; however, the manifestations of phobic reactions to the signals were markedly diminished. Extreme space-constriction with the lid of the food-box partly open occasionally induced complete or abortive feeding responses, yet the light-and-bell signals given as the cat began to feed sent the animal rushing away from the box. If, now, the lid of the food-box and the barrier were both manipulated from outside the cage, the inverse influence of the two on the feeding response could be demonstrated. With slight constriction the lid had to be fully opened for feeding to follow; with extreme constriction the lid could be almost fully closed; moreover, this relationship held true in the entire range between the extremes.*

Reinforcement of constriction by other stimuli associated with feeding. – Cat 15 was subjected to a single air-blast plus grid-shock stimulus as he responded to his accustomed feeding signal; he immediately retreated to a far corner, showed piloerection, mydriasis, and rapid, disturbed respiration, and remained in the same crouching position for several hours. On the six succeeding days the animal was repeatedly constricted against the food-box and subjected to feeding signals irregularly followed by blast-plus-shock stimuli from one to four signals apart. This procedure did not re-establish the feeding responses until, on one occasion, maximal constriction was accidentally reinforced by a scratching noise emanating from the direction of, and similar to, the sound made by the feeder-mechanism. After this, not only did the same sound and that of the feeder precipitate feeding responses but so also did widely divergent auditory stimuli, such as tapping the feeder, whistling, clapping hands, etc. An added feature of these feedings was that they could be elicited within a second or two after a blast-plus-shock stimulus to which the animal had reacted with shudders, crouching, and retreat; in fact, fifteen such blasts plus shocks in a single day failed to abolish the feeding responses when these were encouraged by constriction and auditory reinforcement.

V. Effects of normal behavior of a cage-mate

During the course of the work a fifth possibility of influencing the behavior of neurotic animals was investigated, namely, the

* Such quantitative observations in our experiments suggested the possibility of working out a vector formula in which the hunger of the animal, the distance from the food, the reactive space, the intensity of visual and auditory reinforcements, and other contingent factors could be given a mathematical or topological weighting in accordance with the observed behavioral results.

method of placing a cat with normal responses to the feeding signals together with the neurotic animal in the experimental situation. The psychological significance of this technic with regard to the problem of the 'social interaction' of animal or human subjects will be discussed in chapter IX [in *Behavior and neurosis*]; however, typical data showing the variable results with this procedure in nine experiments may here be cited.

1. Cat 29 had been subjected to an air-shock combination which eliminated her feeding responses and caused typical anxiety and phobic reactions to the conditional signals. After a control period of seven days, during which these reactions remained constant despite hunger and constriction, Cat 31, a normal, active animal with prompt feeding responses to the same signals, was put into the experimental apparatus with her. At first Cat 29 continued her cowering at the food-signals; gradually, however, she showed interest in 31's feeding behavior and, after eighteen signals, began to approach the box when Cat 31 opened it. Following twelve additional signals, Cat 29 began pushing the normal animal aside and joining in the feeding. Finally, on the last five signals of the day she was beating 31 in the race to the box, opening it herself, and constantly keeping 31 from feeding as she gorged herself on all the food offered. The normal animal now retired to the other side of the barrier, which had been advanced halfway to the box. This did not affect 29's behavior; moreover, when the normal cat was removed, 29 retained her feeding response, although the following day a few additional reinforcements by 'social example' were necessary.

2. Cat 52 was treated in the same way. She, however, fed hesitantly and irregularly when the normal cat opened the box; and, after the normal cat was removed, even this partial response was discontinued. Repetition of the procedure every day for a week produced no further significant changes in the behavior of Cat 52.

3. A third neurotic cat, 26, did not feed on conditioned signal, despite prolonged hunger. The example of a normally responding cat in the cage with him had no apparent effects during numerous trials over a period of two weeks.

In none of the nine experiments, in which the effects on the neurotic animal were distributed between the extremes shown by Cats 29 and 26, did the presence of the abnormally reacting cat affect the responses of the normal animal, except as the ravenous appetite of the 'cured' neurotic animal kept the normal one from feeding. Even the latter circumstance did not occasion any behavior changes, since in nearly every instance the normal cat had satiated her appetite by the time the other displaced her at the box.

VI. Partial control of the experimental situation by the animal

Subject

A final method of influencing and possibly correcting the behavioral aberrations of neurotic animals was suggested by numerous clinical observations that, if a neurotic human subject was given some degree of manipulative control of a motivationally conflictful situation, he was much more likely to 'work through' a solution of it than if he were merely the passive pawn of circumstances which he could in no way influence. The application of this clinical principle to animal behavior was investigated by means of an experimental device described in chapter II [in *Behavior and neurosis*], i.e., the animal was first trained to feed after certain sensory signals and was then further trained to depress a switch which actuated these signals preparatory to receiving the reward of food. Once this pattern was established many variations of procedure were possible; for example, (*a*) the animal could be barred from either the food or the switch; (*b*) the latter could be turned off so that its operation would not actuate the signals; (*c*) the switch could be placed in positions that demanded modified technics of closure by the animal; (*d*) the food reward could be given (1) only after every second or third manipulation of the switch, (2) irregularly, or (3) withheld altogether; (*e*) feeding or other conditional signals could be interposed by the examiner; and, finally, (*f*) air-blasts or other stimuli that induced motivational conflicts could be given when the animal worked the switch or when it attempted to secure the food reward. Obviously, a cat trained in the normal use of the switch and then made to develop feeding inhibitions by the last-named procedure would nevertheless have an advantage over one trained only to given signals, in that (*a*) the former could proceed to try out the feeding pattern by further spontaneous manipulation of the switch, (*b*) it could refrain from doing so, or (*c*) it could develop a repertoire of normal or 'neurotic' adaptations to the new problem situation. Typical observations with various combinations of these procedures in experiments with twelve animals are described in the following sections.

Control observations

By the use of one or another of the training technics described above, nearly all animals, in from ten to sixty trials over a period of one to six days, learned to depress the switch disk vertically in order to actuate the feeding signals and thus secure the reward of food. The learning process was at first facilitated by placing the switch near the food-box (i.e., in the immediate gestalt field); however, after this the switch could be moved anywhere in the cage or hidden behind an opaque barrier, since the animal would reach around or struggle past obstacles to manipulate the switch before taking food, even when the latter was openly displayed in the box. Once it had sounded the signals, the animal would then struggle past the barrier in the opposite direction to secure the food. Nevertheless, that the signals rather than the switch-manipulation were prerequisite to feeding was demonstrated in most instances (although a significant exception will be cited) by the fact that, if the feeding signals were independently given by the operator, the cat fed forthwith.

Experience in training the various animals showed that cats differed widely not only in the speed and efficiency with which they associated manipulation of the switch with the signal-feeding pattern but also in their ability to grasp the 'principle' that compression of the switch from any direction would elicit the desired signals. Thus, one animal which had been accustomed to depress the switch with a forepaw, seemed completely puzzled when the switch was upended so that the same motion no longer closed the circuit. Interestingly, the animal refused to feed, became restless and disturbed, and went about the cage pressing down on other objects in lieu of the now intractable switch. When, however, the position of the disk was gradually changed from horizontal to vertical through angles of only about 20° at a time, the animal learned to compress the switch at each new angle, finally began to work it effectively in any position before feeding and thereafter showed no further behavior disturbances. In contrast, other animals, after only one or two successful manipulations, readily grasped the 'principle' of the switch and acquired a facility in manipulating it in any position and with almost any portion of their bodies.

Frustration of the goal-directed behavior by the interposition of an impassable barrier between the cat and the food or by failing to feed the animal after it had depressed the switch produced significant effects: the animal showed neither rapid extinction of the response nor behavior indicative of anxiety, but instead continued for long periods to actuate the signals, look up at the light, and even reach for it as though by doing so it was attaining some substitutive satisfaction.* When, however, there was no barrier to

* The prayer-like attitudes assumed by animals under these circumstances were described on one occasion by a rather sacrilegious visitor to the labora-

feeding but the current was turned off so that manipulation of the switch did not actuate the sound or light signals, the animal developed more marked behavioral disturbances; it refused to feed, vocalized almost continually, paced searchingly about between periods of energetic manipulation of the switch, or even attacked the latter with teeth and claws as though to vent its anger and frustration.† When the current was again turned on so that the next compression of the switch worked the signals, this behavior disappeared immediately, and the animal resumed its normal feeding pattern.

Significantly, a quite different series of reactions was produced when, instead of being mechanically thwarted in its ultimate (food) or intermediate (symbolic) goals, the animal was permitted to work the signal-switch and thereafter to open the food-box, but was then given an air-blast or grid-shock at the moment of feeding. Such animals developed all the neurotic behavioral abnormalities noted previously – anxiety, signal-phobias, regressions, compulsions, etc. – although generally in a milder form. In addition, they showed a number of specific reactions to the switch itself, i.e., either they ignored it as though they had never learned its use, or else they actively avoided it as though it had become an instrument of danger. Examples of the latter reaction were seen in an animal which despite two days of starvation, refused to approach the open food-box as long as the switch was in its vicinity and in another animal, which avoided the switch when it was in its accustomed place behind the barrier but which worked the signals – at first hesitantly, then efficiently – when the switch was moved to a new location between the barrier and the food-box. Nevertheless, animals trained in the use of the switch and then made neurotic by the air or shock technic possessed a definite advantage over others not so trained, in that the former, either spontaneously or under additional pressure from increased hunger or spatial constriction, began once again to approach the switch, to re-explore its possibilities, and to manipulate it with increasing confidence until they had re-established their individual signal-sounding and feeding patterns. When this occurred, their neurotic abnormalities rapidly diminished and normal behavior returned.

† Much as we smash a tennis racket or a mashie that no longer seems to obey our wishes under crucial circumstances.

tory as a 'worshipful reaching for heavenly light after its promise below had failed.'

Representative observations in the eighteen animals trained to manipulate the switch are quoted in the following examples:

Manipulative learning. – The behavior of Cat 55 is a typical instance of the adaptive and goal-directed rather than stereotyped nature of the learned activity. When the control switch was placed to the right of the barrier away from the food-box, Cat 55 at first passed completely around the barrier to manipulate the switch with a direct downward push of the right forepaw. After only seven trials, however, she began to short-circuit this energetic activity by merely reaching either forepaw past the barrier to depress the switch. When the control was then placed just out of reach, the cat began to struggle completely through the opening; however, she soon discovered the roomier passage to the rear and thereafter utilized this indirect but easier way of access to the switch. Moreover her behavior was now even less stereotyped, in that she manipulated the switch with any portion of her body – paw, head, or rump – best suited to its relative position.

Incorporation of signals into habit-patterns. – The compulsion most animals felt to manipulate the switch and actuate the signals before feeding was apparent in many observations. Thus, in experiments with Cats 30 and 102, the current from the switch was interrupted so that depression of the disk no longer produced the light-and-bell signals. Under such circumstances the cats remained at the control, continually rubbing against it or stepping on it until at length the current was again turned on. However, as soon as the feeding signals were actuated, the cats immediately left the control and rushed to feed. Cat 30 several times left the switch when it was turned off and approached the box but, instead of opening it, returned to the switch; when this was turned on, she depressed it once more and, as the signal was given, promptly went to feed.

Effects of frustration. – Cat 60 was placed with the switch to the right of the barrier and permitted several feeding responses, after which the side guards were mounted on the barrier to prevent the animal's return to the food-box. The cat worked the switch and gave the signal as usual, then proceeded vigorously to claw at the sides of the barrier. Finding this futile, she showed agitation and restlessness but returned to press the switch, first with one paw, then with both; finally, she sat continuously on the disk control for ten minutes, constantly actuating the signals until the guards were removed and she was allowed to rush to the box and feed.

'Repression' of learned behavior produced by air-blasts, air-blasts plus grid-shocks, and space-constriction. – Cat 37, a normally active animal, easily learned to use the control switch. However, when the feeding responses were disrupted by air-blasts given at the time he opened the food-box, he abandoned the use of the control, vocalized excessively, and paced about continually. Moreover, while he did not avoid the switch, he seemed to ignore it precisely as he had done before he became familiar with its use, even when restricted very close to it by the barrier.

Under these circumstances he closed the switch twice, apparently accidentally, but showed no manifest reactions to the signals. After two days of starvation the animal approached the food-box but would not feed without the use of the control. Later, however, abortive attempts to manipulate the switch began to appear, e.g., touching the switch lightly but not hard enough to activate the feeding signal. Space-constriction elicited use of the switch and feeding, but this response was again completely abolished by another air-blast. During this period Cat 37, although he had previously run directly from the animal room to jump into the experimental apparatus, now took many wrong turns in the hall and finally began to resist being placed in the apparatus, in spite of the fact that that was the only place he could expect to be fed. Following two days of complete starvation, however, the animal spontaneously began again to paw the switch delicately until it had actuated the signals; after a series of decreasing phobic reactions to these, he began to manipulate the switch with increasing effectiveness and so re-establish his feeding responses and normal general behavior.

Cat 15 had been used in previous experiments with air-blasts and grid-shocks but had been retrained to respond to the signals and had learned to use the control switch with no difficulty. However, air-blasts again given when he manipulated the switch abolished this newly learned behavior but did not prevent him from feeding when the signal was given by the experimenter. Nevertheless, when space-constriction was introduced, he began using the control once or twice each time the barrier was moved to the left, and further constriction finally induced him to open the food-box.

Cat 53 required nine days of training before she learned the use of the switch. She then received only one air-blast plus grid-shock at the time of opening the lid, yet this abolished her response for the following five days. Starvation and some retraining finally induced her to resume manipulation of the switch and even to feed despite air-blasts, but her spontaneous use of the control subsequent to such experiences was usually again abolished or impaired. For instance, she would depress the switch but would not respond to the feeding signal she elicited, or occasionally she would go through successful or abortive manipulations of the switch several times before moving up to feed, even when constricted into a small space with the switch and food-box. Under these circumstances, however, the animal would sometimes feed furtively without using the control. Space-constriction with only the switch available also favored use of the control for the signals alone, but only when the response had been abolished by air-blasts; after the greater psychological trauma of blasts plus shock, constriction produced only feeding directly from the box without the use of the control switch. Nevertheless, when direct feeding was prevented for four days of near-starvation, the excessive hunger finally induced the animal to manipulate the switch successfully before feeding. Thereafter, responses to conditional signals given by the operator were variable; sometimes the animal came to feed, while at other times she either cowered or ignored the signals and lay still.

On being placed in the cage each day she operated the switch and responded to the signals once or twice but then settled back at the rear and lay quiet. After the blast plus shock the animal usually became exceedingly quiet, but on the following day would actively resist entry to the cage and would show agitation when forced into it. However, after a terminal week of partial starvation and intensive retraining, the use of the switch and signal-feeding behavior was re-established, and the neurotic manifestations disappeared.

Spontaneous working-through of the conflict situation. – Cat 74, after a month of normal responses, was exposed to air-blasts at the time of delivery of food. She at first abandoned the use of the switch but in five days progressed through partial tolerance of air-blasts, with delayed, hesitant, tentative trials of the switch, to complete tolerance of the blasts and normal use of the control. This was accomplished with the use of no therapeutic technic other than maintaining the animal's hunger by subliminal feedings and permitting her an hour daily in the experimental apparatus.

Differentiation of externally given from manipulated feeding signals

As has been indicated, many cats which abandoned the use of the control switch nevertheless continued to respond to feeding signals given by the experimenter. However, a special experiment demonstrated that this effect could be reversed under circumstances in which the externally given signals were directly reminiscent of an unpleasant motivational conflict, whereas the use of the switch represented a means of indirect or manipulative avoidance of that conflict. The experiment was as follows:

Cat 204 was trained to respond to a bell feeding signal and subsequently taught the use of the switch that controlled the signal. The switch was then removed from the cage, and the signal was given by the experimenter, followed by air-blasts at the moment of feeding. This technic induced behavior disturbances of a severe degree: bodily manifestations of anxiety, self-starvation, exaggerated startle reactions, panic states during constriction, etc. The animal was then permitted to rest for several weeks without further experimentation. On its return to the experimental situation, it still refused to feed if the signal was given by the experimenter. When, however, the control switch was reintroduced, the cat immediately began using it to sound the same bell, after which the animal fed promptly and with complete freedom, *although it continued to cower at all feeding signals given by the experimenter*. In this animal, then, signals not preceded by spontaneous switch-manipulation had apparently come to represent a conflictful and anxiety-ridden situation, whereas the same signals, when self-administered, had no such connotation and were therefore conducive to 'normal' adaptive behavior.

Differentiation of successive responses

In an attempt to produce specifically repetitive patterns of adaptation ('counting behavior') seven cats, after being trained to use the control switch, were then given food through the feeder-mechanism only at every second feeding signal in four instances, and at every third feeding signal in the three others. The results were these:

Cat 33, which received food from alternate cups, began to respond more slowly to the feeding signal which was not followed by food and to look only momentarily into the box before returning to the switch to work the next signal, following which he dashed to the box for the expected reward. After some days he began walking to the box without opening it on the alternate (negative) trials, but for some undetermined reason lost this differential reaction after about a month. In four weeks of further training, however, partial differentiation reappeared and progressed to the point at which the animal no longer made a detectable motion toward the food-box on alternate trials, but instead efficiently pressed the switch twice in succession before attempting to feed. Complete differentiation of alternate trials (i.e., 'counting to two') was similarly established in another animal and partial differentiation in two more.

Cat 29 had food delivered only after every third manipulation of the switch. Initially, every time she gave the signal she opened the box and explored it thoroughly for food; however, after five days she began to drop the lid more promptly and return to the switch on the two trials when no food was delivered. Finally her activity became less well-co-ordinated with the sequence of signals, and she again came to open the box after every signal, although not bothering to explore it if no food was evident at first glance. After passage to the food-box was made more difficult by placing the switch behind the barrier, the animal showed a lesser degree of energy in struggling through the opening on the two negative trials – indicating the acquisition of a significant triplicate sequence; nevertheless, she always came through and made no further progress toward learning to depress the switch thrice in succession before feeding. Two other animals, subjected to a similar procedure, were even less successful in learning the differentiation.* However, no animal, despite months of such arithmetically determined frustration, developed significant signs of neurotic behavior.

Comparative efficacy of the methods of alleviating experimental neuroses

Of the six methods – (1) rest from the conflictful situation; (2) diminution of the conflictful hunger drive by forced feeding;

* Recently, one cat genius has been taught to 'count to three'; i.e., to press the switch-disk three times before feeding (Masserman and Rubinfine, 1943).

(3) petting and reassuring handling by the experimenter; (4) environmental manipulations by the experimenter leading to a break-through of inhibitions on the part of the animal; (5) 'inter-cat example', and (6) manipulative 'working-through' of the conflict by the animal itself – methods (6) and (4) were nearly always most effective in that order in producing lasting alleviation of the experimentally produced 'symptoms' and in restoring normal adaptive behavior in the neurotic animals. In this con-nexion it is significant that these methods also required the great-est amount of *spontaneous* readaptation on the part of the animal, whereas methods (2), (3), and (5) required various degrees of manipulation by others. Needless to say, a combination of all the methods, with the possible exception of (4), produced he most satisfactory therapeutic results when used as indicated in the individual neurotic animal.

Production of behavior changes in dogs

As a preliminary extension of these studies to animals of other species, two dogs were trained to respond by feeding to the light-and-bell signals and were then given air-blasts during these responses. This was at first done in the cage used for the cat experi-ments, but later the dogs were transferred to a special room built for the study of conflictful behavior in larger animals. Essentially this room was an expanded version of the experimental cat cage seven feet square and eight feet high, equipped with three half-mirrored glass panes placed so that the animal could not see the experimenter, whereas the latter could observe and photograph the entire room. A long chute carried food to a food-box near the center of the room; this box had a hinged lid which could be raised or lowered by cords leading to the outside. Overhead lights and a bell served as conditional signals and were either manually oper-ated from a switchboard outside the cage or else mechanically actuated at selected intervals by an automatic rotary governor. A nozzle was placed to throw a jet of air across the food-box when desired, and a grid-panel covered the floor around the food-box to make possible application of grid-shocks.

Dog 1 was trained in the cat cage in the usual manner but with some initial difficulty because of his intense interest in exploring the cage and watching the experimenter. Even after adequate training he remained rather active, moved around constantly, whined occasionally, and continued to be very sensitive to extraneous stimuli; nevertheless, he always stopped other activities and came directly to feed at the condition-al bell-and-light signals. After being trained to open the box for food at the combined stimuli, the animal invariably responded to the light alone, the bell alone, or the feeder alone, although in the latter instance occasionally with some hesitation.

One air-blast at the time of his feeding response to a conditional signal caused a frenzied rush away from the food-box and constant running, turning, and twisting until the next signal, at which he whined excessively and then sat quietly trembling and panting with obvious respiratory irregularity. Subsequent feeding signals again induced whining, twisting movements and, later, peculiarly abortive and self-frustrative attempts to open the lid of the food-box. When this was done by the experimenter from outside the cage, the animal came up to feed, but a feeding signal administered as he was eating caused another scurry to the rear. On subsequent days pronounced trembling occurred between and during the signals, and at times there appeared excited pacing about, pawing the sides of the cage, and barking. At this time the dog began to manifest uneasiness at the approach of the experimenter and to show increasing reluctance and resistance to being taken to the experimental room.

After a month's vacation the animal was again placed in the special experimental dog room. He was very restless, crouched at the feeding signal, and ate only hesitantly from the open food-box. However, when he was allowed to feed from the open box without being given any signals he soon showed a return to his normal curiosity and mobility. Then, over a fourteen-day period the light-and-bell signals were reintroduced and the lid gradually lowered until a good feeding response was obtained.

A singular behavioral pattern strikingly analogous to compulsive behavior in the human then appeared. Regardless of where the dog happened to be – even if sitting immediately in front of the food-box or tentatively sniffing at it – the moment the feeding signal was given, the animal invariably circled the room twice in succession, 'bowed' on his forepaws in a far corner, and then furtively stalked to the box from the left before opening it and feeding. Sometimes after the completion of this pre-feeding ritual and just as he was about to feed, he would suddenly run once or twice more around the food-box itself. This behavior pattern appeared unchanged after each feeding signal for ten days, during which no other experimental procedures were introduced. A single air-blast was then again administered after a feeding response; this pre-cipitated a rush to hide in a far corner of the room, where the dog then remained, trembling, in one position, except to cower tensely at each later feeding signal. During the succeeding four daily sessions he sat sulking in the same corner, refusing to feed even when the lid was widely opened and feeding signals were not given. By this time the animal had become somewhat emaciated, and the experiment was discontinued; however, even in its home cage and with the kindest of care, the animal, contrary to its previous characteristics, continued to be restless, sensitive, fearful of unusual lights and noises, suspicious of strangers, and un-predictable in its feeding habits.

Dog 2 was a rather timid animal which, when placed in the experimental room, sat quietly behind the food-box. She was hesitant about feeding from the open box and was severely frightened by the feeding signal. After another day without food she began eating from the box more regularly as food was given, and after a week began to show more freedom of movement. This spontaneity was markedly enhanced when the experimenter was in the room with the dog. At such times the animal seemed at ease and even playful; in fact, only under these conditions could the feeding response to the light-and-bell signal be initiated even with the lid of the box wide open. The experimenter then left the room, and during the next five days the lid was gradually lowered until the complete box-opening behavior was firmly established. The animal's normal feeding response to the signal then evolved as a ludicrously sedate approach from behind and to the left of the food-box to open the lid. Between signals she usually sat near the box and occasionally got up to wander around the room. After one air-blast, which sent the animal cowering against the door of the room, no further feeding responses to the signals appeared. Instead, the animal remained crouched near the door and at each signal scratched at the door for several seconds. When the food-box was opened by the experimenter from outside the cage, the animal continued to abstain from feeding, even after three days of hunger. However, as soon as the experimenter stepped into the room, the dog once again rushed to the food-box and fed as readily as she had done during her initial training. This feeding reaction to the experimenter's presence invariably occurred when the lid of the box was down and occasionally even during an air-blast, although the light-and-bell signals continued to disrupt the feeding every time they were given. Moreover, as soon as the experimenter left the room, the feeding responses disappeared, the animal again became restless and fearful, and the other neurotic manifestations returned.

Both dogs, before exposure to the air-blast, found their own way to the experimental chamber and freely entered it. However, after experiencing the air-blast during feeding, their behavior outside of the experimental situation was noticeably changed; they followed the experimenter downstairs but huddled in the corridor outside the experimental room and had to be dragged into it. Moreover, both animals were definitely more restless, irritable, excitable, and fearful even under favorable circumstances in their home cages.

Summary of Experimental Results

Résumé of methods and control observations

Eighty-two cats and two dogs were trained in an automatic apparatus to lift the lid of a box to secure food at a sound and/or light signal, thus establishing a simple or compound sensory symbolism which regularly initiated goal-directed behavior. Animals so trained readily entered the conditioning cage, resisted removal, and showed no adverse reactions to any of the training procedures. When the feeding responses were prevented by locking the lid of the food-box, by interposing an impassable barrier between the cat and the food, or by failing to drop food into the box after the signal, the animal soon ceased to respond to the food-signals and later appeared to ignore these completely; significantly, however, such 'frustrated' animals did not resist being put into the cage and displayed no anxiety or phobic reactions in the experimental situations.

Technic of production of an experimental neurosis

The animal was permitted to open the food-box on signal but was then subjected to a physically harmless but apparently fear-inspiring air-blast across the box at the moment of food-taking. One or two repetitions of the procedure apparently engendered a motivational conflict (fear versus hunger) of sufficient intensity to produce an 'experimental neurosis' characterized by the following 'symptoms':

1. *Chronic 'anxiety' in or out of the experimental situation* – This was manifested by restlessness, trembling, crouching, hiding, marked startle responses to minor sensory stimuli, and recurrent or chronic disturbances of pulse and respiration.

2. *The development of 'phobic' responses to stimuli symbolic of the emotionally conflictful stimulation* – The neurotic animal, despite its hunger, now reacted to the formerly welcomed feeding signal with marked accentuation of the symptoms of anxiety and with immediate attempts to escape from the vicinity of the food-box. Some animals actually starved themselves into severe cachexia with the food openly displayed and readily available, whereas others accepted only small amounts of food from the hand of the experimenter, provided that it differed materially from that used in the conflict situation.

3. *Other 'neurotic' phenomena* – During their neurosis many animals licked, cleaned, and preened themselves excessively, courted an unusual amount of fondling by the experimenter, and often reacted aggressively toward other animals. 'Fixation' of reaction patterns was also observed; e.g., once an animal learned a specific method of escaping from the vicinity of the food, it persisted in this pattern, no matter how difficult or apparently painful, even when much easier avenues of escape were made available. 'Compulsive' and 'counterphobic' acts likewise appeared; for instance, during the neurosis the animal would

circumvent the food-box in a peculiarly ritualistic manner or hide its head in the box at the signal without taking food despite days of starvation.

4. *Exacerbation of the 'neurotic' behavior during accentuation of the motivational conflict* – The behavior abnormalities noted above were usually most marked on the third day of self-starvation when the conflict between hunger and fear of feeding was apparently at its height. However, an increase in the anxiety and desperate attempts to escape could be produced at any time if the hungry animal was forced towards the food-box by a movable transparent barrier. This psychological effect was more marked when the barrier was fitted with an opaque screen, i.e., behavior reactions characteristic of severe 'claustrophobia' appeared. Similarly, the disturbing effects of the feeding signals increased as the animal was pushed toward the food – the locale and nidus of its conflict – by the movable barrier.

Methods of 'psychotherapy'

The 'neurotic' behavior patterns generally persisted in overt form for many months after experimental induction and could readily be re-established in full strength thereafter by only a single repetition of the conflict situation. However, six types of procedure, alone or in combination, were found to be effective in mitigating or abolishing the neurotic manifestations. Dynamically analyzed, the 'therapeutic' technics were these:

1. *A period of rest from the situation which had induced the motivational conflict* – This, however, produced only an unstable recovery, and the neurosis could be precipitated again by a single repetition of the conflictful situation.

2. *Diminution of the intensity of the conflictful hunger drive* – If the neurotic animal were fed outside the cage before being replaced in the experimental situation, its anxiety and phobic reactions to the feeding signals and to space-constriction were less marked than those that occurred when its hunger was intense.

3. *'Reassurance' and 'suggestion' ('transference technic')* – If the animal in the experimental situation was gently brought to the food-box by an experimenter it trusted, hand-fed by him, and then patiently retrained to take the food directly from the box, it gradually resumed normal feeding responses on signal and, despite residua of neurotic behavior, the anxiety, phobic, and regressive reactions gradually disappeared. This technic likewise partook of some of the elements of 'transference', since the animal apparently utilized the security it had previously associated

with the experimenter in resolving the fear component in its fear-hunger motivational conflict. Conversely, if the animal had always feared the experimenter or had grown to distrust him, the technic was ineffectual.

4. *Forced solution of the motivational impasse through environmental manipulation* – If the animal, on its third day of starvation, was forced by the barrier into the vicinity of an open food-box containing highly attractive food seasoned with catnip, the inhibitions were in most cases suddenly overwhelmed by the maximally reinforced hunger drive, with the result that rapid, compulsive eating from the box ensued. Once this more normally adaptive response broke through, the animal quickly lost its phobic reactions to the food, the signals, and other elements in the experimental situation; in fact, the air-blast itself – previously so fear-inspiring – in some instances became an eagerly awaited signal for feeding. Concurrently, the anxious, fixated, substitutive, and regressive behavior patterns present during the preceding period of neurosis rapidly diminished.

5. *'Social imitation'* – If a cat with normal responses to the food-signal was placed in the cage with the hungry neurotic animal, the latter gradually began to join in the feeding behavior and eventually again responded to the feeding signal by opening the box. However, the normal responses never became so completely re-established as those obtained by the preceding methods, nor were the neurotic behavior patterns as rapidly overcome.

6. *'Working through'* – Cats could readily be trained to depress a switch which operated various conditional sensory signals that they had previously learned to associate with the deposition of food in the box. An animal so trained rarely attempted to feed unless it had first flashed or sounded the appropriate feeding signals and would accordingly make every effort to circumvent barriers experimentally placed between it and the control switch. When the circuit was turned off so that manipulation of the switch no longer operated the signals, the animal still did not attempt to feed but instead spent a great deal of time and energy in pressing the switch or other objects in efforts to make the signals work, i.e., the animal displayed substitutive goal-directed activity but *did not develop neurotic behavior patterns*. If, however, the animal were given free access to both the signal-switch and the food but if food-taking were now rendered *conflictful* by the air-blast technic, the neurotic manifestations described above quickly appeared. The animal then began to avoid the switch or else ignored it as though the 'emotionally traumatic' memory of its function had been

'repressed'. Nevertheless, as hunger mounted, the animal once more began to work the signals and take the food reward with increasing confidence despite repetitions of the air-blast, until, through trial activity at optimum moments of its own selection, it had spontaneously resolved its motivational conflicts and dissipated the 'neurosis'.

References
1. BROSIN, H. W., 'Anorexia nervosa', *J. clin. Endocrinol.*, 1941, 1: 269.
2. MASSERMAN, J. H., 'Psychodynamisms in anorexia nervosa and neurotic vomiting', *Psychoanalyt. Quart.*, 1941, 10: 211.
3. MASSERMAN, J. H., and RUBINFINE, D. L., '"Counting" behaviour in cats', *J. gen. Psychol.*, 1943, 30: 87–8.
4. SKINNER, B. F., *The behavior of organisms: an experimental analysis*, Appleton-Century-Crofts, 1938.

Part Four CLASSICAL PSYCHODYNAMICS

The paper by Breuer and Freud is generally regarded as the foundation of psychoanalytical theory. It exemplifies the modesty and diffidence as well as the caution of the earlier writings of Freud. It has not been possible to include the case reports which accompany it, but I hope that this will not impair its value.

Later in their work both Freud and Jung became very much more interested in theory and speculation but the early paper of Jung's included here is a clear illustration of that remarkable combination of clinical insight and down-to-earth adherence to facts which are characteristic of his earlier work. As with the previous paper, it can still be the basis for much vigorous discussion and criticism and this is as good a reason as any for including it.

The paper by Adler is one of the few which are sufficiently complete in themselves to stand on their own.

The work of Janet has tended to be overshadowed by that of Freud and a renewed interest in his work is long overdue. His theory on the nature of hysteria has become much more important since it has been generally recognized that hysterical symptoms may appear in anybody under conditions of sufficient stress and fatigue. I hope that this final chapter of his book will give an adequate impression of his work.

11 J. Breuer and S. Freud

On the Psychical Mechanisms of Hysterical Phenomena:
Preliminary Communication

J. Breuer and S. Freud, *Studies on hysteria*, Basic Books Inc., 1957, chapter
1: *The complete works of Sigmund Freud* (ed. J. Strachey), Hogarth
Press, 1955, vol. 2.

I

A chance observation has led us, over a number of years, to investigate a great variety of different forms and symptoms of hysteria,
with a view to discovering their precipitating cause – the event
which provoked the first occurrence, often many years earlier, of
the phenomenon in question. In the great majority of cases it is
not possible to establish the point of origin by a simple interrogation of the patient, however thoroughly it may be carried out. This
is in part because what is in question is often some experience
which the patient dislikes discussing; but principally because he is
genuinely unable to recollect it and often has no suspicion of the
causal connection between the precipitating event and the pathological phenomenon. As a rule it is necessary to hypnotize the
patient and to arouse his memories under hypnosis of the time at
which the symptom made its first appearance; when this has been
done, it becomes possible to demonstrate the connexion in the
clearest and most convincing fashion.

This method of examination has in a large number of cases produced results which seem to be of value alike from a theoretical
and a practical point of view.

They are valuable theoretically because they have taught us that
external events determine the pathology of hysteria to an extent
far greater than is known and recognized. It is of course obvious
that in cases of 'traumatic' hysteria what provokes the symptoms
is the accident. The causal connexion is equally evident in hysterical
attacks when it is possible to gather from the patient's utterances
that in each attack he is hallucinating the same event which provoked the first one. The situation is more obscure in the case of
other phenomena.

Our experiences have shown us, however, that the most various
symptoms, which are ostensibly spontaneous and, as one might say,
idiopathic products of hysteria, are just as strictly related to the

precipitating trauma as the phenomena to which we have just alluded and which exhibit the connexion quite clearly. The symptoms which we have been able to trace back to precipitating factors of this sort include neuralgias and anaesthesias of very various kinds, many of which had persisted for years, contractures and paralyses, hysterical attacks and epileptoid convulsions, which every observer regarded as true epilepsy, *petit mal* and disorders in the nature of *tic*, chronic vomiting and anorexia, carried to the pitch of rejection of all nourishment, various forms of disturbance of vision, constantly recurrent visual hallucinations, etc. The disproportion between the many years' duration of the hysterical symptom and the single occurrence which provoked it is what we are accustomed invariably to find in traumatic neuroses. Quite frequently it is some event in childhood that sets up a more or less severe symptom which persists during the years that follow.

The connexion is often so clear that it is quite evident how it was that the precipitating event produced this particular phenomenon rather than any other. In that case the symptom has quite obviously been determined by the precipitating cause. We may take as a very commonplace instance a painful emotion arising during a meal but suppressed at the time, and then producing nausea and vomiting which persists for months in the form of hysterical vomiting. A girl, watching beside a sick-bed in a torment of anxiety, fell into a twilight state and had a terrifying hallucination, while her right arm, which was hanging over the back of her chair, went to sleep; from this there developed a paresis of the same arm accompanied by contracture and anaesthesia. She tried to pray but could find no words; at length she succeeded in repeating a children's prayer in English. When subsequently a severe and highly complicated hysteria developed, she could only speak, write and understand English, while her native language remained unintelligible to her for eighteen months – The mother of a very sick child, which had at last fallen asleep, concentrated her whole will-power on keeping still so as not to waken it. Precisely on account of her intention she made a 'clacking' noise with her tongue. (An instance of 'hysterical counter-will'.) This noise was repeated on a subsequent occasion on which she wished to keep perfectly still; and from it there developed a *tic* which, in the form of a clacking with the tongue, occurred over a period of many years whenever she felt excited – A highly intelligent man was present while his brother had an ankylosed hip-joint extended under an anaesthetic. At the instant at which the joint gave way with a crack, he felt a violent pain in his own hip-joint, which persisted for nearly a year – Further instances could be quoted.

In other cases the connexion is not so simple. It consists only in what might be called a 'symbolic' relation between the precipitating cause and the pathological phenomenon – a relation such as healthy people form in dreams. For instance a neuralgia may follow upon mental pain or vomiting upon a feeling of moral disgust. We have studied patients who used to make the most copious use of this sort of symbolization. In still other cases it is not possible to understand at first sight how they can be determined in the manner we have suggested. It is precisely the typical hysterical symptoms which fall into this class, such as hemi-anaesthesia, contraction of the field of vision, epileptiform convulsions, and so on. An explanation of our views on this group must be reserved for a fuller discussion of the subject.

Observations such as these seem to us to establish an analogy between the pathogenesis of common hysteria and that of traumatic neuroses, and to justify an extension of the concept of traumatic hysteria. In traumatic neuroses the operative cause of the illness is not the trifling physical injury but the affect of fright – the psychical trauma. In an analogous manner, our investigations reveal, for many, if not for most, hysterical symptoms, precipitating causes which can only be described as psychical traumas. Any experience which calls up distressing effects – such as those of fright, anxiety, shame or physical pain – may operate as a trauma of this kind; and whether it in fact does so depends naturally enough on the susceptibility of the person affected (as well as on another condition which will be mentioned later). In the case of common hysteria it not infrequently happens that, instead of a single, major trauma, we find a number of partial traumas forming a *group* of provoking causes. These have only been able to exercise a traumatic effect by summation and they belong together in so far as they are in part components of a single story of suffering. There are other cases in which an apparently trivial circumstance combines with the actually operative event or occurs at a time of peculiar susceptibility to stimulation and in this way attains the dignity of a trauma which it would not otherwise have possessed but which thenceforward persists.

But the causal relation between the determining psychical trauma and the hysterical phenomenon is not of a kind implying that the trauma merely acts like an *agent provocateur* in releasing the symptom, which thereafter leads an independent existence. We must presume rather that the psychical trauma – or more precisely the memory of the trauma – acts like a foreign body which long after its entry must continue to be regarded as an agent that is still at work; and we find the evidence for this in a highly remarkable phenomenon which at the same time lends an important *practical* interest to our findings.

For we found, to our great surprise at first, that *each individual hysterical symptom immediately and permanently disappeared when we had succeeded in bringing clearly to light the memory of the event by which it was provoked and in arousing its accompanying affect, and when the patient had described that event in the greatest possible detail and had put the affect into words.* Recollection without affect almost invariably produces no result. The psychical process which originally took place must be repeated as vividly as possible; it must be brought back to its *status nascendi* and then given verbal utterance. Where what we are dealing with are phenomena involving stimuli (spasms, neuralgias and hallucinations) these re-appear once again with the fullest intensity and then vanish for ever. Failures of function, such as paralyses and anaesthesias, vanish in the same way, though, of course, without the temporary intensification being discernible.*

It is plausible to suppose that it is a question here of unconscious suggestion: the patient expects to be relieved of his sufferings by this procedure, and it is this expectation, and not the verbal utterance, which is the operative factor. This, however, is not so. The first case of this kind that came under observation dates back to the year 1881, that is to say to the 'pre-suggestion' era. A highly complicated case of hysteria was analyzed in this way, and the symptoms, which sprang from separate causes, were separately removed. This observation was made possible by spontaneous

---

* The possibility of a therapeutic procedure of this kind has been clearly recognized by Delboeuf and Binet, as is shown by the following quotations: 'On s'expliquerait dès lors comment le magnétiseur aide à la guérison. Il remet le sujet dans l'état où le mal s'est manifesté et combat par la parole le même mal, mais renaissant.' ['We can now explain how the hypnotist promotes cure. He puts the subject back into the state in which his trouble first appeared and uses words to combat that trouble, as it now makes a fresh emergence.'] (Delboeuf, 1889.) – '. . . peut-être verra-t-on qu'en reportant le malade par un artifice mental au moment même où le symptome a apparu pour la première fois, on rend ce malade plus docile à une suggestion curative.' ['. . . we shall perhaps find that by taking the patient back by means of a mental artifice to the very moment at which the symptom first appeared, we may make him more susceptible to a therapeutic suggestion.'] (Binet, 1892, 243.) – In Janet's interesting study on mental automatism (1889), there is an account of the cure of a hysterical girl by a method analogous to ours.

auto-hypnoses on the part of the patient, and came as a great surprise to the observer.

We may reverse the dictum *'cessante causa cessat effectus'* ['when the cause ceases the effect ceases'] and conclude from these observations that the determining process continues to operate in some way or other for years – not indirectly, through a chain of intermediate causal links, but as a *directly* releasing cause – just as a psychical pain that is remembered in waking consciousness still provokes a lachrymal secretion long after the event. *Hysterics suffer mainly from reminiscences.**

II

At first sight it seems extraordinary that events experienced so long ago should continue to operate so intensely – that their recollection should not be liable to the wearing away process to which, after all, we see all our memories succumb. The following considerations may perhaps make this a little more intelligible.

The fading of a memory or the losing of its affect depends on various factors. The most important of these is *whether there has been an energetic reaction to the event that provokes an affect*. By 'reaction' we here understand the whole class of voluntary and involuntary reflexes – from tears to acts of revenge – in which, as experience shows us, the affects are discharged. If this reaction takes place to a sufficient amount a large part of the affect disappears as a result. Linguistic usage bears witness to this fact of daily observation by such phrases as 'to cry oneself out' ['*sich ausweinen*'], and to 'blow off steam' ['*sich austoben*', literally 'to rage oneself out']. If the reaction is suppressed, the affect remains attached to the memory. An injury that has been repaid, even if only in words, is recollected quite differently from one that has had to be accepted. Language recognizes this distinction, too, in its mental and physical consequences; it very characteristically describes an injury that has been suffered in silence as 'a mortification' ['*Kränkung*', lit. 'making ill']. The injured person's reaction to the trauma only exercises a completely 'cathartic' effect if it is an *adequate* reaction – as, for instance, revenge. But language serves as a substitute for action; by its help, an affect can be 'abreacted' almost as effectively.† In other cases speaking is

---

* In this preliminary communication it is not possible for us to distinguish what is new in it from what has been said by other authors.

† ['Catharsis' and 'abreaction' made their first published appearance in this passage. Freud had used the term 'abreaction' previously (June 28, 1892), in a letter to Fliess referring to the present paper.]

itself the adequate reflex, when, for instance, it is a lamentation or giving utterance to a tormenting secret, e.g. a confession. If there is no such reaction, whether in deeds or words, or in the mildest cases in tears, any recollection of the event retains its affective tone to begin with.

'Abreaction', however, is not the only method of dealing with the situation that is open to a normal person who has experienced a psychical trauma. A memory of such a trauma, even if it has not been abreacted, enters the great complex of associations, it comes alongside other experiences, which may contradict it, and is subjected to rectification by other ideas. After an accident, for instance, the memory of the danger and the (mitigated) repetition of the fright becomes associated with the memory of what happened afterwards – rescue and the consciousness of present safety. Again, a person's memory of a humiliation is corrected by his putting the facts right, by considering his own worth, etc. In this way a normal person is able to bring about the disappearance of the accompanying affect through the process of association.

To this we must add the general effacement of impressions, the fading of memories which we name 'forgetting' and which wears away those ideas in particular that are no longer affectively operative.

Our observations have shown, on the other hand, that the memories which have become the determinants of hysterical phenomena persist for a long time with astonishing freshness and with the whole of their affective colouring. We must, however, mention another remarkable fact, which we shall later be able to turn to account, namely, that these memories, unlike other memories of their past lives, are not at the patients' disposal. On the contrary, *these experiences are completely absent from the patients' memory when they are in a normal psychical state, or are only present in a highly summary form.* Not until they have been questioned under hypnosis do these memories emerge with the undiminished vividness of a recent event.

Thus, for six whole months, one of our patients reproduced under hypnosis with hallucinatory vividness everything that had excited her on the same day of the previous year (during an attack of acute hysteria). A diary kept by her mother without her knowledge proved the completeness of the reproduction. Another patient, partly under hypnosis and partly during spontaneous attacks, re-lived with hallucinatory clarity all the events of a hysterical psychosis which she had passed through ten years earlier and which she had for the most part forgotten till the moment at which it re-emerged. Moreover, certain memories of aetiological importance which dated back from fifteen to twenty-five years were found to be astonishingly intact and to possess remarkable sensory force, and when they returned they acted with all the affective strength of new experiences.

This can only be explained on the view that these memories constitute an exception in their relation to all the wearing-away processes which we have discussed above. *It appears, that is to say, that these memories correspond to traumas that have not been sufficiently abreacted;* and if we enter more closely into the reasons which have prevented this, we find at least two sets of conditions under which the reaction to the trauma fails to occur.

In the first group are those cases in which the patients have not reacted to a psychical trauma because the nature of the trauma excluded a reaction, as in the case of the apparently irreparable loss of a loved person or because social circumstances made a reaction impossible or because it was a question of things which the patient wished to forget, and therefore intentionally repressed from his conscious thought and inhibited and suppressed. It is precisely distressing things of this kind that, under hypnosis, we find are the basis of hysterical phenomena (e.g., hysterical deliria in saints and nuns, continent women and well-brought-up children).

The second group of conditions are determined, not by the content of the memories but by the psychical states in which the patient received the experiences in question. For we find, under hypnosis, among the causes of hysterical symptoms ideas which are not in themselves significant, but whose persistence is due to the fact that they originated during the prevalence of severely paralysing affects, such as fright, or during positively abnormal psychical states, such as the semi-hypnotic twilight state of day-dreaming, auto-hypnoses, and so on. In such cases it is the nature of the states which makes a reaction to the event impossible.

Both kinds of conditions may, of course, be simultaneously present, and this, in fact, often occurs. It is so when a trauma which is operative in itself takes place while a severely paralysing affect prevails or during a modified state of consciousness. But it also seems to be true that in many people a psychical trauma *produces* one of these abnormal states, which, in turn, makes reaction impossible.

Both of these groups of conditions, however, have in common the fact that the psychical traumas which have not been disposed of by reaction cannot be disposed of either by being worked over by means of association. In the first group the patient is determined to forget the distressing experiences and accordingly excludes them so far as possible from association; while in the second group the associative working-over fails to occur because there is no extensive associative connexion between the normal state of consciousness and the pathological ones in which the ideas made their appearance. We shall have occasion immediately to enter further into this matter. *It may therefore be said that the ideas which have become pathological have persisted with such freshness and affective strength because they have been denied the normal wearing-away processes by means of abreaction and reproduction in states of uninhibited association.*

III

We have stated the conditions which, as our experience shows, are responsible for the development of hysterical phenomena from psychical traumas. In so doing, we have already been obliged to speak of abnormal states of consciousness in which these pathogenic ideas arise, and to emphasize the fact that the recollection of the operative psychical trauma is not to be found in the patient's normal memory but in his memory when he is hypnotized. The longer we have been occupied with these phenomena the more we have become convinced that *the splitting of consciousness which is so striking in the well-known classical cases under the form of* 'double conscience'* *is present to a rudimentary degree in every hysteria, and that a tendency to such a dissociation, and with it the emergence of abnormal states of consciousness (which we shall bring together under the term 'hypnoid') is the basic phenomenon of this neurosis.* In these views we concur with Binet and the two Janets,† though we have had no experience of the remarkable findings they have made on anaesthetic patients.

We should like to balance the familiar thesis that hypnosis is an artificial hysteria by another – the basis and *sine qua non* of hysteria is the existence of hypnoid states. These hypnoid states share with one another and with hypnosis, however much they may differ in other respects, one common feature: the ideas which emerge in them are very intense but are cut off from associative communication with the rest of the content of consciousness. Associations may take place between these hypnoid states, and their ideational content can in this way reach a more or less high degree of psychical organization. Moreover, the nature of these states and the extent

* [The French term 'dual consciousness'.]
† [Pierre and Jules.]

to which they are cut off from the remaining conscious processes must be supposed to vary just as happens in hypnosis, which ranges from a light drowsiness to somnambulism, from complete recollection to total amnesia.

If hypnoid states of this kind are already present before the onset of the manifest illness, they provide the soil in which the affect plants the pathogenic memory with its consequent somatic phenomena. This corresponds to *dispositional* hysteria. We have found, however, that a severe trauma (such as occurs in a traumatic neurosis) or a laborious suppression (as of a sexual affect, for instance) can bring about a splitting-off of groups of ideas even in people who are in other respects unaffected; and this would be the mechanism of *psychically acquired* hysteria. Between the extremes of these two forms we must assume the existence of a series of cases within which the liability to dissociation in the subject and the affective magnitude of the trauma vary inversely.

We have nothing new to say on the question of the origin of these dispositional hypnoid states. They often, it would seem, grow out of the day-dreams which are so common even in healthy people and to which needlework and similar occupations render women especially prone. Why it is that the 'pathological associations' brought about in these states are so stable and why they have so much more influence on somatic processes than ideas are usually found to do – these questions coincide with the general problem of the effectiveness of hypnotic suggestions. Our observations contribute nothing fresh on this subject. But they throw a light on the contradiction between the dictum 'hysteria is a psychosis' and the fact that among hysterics may be found people of the clearest intellect, strongest will, greatest character and highest critical power. This characterization holds good of their waking thoughts; but in their hypnoid states they are insane, as we all are in dreams. Whereas, however, our dream-psychoses have no effect upon our waking state, the products of hypnoid states intrude into waking life in the form of hysterical symptoms.

IV

What we have asserted of chronic hysterical symptoms can be applied almost completely to hysterical *attacks*. Charcot, as is well known, has given us a schematic description of the 'major' hysterical attack, according to which four phases can be distinguished in a complete attack: (1) the epileptoid phase, (2) the phase of large movements, (3) the phase of '*attitudes passionnelles*' (the hallucinatory phase), and (4) the phase of terminal delirium.

Charcot derives all those forms of hysterical attack which are in practice met with more often than the complete '*grande attaque*', from the abbreviation, absence or isolation of these four distinct phases.

Our attempted explanation takes its start from the third of these phases, that of the '*attitudes passionelles*'. Where this is present in a well-marked form, it exhibits the hallucinatory reproduction of a memory which was of importance in bringing about the onset of the hysteria – the memory either of a single major trauma (which we find *par excellence* in what is called traumatic hysteria) or of a series of interconnected part-traumas (such as underlie common hysteria). Or, lastly, the attack may revive the events which have become emphasized owing to their *coinciding* with a moment of special disposition to trauma.

There are also attacks, however, which appear to consist exclusively of motor phenomena and in which the phase of *attitudes passionelles* is absent. If one can succeed in getting into *rapport* with the patient during an attack such as this of generalized clonic spasms or cataleptic rigidity, or during an *attaque de sommeil* [attack of sleep] – or if, better still, one can succeed in provoking the attack under hypnosis – one finds that here, too, there is an underlying memory of the psychical trauma or series of traumas, which usually comes to our notice in a hallucinatory phase.

Thus, a little girl suffered for years from attacks of general convulsions which could well be, and indeed were, regarded as epileptic. She was hypnotized with a view to a differential diagnosis, and promptly had one of her attacks. She was asked what she was seeing and replied 'The dog! the dog's coming!'; and in fact it turned out that she had had the first of her attacks after being chased by a savage dog. The success of the treatment confirmed the choice of diagnosis.

Again, an employee who had become a hysteric as a result of being ill-treated by his superior, suffered from attacks in which he collapsed and fell into a frenzy of rage, but without uttering a word or giving any sign of a hallucination. It was possible to provoke an attack under hypnosis, and the patient then revealed that he was living through the scene in which his employer had abused him in the street and hit him with a stick. A few days later the patient came back and complained of having had another attack of the same kind. On this occasion it turned out under hypnosis that he had been re-living the scene to which the actual onset of the illness was related: the scene in the law-court when he failed to obtain satisfaction for his maltreatment.

In all other respects, too, the memories which emerge, or can be aroused, in hysterical attacks correspond to the precipitating causes which we have found at the root of *chronic* hysterical symptoms. Like these latter causes, the memories underlying hysterical attacks relate to psychical traumas which have not been disposed of by abreaction or by associative thought-activity. Like them, they are, whether completely or in essential elements, out of reach of the memory of normal consciousness and are found to belong to the ideational content of hypnoid states of consciousness with restricted association. Finally, too, the therapeutic test can be applied to them. Our observations have often taught us that a memory of this kind which had hitherto provoked attacks, ceases to be able to do so after the process of reaction and associative correction have been applied to it under hypnosis.

The motor phenomena of hysterical attacks can be interpreted partly as universal forms of reaction appropriate to the affect accompanying the memory (such as kicking about and waving the arms and legs, which even young babies do), partly as a direct expression of these memories; but in part, like the hysterical stigmata found among the chronic symptoms, they cannot be explained in this way.

Hysterical attacks, furthermore, appear in a specially interesting light if we bear in mind a theory that we have mentioned above, namely, that in hysteria groups of ideas originating in hypnoid states are present and that these are cut off from associative connexion with the other ideas, but can be associated among themselves, and thus form the more or less highly organized rudiment of a second consciousness, a *condition seconde*. If this is so, a chronic hysterical symptom will correspond to the intrusion of this second state into the somatic innervation which is as a rule under the control of normal consciousness. A hysterical attack, on the other hand, is evidence of a higher organization of this second state. When the attack makes its first appearance, it indicates a moment at which this hypnoid consciousness has obtained control of the subject's whole existence – it points, that is, to an acute hysteria; when it occurs on subsequent occasions and contains a memory, it points to a return of that moment. Charcot has already suggested that hysterical attacks are a rudimentary form of a *condition seconde*. During the attack, control over the whole of the somatic innervation passes over to the hypnoid consciousness. Normal consciousness, as well-known observations show, is not always entirely repressed. It may even be aware of the motor phenomena of the attack, while the accompanying psychical events are outside its knowledge.

The typical course of a severe case of hysteria is, as we know, as follows. To begin with, an ideational content is formed during hypnoid states; when this has increased to a sufficient extent, it gains control, during a period of 'acute hysteria', of the somatic innervation and of the patient's whole existence, and creates chronic symptoms and attacks; after this it clears up, apart from certain residues. If the normal personality can regain control, what is left over from the hypnoid ideational content recurs in hysterical attacks and puts the subject back from time to time into similar states, which are themselves once more open to influence and susceptible to traumas. A state of equilibrium, as it were, may then be established between the two psychical groups which are combined in the same person: hysterical attacks and normal life proceed side by side without interfering with each other. An attack will occur spontaneously, just as memories do in normal people; it is, however, possible to provoke one, just as any memory can be aroused in accordance with the laws of association. It can be provoked either by stimulation of a hysterogenic zone* or by a new experience which sets it going owing to a similarity with the pathogenic experience. We hope to be able to show that these two kinds of determinant, though they appear to be so unlike, do not differ in essentials, but that in both a hyperaesthetic memory is touched on.

In other cases this equilibrium is very unstable. The attack makes its appearance as a manifestation of the residue of the hypnoid consciousness whenever the normal personality is exhausted and incapacitated. The possibility cannot be dismissed that here the attack may have been divested of its original meaning and may be recurring as a motor reaction without any content.

It must be left to further investigation to discover what it is that determines whether a hysterical personality manifests itself in attacks, in chronic symptoms or in a mixture of the two.

V

It will now be understood how it is that the psychotherapeutic procedure which we have described in these pages has a curative effect. *It brings to an end the operative force of the idea which was not abreacted in the first instance, by allowing its strangulated affect to find a way out through speech; and it subjects it to associative correction by introducing it into normal consciousness (under light*

* [This is a term regularly used by Charcot.]

hypnosis) or by removing it through the physician's suggestion, as is done in somnambulism accompanied by amnesia.

In our opinion the therapeutic advantages of this procedure are considerable. It is of course true that we do not cure hysteria in so far as it is a matter of disposition. We can do nothing against the recurrence of hypnoid states. Moreover, during the productive stage of an acute hysteria our procedure cannot prevent the phenomena which have been so laboriously removed from being at once replaced by fresh ones. But once this acute stage is past any residues which may be left in the form of chronic symptoms or attacks are often removed, and permanently so, by our method, because it is a radical one; in this respect it seems to us far superior in its efficacy to removal through direct suggestion, as it is practised today by psychotherapists.

If by uncovering the psychical mechanism of hysterical phenomena we have taken a step forward along the path first traced so successfully by Charcot with his explanation and artificial imitation of hystero-traumatic paralyses, we cannot conceal from ourselves that this has brought us nearer to an understanding only of the *mechanism* of hysterical symptoms and not of the internal causes of hysteria. We have done no more than touch upon the aetiology of hysteria and in fact have been able to throw light only on its acquired forms – on the bearing of accidental factors on the neurosis.

Vienna, *December* 1892

12 C. G. Jung

The Content of the Psychoses

C. G. Jung, 'The content of the psychoses', *Collected works of C. G. Jung* (translated by R. F. C. Hull), Bolligen Series, Pantheon Books, Routledge & Kegan Paul, 1960, vol. 3, pp. 158–78.

Psychiatry is a stepchild of medicine. All the other branches of medicine have one great advantage: the scientific method. In all other branches there are things that can be seen and touched, physical and chemical methods of investigation to be followed. The microscope reveals the dreaded bacillus, the surgeon's knife halts at no anatomical difficulty and gives us glimpses into the most vital and inaccessible organs. Psychiatry, the art of healing the soul, still stands at the door, seeking in vain to weigh and measure as in the other departments of science. We have long known that we have to do with a definite organ, the brain; but only beyond the brain, beyond the anatomical substrate, do we reach what is important for us – the psyche, as indefinable as ever, still eluding all explanation, no matter how ingenious.

Former ages, endowing the soul with substance and personifying every incomprehensible occurrence in nature, regarded mental illness as the work of evil spirits; the patient was looked upon as one possessed, and the methods of treatment were such as befitted this conception. It is not unknown for this medieval view to find credence and expression even today. A classic example is the expulsion of the devil which was successfully performed by the elder Pastor Blumhardt in the famous case of the Dittus sisters*. To the honour of the Middle Ages be it said that there were also early evidences of a sound rationalism. Thus, in the sixteenth century at the Julius Hospital in Würzburg, mental patients were already being treated side by side with the physically sick, and the treatment seems to have been really humane. With the opening of the modern era and the dawn of the first scientific ideas, the original barbaric personification of unknown powers gradually disappeared; a change arose in the conception of mental disease in favour of a more philosophic moral attitude. The ancient view

* Bresler, 'Kulturhistorischer Beitrag zur Hysterie' (1897); Zündel, *Pfarrer J. C. Blumhardt* (1880).

that every misfortune was the vengeance of offended gods returned in a new guise to suit the times. Just as physical diseases can, in many cases, be traced back to some frivolous self-injury, so mental diseases were believed to be due to some moral injury, or sin. Behind this conception, too, lurks the angry deity.

Such views played a great role right up to the beginning of the last century, especially in German psychiatry. In France, however, at about the same time, a new idea was appearing, destined to sway psychiatry for a hundred years. Pinel, whose statue fittingly stands at the gateway of the Salpêtrière in Paris, removed the chains from the insane and thus freed them from the stigma of the criminal. In this way he gave the most effective expression to the humane and scientific conceptions of modern times. A little later Esquirol and Bayle made the discovery that certain forms of insanity ended in death after a relatively short time, and that regular changes in the brain could be demonstrated *post mortem*.* Esquirol had discovered general paralysis of the insane (or, as it was popularly called, 'softening of the brain'), a disease which is always accompanied by chronic inflammatory shrinkage of the cerebral tissue. Thus was laid the foundation of the dogma which you will find repeated in every text-book of psychiatry: 'Mental diseases are diseases of the brain.'

Further confirmation of this view was furnished about the same time by the discoveries of Gall, who traced partial or complete loss of the power of speech – a psychic faculty – to a lesion in the region of the lower left frontal convolution. Later this view proved to be exceedingly fruitful. Innumerable cases of extreme idiocy and other serious mental disorders were found to be caused by tumours of the brain. Towards the end of the nineteenth century Wernicke (recently deceased) localized the speech-centre in the left temporal lobe. This epoch-making discovery raised hopes to the highest pitch. It was expected that the time was not far off when every characteristic and every psychic activity would be assigned its place in the cortical grey matter. Gradually, more and more attempts were made to trace the primary mental changes in the psychoses back to parallel changes in the brain. Meynert, the famous Viennese psychiatrist, propounded a regular system in which the alteration of the blood-supply to certain areas of the cortex was to play the chief role in the origin of the psychoses. Wernicke made a similar but far more ingenious attempt at an anatomical explanation of psychic disturbances. One visible result

* [For these and other historic medical personages mentioned in this volume, cf. Zilboorg and Henry, *History of Medical Psychology* – EDITORS.]

of this tendency can be seen in the fact that nowadays even the smallest and most out of the way asylum has its anatomical laboratory, where cerebral sections are cut, stained, and examined under the microscope. Our numerous psychiatric journals are full of morphological contributions, investigations on the path of the fibres in the brain and spinal cord, on the structure and distribution of cells in the cerebral cortex, and the various ways they are destroyed in different mental diseases.

Psychiatry has been charged with gross materialism. And quite rightly, for it is on the road to putting the organ, the instrument, above the function – or rather, it has long been doing so. Function has become the appendage of its organ, the psyche an appendage of the brain. In modern psychiatry the psyche has come off very badly. While immense progress has been made in cerebral anatomy, we know practically nothing about the psyche, or even less than we did before. Modern psychiatry behaves like someone who thinks he can decipher the meaning and purpose of a building by a mineralogical analysis of its stones. Let us try to form a statistical picture of the number and types of mental patients who show any clear lesions of the brain.

In the last four years we have admitted 1,325 mental patients to Burghölzli Mental Hospital – some 331 a year – of whom 9% suffer from *constitutional* psychic anomalies. By this I mean an inborn defect of the psyche. Of the 9%, about a quarter are imbeciles, congenitally feeble-minded. In them we find definite cerebral changes such as congenital microcephalus, pronounced hydrocephalus, and malformation of certain parts of the brain. The remaining three quarters of the psychopathically inferior show no trace of typical findings in the brain.

Three per cent of our patients suffer from epileptic mental disturbances. In the course of epilepsy a typical degeneration of the brain gradually sets in, which I cannot describe more closely here. The degeneration is demonstrable only in severe cases and after the illness has lasted a long time. If the attacks have been present for a relatively short time only, not more than a few years, as a rule nothing can be discovered in the brain.

Seventeen per cent of our patients suffer from progressive paralysis and senile deterioration. Both diseases present characteristic cerebral findings. In progressive paralysis there is regularly an extensive shrinkage of the brain, so that the cerebral cortex in particular is often reduced by one half. Especially the frontal portions of the brain may be reduced to a third of the normal weight. A similar destruction occurs in senile deterioration.

Fourteen per cent of the patients admitted annually suffer from poisoning, at least 13% of the cases being due to alcohol. As a rule, in milder cases nothing can be found in the brain; only in relatively few of the more severe cases is there a slight shrinkage of the cortex. The number of these severe cases amounts to less than 1% of the yearly cases of alcoholism.

Six per cent of the patients suffer from so-called manic-depressive insanity, which comprises the manias and the melancholias. The essence of this disease can be understood even by the layman. Melancholia is a condition of abnormal sadness with no disturbance of intelligence and memory. Mania is the opposite, the rule being an abnormally excited state with great restlessness, but without any deeper disturbance of intelligence and memory. In this disease no morphological lesions of the brain can be demonstrated.

Forty-five per cent of the patients suffer from the authentic and common disease known as dementia praecox. The name is a very unhappy one, for the dementia is not always precocious, nor in all cases is there dementia. Unfortunately the disease is too often incurable; even in the best cases, in recoveries where the layman would notice no abnormality, one always finds some defect in the patient's emotional life. The clinical picture is incredibly varied; usually there is some disturbance of feeling, very often there are delusions and hallucinations. As a rule there is nothing to be found in the brain. Even in cases of the most severe type, lasting for years, an intact brain is not infrequently found *post mortem*. Only in a few cases are slight changes to be found, which cannot yet, however, be proved to be regular.

To sum up: in round figures about a quarter of our patients show more or less extensive alterations and lesions of the brain, while three-fourths have a brain which seems to be generally unimpaired or at most exhibits changes such as afford absolutely no explanation of the psychological disturbance.

These figures offer the best possible proof that the purely anatomical approach of modern psychiatry leads – to put it mildly – only very indirectly to the goal, which is the understanding of the psychic disturbance. In addition, it must be remembered that the mental patients who show the most striking lesions of the brain die after a relatively short time; consequently, the chronic inmates of the asylum, who form its real population, consist of up to 70 or 80% cases of dementia praecox, that is, of patients in whom anatomical changes are practically non-existent. The way to a psychiatry of the future, which is to come to grips with the essence of the matter, is therefore clearly marked out: it can only be by way of psychology. For this reason we have entirely abandoned the anatomical approach in our Zurich Clinic and have turned to the psychological investigation of mental disease. Since most of our patients suffer from dementia praecox, this disease is naturally our chief problem.

The older clinicians paid great attention to the psychological precursors of insanity, just as the lay public still does, following a true instinct. We took up this trail and carefully investigated the previous psychological history whenever possible. Our efforts were richly rewarded, for we found surprisingly often that the illness broke out at a moment of some great emotion which, in its turn, had arisen in a more or less normal manner. We also found that in the mental disease which ensued there were a number of symptoms that could not be understood at all from the anatomical standpoint. These symptoms immediately became comprehensible when considered from the standpoint of the individual's previous history. Freud's pioneering investigations into the psychology of hysteria and dreams afforded us the greatest stimulus and help in our work.

A few examples of the most recent departures in psychiatry will, I think, make the subject clearer than any amount of dry theory. In order to bring home to you the difference in our conception, I shall in each case, first describe the medical history in the older fashion, and then give the solution characteristic of the new approach.

The first case to be considered is that of a cook, aged 32. She had no hereditary taint, was always very industrious and conscientious, and had never been noticeable for eccentric behaviour or the like. Quite recently she became acquainted with a young man who wanted to marry her. From that time on she began to show certain peculiarities. She often spoke of his not liking her very much, was frequently out of sorts, moody, and sat alone brooding. Once she ornamented her Sunday hat very strikingly with red and green feathers; another time she bought a pair of pince-nez to wear when she went out walking with her fiancé. One day the sudden idea that there was something the matter with her teeth would not let her rest, and she decided to get a new set, although it wasn't absolutely necessary. She had all her teeth out under an anaesthetic. The following night she suddenly had a severe anxiety attack. She cried and moaned that she was damned for ever, for she had committed a great sin: she should not have allowed her teeth to be extracted. She must be prayed for, so that God would pardon her sin. In vain her friends tried to talk her out of her fears, to assure her that the extraction of teeth was not really a sin; it availed nothing. At daybreak she became somewhat quieter, and worked throughout the day. On the following nights the attacks were repeated. On being consulted I found the patient quiet, but with a rather vacant expression. I talked to her about the operation, and she assured me that it was not so dreadful to have teeth extracted, but still it was a great sin, from which position, despite every persuasion, she could not be moved. She continually repeated in plaintive, pathetic tones: 'I should not have allowed my teeth to be taken out, yes, yes, it was a great sin and God will never forgive me.' She gave the impression of real insanity. A few days later her condition grew worse and she had to be brought to the asylum. The anxiety attack persisted and did not stop; it was a disturbance that lasted for months.

This history shows a series of symptoms which are all quite absurd. Why this queer story of the hat and the pince-nez? Why these anxiety attacks? Why this delusion that the extraction of her teeth was an unpardonable sin? Nothing is clear. The anatomically-minded psychiatrist would say: This is just a typical case of dementia praecox. It is the essence of insanity, of 'madness', to talk of nothing but absurdities; the view the diseased mind has of the world is deranged, crazy. What is no sin for a normal person is a sin for a mad one. It is a bizarre delusion characteristic of dementia praecox. The extravagant lamentation about this supposed sin is the result of 'inappropriate' emotional emphasis. The eccentric ornamentation of the hat, the pince-nez, are bizarre notions such as are very common in these patients. Somewhere in the brain a few cells have got out of order and produce illogical, senseless ideas of one kind or another which are quite without psychological meaning. The patient is obviously a congenital degenerate with a feeble brain, having from birth a kink which contained the seed of the disorder. For some reason or other the disease suddenly broke out now; it could just as easily have broken out at any other time.

Perhaps we should have had to capitulate to these arguments had not fate come to the aid of our psychological analysis. In connexion with the formalities required for her admission to the asylum it was found that many years ago the patient had an affair which came to an end when her lover left her with an illegitimate child. The otherwise respectable girl sought to hide her shame and had the child secretly brought up in the country. Nobody knew of this. When she got engaged she was in a dilemma: what would her fiancé say? At first she put off the marriage, becoming more and more worried, and then the eccentricities began. In order to understand them, we have to feel our way into the psychology of the naïve mind. If we have to disclose some painful secret to a person we love, we usually try to strengthen his love beforehand so as to obtain a guarantee of his forgiveness. We do it by flattery or by sulking, or we try to show off the value of our own personality so as to raise it in the eyes of the other. Our patient decked herself out with 'fine feathers', which to her simple taste seemed worthy of esteem. The wearing of pince-nez increases the respect of children, even when they are older. And who does not know people who will have their teeth extracted out of sheer vanity, simply in order to wear a denture?

After such an operation most people find themselves in a slightly nervous state, when everything becomes much more difficult to bear. And it was just at this moment that the catastrophe occurred: her fear lest her fiancé should break with her when he heard of her previous life. That was the first anxiety attack. Just as the patient had not admitted her fault all these years, so now she still sought to guard her secret, and shifted her pangs of conscience on to the extraction of her teeth. In this she followed the well-known pattern, for when we cannot admit a great sin, we deplore a small one with all the greater emphasis.

The problem seemed insoluble to the weak and sensitive mind of the patient, hence the affect became insurmountably great. That is how mental illness looks from the psychological side. The series of apparently meaningless happenings, the so-called 'absurdities', suddenly take on meaning. We understand the method in the madness, and the insane patient becomes more human to us. Here is a person like ourselves, beset by common human problems, no longer merely a cerebral machine thrown out of gear. Hitherto we thought that the insane patient revealed nothing to us by his symptoms except the senseless products of his disordered brain-cells, but that was academic wisdom reeking of the study. When we penetrate into the human secrets of our patients, the madness discloses the system upon which it is based, and we recognize insanity to be simply an unusual reaction to emotional problems which are in no wise foreign to ourselves.

The light that is shed by this view seems to me exceedingly great, for it penetrates into the innermost depths of the mental disturbance which is the commonest in our asylums and the least understood; indeed, because of the craziness of its symptoms, it is the type that strikes the layman as madness *in excelsis*.

The case I have just sketched is a simple one. It is, in fact, quite transparent. My second example is somewhat more complicated. It is the case of a man between 30 and 40 years of age; he is a foreign archaeologist of great learning and extraordinary intelligence. He was an intellectually precocious boy, very sensitive, with excellent qualities of character and unusual gifts. Physically he was small, weakly, and afflicted with a stammer. Brought up and educated abroad, he afterwards studied for several terms in B. Up to this point there had been no disturbances of any kind. On completing his university studies he immersed himself in his archaeological work, which gradually absorbed him to such an extent that he was dead to the world and all its pleasures. He worked incessantly, and buried himself entirely in his books. He became thoroughly unsociable; awkward and shy in society before, he now shunned it altogether, and saw no one beyond a few friends. He thus led the life of a hermit devoted entirely to science.

A few years later, on a holiday tour, he revisited B., where he remained a few days. He walked a great deal in the environs of the town. The few acquaintances he had there found him strange, taciturn, and nervous. After a rather long walk he seemed very tired, and remarked that he did not feel very well. He then talked of getting himself hypnotized, as he felt nervously run down. On top of this he fell physically ill with inflammation of the lungs. Soon afterwards a peculiar state of excitement supervened, which rapidly passed over into frenzy. He was brought to the asylum, where for weeks he remained in an extremely excited state. He was completely deranged, did not know where he was, spoke in broken sentences which no one could understand. Often he was so excited and aggressive that it took several attendants to hold him down. He gradually became quieter, and one day he came to himself as if waking out of a long, confused dream. He quickly obtained complete insight into his illness and was soon discharged as cured. He returned home and again immersed himself in his books. In the following years he published several outstanding works, but, as before, his life was that of a hermit living entirely in his books and dead to the world. Gradually he got the reputation of being a dried-up misanthropist, with no feeling for the beauty of life.

A few years after his first illness a short holiday trip again brought him to B. As before, he took his solitary walks in the environs. One day he was suddenly overcome by a feeling of faintness and lay down in the street. He was carried into a neighbouring house, where he immediately became violently excited.

277

He began to perform gymnastics, jumped over the rails of the bed, turned somersaults in the room, started declaiming in a loud voice, sang improvised poems, etc. Again he was brought to the asylum. The excitement continued. He extolled his wonderful muscles, his beautiful figure, his enormous strength. He believed he had discovered a law of nature by which a marvellous voice could be developed. He regarded himself as a great singer and a unique orator, and at the same time he was a divinely inspired poet and composer to whom the verse came simultaneously with the melody.

All this was in pathetic but very significant contrast to reality. He was a small weakly man of unimposing build, with poorly developed muscles, betraying at the first glance the atrophying effect of his studious life. He was unmusical, his voice was squeaky and he sang out of tune; he was a bad speaker because of his stammer. For weeks he occupied himself in the asylum with peculiar jumpings and contortions of the body which he called gymnastics, now and then singing and declaiming. Then he became quieter and dreamy, often stared musingly in front of him for long periods of time, sometimes softly singing a love-song which, despite its lack of musical expression, showed a pretty feeling for the yearnings of love. This, too, was in complete contrast to the aridity and isolation of his normal life. Gradually he became more accessible for conversations.

Let us break off the case-history here and sum up what has been furnished simply by the observation of the patient.

In the first attack of illness the delirium broke out unexpectedly, and was followed by a mental disturbance with confused ideas and violence which lasted for several weeks. Afterwards complete recovery appeared to have taken place. Six years later there was a sudden outbreak of excitement, with delusions of grandeur and bizarre actions, followed by a twilight stage gradually leading to recovery. Again it is a typical case of dementia praecox, of the catatonic variety, which is especially characterized by peculiar movements and actions. And here again the views now prevailing in psychiatry would regard this as a localized deterioration of the brain-cells in some part of the cortex, causing now delirium and confusional ideas, now delusions of grandeur, now peculiar contortions of the muscles, now twilight states, which taken all together have as little psychological meaning as the weird shapes of a drop of molten lead thrown into water.

This is not my view. It was certainly no accidental freak of diseased brain-cells that created those dramatic contrasts in the second attack. We can see that these contrasts, the so-called delusions of grandeur, are very subtly attuned to the deficiencies in the patient's personality. They are deficiencies which any one of us would certainly feel as a lack. Who has not felt the need to console himself for the aridity of his profession and of his life with the joys of poetry and music, and to restore to his body the natural strength and beauty stolen from it by the atmosphere of the study? Finally, who does not recall with envy the energy of Demosthenes who, despite his stammer, became a great orator? If our patient filled the obvious gaps in his physical and psychic life by delusionally fulfilled wishes, we may also conjecture that those soft love-songs which he sang from time to time filled a painful blank in his being, making up for a lack which became the more agonizing the more it was concealed.

I did not have to search for long. It was the same old story, born anew in every human soul, in a guise suited to the sensibilities of the predestined victim.

When our patient was a student he learnt to know and love a girl student. Together they took many solitary walks in the environs of the town, but his exceeding timidity and bashfulness (the lot of the stammerer) never allowed him an opportunity to get out the appropriate words. Moreover he was poor and had nothing to offer her but hopes. The time came for the termination of his studies; she went away, and he also, and they never saw one another again. And not long afterwards he heard she had married someone else. Then he relinquished his hopes, but he did not know that Eros never emancipates his slaves.

He buried himself in abstract learning, not to forget, but to work for her in his thoughts. He wanted to keep the love in his heart quite secret, and never to betray that secret. He would dedicate his works to her without her ever knowing it. The compromise succeeded, but not for long. Once he travelled through the town where he had heard she lived – he said it was quite by chance that he travelled through that town. He did not leave the train, which made only a short halt there. From the window he saw in the distance a young woman with a small child, and thought it was she. Impossible to say whether it really was or not; not even he knew. He did not think he felt any particular sensation at that moment; anyway he did not trouble to find out whether it was she or not, and this suggests that it wasn't. The unconscious wanted to be left in peace with its illusion. Shortly afterwards he again came to B., the place of old memories. Then he felt something strange stir in his soul, an uneasy feeling presciently described by Nietzsche:

Yet not for long shalt thou thirst, O burnt-out heart!
There is promise in the air,
From unknown mouths I feel a breath
—The great coolness cometh.*

Civilized man no longer believes in demons, he calls in the doctor. Our patient wanted to be hypnotized. Then madness overcame him. What was going on?

He answered this question in broken phrases, with long pauses in between, in that twilight stage which precedes convalescence. I follow his own words as faithfully as possible. When he fell ill he suddenly left the orderly world and found himself in the chaos of an overmastering dream: a sea of blood and fire, the world was out of joint, everywhere conflagrations, volcanic outbursts, earthquakes, mountains caved in, then came tremendous battles in which nation was hurled on nation, more and more he found himself involved in the struggle of nature, he was in the midst of the fighters, wrestling, defending himself, enduring unutterable misery and pain, but gradually exalted and strengthened by a strange, soothing feeling that someone was watching his struggles – that his loved one saw all this from afar. (That was the time when he showed real violence towards the attendants.) He felt his strength increasing and saw himself at the head of great armies which he would lead to victory. Then more battles, and victory at last. As the victor's prize he gained his loved one. As he drew near her the illness ceased, and he awoke from a long dream.

His daily life now resumed its ordered course. He shut himself up in his work and forgot the abyss within him. A few years later he was again in B. Demon or destiny? Again he followed the old trail and again was overborne by old memories. But this time he did not sink into the depths of confusion. He remained oriented and en rapport with his surroundings. The struggle was considerably milder; he merely did gymnastics, practised the masculine arts, and made up for his deficiencies. Then followed the dreamy stage with the love-songs, corresponding to the period of victory in the first psychosis. In this state – I follow his own words – he had a dreamy feeling, as if he stood on the border between two different worlds and did not know whether reality was on the right or on the left. He said: 'They tell me she is married, but I believe she is not; she is still waiting for me. I feel that it must be so. For me it is always as if she were not married, as if success must still be attainable.' What our patient has here described is but a pale

* ['The Sun Sinks', *Complete Works*, XVII, p. 182.]

reflection of that scene in the first attack of psychosis, when he stood as the victor before his bride. A few weeks after this conversation, his scientific interests began to reassert themselves. He spoke with obvious unwillingness about his intimate life, he repressed it more and more, and finally turned away from it as if it did not belong to him. Thus the door of the underworld gradually closed. There remained nothing but a certain tenseness of expression, and a look which, though fixed on the outer world, was at the same time turned inwards; and this alone hinted at the silent activity of the unconscious, preparing new solutions for his insoluble problem. Such is the so-called cure in dementia praecox.

Hitherto we psychiatrists were unable to suppress a smile when we read of a poet's attempts to describe a psychosis. These attempts have generally been regarded as quite useless, on the ground that a poet introduces into his conception of psychosis psychological relationships that are quite foreign to the clinical picture of the disease. But if the poet has not actually set out to copy a case from a text-book of psychiatry he usually knows better than the psychiatrist.

The case I have just described is not unique, it is typical of a whole class, for which one of our poets has created a universally valid model. The poet is Spitteler, and the model is *Imago*. I take it that the course of *that* case is known. However, the psychological gulf between the creation of the artist and the insane person is great. The world of the artist is a world of solved problems; the world of reality, that of unsolved problems. The insane person is a faithful reflection of this reality. His solutions are unsatisfying illusions, his cure a temporary relinquishing of the problem, which yet goes on working unsolved in the depths of the unconscious, and at the appointed time rises again to the surface and creates new illusions with new scenery – the history of mankind writ small.

Psychological analysis is far from being able to explain in a clear and illuminating fashion all cases of the disease with which we are here concerned. On the contrary, the majority remain exceedingly obscure and difficult to understand, not least because only a fraction of the patients recover. Our last case was exceptional in that the patient's return to a normal state enabled us to survey the period of his illness. Unfortunately we do not always enjoy the advantage of this standpoint, because a large number of patients never find their way back from their dreams. They are lost in the maze of a magic garden where the same old story is repeated again and again in a timeless present. For them the hands of the world's clock remain stationary; there is no time, no further development. It makes no difference to them whether they dream for two days or thirty years. I had a patient in my ward who had lain in bed for five years without uttering a word, completely buried in himself. For years I visited him twice daily, and as I reached his bedside I could always see at once that there was no change. One day I was on the point of leaving the room when a voice I did not recognize called out, 'Who are you? What do you want?' I saw with amazement that it was our dumb patient who had suddenly recovered his voice, and obviously his senses as well. I told him I was his doctor, whereupon he asked angrily why he was kept a prisoner here, and why no one ever spoke to him? He said this in an injured voice just like a normal person whom one had not greeted for a couple of days. I informed him that he had been laid in bed quite speechless for five years and had responded to nothing, whereat he looked at me fixedly and without understanding. Naturally I tried to discover what had gone on in him all these years, but could learn nothing. Another patient with a similar symptom, when asked why he had remained silent for years, declared, 'Because I wanted to spare the German language.'* These examples show that it is often quite impossible to lift the veil, because the patients themselves have neither the desire nor the interest to explain their strange experiences; as a rule they do not even find them strange.

Occasionally, however, the symptoms themselves are pointers to the psychological content of the disease.

We had a patient who for thirty-five years was an inmate of Burghölzli. For decades she lay in bed, she never spoke or reacted to anything, her head was always bowed, her back bent and the knees slightly drawn up. She was always making peculiar rubbing movements with her hands, so that in the course of the years thick horny patches developed on the palms. She kept the thumb and index finger of her right hand together as if sewing. When she died, some two years ago, I tried to discover what she had been like formerly. Nobody in the asylum recalled ever having seen her out of bed. Only our old chief attendant had a memory of having seen her sitting in the same attitude in which she afterwards lay in bed. In those days she made rapid sweeping movements of the arms across her right knee; she was said to be 'sewing shoes' and, later, 'polishing shoes'. As time went on the movements became

---

* I am indebted to my colleague Dr Abraham, in Berlin, for this example. [Karl Abraham had been Jung's associate on the staff of the Burghölzli Mental Hospital, Zurich, from 1904 to 1907.— EDITORS.]

more restricted till finally nothing but a little rubbing movement remained, and only the thumb and forefinger kept the sewing position. In vain I consulted our old records; they contained nothing about the patient's previous history. When her seventy-year-old brother came to the funeral I asked him if he remembered what had been the cause of his sister's illness. He told me that she had had a love-affair, but for various reasons it had come to nothing, and the girl had taken this so much to heart that she became melancholic. I asked who her lover was: he was a shoemaker.

Unless we choose to see here some very strange play of chance, we must assume that the patient had kept the memory-image of her lover unaltered in her heart for thirty-five years.

It might easily be thought that these patients, who give the impression of being imbeciles, are in fact nothing but burnt-out ruins of humanity. But in all probability that is not so. Very often one can prove directly that such patients register everything going on around them, sometimes even with curiosity, and that they have an excellent memory for it all. This explains why many patients often become quite sensible again for a time, and develop mental powers which one believed they had long since lost. Such intervals occasionally occur during serious physical illness or shortly before death. For example, we had a patient with whom it was impossible to carry on a sane conversation; he produced only a crazy mixture of delusional ideas and queer words. This man once went down with a serious physical illness, and I expected it would be very difficult to treat him. But not at all. He was entirely changed; he became friendly and obliging, and carried out all the doctor's orders with patience and gratitude. His eyes lost their evil darting looks, and shone quietly and with understanding. One morning I came to his room with the usual greeting: 'Good morning, how are you?' But the patient forestalled me with his well-known refrain: 'Here comes another of the dog and monkey troupe wanting to play the Saviour.' Then I knew his physical trouble was over. From that moment the whole of his reason was as if blown away again.

We can see from this that reason still survives, but is pushed away into some remote corner by the mind's preoccupation with pathological ideas.

Why is the mind compelled to expend itself in the elaboration of pathological nonsense? Our new method of approach gives us a clue to this difficult question. Today we can assert that the pathological ideas dominate the interests of the patient so completely because they are derived from the most important questions that occupied him when he was normal. In other words, what in insanity is now an incomprehensible jumble of symptoms was once a vital field of interest to the normal personality.

I will cite as an example a patient* who has been over twenty years in the asylum. She was always a puzzle to the doctors, for the absurdity of her delusions exceeded anything the boldest imagination could devise.

She was a dressmaker by trade, born in 1845, of very poor family. Her sister early went to the bad and was finally lost in the morass of prostitution. The patient herself led an industrious, respectable, secluded life. She fell ill in 1886 in her thirty-ninth year – on the threshold of the age when so many dreams are brought to naught. Her illness consisted of delusions and hallucinations which increased rapidly, and soon became so absurd that no one could understand her wishes and complaints. In 1887 she came to the asylum. By 1888 her speech, so far as it concerned her delusions, had degenerated into complete unintelligibility. She maintained such monstrous things as this: At night the spinal marrow is torn out of her; pains in the back are caused by substances going through the walls covered with magnetism. The monopoly establishes the pains that do not stick in the body and do not fly about in the air. Extracts are made by an inhalation of chemistry and legions perish of death by suffocation.

In 1892 the patient styled herself 'The Bank-note Monopoly, Queen of the Orphans, Proprietress of Burghölzli Asylum', saying that 'Naples and I must supply the whole world with macaroni.'

In 1896 she became 'Germania and Helvetia of exclusively sweet butter,' and said: 'I am Noah's Ark, the boat of salvation and respect.'

Since then the pathological nonsense has greatly increased; her latest creation is the delusion that she is the 'lilac new-red sea-wonder and the blue.'

These examples show how far the unintelligibility of such pathological formations can go. For this reason our patient became the classic example of 'meaningless delusional ideas' in dementia praecox, and many hundreds of medical students received from her a lasting impression of the sinister power of insanity. But even this case has not withstood the newest technique in modern analysis. What the patient says is not at all meaningless; it is full of significance, so that he who knows the key can understand her without undue difficulty.

Unfortunately time does not permit me to describe the tech-

* [Cf. 'The Psychology of Dementia Praecox', pars. 198 ff.– EDITORS.]

nique by means of which I succeeded in lifting the veil from her secret. I must content myself with a few examples which will make clear the strange changes of thought and speech in this patient.

She said of herself that she was *Socrates*. Analysis of this delusional idea reveals the following train of thought: Socrates was the greatest sage, the greatest man of learning; he was slanderously accused and had to die at the hands of strange men in prison. She – the patient – is the best dressmaker, has 'never cut a thread', 'never left a bit of cloth on the floor'. She has worked incessantly, and now she has been falsely accused, wicked men have shut her up, and she will have to die in the asylum. Therefore she is Socrates. This, as you see, is a simple metaphor based on an obvious analogy.

Take another example: 'I am the finest professorship and the finest world of art.' Analysis shows that she is the best dressmaker and chooses the most beautiful models which show up well and waste little material; she puts the trimming on only where it can be seen. She is a professor, an artist in her work. She makes the best clothes, which she grandly calls the 'Schneckenmuseum clothing'. Only such persons as frequent the Hans zur Schnecke and the Museum are her customers, for she is the best dressmaker who makes only Schneckenmuseum clothing.

The patient also calls herself Mary Stuart. Analysis shows the same analogy as with Socrates: wrongful suffering and death of the heroine.

'I am the Lorelei.' Analysis: This refers to Heine's well-known song, 'Ich weiss nicht, was soll es bedeuten' (I know not what it means). Whenever she wants to speak about her affairs people do not understand her, and say they don't know what it means; therefore she is the Lorelei.

'I am a Switzerland.' Analysis: Switzerland is free, no one can rob Switzerland of her freedom. The patient does not belong in the asylum; she should be free like Switzerland; therefore she is a Switzerland.

'I am a crane.' Analysis: In the *Cranes of Ibycus* it is said: 'Whoso is free of guilt and sin/Shall keep the child's pure soul within.' She has been wrongfully brought to the asylum and has never committed a crime. Therefore she is a crane.

'I am Schiller's *Bell*.' Analysis: Schiller's *Bell* is the greatest work of the greatest master. She is the best and most industrious dressmaker, and has achieved the highest rung in the art of dressmaking. Therefore she is Schiller's *Bell*.

'I am Hufeland.' Analysis: Hufeland was the best doctor. She suffers infinite torments in the asylum and on top of that is treated by the worst doctors. But she is such a distinguished personality that she is entitled to the very best doctors, a doctor like Hufeland. Therefore she is Hufeland.

The patient uses the form 'I am' in a very capricious way. Sometimes it means 'it belongs to me' or 'it is proper for me', sometimes it means 'I ought to have'. This can be seen from the following analysis:

'I am the master-key.' The master-key is the key that opens all the doors in the asylum. Properly, by rights, she should have obtained this key long ago, for she has been for many years the 'Proprietress of Burghölzli Asylum'. She expresses this argument very much simplified in the sentence: 'I am the master-key.'

The chief content of her delusional ideas is concentrated in the following statement:

'I am the monopoly.' Analysis: By this she means the bank-note monopoly, which has belonged to her for some time. She believes that she possesses the monopoly of all the bank-notes in the world, thus creating enormous riches for herself, in compensation for the poverty and wretchedness of her life. Her parents died early; therefore she is 'Queen of the Orphans'. Her parents lived and died in great poverty, and to them too she extends her blessings, in fancy pouring out her riches with both hands. She said in her own words: 'By me my parents are clothed, my sorely tried mother, full of sorrows – I sat with her at the table, covered white with abundance.'

This is one of those vivid hallucinations which the patient has daily. It is a wish-fulfilment, the poverty in this world contrasting with the riches in the next, reminiscent of Gerhardt Hauptmann's *Hannele*, more especially of that scene where Gottwald says: 'She was hung with rags – now she is bedecked in silken robes; she ran about barefoot, now she has shoes of glass to her feet. Soon she will live in a golden castle and eat each day of baked meats. Here she lived on cold potatoes . . .'

The wish-fulfilments of our patient go even further. Switzerland has to pay her an annuity of 150,000 francs. The director of Burghölzli owes her 80,000 francs damages for wrongful incarceration. She is the owner of a distant island with silver mines, 'the mightiest silver island in the world'. That is why she is also the 'greatest orator', possessing the 'highest eloquence', because, as she says, 'Speech is silver, silence is golden.' To her all the finest estates belong, all the wealthy quarters, all cities and countries, she is the owner of the world, actually the 'triple owner of the world'. Whilst poor Hannele was only elevated to the side of the Heavenly Bridegroom, our patient possesses the 'key of heaven'; she is not only the honoured earthly queens Mary Stuart and Queen Louise of Prussia, she is also the Queen of Heaven, the Mother of God, and at the same time the Godhead. Even in this earthly world where she was nothing but a humble dressmaker she has attained the fulfilment of her human wishes, for she chose three husbands from the best families in the town and her fourth was the Emperor Francis. From these marriages sprouted two phantom children, a little boy and a little girl. Just as she clothed and regaled her parents with food and drink, so she provided for the future of her children. To her son she bequeathed the big bazaars of Zurich, therefore her son is a Czar, for the owner of a bazaar is a Czar. The little daughter resembles her mother, therefore she becomes the proprietress of the asylum and takes her mother's place so that the mother shall be released from captivity. The daughter therefore receives the title of the 'Socrates deputy', since she acts for Socrates in captivity.

These examples by no means exhaust the delusional ideas of the patient. But they will give you, I hope, some idea of the richness of her inner life although she was apparently so dull and apathetic, sitting like an 'imbecile' for twenty years in her workroom, mechanically darning her linen and occasionally mumbling a few meaningless phrases which nobody had been able to understand. Her baroque jumble of words can now be seen in a different light: they are fragments of an enigmatic inscription, bits and pieces of fairy-tale fantasies, which have broken away from hard reality to build a far-off world of their own. Here the tables are ever laden, and a thousand banquets are held in golden palaces. The patient can spare only a few mysterious symbols for the dim, dismal realm of reality; they need not be understood, for our understanding has long ceased to be necessary to her.

Nor is this patient at all unique. She is one of a type. Similar fantasies are always found in patients of this kind, though not always in such perfection.

The parallels with Hauptmann's *Hannele* show that once again a poet has pointed the way, freely drawing on his own fantasy. From this conjecture, which is not due to chance, we may conclude that what the artist and the insane have in common is common also to every human being – a restless creative fantasy which is constantly engaged in smoothing away the hard edges of reality. Anyone who observes himself, carefully and unsparingly, will know that there is something within him which would gladly hide and cover up all that is difficult and questionable in life, in order to smooth a path for itself. Insanity gives it a free hand. And once it has gained ascendency, reality is veiled, more quickly or less; it becomes a distant dream, but the dream becomes a reality which holds the patient enchained, wholly or in part, often for the rest of his life. We healthy people, who stand with both feet in reality, see only the ruin of the patient in *this* world, but not the richness of that side of the psyche which is turned away from us. Unfortunately only too often no further knowledge reaches us of the things that are being played out on the dark side of the soul, because all the bridges have broken down which connect that side with this.

We still do not know at present whether these new insights have a general or only a limited validity. The more carefully and patiently we examine the mentally sick, the more we find cases which, despite the appearance of total imbecility, allow us at least fragmentary glimpses of a shadowy psychic life, far removed from that spiritual impoverishment which the prevailing theories have obliged us to accept.

Though we are still far from being able to explain all the relationships in that obscure world, we can maintain with complete assurance that in dementia praecox there is no symptom which could be described as psychologically groundless and meaningless. Even the most absurd things are nothing other than symbols for thoughts which are not only understandable in human terms but dwell in every human breast. In insanity we do not discover anything new and unknown; we are looking at the foundations of our own being, the matrix of those vital problems on which we are all engaged.

13 A. Adler

Position in Family Constellation Influences Life-Style

A. Adler, 'Position in family constellation influences life-style', *Int. J. individ. Psychol.*, no. 3, vol. 3. (1937), pp. 211–27.

It is a common fallacy to imagine that children of the same family are formed in the same environment. Of course there is much which is the same for all children in the same home, but the psychic situation of each child is individual and differs from that of others, because of the order of their succession.

There has been some misunderstanding of my custom of classification according to position in the family. It is not, of course, the child's number in the order of successive births which influences his character, but the *situation* into which he is born and the way in which he *interprets* it. Thus, if the eldest child is feeble-minded or suppressed, the second child may acquire a style of life similar to that of an eldest child; and in a large family, if two are born much later than the rest, and grow up together separated from the older children, the elder of these may develop like a first child. This also happens sometimes in the case of twins.

Position of the First Child

The first child has the unique position of having been the only one at the beginning of his life. Being thus the central interest he is generally spoiled. In this he resembles the only child, and spoiling is almost inevitable in both cases. The first child, however, usually suffers an important change of situation, being dethroned when the second baby is born. The child is generally quite unprepared for this change, and feels that he has lost his position as the center of love and attention. He then comes into great tension for he is far from his goal and there begins a striving to regain favor. He uses all the means by which he has hitherto attracted notice. Of course he would like to go the best way about it, to be beloved for his goodness; but good behavior is apt to pass unnoticed when everyone is busied with the new-comer. He is then likely to change his tactics and to resort to old activities which have previously attracted attention – even if it was unfavorable attention.

If intelligent, he acts intelligently, but not necessarily in harmony with the family's demands. Antagonism, disobedience, attacks on the baby, or even attempts to play the part of a baby, compel the parents to give renewed attention to his existence. A spoiled child must have the spotlight upon himself, even at the cost of expressing weakness or imitating a return to babyhood. Thus, under the influence of the past, he attains his goal in the present by unsuitable means; suddenly showing inability to function alone, needing assistance in eating and excretion and requiring constant watching, or compelling solicitude by getting into danger and terrifying the parents. The appearance of such characteristics as jealousy, envy, or egotism has an obvious relation to the outside circumstances, but he may also indulge in – or prolong – illnesses such as asthma and whooping cough. The tension in certain types (depending upon the bodily organization) may produce headache, migraine, stomach trouble, *petit mal*, or hysterical chorea. Slighter symptoms are evinced in a tired appearance and a general change of behavior for the worse, with which the child impresses his parents. Naturally, the later the rival baby is born, the more intelligible and understandable will the methods appear which the first child uses in his change of behavior. If dethroned very early, the eldest child's efforts are largely 'instinctive' in character. The style of his striving will in any case be conditioned by the reaction of others in the environment and his evaluation of it. If, for instance, the dethroned child finds that fighting does not pay, he may lose hope, become depressed, and score a success by worrying and frightening the parents. After learning that such ways are successful for him he will resort to ever more subtle uses of misfortune to gain his end.

The type of activity which in later life will be based on the prototype was shown in the case of a man who became afraid to swallow for fear of choking. Why did he select this symptom instead of another? The patient had an immediate social difficulty in the behavior of an intimate friend, who attacked him violently. Both the patient and his wife had come to the conclusion that he must put up with it no longer, but he did not feel strong enough to face the struggle. Upon inquiry into his childhood, it appeared that he had had such a difficulty in connexion with swallowing before. He was the eldest child, and had been surpassed by his younger brother, but he had at that time been able, by means of difficulty in eating, to make his father and mother watch over him. Now faced with a personal defeat in later life, and not knowing what to do about it, he fell back upon this old line of defense, as though it might make someone watch over him and help him.

Effects of Dethronement

The dethronement of the first child by another may make it turn away from the mother towards the father, and a very critical attitude towards the mother will then persist ever after. A person of this type is always afraid of being 'pushed back' all through life; and we notice that in all his affairs he likes to make one step forward and then one backward, so that nothing decisive can happen. He always feels justified in fearing that a favorable situation will change. Towards all the three life-questions he will take up a hesitative attitude, with certain problem behavior and neurotic tendencies. Problem behavior and symptoms will be felt by him to be a help and a security. He will approach society, for example, with a hostile attitude; he may constantly be changing his occupation; and in his erotic life he may experience failure in functioning, and may show polygamous tendencies – if he falls in love with one person he very quickly falls in love with another. Dubious and unwilling to decide anything, he becomes a great procrastinator. I met a very perfect example of this type once, and his earliest remembrance was this: 'At three years of age I caught scarlet fever. By mistake my mother gave me carbolic acid for a gargle, and I nearly died.' He had a younger sister who was the favorite of his mother. Later in life this patient developed a curious fantasy of a young girl ruling and bullying an older one. Sometimes he imagined her riding the old woman like a horse.

First Child May Keep Position

The eldest child may, however, be so firmly fixed in the parents' favor that he cannot be supplanted. This may be either by virtue of his own good native endowment and development, or because of the second child's inferiority, if the latter is ugly, organically handicapped, or badly brought up. In such a case it is the second child who becomes the problem, and the eldest may have a very satisfactory development, as in the following case:

Of two brothers, differing four years in age, the elder had been much attached to the mother, and when the younger was born the father had been ill for some time. Caring for the father took the entire time and most of the attention of the mother. The elder boy, trained in friendship and obedience to her, tried to help and relieve her, and the younger boy was put into the care of a nurse, who spoiled him. This situation lasted for some years, so that the younger child had no reasonable chance to compete with the elder for the love of the mother; and he soon abandoned the useful side of life, and became wild and disobedient. His behavior became still worse four years later, when a little sister was born, to whom the mother was able to devote herself owing to the death of the father. Thus twice excluded from the mother's attention and spoiled by the nurse, this second child turned out to be the worst pupil in his class, while the elder boy was always the best. Feeling hopelessly handicapped in competitition with his brother, unloved at home, and reproached at the school (from which he was finally expelled), this second son could find no goal in life but to dominate his mother by worrying her. Being physically stronger than either the brother or sister, he took to tyrannizing over them. He trifled away his time, and at puberty he began to waste money and to incur debts. His honest and well-meaning parent provided a very strict tutor for him who did not, of course, grasp the situation, and dealt with it superficially by punishments. The boy grew into a man who strove to get rich quickly and easily. He fell an easy prey to unscrupulous advisers, followed them into fruitless enterprises, and not only lost his money but involved his mother in his dishonorable debts.

The facts of the case clearly showed that all the courage this man ever displayed resulted from his unsatisfied desire to conquer. He played a queer game from time to time, especially when things went against him. His nurse was now an old woman, earning her living in the family as a superior servant; she still worshipped the second boy and always interceded for him in his numerous scrapes. The odd sport in which he indulged was to lock her in a room with him and make her play at soldiers with him, commanding her to march, to fall and to jump up again at his orders; and sometimes he quickened her obedience by beating her with a stick. She always obeyed although she screamed and resisted.

This singular sport revealed what he really wanted, the completest domination in the easiest way. Some writers would describe this as sadistic conduct, but I demur at the use of a word which implies a sexual interest, for I could discover nothing of the kind in it. In sexual matters the man was practically normal, except that he changed his mates too frequently and always chose inferiors. Genuine sadism itself is a domineering tendency availing itself of the sexual urge for its expression, owing to the discouragement of the individual in other spheres.

In the end this man brought himself into very bad circumstances, while the elder brother became very successful and highly respected.

Attitude of Eldest Toward Authority

The eldest child, partly because he often finds himself acting as representative of the parental authority, is usually a great believer in power and the laws. The intuitive perception of this fact is shown in the ancient and persistent custom of primogeniture. It is often observable in literature. Thus Theodore Fontane wrote of his perplexity at his father's pleasure in hearing that ten thousand Poles had defeated twenty thousand Russians. His father was a French emigrant who had sided with the Poles, but to the writer it was an inconceivable idea that the stronger could be beaten; he felt that the status quo should be preserved and that might must, and ought to, succeed. This was because Theodore Fontane was a first child. In any case the eldest child is readier than others to recognize power, and likes to support it. This is shown in the lives of scientists, politicians, and artists, as well as in those of simpler people. Even if the person is a revolutionary we find him harboring a conservative tendency, as in the case of Robespierre.

Position of Second Child

The second child is in a very different situation, never having had the experience of being the only one. Though he is also petted at first, he is never the sole center of attention. From the first, life is for him more or less of a race; the first child sets the pace, and the second tries to surpass him. What results from competition between two such children depends on their courage and self-confidence. If the elder becomes discouraged he will be in a serious situation, especially if the younger is really strong and outstrips him.

If the second child loses hope of equality he will try to *shine* more rather than to *be* more. That is, if the elder is too strong for him, the younger will tend to escape to the useless side of life. This is shown in many cases of problem behavior in children where laziness, lying or stealing begins to pave the way towards neurosis, crime, and self-destruction.

As a rule, however, the second child is in a better position than the first. His pacemaker stimulates him to effort. Also, it is a common thing for the first child to hasten his own dethronement by fighting against it with envy, jealousy and truculence, which lower him in the parental favor. It is when the first child is brilliant that the second child is in the worst situation.

But the elder child is not always the worst sufferer, even when dethroned. I saw this in the case of a girl who had been the center of attention and extremely spoiled until she reached the age of three, when a sister was born. After the birth of her sister she became very jealous and developed into a problem-child. The younger sister grew up with sweet and charming manners, and was much the more beloved of the two. But when this younger sister came to school the situation was not to her taste; she was no longer spoiled and, being unprepared to encounter difficulties, was frightened and tried to withdraw. To escape defeat both in fact and in appearance, she adopted a device very common among the discouraged – she never finished anything she was doing, so that it always escaped final judgment, and she wasted as much time as possible. We find that time is the great enemy of such discouraged people, for under the pressure of the requirements made on them by social living, they feel as if time were persecuting them continually with the question, 'How will you use me?' Hence their strange efforts to 'kill time' with silly activities. This girl always came late and postponed every action. She did not antagonize anyone, even if reproved, but her charm and sweetness, which were maintained as before, did not prevent her from being a greater worry and burden than her fighting sister.

When the elder sister became engaged to be married the younger sister was desperately unhappy. Though she had won the first stage of the race with her rival by gentleness and obedience, she had given up in the later stages of school and social life. She felt her sister's marriage as a defeat, and that her only hope of regaining ground would be to marry also. However, she had not courage enough to choose a suitable partner, and automatically sought a second-best. First she fell in love with a man suffering seriously from tuberculosis. Can we regard this as a step forward? Does it contradict her pre-established custom of leaving every task unfinished? Not at all. The poor health of her lover and her parents' natural resistance to the match were sure causes of delay and frustration. She preferred an element of impossibility in her choice. Another scarcely eligible partner appeared later in her life, in a man thirty years older than herself. He was senile, but did not die as the previous one had done, and the marriage took place. However, it was not a great success for her, as the attitude of hopelessness in which she had trained herself did not allow her to undertake any useful activity. It also inhibited her sexual life, which she considered disgusting, feeling humiliated and soiled by it. She used her usual methods to evade love and postpone relations at the appropriate times. She did not quite succeed in this, however, and became pregnant, which she regarded as another hopeless state, and from that time onward not only rejected caresses but complained that she felt soiled, and began to wash and clean all day long. She not only washed herself, but cleaned everything that had been touched by her husband, by the maid servant or the visitors, including furniture, linen, and shoes. Soon she allowed no one to touch any of the objects in her room, and lived under the stress of a neurosis – in this case, a washing-compulsion. Thus she was excused from the solution of her problems, and attained a very lofty goal of superiority – she felt more fastidiously clean than anyone else.

Exaggerated striving for a lofty goal of high distinctiveness is well expressed in the neurosis of 'washing-compulsion'. As far as I have been able to ascertain, this illness is always used as a means of avoiding sexual relations by a person who feels that sex is 'dirty'. Invariably it gives the fantastic compensation of feeling cleaner than everybody else.

However, due to his feeling life to be a race, the second child usually trains himself more stiffly and, if his courage holds, is well on the way to overcome the eldest on his own ground. If he has a little less courage he will choose to surpass the eldest in another field, and if still less, he will become more critical and antagonistic than usual, not in an objective but in a personal manner. In childhood this attitude appears in relation to trifles: he will want the window shut when the elder opens it, turn on the light when the other wants it extinguished, and be consistently contrary and opposite.

This situation is well described in the Bible story of Esau and Jacob, where Jacob succeeds in usurping the privileges of the eldest. The second child lives in a condition like that of an engine under a constantly excessive head of steam. It was well expressed by a little boy of four, who cried out, weeping, 'I am so unhappy because I can *never* be as old as my brother.'

The fact that children repeat the psychic behavior of older brothers and sisters and of parents is, by some writers, attributed to an 'instinct' of imitation or to 'identification' of the self with another; but it is explained better when we see that a child imitates only that kind of behavior which he finds to be a successful way of asserting an equality which is denied to him on other grounds. Psychic resemblances to the conduct of ancestors or even of savages do not signify that the pattern of psychic reaction is hereditary, but that many individuals use the same means of offense and defense in similar situations. When we find so much resemblance between all first children, all second, and all youngest children, we may well ask what part is left for heredity to play in determining those resemblances. Thus, as psychologists we have also not sufficient evidence to accept the theory that the mental development of the individual ought to repeat the development of the race of mankind in successive stages.

In his later life, the second child is rarely able to endure the strict leadership of others or to accept the idea of 'eternal laws'. He will be much more inclined to believe, rightly or wrongly, that there is no power in the world which cannot be overthrown. Beware of his revolutionary subtleties! I have known quite a few cases in which the second child has availed himself of the strangest means to undermine the power of ruling persons or traditions. Not everybody, certainly not these rebels themselves, would easily agree with my view of their behavior. For though it is possible to endanger a ruling power with slander, there are more insidious ways. For example, by means of excessive praise one may idealize and glorify a man or a method until the reality cannot stand up to it. Both methods are employed in Mark Antony's oration in 'Julius Caesar'. I have shown elsewhere how Dostoievsky made masterly use of the latter means, perhaps unconsciously, to undermine the pillars of old Russia. Those who remember his representation of Father Zosima in 'The Brothers Karamazov', and who also recall the fact that he was a second son, will have little difficulty agreeing with my suggestion regarding the influence played by position in the family.

I need hardly say that the style of life of a second child, like that of the first, may also appear in another child – one in a different chronological position in the family – if the *situation* is of a similar pattern.

Situation of Youngest Child

The youngest child is also a distinct type, exhibiting certain characteristics of style which we seldom fail to find. He has always been the baby of the family, and has never known the tragedy of being dispossessed by a younger, which is more or less the fate of all other children. In this respect his situation is a favored one, and his education is often relatively better, as the economic position of the family is likely to be more secure in its later years. The grown-up children not infrequently join with the parents in spoiling the youngest child, who is thus likely to be too much indulged. On the other hand, the youngest may also be too much stimulated by elders – both mistakes are well known to our educationists. In the former case (of over-indulgence) the child will strive throughout life to be supported by others. In the latter case the child will rather resemble a second child, proceeding competitively, striving to overtake all those who set the pace for him, and in many cases failing to do so. Often, therefore, he looks for a field of activity remote from that of the other members of the family – in which case, I believe, he gives a sign of hidden cowardice. If the family is commercial, for instance, the youngest often inclines to art or poetry; if scientific, he wants to be a salesman. I have remarked elsewhere that many of the most successful men of our time were youngest children, and I am convinced this is also the case in any other age. In biblical history we find a remarkable number of youngest children among the leading characters, such as David, Saul, and Joseph. The story of Joseph is a particularly good example, and illustrates many of the views we have advanced. His younger brother Benjamin was seventeen years his junior and, therefore, played little part in Joseph's development. Joseph's psychological position, therefore, was that of a youngest child.

It is interesting to note how well Joseph's brethren understood his dreams. More precisely, I should say that they understood the feeling and emotion of the dreamer, a point to which I shall return later. The purpose of a dream is not to be understood but to create a mood and a tension of feeling.

In the fairy tales of all ages and peoples the youngest child plays the role of a conqueror. I infer that in earlier times, when both circumstances and men's apprehension of them were simpler, it was easier to collect experiences and to understand the coherent current of the life of the latest-born. This traditional grasp of character survives in folk-lore when the actual experiences are forgotten.

A strange case of the type of youngest child who is spoiled, which I have already given elsewhere, is that of a man with a 'begging' style of life. I found another such case in that of a physician who was having difficulties with his mouth and was fearful of cancer. For twenty years he had been unable to swallow normally and could take only liquid food. He had recently had a dental plate made for him, which he was continually pushing up and down with his tongue, a habit which caused pain and soreness of the tongue, so that he feared he was developing cancer.

He was the youngest of a family of three, with two older sisters, and had been weakly and much indulged. At the age of forty he could eat only alone or with his sisters. This is a clear indication that he was comfortable only in his favorite situation – of being spoiled by the sisters. Every approach to society had been difficult for him. He had no friends, and only a few associates whom he met weekly in a restaurant. His attitude towards the three questions of life being one of fear and trembling, we can understand that his tension when with other people made him unable to swallow food. He lived in a kind of stage fright, fearful that he was not making a sufficiently good impression.

This man answered the second life-question (that of occupation) with tolerable competence, because his parents had been poor and he could not live without earning, but he suffered exceedingly when he had to take his examinations. His ambition, as a general practitioner, was to obtain a position with a fixed salary, and, later on, a pension. This great attraction to a safe official position is a sign of a feeling of insecurity. People with a deep sense of inadequacy commonly aspire to the 'safe job'. For years he gave himself up to his symptoms. When he became older he lost some of his teeth, and decided to have a plate made, which became the occasion of the development of his latest symptom.

When he came to me, the patient was sixty years of age, and was still living in the care of his two sisters. Both were suffering from their age, and it was clear to me that this man, aging, and spoiled by two unmarried and much older women, was facing a new situation. He was very much afraid his sisters would die. What should he do in that case – he who needed to be continually noticed and watched over? He had never been in love, for he could never find a woman whom he could trust with his fragile happiness! How could he believe that anyone would spoil him as his mother and older sisters had done. It was easy to guess the form of his sexuality – masturbation, and some petting affairs with girls. But recently an older woman had wanted to marry him; and he wished to appear more pleasant and attractive in behavior. The beginning of a struggle seemed imminent, but his new dental plate came to the rescue. In the nick of time he became anxious about contracting cancer of the tongue.

He himself, as a doctor, was very much in doubt about the reality of this cancer. The many surgeons and physicians he consulted all tried to dissuade him from belief in it; but he persisted in his uncertainty, continued to press his tongue against the plate until it hurt; then he consulted another doctor.

Such preoccupations – 'overvalued ideas', as Wernicke calls them – are carefully cherished in the arrangement of a neurosis. The patient shies away from the right objective by fixing his glances more and more firmly upon a point somewhere off a good, productive course. He does this in order to swerve out of a direction which is beginning to be indicated by logical necessity. The logical solution of his problem would be antagonistic to his style of life, and as the style of life rules (since it is the only way of approach to life the individual has learned), he has to establish emotions and feelings which will support his life-style and will ensure his escape.

In spite of the fact that this man was sixty years old, the only logical solution was to find a trustworthy substitute for his spoiling sisters before their departure. His distrustful mind could not rise to the hope of achieving this possibility; nor could his doubts be dissipated by logic, because he had built up throughout his life a definite resistance to marriage. Because it improved his appearance, the dental plate should have been a help towards marriage but he made it into an insuperable impediment.

In the treatment of this case it was useless to attack the belief in the cancer. When he understood the coherence of his behavior the patient's symptoms were very much alleviated. The next day he told me of a dream: 'I was sitting in the house of a third sister at a birthday celebration of her thirteen-year-old son. I was entirely healthy, felt no pain, and could swallow anything.' But this dream was related to an episode in his life which took place fifteen years before. Its meaning is very obvious: 'If only I were fifteen years younger.' Thus is the style maintained.

Difficulties of Only Child

The only child also has his typical difficulties. Retaining the center of the stage without effort, and generally pampered, he forms a style of life that calls for his being supported by others and at the same time ruling them. Very often he grows up in an intimate environment. The parents may be fearful people and afraid to have more children. Sometimes the mother, neurotic before this advent, does not feel equal to rearing more children, and develops such behavior that everyone must feel, 'It is a blessing that this woman has no more children.' Birth control may absorb much of the attention of the family, in which case we may infer tension, and that the two parents are united to carry on their life in anxiety. The care then devoted to the only child never ceases by day or night, and often impresses the child with a belief that it is an almost mortal danger not to be watched and guarded. Such children often grow up cautious, and sooner or later they may often become successful and gain the esteem and attention they desire. But if they come into wholly different conditions where life is difficult for them, they may show striking insufficiency.

Only children are often sweet and affectionate, and later in life they may develop charming manners in order to appeal to others, because they have trained themselves this way both in early life and later. They are usually closer to the more indulgent parent, which is generally the mother; and in some cases develop a hostile attitude towards the other parent.

The proper upbringing of an only child is not easy, but it is possible for parents to understand the problem and to solve it correctly. We do not regard the only child's situation as dangerous, but we find that, in the absence of the best educational methods, very bad results frequently occur which would have been avoided if there had been brothers and sisters.

Case of Homosexual Development

I will give a case of the development of an only child, a boy whose attachment was entirely to the mother. The father was of no importance in the family; he contributed materially but was obviously without interest in the child. The mother was a dressmaker who worked at home, and the little boy spent all his time with her, sitting or playing beside her. He played at sewing, imitating his mother's activity, and ultimately became very proficient in it, but he never took any part in boys' games. The mother left the house each day at five p.m. to deliver her work, and returned punctually at six. During that time the boy was left alone with an older girl cousin, and played with sewing materials. He became interested in timepieces, because he was always looking for his mother's return. He could tell the time when he was only three years old.

The cousin played games with him in which she was the bridegroom and he was the bride, and it is noteworthy that he looked more like a girl than she did. When he came to school he was quite unprepared to associate with boys, but he was able to establish himself as a favored exception, for others liked his mild and courteous disposition. He began to approach his goal of superiority by being attractive, especially so to boys and men. At fourteen years of age he acted the part of a girl in a school play. The audience had not the slightest doubt that he was a girl; a young fellow began to flirt with him and he was much pleased to have excited such admiration.

He had worn girlish dress during his first four years, and until the age of ten he did not know whether he was a boy or a girl. When his sex was explained to him he began to masturbate, and in his fantasy he soon connected sexual desire with what he had felt when boys touched him or kissed him. To be admired and wooed

was his goal in life; to this end he accommodated all his characteristics in such a way that he might be admired especially by boys.
His older cousin was the only girl he had known, and she was gentle
and sweet, but she had played the man's role in their games and
otherwise she had ruled him like his mother. A great feeling of
inferiority was his legacy from his mother's over-indulgent and
excessive care. She had married late, at the age of thirty-eight,
and she did not wish to have more children by the husband she
disliked. Her anxiety then was doubtless of earlier origin, and her
late marriage indicative of a hesitant attitude to life. Very strict
in sexual matters, she wanted her child to be educated in ignorance
of sex.

At the age of sixteen this patient looked and walked like a
flirtatious girl, and he soon fell into the snare of homosexuality.
In order to comprehend this development we must remember that
he had had, in a psychological sense, the education of a girl, and
that the difference between the sexes had been made clear to him
much too late in his development. Also he had experienced his
triumphs in the feminine role, and had no certainty of gaining as
much by playing the man. In the imitation of girlish behavior he
could not but see an open road to his goal of superiority.

It is my experience that boys who have this type of upbringing
always look like girls. The growth of the organs and probably also
of the glands is partially ruled by the environment and the child's
attitude toward it; and they are adapted to them. Thus if such an
early environmental training towards femininity is succeeded by a
personal goal of the same tendency, the wish to be a favored girl
will influence not only the mind, but also the carriage and even the
body.

This case illustrates very clearly how a pervert trains himself
mentally into his abnormal attitude towards sex. There is no
necessity to postulate an inborn or hereditary organic deviation.

When the boy in question came to me he was involved in a
relationship with another boy who was the neglected second child
of a very domineering mother; this boy's striving was to overcome
men by his personal charm. It was by his charm that he had succeeded early in ruling his weak father. When he reached the age of
sexual expression he was shocked. His notion of women was
founded upon experience of his domineering mother, who had
neglected him. He felt the need to dominate but he entertained no
hope of dominating women for, in accordance with the generalization he had made of his early experiences connected with a strong
and ruling mother, he had come to feel that a woman was too

powerful to control. His only chance to be the victor, he felt, was in relationship with men; so he turned homosexual. Consider then the hopeless situation of my patient! He wanted to conquer by female means – by having the charm of a girl – but his friend wanted to be a conqueror of men.

I was able to make my patient realize that, whatever he himself thought or felt in this liaison, his friend felt himself to be a conquering man-charmer. My patient, therefore, could not be sure that his was the real conquest, and his homosexuality was accordingly checked. By this means I was able to break off the relationship for he saw that it was stupid to enter into such a fruitless competition. This also made it easier for him to understand that his abnormality was due to a lack of interest in others, and that his feeling of inadequacy, as the result of being pampered, had led him to measure everything in terms of personal triumph. He then left me for some months; when he visited me again he had had sexual relations with a girl, but had tried to play a masochistic part towards her. He obviously wished, in order to prove to himself that his original view of the world was correct, to experience with her the same inferiority that he had felt with his mother and cousin. This masochistic attitude was shown in the fact that his goal of superiority required that the girl should do to him what he commanded, and he wished to complete the act at this point, without achieving sexual intercourse, so that the normal was still excluded.

The great difficulty of changing a homosexual lies not only in his lack of general social adjustment, but also in the invariable absence of right training toward the sexual role, which ought to begin in early childhood. The attitude towards the other sex is strained in a mistaken direction almost from the beginning of life. In order to realize this fact one must note the kind of intelligence, of behavior, and of expectations which such a case exhibits. Compare normal persons walking in the street or mixing in society with a homosexual in the same situations! Those who are normal are chiefly interested in the opposite sex, the homosexuals only in their own. The latter evade normal sexuality not only in behavior but even in dreams. The patient I have just described used frequently to dream that he was climbing a mountain, and ascending it by a serpentine road. The dream expresses his discouraged and circuitous approach to life. He moved rather like a snake, bending his head and shoulders at every step.

In conclusion I will recall some of the most disastrous cases I have known among only children. A woman asked me to help her and her husband in the case of their only boy, who tyrannized over them terribly. He was then sixteen, a very good pupil at school, but quarrelsome and insulting in behavior. He was specially combative toward his father, who had been stricter with him than had the mother. He antagonized both parents continually, and if he could not get what he wanted he made open attack, sometimes wrestling with his father, spitting at him, and using bad language. Such a development is possible in the case of a pampered and only child who is trained to give nothing but to expect everything – and gets it, until the time comes when indulgence can go on no longer. In such cases it is difficult to treat the patient in his old environment, because too many old recollections are revived, which disturb the harmony of the family.

Another case was brought to me, a boy of eighteen, who had been accused of murdering his father. He was an only child, and a spoiled one, who had stopped his education and was wasting, in bad company, all the money he could extort from his parents. One day when his father refused to give him money, the boy killed him by hitting him on the head with a hammer. No one but the lawyer who was defending him knew that he had killed another person several months before. It was obvious that he felt perfectly sure of escaping discovery this second time.

In yet another case of criminal development, an only boy was brought up by a very well-educated woman who wanted him to be a genius. At her death another experienced woman continued his nurture in the same way, until she became aware of his tyrannical tendencies. She believed it to be due to sexual repression, and had him analyzed. His tyrannical attitude did not cease, however, and she then wished to be rid of him. But he broke into her house one night intending to rob her, and strangled her.

All the characteristics which I have described as typical of certain positions in the family can, of course, be modified by other circumstances. With all their possibilities of variation, however, the outlines of these patterns of behavior will be found to be substantially correct. Among other possibilities, one may mention the position of a boy growing up among girls. If he is older than they are he develops very much the same as an elder brother close to a younger sister. Differences in age, in the affection of the parents, and in the preparation for life, are all reflected in the individual pattern of behavior.

Where a female majority and feminine influence dominates the whole environment, a single boy is likely to have a goal of superiority and a style of life which are directed towards femininity.

This occurs in various degrees and various ways: in a humble devotion to women and worship of them, in an imitative attitude, tending towards homosexuality, or in a tyrannical attitude towards women. People usually avoid educating boys in a too-feminine environment; for it seems to be a matter of general experience that such children develop towards one of two extremes – either exaggerated vanity or audacity. In the story of Achilles there are many points from which we may assume that the latter case was well understood in antiquity.

Importance of Evaluation of Women and Men

We find the same contradictory possibilities in the cases of only girls who grow up among boys or in a wholly masculine environment. In such circumstances a girl may, of course, be spoiled with too much attention and affection; but she may also adopt boys' attitudes and wish to avoid looking like a girl. In any case, what happens is largely dependent upon how men and women are *valued* in the environment. In every environment there is always a prevailing attitude of mind in regard to this question; and it is largely in accordance with the relative value given to men and women in that attitude that the child will wish to assume the role of a man or of a woman.

Other views of life which prevail in the family may also influence the pattern of a child's behavior, or bring it into difficulties, as for example the superstition about character being inherited, and the belief in fancy methods of education. Any exaggerated method of education is likely to cause injury to the child, a fact we can often trace in the children of teachers, psychologists, doctors, and people engaged in the administration of laws – policemen, lawyers, officers, and clergymen. Such educational exaggerations often come to light in the life-histories of problem-children, delinquents, and neurotics. The influence of both factors – the superstition regarding heredity and a fanatical mode of training – appear in the following case:

A woman came to me with a daughter of nine, both of them in tears and desperation. The mother told me that the girl had only recently come to live with her, after having spent years under the care of foster parents in the country. There she had completed the third grade of her schooling, and she had entered the fourth grade in the city school, but her work became so bad that her teacher had her put back into the third grade. Soon afterwards her work had become still worse, and she was graded still lower and put in the second. The mother was thoroughly upset at this and obsessed with the idea that her daughter's deficiency was inherited from the father.

At first sight it was evident to me that the mother was treating the child with exaggerated educational insistence, which in this case was particularly unfortunate, because the girl had been brought up in a congenial, easy environment and expected still greater kindness from the mother. But in her eagerness that her child should not be a failure the mother was overstrict, and this gave the child the keenest disappointment. She developed a great emotional tension which effectually blocked her progress both at school and at home. Exhortation, reproaches, criticism, and spanking only intensified the emotion, with consequent hopelessness on both sides. To confirm my impression, I spoke with the girl alone about her foster parents. She told me how happy her life with them had been; and then, bursting into tears, told me also how she had at first enjoyed being with her mother.

I had to make the mother understand the mistakes in which she had become involved. The girl could not be expected to put up with such a hard training. Putting myself in her place I could perfectly understand her conduct as an intelligent reaction – that is, as a form of accusation and revenge. In a situation of this type, but where there is less social feeling, it is perfectly possible for a child to turn delinquent, neurotic, or even to attempt suicide. But in this case I was sure it would not be difficult for the girl to improve if the mother could be convinced of the truth, and could impress the child with a sufficiently definite change of attitude. I therefore took the mother in hand, and explained to her that the belief in inheritance was nothing but a nuisance, after which I helped her to realize what her daughter had not unreasonably expected when she came to live with her, and how she must have been disappointed and shaken by such disciplinary treatment, to the point of utter inability to do what was expected of her. I wanted the mother to confess to the child that she had been mistaken and would like to reform her method, so I told her I did not really believe she could bring herself to do it, but that it was what I would do in the circumstances. She answered decidedly, 'I will do it'. In my presence and with my help, she explained her mistake to the child, and they kissed and embraced and cried together. Two weeks later they both visited me, gay and smiling and very well satisfied. The mother brought me a message from the third-grade teacher: 'a miracle must have happened. The girl is the best pupil in the class.'

14 P. Janet

The Major Symptoms of Hysteria

Excerpts from P. Janet, *The major symptoms of hysteria*, Lecture 15 'General definitions', Macmillan, 1907, pp. 317–37.

General Definitions

[. . .] In these lectures on the great symptoms of hysteria, I have tried to present a rapid picture, not of all the symptoms of hysteria, but of the essential ones, in order that you might form a just idea of a singular malady, of which everybody speaks and which but few physicians know well. I have only presented to you the typical cases and forms, around which it is easy for you to group the degraded forms and confused aspects which most diseases offer in practice. We must try now to sum up these descriptions and to derive from them some general conception of the whole disease.

I

Allow me, first, to remind you in a few words of the essential pictures you should keep before your eyes in order to form a general idea of the hysterical disease. We have studied somnambulism together. I no longer say 'hysterical somnambulism', for there is no more any somnambulism for us, outside of hysteria. We have studied it under its simple and typical form of monoideic somnambulism, then in its more complete forms of fugues, of polyideic somnambulisms, of artificial somnambulisms. You remember that we have always recognized in it the exaggerated development of an idea, of a feeling, of a psychological state, in a word, of a system of thoughts, which takes place outside the memory and the normal consciousness. This dissociation of a psychological system is manifested not only by the preceding development, but also by amnesia, bearing not only on the somnambulic period, but even, in remarkable cases, on the whole of the idea and of the feeling.

When later we studied various accidents bearing on the movements of the limbs, we recognized that small systems of movements, and sometimes great systems, rich and old, constituting real functions, develop themselves without control to an exaggerated degree, and give rise to tics and choreas of various kinds. This lack of control is manifested through negative phenomena closely connected with the preceding ones, paralyses and anaesthesias, which seem to play here the same role as the amnesias of somnambulism. When we came to the sensorial functions, we saw the same agitations under the forms of tics, of pains, and of hallucinations, accompanied with certain losses of control which constitute various anaesthesias bearing on the special senses as well as on the general sensibilities.

In connexion with these anaesthesias, we remarked more clearly than we had done in connexion with the preceding phenomena, the real nature of these amnesias, of these paralyses; in a word, of these disappearances of functions. The function is far from being destroyed. It continues to exist and often even develops to an exaggerated degree. It is only suppressed from one very special standpoint; it is no longer at the disposal of the will or the consciousness of the subject. Surprising as it is, we recognized the same facts not only in the complex function of speech, but even in the visceral functions. The refusal to eat, vomitings, hysterical dyspnoeas, are not diseases of the stomach or lungs. They consist in a kind of emancipation of the cerebral and psychological function relative to these organs. There is now an exaggeration independent of the function; again and more often, a disappearance from consciousness of these organic wants and of the acts that are connected with them.

Finally, in our last lectures, we sought in the very character of these patients, in the status of their minds, for fundamental stigmata allowing us to recognize and understand the malady. We succeeded in bringing into evidence, on the one hand, stigmata proper to hysteria: suggestion, absent-mindedness carried to unconsciousness, alternation, which we summarized in the general idea of *retraction of the field of consciousness*; and, on the other hand, general stigmata, the absence of attention, the lack of feeling and of will, which are connected with depression, with the *lowering of the mental level*.

This is a clinical picture that must suffice us in practice. If we remember these chief facts, by comparing with them the complex and less clear cases that practice presents to us, we shall succeed in appreciating the hysterical disease fairly justly while avoiding many prejudices and errors that are still very common nowadays.

Unfortunately, the human mind is not so easily content; it is fond of dangers and quarrels, and we feel the need of formulating concerning hysterical disease, general conceptions, interpretations, definitions, which are much more exposed to criticism and error. It seems to me that it is in some way a medical fashion to give definitions on hysteria. Already, in the old book of Brachet, in 1847, there were, at the beginning, about fifty formulas passed in review. Though Lasègue said that hysteria could never be defined and that the attempt should not be made, since that declaration everybody has tried to define it. I have discussed, in my little book on hysteria, about ten definitions, and I have been foolish enough to present a new one. Of course, physicians have continued to define it, and, since that time, ten others or so have been proposed. We must obey the fashion by saying a few words about these definitions. Let us try to derive from them, without attaching too great importance to the terms, a general idea that suffices us in practice.

II

I am wrong in laughing at the definitions of hysteria and observing to you their abundance, which, in these matters, is not a proof of truth. These definitions have evolved; they have made visible progress, and, though they appear numerous nowadays, they come so close to one another that they blend together. Do not forget that we are speaking of medicine, and that this is rather a special domain, less calm and serene than high mathematics. You should not ask too much of the virtue of a physician, or hope that he will confine himself to repeating the definition of a predecessor, even if he does not cite his name. What would be left for him? He must needs change something in these definitions, were it but a single word, in order to appear to innovate, which, in medicine, is indispensable. I do not exaggerate in telling you that, nowadays, three-fourths of the definitions of hysteria are nearly identical.

Thus, I shall perhaps surprise you by telling you that there is no opposition between the definitions that gloriously entitle themselves physiological and those that modestly call themselves psychological. No doubt, there would be a great difference if these authors had seen, really seen, a lesion characteristic of the neurosis, and if they had connected the evolution of the disease with this lesion. Never fear, one can make, nowadays, a so-called physiological definition at smaller cost. It is enough to take the most commonplace psychological definitions and replace their terms with words vaguely borrowed from the language of anatomy and the current physiological hypotheses. Instead of saying, 'The function of language is separated from the personality', one will proudly say, 'The centre of speech has no longer any communication with the higher centres of association'. Instead of saying, 'The mental synthesis appears to be diminished', one will say, 'The higher centre of association is benumbed', and the feat will be done. I recommend to you in this connexion to read the last book of M. Jose Ingenieros, published at Buenos Ayres, in 1906. In the first chapter, which I do not understand very well on account of my imperfect knowledge of Spanish, he shows that many of the definitions of modern physicians are equivalent, and I am quite of his opinion. So there is an ensemble of points on which all the authors agree, and it is those which we shall have to bring into evidence.

Charcot used to say that hysteria is an entirely psychic malady. This opinion was discussed at his time. There were still some remainders of the old uterine and genital theories; there were still some attempts to connect hysteria with various nervous lesions. Dr Bastian's book* in England, a very interesting book, is very courageous. He had the pretension to localize different hysterical accidents in different corners of the medulla, of the bulb, or of the lower centres of the encephalon. That there is no truth in those old conceptions, that hysteria will not be recognized later as resulting from some unknown disturbance of the secretion of a vascular gland or from some lesion of a nowadays badly defined nervous system, I should not dare assert; but one thing is certain; namely, that for twenty years everybody has departed from this view of the matter, and that the psychological conception has the mastery. I again observe to you that I consider the pretended physiological definitions as mere translations of the psychological ideas. This point is almost agreed on by every one.

But now, difficulties begin. Of what kind of psychological disturbance is it a question? We should not, under pretence of psychology, confusedly link hysteria with the vague group of mental diseases and the old nervosismus. On this point, the work of a distinguished physician, Dr Dubois, of Bern, interesting from other standpoints, is, in my opinion, absolutely pernicious. The psychological interpretation should not suppress what is good, what is excellent, in our ancestors' works. Now the last century produced a monumental work; namely, clinical work. With infinite patience and penetration, all those great clinicians introduced order into a real chaos; they ranged the diseases in groups, they enabled us to recognize these groups. Improvements should consist in consolidating this edifice and not in throwing it down. To say, under pretence of psychology, that a somnambulism is identical with any delirium, that hysterical vomiting is a mere derangement to be confounded with manias of doubt or with melancholias, or even,

* Charlton Bastian, 'Various Forms of Hysterical or Functional Paralysis', 1893.

perhaps, with the tics of idiots, is to go two hundred years back, and it would be much better to suppress the psychological interpretation and be content with the clinical description. Consequently, in making hysteria a psychological affection, we do not intend at all, as M. Grasset seemed to believe, to confound it with some sort of other, or mental, malady. We even say that it is nowadays the most characteristic disturbance of all, and that it is important to distinguish it well.

The first psychological notion that appears to me to result with the greatest clearness from all the contemporary works is a notion relative to *the importance of ideas* in certain hysterical accidents. Charcot, studying the paralyses, had shown that the disease is not produced by a real accident, but by the idea of this accident. It is not necessary that the carriage wheel should really have passed over the patient; it is enough if he has the idea that the wheel passed over his legs. This remark is easy to generalize. There are such kinds of fixed ideas in somnambulisms and fugues; the idea of one's mother's death, the idea of visiting tropical countries, etc. There are such ideas in systematic contractures, for instance, when a patient seems to hold her feet stretched because she thinks herself on the cross. There are such ideas in visceral disturbances, and I have shown you the observation of a patient who died of hunger because she had the fixed idea of the turnips she had eaten when at school. These remarks have been well made on every side. It has also been established that, with hystericals, ideas have a greater importance, and, above all, a greater bodily action than with the normal man. They seem to penetrate more deeply into the organism, and to bring about motor and visceral modifications. It is a point which was again emphasized by MM. Mathieu and Roux, in a recent paper they devoted to hysterical vomiting. 'What characterizes hystericals,' they said, 'is less the fact of accepting some idea or other than the action exercised by this idea on their stomachs or intestines.'

At the same time, the studies on suggestion, which have been very numerous, have allowed clinicians to realize experimentally, through the action of ideas, many phenomena analogous to hysterical accidents. So it may be said that the most common conceptions of hysteria turn on this character. Moebius in 1888, after Charcot, said: 'We may consider as hysterical all morbid modifications of the body that are caused by representations.' Strümpell, in 1892, Bernheim, Oppenheim, and more recently, Babinski, have repeated, each of them of course with a slight change in the words, quite similar definitions. 'A phenomenon is hysterical,' said

Babinski, 'when it can be produced through suggestion and cured through persuasion'. Let us take no account of the end of the sentence. The treatment and cure are delicate things; much might be said on those cures through persuasion. Let us only retain the beginning: *hysteria is defined by suggestion*. It is absolutely the conception of Charcot and Moebius, hysteria through fixed ideas and hysteria through representation. This word 'suggestion', which, besides, one takes care not to define, is taken simply in the sense attached to it by all the preceding authors, namely that of a too-powerful idea acting on the body in an abnormal manner. It is easy to remark here a unity of a great number of contemporary conceptions.

III

I do not object very much to the preceding definitions. If more precision were given to the meaning of the word 'suggestion', these definitions would be agreed on by everybody. Besides, these definitions bring back all the accidents of the neurosis to a symptom we have put in the first rank among the stigmata, to the suggestibility. So they are very scientific and useful. It is one of the first results of all the psychological work that has been done on hysteria. However, I had already discussed them in 1894, and still think them insufficient. As my arguments have been very little contradicted I will try to formulate them more clearly.

In the first place, I believe that this conception of hysteria is more just in theory than in practice. It rather summarizes a systematic interpretation than the clinical observation. It is we who have repeated that the accidents seem to be brought about by ideas. It is not quite exact that we always observe these ideas. In a few cases – and they are always the ones that are repeated – the patient, it is true, has the idea that he is paralyzed. 'I thought,' he says, 'that my leg was crushed; I had the idea that my leg no longer existed.' The consecutive paralysis with anaesthesia of the limb seems to be the exact translation of his idea. But it is a singular exaggeration to apply this indifferently to all hysterical accidents, and to say unreservedly with M. Bernheim, 'The hysterical realizes his accident just as he conceives it.'

This is to come back to a kind of contemptuous accusation against the patient. Formerly, the physician said to the patient: 'You are paralyzed, you have crises of sleep because you are willing to have these accidents.' Now, it is recognized that he is not willing to have them, but it is still maintained that he thinks of them. 'You have such or such a crisis with such or such an accident

311

because you think of it.' I say that this is not true: there are many hystericals who do not think of the accidents they have. First of all, with some patients, the accidents develop insidiously, unknown to them. They become anaesthetic, paralytic, anorexic, amaurotic, without in the least suspecting it. Clinical practice shows you this every day. What shall we do, then, with the observations already cited by Lasègue, in which it is the physician who reveals to the subject an anaesthesia, or the blindness of one eye, which he was not aware of. In other cases, it is incontestable that the accident develops with details, with an evolution that the patient does not know. Whatever M. Bernheim may say about it, I do not admit at all that hystericals have, at will, paralyses, with or without anaesthesias. I do not admit that these patients know what happens in their somnambulisms, that they combine the disease beforehand.

If these patients have fixed ideas – and I acknowledge that this is very frequent – it should be well remarked that these fixed ideas have no relation to the medical form of their accident. One has the fixed idea of her mother's death; it is not at all the fixed idea of somnambulism and of its laws. Another has a fixed idea relative to the flight of his wife, who robbed him; it is not the fixed idea of dumbness. Much oftener than is believed, the accident develops independently of the ideas of the subject, whether the subject does not think of it or thinks of something else.

I should like to present, in the second place, an argument which is still weak, but the importance of which will grow more and more. It relates to the physiological and psychological laws of hysterical accidents, laws of which we are ignorant, and of which the subjects are ignorant like us. When we see a crowd of accidents evolve according to these laws, which we painfully describe, we cannot say that they are due to auto-suggestion.

I remind you of the laws of somnambulisms, which, in my opinion, are capital. Somnambulism is followed by an amnesia which bears not only on the abnormal period, but often also on the idea itself that fills it and on all the feelings connected with it. This amnesia disappears and all the apparently lost remembrances are restored when the subject comes back into the same somnambulism. In the case of Irène, which I take as a type, there is in the waking state an amnesia not only of the crisis, but also of her mother's death, of the three preceding months, and of all that is connected with her affection for her mother, and during the fits all these remembrances are perfect. Do the subjects who show us applications of these laws – and, in my opinion, they are very numerous – do these subjects know them? Have they the idea of having such an oblivion in connexion with their somnambulism? How very unlikely! They would much rather have the contrary idea, that of being obsessed by their remembrance like the psychasthenics.

The more hysterical paralyses are studied, the more laws of a similar kind will be discovered. I have observed to you that the accidents bear on functions. It is true that these functions oftenest appear to be identical with those which the vulgar have themselves recognized, the function of alimentation, the function of walk, the function of the movements of the hand. In this case, you will tell me, the paralysis might very well be brought about by an idea, since the popular idea coincides with the very limits of the paralysis. This is true in general, simply because the popular ideas are true. The great divisions of the functions correspond to the great divisions of the organs, and the popular analysis has been correct, that is all. But there are some cases in which the popular analysis proves ignorant and in which hysterical paralysis analyzes the functions much better than good sense does. Why are the disturbances of speech accompanied with right-sided hemiplegy? Why are there cases of hemianopsia? How is it that there are distinct paralyses of monocular vision and of binocular vision? Why are there disturbances of accommodation? If you pass on to contractures, do you really believe that the patient has the idea of rigidity without fatigue, without increase of the temperature? That he has the idea of that modification of the reactions, of that slowness of the muscular shake? I am convinced, for my part, that hysterical contracture has its own laws, quite peculiar to it, presenting us, as I told you, a degradation of the contraction of the striated muscles. All this is outside of the thought of the subject. As I told you at the beginning, it will be, later, a matter of astonishment that physicians should have attributed to the caprice of the subject all the psychological and physiological laws that will be discovered in these various accidents.

Lastly, I insist on a third argument. These definitions have a meaning only on condition that the words 'fixed idea' and 'suggestion' are used in a particular sense. This sense should be that, with hystericals, ideas do not conduct themselves as with everybody. It is of no use for me to represent to myself that I am asleep; I do not, therefore, sleep. All these authors imply tacitly that these ideas act in a special manner on the mind and organism. I answer that it is this special action that is the essential point; it is this action that constitutes hysteria, and you have not the right to make a definition in which you tacitly imply what is essential.

Begin by defining what you call suggestion, and afterwards you may say, if you choose and if it is true, that hysteria is a disease due to suggestion. But, to define suggestion, you will be obliged to introduce into your definition certain new notions which are precisely those I asked for.

IV

You will be obliged to recognize that these ideas present themselves in special conditions, that they develop out of measure because they meet with no counterpoise in the mind, because they are isolated, owing to a strange absent-mindedness of the subject; in a word, you will recognize the other stigmata, absent-mindedness and the retraction of the field of consciousness. When you have once admitted this retraction of the field of consciousness as one of the conditions of suggestion itself, why should you maintain that it can produce nothing but suggestions? Why should you not admit that this disease of the mind may be manifested by something else? If this retraction has given too much power to certain ideas, does it not produce, on the other hand, some blanks? Can it not isolate and emancipate one function and suppress another from consciousness?

We then arrive at another group of definitions in which I range mine. They are definitions, in my opinion, more profound, into which enter the phenomena of *dissociation of consciousness*, such as is observed in all hysterical disturbances. Suggestion itself is but a case of this dissociation of consciousness. There are many others beside the one in somnambulisms, in automatic words, in emotional attacks, in all the functional paralyses. Many authors, Gurney, Myers, Laurent, Breuer and Freud, Benedict, Oppenheim, Jolly, Pick, Morton Prince, have thought like me that a place should be made for the disposition to somnambulism. Was not the somnambulic attack for us the type of hysterical accidents in 1889? 'The disposition to this dissociation, and, at the same time, the formation of states of consciousness, which we propose to collect under the name of hypnoid states, constitute the fundamental phenomenon of this neurosis,' said MM. Breuer and Freud, of Vienna, in 1893.

The point which seems to me to be the most delicate in this definition is to indicate to what depth this dissociation reaches. In reality we might say that dementias themselves are dissociations of thought and of the motor functions. We must remember that, in hysteria, the functions do not dissolve entirely, that they continue to subsist emancipated with their systematization. What is dissolved is personality, the system of grouping of the different functions around the same personality. I maintain to this day that, if hysteria is a mental malady, it is not a mental malady like any other, impairing the social sentiments or destroying the constitution of ideas. It is a malady of the *personal synthesis*, and I will take up again, very slightly modified, the formula I have already presented. *Hysteria is a form of mental depression characterized by the retraction of the field of personal consciousness and a tendency to the dissociation and emancipation of the systems of ideas and functions that constitute personality.*

V

Let us leave too-general discussions and come back to a more clinical conception of things. The most important problem is not for me to understand what hysteria in general is, but to account for the practical evolution of the accidents with such or such a person. The difficulty we meet with, then, is a difficulty of *localization*. How is it that with one person the hysteria bears on the arm, with another on the stomach, and that, with a third, it only reaches a system of ideas, which it turns into a somnambulism? It is on this search for an interpretation proper to each subject that one should dwell, to my mind, much more than on general quarrels of definition.

The starting-point of hysteria is the same as that of most great neuroses, it is *a depression, an exhaustion of the higher functions of the encephalon*. All the psychological operations do not present, as I repeat, the same difficulty. There are some operations that are easy for all kinds of reasons, first, because they are simple and only require the union of a small number of elements; second, because they are old, because their systematization was the work of our ancestors and is inscribed in strongly constituted organs. There are some other functions that are difficult because, on the one hand, they are very complex, because they necessitate the systematization of an infinite number of elements, and because, on the other hand, they are very new and require a present synthesis, not yet inscribed in the organism. Now, our nervous strength, which we do not know at all, presents oscillations. When it is high, we easily accomplish the operations of the second group, we have an extended consciousness, we turn back from no new study or action.

But there are many circumstances in which this nervous tension is lowered, especially with those hereditarily predisposed. There are some physiological periods, puberty for instance, at which the vital forces seem to be busy elsewhere and to leave no great resource to the brain. There are diseases that, through a thousand mechanisms, through local lesions, through intoxication, through microbian infection, lower our nervous tension. Even in normal functioning, physical or intellectual fatigue is enough to produce momentarily the same result. Lastly – the fact is more difficult to understand but incontestable – emotion is characterized by this lowering of the nervous strength. Very likely, in emotion, there is a great expense of nervous strength necessitated by the new problem suddenly set, and the emotional disturbance must come close to that of fatigue. However it may be, our patients have been exhausted, through one of the preceding causes. If hereditarily predisposed, they are enfeebled by puberty, or they succumb to intoxication, fatigue, or emotion. The diminution, the lowering of the nervous tension, may bring about a general lowering of all the functions, and especially of the highest. This is what takes place in the psychasthenic neuroses, in which the localization on a special point exists in a rather slight degree.

With hystericals, in consequence of particular dispositions, the lowering of the nervous strength produces, in some manner, a superficial retraction; there is, as it were, an autotomy. Consciousness, which is no longer able to perform too complex operations, gives up some of them. There is, it is true, a general enfeeblement, which manifests itself through the common stigmata, but there is, above all, a localization of the mental insufficiency on such or such particular function. So we find again in hysteria the problem of localization, which is of great importance in this disease.

No doubt, in a certain number of cases, the localization is effected through suggestion. An idea suggested from without attracts the thinking in one direction or another, and brings about, besides, according to laws the subject does not know, such or such automatic functioning and such or such a loss of function.

This is only a particular case. The localization may also be effected through a process akin to suggestion, but which is not identical with it, according to the laws of psychological automatism. I have often drawn your attention to those individuals, who, having had an accident in certain circumstances and having been cured, always recommence the same accident each time they experience an emotion, though it has no relation with the first. The man who was wounded by a railroad engine has a delirium in which he sees an engine coming towards him. This is quite simple. Eleven years afterwards, he sees his wife die, and he recommences the engine delirium. Another has the tic of blowing through one of his nostrils because he had a scab in his nose, in consequence of a bleeding at the nose. He recovers from his tic, but he recommences it now, because he loses his fortune, because his child is ill, etc.

Third law: The dissociation simply bears on a function that, for some reason or other, has remained weak and disturbed. Many of our patients become dumb after an emotion, but they were formerly inclined to stammer, their speech was quite insufficient. A girl's right leg becomes paralyzed; the reason is that, in her childhood, her right leg was affected with rachitis. In the case of another girl, the paralysis of a leg is due to the fact that, in her childhood, the leg was affected with a white tumour and remained long in bandage. This remark relates specially to the very numerous cases of associated hysteria: a disease of any kind bearing on viscera, often an organic lesion of the medulla or of the brain, enfeebles or disturbs some function and it is on this function that the hysteric emancipation is localized. So, in certain cases, hysteria makes conspicuous some light symptoms of organic diseases of the nervous system quite at their beginning by exaggerating them beyond all measure. The fact, for instance, was frequently observed in the cases of tabetic vomiting associated with hysteric vomiting.

Fourth law: The function that disappears is the most complicated and the most difficult for the subject. This law applies chiefly to professional and social paralyses.

Finally, *fifth law:* We remark a very curious fact, which we recognize without always being able to account for it. The dissociation bears on the function that was in full activity at the moment of a great emotion. There are here some physiological laws that cause the chief disturbance to bear on this function, that make it, probably through an association of ideas, through an evocation of the emotion, the most difficult for the subject.

It is the study of these laws, it is the search for these conditions, that constitute the important art of the study of hysteria. Leave the discussions of general definitions; they are premature discussions, which bear on purely verbal differences. Retain from these lessons the importance that attaches to the study of the psychological functions, the necessity of analyzing, in each particular case, the mental state of the patient.

If these lectures have inspired you with some interest for this kind of study, if they can contribute to develop in your beautiful country the researches of pathological psychology, beside the researches of experimental psychology, so brilliantly represented,

I think you will not have lost too much time in trying to understand a barbarous language.

For my part I deeply feel your kind attention and reception, and I am proud of having had, for a few days, the honour of teaching you and of being the colleague of the masters of Harvard University.

Further Reading

It is impossible to give a representative or even a fair introduction to present day literature on the subject of abnormal psychology. The reader's attention is directed to current journals and their book reviews. The following brief list has one element in common, that it is familiar to me. Where the extracts in the present volume come from a book, the reader is urged to get the book and read the whole of it. For the rest, the following few books will give an introduction to new developments in the field.

Part One

BLEULER, P. E., *Dementia praecox or the group of schizophrenias* (trans. J. J. Zinkin), International Universities Press, 1950.

MAYER-GROSS, W., SLATER, E. and ROTH, M., *Clinical psychiatry*, Cassell & Co. Ltd., 2nd Edition, 1960.

SCHNEIDER, K., *Clinical psychopathology* (trans. M. W. Hamilton), Grune & Stratton, 1959.

Part Two

BACHRACH, A. J. (ed.), *Experimental foundation of clinical psychology*, Basic Books, Inc., 1962.

EYSENCK, H. J. (ed.), *Behaviour therapy and the neuroses*, Pergamon Press, 1960.

LORR, M., KLETT, C. J. and MCNAIR, D. M., *Syndromes of psychosis*, Pergamon Press, 1963.

LOVIBOND, S. H., *Conditioning and enuresis*, Pergamon Press, 1964.

YATES, A. J., *Frustration and conflict*, Methuen & Co. Ltd, 1962.

Part Three

IVANOV-SMOLENSKY, A. G., *Essays on the patho-physiology of the higher nervous activity*, Foreign Languages Publishing House, Moscow, 1954.

LORENZ, K. Z., *King Solomon's ring*, Methuen & Co. Ltd, 1961.

MAIER, N. R. F., *Frustration: a study of behavior without a goal*, McGraw Hill, 1949, Ann Arbor Paperbacks.

PAVLOV, I. P., *Conditioned reflexes and psychiatry* (trans. W. H. Gantt), International Publishers, 1941.

Part Four

ADLER, A., *The individual psychology of Alfred Adler: a systematic presentation in selections from his writings* (edited and annotated by H. L. and R. R. Ansbacher), Basic Books, Inc., 1956.

FREUD, S., *The complete psychological works of Sigmund Freud* (ed. J. Strachey), Hogarth Press, 1955.

JUNG, C. G., *The collected works of C. G. Jung* (edited and annotated by H. Read, M. Fordham and G. Adler; trans. R. F. C. Hall), Routledge & Kegan Paul, 1960.

THOMPSON, C., *Psychoanalysis, evolution and development*, George Allen & Unwin Ltd., 1952.

Acknowledgements

Acknowledgements are due to the following for permission to publish extracts in this volume:

American Psychiatric Association, *American journal of psychiatry*, 1929–30, Vol. 9, pp. 719–38. Moore, T.V., 'The empirical determinants of certain syndromes underlying praecox and manic-depressive psychoses.'

American Psychological Association, *Journal of experimental psychology*, 1940, Vol. 26, No. 6, pp. 521–46. Maier, N. R. F., Glaser, N. M., and Klee, J. B., 'Studies in abnormal behaviour in the rat.' *Psychological monographs*, 1938, Vol. 50, No. 1, pp. 1–34. Cameron, N., 'Reasoning, repression and communication in schizophrenics.'

Basic Books, Inc., Publishers, Breuer, J., and Freud, S., *Studies on hysteria*, New York, 1957.

Bollingen Foundation and Routledge & Kegan Paul Ltd., Jung, C. G., 'The content of the psychoses', from 'The psychogenesis of mental disease', in *The collected works of C. G. Jung* (trans. R. F. C. Hull), London: Routledge & Kegan Paul Ltd, New York: Bollingen Series, Pantheon Books, 1960.

Butterworth & Co. Ltd., Kennedy, A., 'The organic reaction types', in *Modern psychological medicine* (ed. J. R. Rees), 1949.

International Publishers Co. Inc. and Lawrence & Wishart Ltd., Pavlov, I. P., *Lectures on conditioned reflexes* (trans. W. Horsley Gantt), 1929.

E. & S. Livingstone Ltd., Kraepelin, E., *Dementia praecox*, 1919, and *Manic depressive insanity and paranoia*, 1921 (trans. R. Mary Barclay).

Royal Society of Medicine, Reproduction of woodcuts in Gull, W., 'Anorexia nervosa', *Trans. clin. Soc.*, Vol. 7, 1874.

Sigmund Freud Copyrights Ltd., Mr James Strachey and The Hogarth Press Ltd., 'On the psychical mechanisms of hysterical phenomena: preliminary communication' (1893), *Studies on hysteria*, Vol. II of the standard edition of *The complete psychological work of Sigmund Freud*, 1955.

University of Chicago Press, Masserman, J., 'Experimental neuroses and therapy', *Behavior and neurosis*, Hafner, 1964.

William Heinemann Medical Books Ltd., Jung, C. G., *Studies in word association* (trans. Dr M. D. Eder), 1918.

Author Index

[Due to the lack of adequate reference in the earlier writings included in this book, many authors are not fully identified by their initials. However, as the omission of these authors from the index would seriously limit its use, the editor has decided to include them.]

Penguin Modern Psychology Readings

Titles available in this series are:

MOTIVATION ed. Dalbir Bindra and Jane Stewart
A collection of papers which deal most directly with the
three central problems of motivation: *drive* (what instigates
an organism to action); *goal direction* (what directs behaviour
toward certain ends); *reinforcement* (what precisely makes
certain events rewarding and others punishing). UPS 1

EXPERIMENTS IN VISUAL PERCEPTION ed.
M. D. Vernon
The volume reviews four central topics – the perception of
form, space and distance, 'constancy' phenomena – and then
explains the variations in perception which occur within the
individual and between individuals. Four excerpts from
Piaget on perception in infancy complete the volume. UPS 2

ATTITUDES ed. Marie Jahoda and Neil Warren
Three sections of readings which cover studies and problems
in concepts, research, and theory and measurement. UPS 3

PERSONALITY ASSESSMENT ed. Boris Semeonoff
Readings on variations in normal personality, which include
Galton and the early writings on typology, and the
applications of psychometric methods and of controlled
observations in selection procedures. UPS 4

INTELLIGENCE AND ABILITY ed. Stephen Wiseman
'The slow emergence of a coherent theory of the structure of
human abilities' is both the subject and the object of this
volume. Professor Wiseman has chosen readings from
philosophers and psychologists, covering a century of
speculation, hypothesis and research on man's intellectual
powers. The earlier papers provide the student with a historical
perspective from which he can appraise the present position.
In the last section of the book Professor Wiseman presents some
of the results of research into learning theory and into
human ability. The integration of these two sectors of
psychological enquiry will, he believes, revolutionize the work
of the educational and vocational psychologists of the
future. UPS 5

Titles to be published in 1967 are:
ANIMAL PROBLEM SOLVING ed. A. J. Riopelle
PERSONALITY ed. R. S. Lazarus and E. Opton Jr

Psychology in Pelicans

Among the books on psychology published in Pelicans which are of particular interest to students of psychology are:

FREUD AND THE POST-FREUDIANS
J. A. C. Brown

FUNDAMENTALS OF PSYCHOLOGY
C. J. Adcock

PSYCHOLOGY OF HUMAN AGEING
D. B. Bromley

THE PSYCHOLOGY OF LEARNING
R. Borger and A. E. M. Seaborne

PSYCHOLOGY: THE SCIENCE OF MENTAL LIFE
George A. Miller

PSYCHOLOGY OF PERCEPTION
M. D. Vernon

PSYCHOLOGY OF STUDY
C. A. Mace

PSYCHOLOGY OF THINKING
Robert Thomson

SCIENTIFIC ANALYSIS OF PERSONALITY
R. B. Cattell

SOCIAL PSYCHOLOGY OF INDUSTRY
J. A. C. Brown

The Psychology of Interpersonal Behaviour
Michael Argyle

Looks, gestures, and tones of voice may be powerful factors when people meet. Moreover these rapid and subtle messages are highly co-ordinated.

Experimental techniques have recently been developed for studying the minutiae of social behaviour scientifically: these are described here by a social psychologist. The study of social interaction demands a 'language' of its own, to which Michael Argyle supplies a clear key. But the reader will not be slow to grasp that 'the motivation of social interaction', 'the synchronization of styles of behaviour' between two or more people, and 'the presentation of a self-image' refer to things we encounter every day.

Certainly specific skills, such as interviewing, group leadership, public speaking, and even child-rearing, are discussed in the light of the latest research, and the author devotes a good deal of space to mental health and to training in social skill. His outline of what amounts to a break-through in psychological analysis makes this a book which the student of psychology may well find indispensable; and the relevance of his material to everyday life offers irresistible reading to the plain man.

New Horizons in Psychology

Edited by Brian M. Foss

Psychology as a science of observation and experiment is 100 years old. In the last decade it has expanded greatly, exploring new fields of human behaviour and using new techniques.

New Horizons in Psychology is both a progress report and a guide to the exciting developments in coming years. All of them will affect scientific thinking in many fields and some of them will influence the way we live.

Visual illusions, information theory, creativity, genetics, motivation, drugs, operant conditioning, programmed learning, behaviour therapy, personal construct psychology, small groups, cross cultural studies – psychology is seething with new ideas and methods today. These and many others are explained here by a distinguished team of experimental psychologists. A linking commentary by the editor, Professor Foss, paints the conceptual background to each topic.